THE COMPLETE
MIDDLE EAST
COOKBOOK

THE COMPLETE
MIDDLE EAST
COOKBOOK

TESS MALLOS

Photographer: Reg Morrison
Illustrator: Walter Stackpool
Designer: Robin James
Editor: Sue Wagner

GRUB STREET • LONDON

Photograph facing title page
Stuffed Grape Vine Leaves: KOUPEPIA, recipe page 84,
or DEREVE PATTOUG, *recipe page 158*

Photograph page 6
RANGINA (Fresh Date Sweet); TAMAR AL GIBNA (Dates with White Cheese)
and AL BATHEETH (Date Sweetmeat) *recipes page 263*

This edition published in Great Britain in 1995 by Grub Street,
The Basement, 10 Chivalry Road, london SW11 HT

Reprinted 1999

Published in conjunction with Lansdowne Publishing Pty Ltd
Level 1, 18 Argyle Street, The Rocks, Sydney 2000

First published by Ure Smith 1979
Reprinted 1982, 1984 (modified edition), 1985, 1986
Reprinted by Weldon Publishing 1990 (modified edition, 1991)
Reprinted by Lansdowne Publishing Pty Ltd 1994, 1995, 1997

British Library Cataloguing in Publication Data

Mallos, Tess
Complete Middle East Cookbook - New Ed
I. Title
641.5956
ISBN 1-898697-36-1

Typeset in Australia by TGC Pty Ltd
Printed in Singapore by Kyodo Printing Co (S'pore) Pty Ltd

CONTENTS

INTRODUCTION

Cooking should be an enjoyable experience. It should also open doors to many cultures and creeds, and its acceptance and appreciation should not be clouded by politics or prejudice. Middle Eastern cooking, as presented here, is open to controversy, but not for these reasons.

First the selection of the countries, as the area covered includes Greece, Cyprus, Turkey and Armenia SSR. More correctly perhaps the title should have been Near and Middle East Cookbook, though Greece and part of Turkey are regarded as the eastern boundaries of Europe. There seemed to be only one course open to me — to delve into the region's early history and justify the inclusion of certain countries from that viewpoint. Pure geography has also played a part, as the area covered fits rather neatly between longitudes 20°E and 70°E, and between latitudes 15°N and 45°N.

The region encompasses the birthplace of civilization and its history goes back as far as 3,500 B.C. with a pre-history dating back to 10,000 B.C. The Mesopotamian, Assyrian, Ancient Egyptian, Phoenecian, Hebrew, Minoan, Mycenaen, Ancient Greek and Persian civilizations all flourished within this area, and their contributions to world knowledge cannot be disputed. In pre-history man first learned to harness nature and farming had its tenuous beginnings in the area now known as Kurdistan, stretching from north-east Turkey across to northern Iran.

It is on this basis that the countries have been selected, for Middle Eastern cookery has evolved over several thousand years.

The second area of controversy relates to the actual recipes. Which dish really originated in which particular country? Again history can solve this in part; however there has been so much interchange of culture through colonization, migration, invasion and counter-invasion that even this presents its difficulties. So many similar recipes turn up in the culinary repertoire of a number of countries that to detect the source of many of them is virtually impossible. There are dolmas with variations in both name and ingredients stretching from Greece to Afghanistan and south to the Arabian Gulf States; Keftethes in Greece gradually change in name and character to kofta in Afghanistan; a sweet preserve made from green walnuts is made in Greece and Cyprus and the same delicacy is prepared in Iran; but nowhere else in between; Kourabiethes in Greece, Ghiraybah in the Gulf States have variations in every other country of the region.

Do not assume that the book is a collection of a group of recipes with countless variations; this has been avoided as far as possible, for the scope of Middle East cooking surprised me as much as it will probably surprise you.

Food and its preparation around the world have almost come full circle. (I say almost, for many aspects have of course changed, and will remain so — this is the essence of civilization. There has been change in the manner of cultivation and the raising of livestock, though there are areas in the region where primitive methods are still employed; and there has been change in cooking methods.)

Modern man has realized that highly refined foods are responsible for a number of his ailments; what nutrition experts now advocate is a diet based on simple, natural foods — meats, fish, poultry, less-refined cereals, pulses, vegetable oils, pure butter and ghee, vegetables, fruit, nuts, yoghurt and cheese. And these, along with herbs and spices, are what Middle Eastern cooking is all about — a diet basically unchanged for thousands of years.

The Western kitchen, with its electric blender, food grinder, mixer and food processor, cuts down on preparation time considerably. Many ingredients you will already have or be familiar with; the others are readily available at Middle East, Greek and Armenian food stores and at specialized food stores such as those stocking natural foods. The glossary will assist you greatly as it gives the various names for particular ingredients, and which substitutes, if any, may be used for unusual or hard-to-come-by ingredients.

Now let us mount the magic carpet for a culinary tour of the mystical, exotic world of Homer, the Arabian Nights and Omar Khayyam. Ahlan wasah'lan! (Welcome!)

Tess Mallos

ACKNOWLEDGEMENTS

Writing a book such as this could not be possible without assistance from many quarters. Organizations and numerous individuals were responsible for this assistance and thanking each and every one of them is the least I can do.

It is to my family that I owe deep and heartfelt gratitude. John and I have had over a quarter of a century of partnership, and nothing can test its strength more than writing a book of this magnitude. If this book symbolizes anything, then it has to be the strength of the family bond. With the constantly taxing effort involved in testing, research and writing I barely had time to be part of my family, but they were always there, encouraging, supportive, loving and very willing taste-testers — could be that willingness stemmed from pure hunger!

My sincere gratitude to Singapore Airlines for making it possible to travel to their Middle East destinations and Greece for the very necessary on-the-spot research.

To my sister-in-law Irene Harris for looking after our family while John and I travelled to such exotic and intriguing places.

The Australian Meat and Live-stock Corporation and their representatives in Middle East countries, without whose valuable assistance and advice much of this research would not have been possible.

The Ethnic Communities Council of New South Wales were wholeheartedly behind my task and gave me contacts in the various ethnic groups of Sydney.

The skill of photographer Reg Morrison is self-evident, and I thank him for his patience and creativity. During my long career I have worked with many photographers, all with considerable professional skill and the most up-to-date equipment. Reg has shown what can be done with a maximum of skill and a minimum of equipment — he says he does not need more equipment than he has, and I believe him.

Preparing the food for photography is an enormous task, and I am grateful to Maggie Williams for her assistance.

Sue Wagner, my editor and a long-time fan of Middle East cooking. Her co-operation, editorial skills, patience, guidance and friendship are much appreciated and valued.

Designer Robin James for her enthusiasm and for putting the book together with so much thought and skill; Walter Stackpool for his excellent artwork, adding a vital extra dimension to the book.

Stirling Macoboy, long-time friend and author of garden books, for his assistance with the botanical details necessary for the Glossary. The Dondurmas in the Turkish chapter are dedicated to him.

To my publishers for having faith in my ability to prepare such a book.

My thanks also to those who advised me regarding various countries, their foods, names of ingredients and general information.

Claire Truscott, who, as a diplomat's wife, spent many years in the Middle East.

Greece: Much of my knowledge of Greek cooking has come through a lifetime of contact with excellent Greek cooks beginning with my mother, Kaliope Calopades, then my mother-in-law Marika Mallos. My sister, Eleni Argyriou of Athens, gave me much information and it was through her, years ago, that I learned the cookery skills involved in recipe development and preparation of food for photography. Sylvia Glytsos, Efthalia Serafim, Koula Simos, and Zoe Kominato for correcting my Greek transliteration.

Cyprus: Tatia Phillipides of Nicosia; Sophia Agathocleous, Olga Constantine, Erato Christoforou, Anna Adamon, Socrates Andoniou and Chris Jacovides.

Turkey: Gulcin Incekara for a great deal of invaluable assistance, and Ayse Oztunc.

Armenia: Chake and Berdj Sebefdjian, Anny and Joyce Tshaglassian.

Lebanon: Len Obeid and George Habib of Lebanese Import Export, distributors of Middle East foods, for answering innumerable queries about the foods they sell and for lending Lebanese props for photography; Evelyn Bobb.

Syria: Jimmy Antoun and Laudy Jammal of the Al-Sahara Restaurant, Chatswood, Sydney; and Rene Jammal.

Jordan: Idlid Arida and her brother-in-law Nazih Arida.

Egypt: Solange Mattar and Nargus Youssof.

Yemen: Zdenka Underwood of Perth, W.A., who worked for 2 years in North Yemen with her husband, Dr Peter Underwood. Zdenka was made an honorary male, enabling her to be present at many special feasts, so gaining further insight into the manners and customs of the Yemenis. Doreen Ingrams' book *A Time in Arabia* was a source of many anecdotes and much information regarding South Yemen.

Iran: Akhtar Ostowari, an excellent cook with a vast knowledge of Iranian foods, although living in other countries for much of her life. Helen and Keith Weymouth, now of Melbourne, who spent 10 years in Iran, were most helpful in providing information and props for photographs.

Afghanistan: Faizi and Fahima Seddiq; Anwar and Pari Afzali of the Shah Restaurant, Manhattan Beach, California.

For general assistance, and for lending props and treasures for photography, my thanks to: Chris and Judy Jacovides; Howard Ewins; Bernard King, king of the TV kitchen, staunch friend and avid collector; Carol Wilkinson of Darling Street Antiques, Balmain; Dr Peter Lansky of Galerie elle, Paddington, Sydney; Chaudhary's Oriental Carpet Palace, Melbourne; June Hazel of the Bay Tree, Woollahra; Saywell Imports; Breville, Thorn Kenwood and Email Ltd, makers of Frigidaire for electrical appliances; Kevin Moses and Doreen Badger of the Bread Research Institute of Australia; The Australian Dairy Corporation; Dairy Farmers Pty Ltd.

TESS MALLOS

BASICS OF MIDDLE EAST COOKING

Many foods are common to most Middle Eastern countries. Though most recipes give full details of preparation, there is a need for basic information for easy reference.

PREPARATION OF EXOTIC VEGETABLES

Okra (Ladies' Fingers)

Wash well, handling okra gently. Trim stem end without cutting pod. If desired trim around conical stem attached to pod, removing a thin layer. This is the correct way to prepare okra, but it is time-consuming and only serves to remove the fine brown ring just above the pod and the outer layer of the stem. Middle Eastern cooks prefer to do this as the whole vegetable is then edible.

Fuzz can be removed if desired by rubbing pod gently with a fine nylon scourer. Do this under running water. If okra is young, there is no need to remove fuzz. Dry okra well in a cloth, or spread out and leave until dry. Place in a bowl and pour on ½ cup vinegar to each 500 g (1 lb) okra. Toss gently with hand so that vinegar coats okra. Leave for 30 minutes, drain and rinse well. Dry and use as directed in recipes. The vinegar treatment prevents okra from becoming slimy during cooking.

Freezing Okra

As okra are available only for a short time it is worthwhile freezing some if canned or frozen okra are not readily available.

Method I

Prepare as above and dry. In a deep pan heat 2 tablespoons oil to each 500 g (1 lb) okra and fry okra for 5 minutes, tossing gently with a wooden spoon. Cool, place in freezer bags, expel air, seal and label. Pack into freezer.

Method II

Prepare as above. Bring a large pot of water to the boil. Have ready a bowl of iced water. Place prepared okra in a frying basket and lower into boiling water. Boil for 3 minutes, timed from when water returns to the boil. Lift out and place in iced water for 3 minutes. Drain well, pack and store.

Globe Artichokes

Wash artichokes well and cut off stem close to base. Have ready a bowl of cold water with the juice of 1 lemon and some lemon slices added. If desired stir in 2-3 tablespoons flour as this is quite effective in preventing discoloration.

As each artichoke is prepared to requirements, rub cut surfaces with a lemon slice from the bowl and place in the bowl until all are prepared. Cook as soon as possible after preparation.

Whole Artichokes: Remove tough outer leaves and trim carefully around base just enough to neaten. Cut off 3 cm (1¼ inches) from top and trim remaining leaf ends with scissors. If artichokes are of good shape and quality, it is not necessary to trim leaf ends.

Artichoke Hearts: As for whole artichokes, only remove 3 or 4 layers of leaves until the tender inner leaves remain. Scoop out choke and pink thorny leaves from centre, using a spoon or melon ball scoop. Leave whole or cut in half.

Artichoke Bases (Fonds): Pull off all leaves. Remove choke and trim base into a neat cup shape. Do not over-trim as you will lose too much of the best part of the artichoke.

Eggplant (Aubergine)

Recipes give details of preparation in most instances. However, as a general rule, leave skin on, removing the green stem for general usage. Stem is left on if baking or grilling as it provides a convenient handle.

Slice, cube or slit as directed in recipe and either sprinkle generously with salt or place in well-salted, cold water. Leave for 30 minutes so that bitter juices are removed. Drain and pat dry with a clean cloth or paper towels.

Baked Eggplant for Purées

Recipes give detailed instructions as methods vary in different countries. However, if you have a microwave oven, it is an excellent means of cooking whole eggplant. Pierce in several places with a fork or fine skewer, place on a suitable dish and cook for 3-5 minutes according to size. Eggplant flesh becomes

soft and creamy in texture and remains light in colour.

Whichever way eggplant is baked, skin must be removed quickly and flesh combined with some of the lemon juice or vinegar in the recipe to prevent discoloration.

Spinach and Silverbeet (Swiss chard)

Spinach should not be confused with silverbeet — the two vegetables are not even related botanically. Spinach is native to Iran and widely used there and in other countries of the region. As spinach has a short season, from mid-winter to late spring, frozen leaf spinach may be substituted at other times.

Silverbeet can be used instead of spinach, but in some recipes the result is not quite the same, particularly for Iranian recipes. However there are instances where silverbeet is the desired vegetable, with spinach an impractical substitute. Individual recipes indicate whether one can be substituted for the other.

Whether spinach or silverbeet is being prepared, it is preferable to cook either vegetable in a stainless steel, enamelled or tinned pan as aluminium can cause discoloration.

As bunch sizes vary, I have given a weight as the amount required for a recipe. If your bunch is above the weight given, the success of the recipe will not be affected if the whole bunch is used. Some recipes give amounts in cups of shredded spinach leaves or number of silverbeet leaves.

Preserved Grape Vine Leaves

Pick leaves early in their growth period, that is early summer, when vines are well covered with leaves.

Choose leaves of medium light colour, not too young. If vines have been sprayed, wait for period recommended for general harvest by manufacturer of insecticide. When picking, snip off stem.

Wash leaves and stack in piles of 24, with shiny side up. Roll up and tie with string.

Bring 8 cups water to the boil with ¼ cup salt. Drop in 4 bundles at a time, return to the boil and blanch for 3 minutes, turning rolls over to blanch evenly. Lift out and drain. Repeat with remaining rolls.

Make a brine with 8 cups water boiled with 1 cup rock salt.

Pack rolls upright into warm sterilized jars and pour hot brine over leaves. Remove air bubbles and seal when cold.

Brine is sufficient for 20 bundles of leaves. Increase according to quantity being preserved.

Parsley

In all recipes flat-leafed parsley (sometimes called Italian parsley) is used. Curly parsley may be used for garnish.

PULSES OR LEGUMES

Either word is correct — pulses are the edible seeds of leguminous plants. The glossary lists them individually with their botanical names and the names by which they are known in the various countries of the region. Following is a general run-down on their basic preparation.

To soak or not to soak? Some require pre-soaking, some do not, just as some cooks prefer to pre-soak while some do not. It all depends on the nature of the seed and on its age. A dried bean less than a year old cooks more quickly than one which has aged somewhat in the pantry or store. As pulses are more readily available, and stores turn over stocks more frequently because of higher demand, the ones you are likely to encounter are relatively fresh. However, as a general guide, I have categorized them.

Lentils, Split Peas, Mung Beans

No need to pre-soak unless a recipe specifically calls for it. Brown lentils are often soaked for certain recipes so that the skin can be removed before cooking (details on this process later). As a general rule, place required amount in a strainer and rinse well under cold running water. If it looks as though small stones have been left in after processing, spread dried peas or lentils in a tray, remove stones and discoloured seeds, then rinse.

Black-eyed, Haricot (Navy), Lima, Red and Cannellini Beans

Pick over and wash well under cold running water. To each cup of beans, add 3 cups cold water and bring slowly to the boil. Boil for 2 minutes, then cover, remove from heat and leave aside until beans are plump. Cook as specified in recipe, using the liquid in which they were soaked.

If overnight soaking is preferred, then wash beans well and use the proportion of 3 cups water to 1 cup beans. If weather is warm, place them in refrigerator to soak. Often beans soaked overnight at room tem-

Dried beans, peas and lentils for Middle East cooking

perature ferment — reason enough for not recommending this method for the beans listed above.

Another method I use, particularly for the quicker cooking black-eyed, lima and haricot beans, is to wash them and add very hot water. In 2 hours they are plump enough for cooking.

Dried Broad Beans (large and small varieties) and Chick Peas (Garbanzo Beans)

Wash well and add 3 cups cold water to 1 cup beans. Soak for 12-48 hours, in refrigerator in warm weather. Soaking time depends on recipe.

Skinning Pulses
(a requirement in certain recipes)

After soaking chick peas, green or brown lentils, take a handful and rub with palms of both hands so that the seeds actually rub against one another. Drop back into bowl and take up another lot. Skim off the floating skins as they accumulate.

Another method for skinning chick peas is to place the drained peas in a shallow dish in a single layer and roll a bottle or rolling pin over them, exerting considerable pressure. Add water so that skins float, skim them off, pour off water and repeat until all are skinned.

There is no short cut to removing skins from large broad beans, none that I know of anyway. After soaking for 48 hours squeeze bean firmly: it should pop easily out of its skin. If not, slit the skin with a fingernail or the point of a knife, then squeeze.

Sometimes these beans are available already skinned — ask for skinned *ful nabed* if the storekeeper is confused.

As you can see, I am not an advocate of the long soak-drain-and-cook method unless absolutely necessary for the success of the dish being prepared. The reason is simple: as well as containing proteins and minerals, pulses are a good source of certain vitamins, in particular B group vitamins such as niacin, riboflavin and thiamine. These are water soluble; by soaking and throwing the water away you are losing valuable nutrients. As the cooking liquid in most pulse recipes forms an integral part of the dish, I advocate thorough washing before soaking so that the soaking water can form part or all of the liquid in the finished dish. For the same reason I do not recommend the addition of bicarbonate of soda when soaking — this also destroys nutrients.

RICE

In many countries of the Middle East rice is as important a part of the daily diet as it is in Asia. However one rice dish you will never find in a Middle Eastern household is plain boiled rice.

In its simplest form it is light and fluffy, tinged with a golden hue from the butter, ghee or oil, each grain glistening separately from the other. This is the riz or timman of the Arab world, the pilav of Turkey, the pilafi of Greece, the chelou of Iran and the chalau of Afghanistan.

Then there are the exotic polous and palaus of Iran and Afghanistan; the more elaborate versions of timman and roz, and numerous other rice dishes of the Arab world; the imaginative and flavourful pilavs and pilafis of Turkey, the Armenians, Greece and Cyprus.

One point all countries have in common is that you will rarely find two cooks agreeing on which is the right way to cook a particular rice dish. On one point they all agree, and that is to wash the rice well until the water runs clear. From that point on there is controversy.

In testing rice recipes, I looked for the simplest methods to give the required results. As to the washing of the grain, in most recipes it is necessary but there are exceptions; I find rice produced in the West is as clean as you could wish it to be, and some dishes benefit from the extra starch not lost in the rinsing process. As to the soaking of the grain before cooking, I found in comparing results that there is no detectable benefit to be derived from so doing. Many cooks believe it to be absolutely necessary and refuse to prepare a rice dish without a pre-soaking time ranging from 10 minutes to several hours.

Not all countries are particular about the type of rice used. Greece, Cyprus and Egypt are flexible in their choice of grain, with a general preference for short grain rice. Turkey prefers long grain rice of good quality for pilavs, but uses any available grain in dolmas, soups and puddings.

Most of the Arabic countries use only high quality, aromatic long grain rice, the basmati rice of Pakistan. Any good quality long grain rice can be used successfully, though others lack that special fragrance of basmati.

In Iran rice is of such importance in the daily diet that none of the rice produced is exported. It is said to be the finest of all the rices — delicate in flavour and aroma and hard of grain. Irrespective of the variety of the grain, rice is available in three main qualities — Berenje Domsiah, Berenje Sadri and Berenje Champa. The first is the whole, long slender grain, the second is grain slightly broken in the polishing process, and the third consists of broken grains. Basmati or any good quality long grain rice may be used successfully for Persian rice dishes.

NUTS!

Middle East cooking calls for lots of them: nuts in pastries, nuts in cakes, nuts in sauces, stuffings and rice dishes — nuts, nuts and more nuts.

Almonds

Purchase in shells or, for easier storage, already shelled but not blanched if they are to be stored for a while. The skin prevents the kernel drying and losing flavoursome oils. Store in a sealed container, in the refrigerator during summer when certain insects decide to multiply.

To blanch: Pour boiling water over the kernels, leave for 2-3 minutes and drain. When cool enough to handle squeeze nut and the kernel will pop out of its skin.

To split almonds: Separate the two halves with a fine-bladed knife.

To sliver almonds: Let them soak a little longer when blanching to soften the kernel, then cut into 3 or 4 slivers. If almonds are very crisp slivers break in the wrong places. Dry out slivers in a low oven.

To chop: Use a nut chopper, food processor or blender and chop to degree required.

To grind: Use a nut grinder or food processor. A blender is likely to cause oils to separate. Almonds should be dry and crisp for grinding finely.

Walnuts

For peak flavour purchase in shells, or buy ready shelled from a reputable retailer. If walnut halves are required it is best to purchase these prepared in this way, as any frustrated walnut cracker will confirm. Store, chop and grind as for almonds.

Pistachio Nuts

Unsalted pistachios are the ones required for cooking. Usually purchased in the shell. Break open and remove kernel. Store, blanch, chop and grind as for almonds.

Hazelnuts

A hard nut to crack! Buy ready shelled. Blanch as for almonds and dry off in a low oven. Alternatively place in a moderate oven, 180°C (350°F) for 15-20 minutes. Rub in a tea towel to remove skins. Store, chop and grind as for almonds.

ALL ABOUT BREAD

This most ancient of foods has sustained man from time immemorial. It is said that bread, or the lack of it, makes history. A profound statement.

However it is not my intention to expound on its history, only on the basics of bread making so that your attempts at producing Middle Eastern breads will be successful. Actually they are worth applying to the baking of any bread.

The Flour

Wheat flour is the most widely used, varying from white to wholemeal (also called whole-wheat, wheatmeal). The gluten in the flour is the protein which, when worked by mixing and kneading, becomes an elastic network to hold in the gases generated by the yeast. The percentage of gluten in flour varies; the higher the percentage, the better the flour for bread making. As flours are rarely labelled with relevant information, your only guide to high gluten content is where the flour was milled, which is usually close to where it was grown.

Wheat grown in the warmer regions of your state or country has a harder grain and is therefore higher in gluten content, so look for flours milled in such areas. If in doubt you can increase the gluten content by adding 1 teaspoon gluten (available from specialist food stores) to each cup flour. Sift together twice to blend thoroughly.

The Yeast

For convenience, a long shelf life and consistently good results, I have used active dried yeast granules in recipes; 1 sachet (7 g or ¼ oz) is equivalent to 2½ teaspoons of granules if puchased loose rather than in sachets. Compressed yeast may be substituted for the active dry yeast in the proportion of 30 g (1 oz) for each sachet. Where cake yeast is available, it should not be confused with compressed yeast; 1 yeast cake (a little over ½ oz) may be used in place of 1 sachet.

Whatever yeast is used it should be dissolved in warm water first — lukewarm for cake or compressed yeast, 30°C (85°F), and a little warmer for active dry yeast, no more than 45°C (115°F). Do not cream cake or compressed yeast with sugar as the sugar slows down the yeast action. Add the balance of the liquid to dissolved yeast, then add the sugar if used and pour

into flour. Stir a little of the flour into the yeast liquid and leave covered for 10-15 minutes in a warm place until frothy to speed up the rising process.

Where fat is used, adding it to the yeast liquid retards the action — it is better to add it after some of the flour has been incorporated; better still, blend the yeast liquid into the flour and work the fat in afterwards.

If you follow these guidelines, your doughs will rise much more quickly.

Testing Yeast Freshness
If unsure about the freshness of the yeast, dissolve yeast in ¼ cup warm water, stir in 2 teaspoons flour, cover and leave in a warm place. If there is no sign of activity in 15 minutes, yeast is stale.

Baking Flat Breads
Basically there are two types of flat breads — those with a pocket and those without. To form a pocket, bread must be rested for a period after shaping and before baking, and it has to be baked in the hottest part of the oven. Heat must be even, otherwise the bread does not puff properly. If oven heat is uneven, an electric frypan may be used with good results. Recipes give details.

For bread without a pocket, prick the shaped dough with a fork or pinwheel, or during cooking press the bread with a folded cloth. Again recipes give details.

Some breads have a higher water content than is normal, in order to give the characteristic chewy texture. Flour with high gluten content is necessary, and as beating must be prolonged so that the water may be absorbed, a high-powered electric mixer with a dough hook attachment is recommended. My 12-year-old Kenwood coped very well indeed with the rigors of the long beating necessary.

Storing Flat Breads
When baking flat breads it is worthwhile preparing enough bread for storing in the freezer for later use. Package cooled breads in freezer bags, sealing well. To reheat, wrap frozen breads individually in foil and heat in a hot oven for 10 minutes.

FILLO PASTRY
Fillo is the Greek name for this delicate, tissue-thin pastry. Frequently it is spelt *phyllo,* which perhaps is a closer transliteration of the Greek word meaning 'leaf', however I prefer the simplified spelling. The Turks call the pastry *yufka,* and in the Arab countries it is generally known as *ajeen,* which can be rather confusing as ajeen is any dough or pastry.

Fillo pastry is available commercially either fresh (chilled) or frozen. If properly sealed, fresh pastry can be stored in the refrigerator for several weeks, but must never be frozen. Frozen fillo pastry is more readily available at supermarkets. It varies slightly from fresh fillo, a different formula being used to withstand the rigours of freezing. For thawing, follow the directions on the pack. Both types of fillo should be left in their packaging and brought to room temperature for 2 hours before using. If opened out while chilled, the pastry could break apart at the folds and can be difficult to handle.

Handling fillo pastry while cooking
Remove fillo from wrap and open out. Spread leaves on a folded dry tea towel and cover with another folded dry tea towel. Moisten a third tea towel with water and wring it well to make it evenly damp. Spread over top cloth. Remove one sheet at a time, re-covering fillo with cloths. If recipe requires pastry to be cut to size, cut all the sheets, stack and cover. Fillo dries out very quickly in the heat of the kitchen, so covering is essential, particularly if the shaping of individual pastries takes time.

HOME-MADE FILLO PASTRY
Equipment required
Mixing bowl, rolling pin, wooden dowel no less than 60 cm (24 inches) long and 2 cm (¾ inch) in diameter, large work surface, large cloth and wax paper.

Sift 4 cups plain flour and 1 teaspoon salt into mixing bowl and add 1⅓ cups tepid water with ¼ cup olive, corn or peanut oil. Stir to a soft dough, then knead in bowl with hand for 10 minutes, using kneading action similar to bread making. It is easier to do this whilst sitting down with bowl placed in lap. Dough will feel sticky at first, but with kneading

BRIAMI (Vegetable Casserole) *recipe page 40.*

the gluten in the flour is developed and the dough becomes smooth and satiny.

When well-kneaded and smooth, wrap pastry in plastic film and leave to rest at room temperature for 1 hour or longer. If all the dough is not to be used for the recipe being followed, wrap unused portion and store in refrigerator for up to 1 week. Bring to room temperature before rolling out.

Divide pastry into 12 even portions, shaping each into a smooth ball. Cover with a cloth.

Dust work surface lightly with flour. Take a ball of pastry and shape it into a square. Place on work surface and dust top with flour. Roll out to a 15 cm (6 inch) square using rolling pin. Dust again with flour. Take dowel and place on one end of pastry. Roll pastry neatly onto dowel, pressing firmly as you roll. Keep hands on each side of pastry. Unroll pastry and dust work surface and pastry again with flour. Roll up again from opposite side of pastry, again exerting pressure. Unroll carefully. After second rolling, pastry should be about 25 x 30 cm (10 x 12 inches) in size.

Using backs of hands (rings removed), place hands under pastry and stretch gently, moving hands to stretch it evenly, working towards edges. Edges can be given a final stretch with finger tips. You will end up with a piece of fillo about 36 x 46 cm (14 x 18 inches) in size. Place on a cloth, cover with wax paper and fold cloth over top.

Repeat using remaining pastry, laying each completed sheet on top of previous one with wax paper in between. Use soon after making, as directed in recipes; for pies and layered pastries where a number of sheets are required, use half the number of homemade fillo sheets to those given in recipes.

Do not be concerned if the pastry tears during stretching. Tears may be mended as fillo is being used, or avoided if cutting into pieces or strips.

Rolling Pastry or Dough Thinly
Many recipes require the pastry to be rolled out thinly. As doughs are often elastic, normal rolling methods can prove very frustrating. This method, widely practised in Greece, Turkey, Armenia and Iran, is referred to in recipes, and is a skill worth developing. A length of wooden dowelling 60 cm (24 inches) long and 1 cm (½ inch) in diameter is required, though dowel used for rolling fillo may be used.

Shape dough into either a ball or a square. Dust work surface and dough with flour and roll out to a 20 cm (8 inch) round or square using rolling pin.

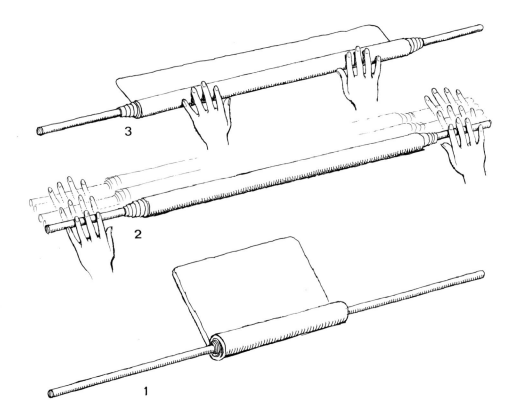

Dust work surface and dough again with flour and place dowel on end nearest you. Roll pastry onto dowel, pressing down firmly as you roll to the end. Unroll carefully, turn pastry round 180° and dust surface and pastry again with flour. Roll up again onto dowel, unroll carefully. Pastry is now ready for use — be guided by dimensions given in recipes, and roll a third time if very thin pastry is required.

Do not grip dowel as you would a rolling pin. Place palms of hand on dowel on each side of pastry, letting dowel roll under your hands. Hands are moved outwards as pastry stretches on dowel.

Perhaps it is worth mentioning another method — a variation on the one just given.

Roll pastry onto dowel to within 5 cm (2 inches) of end of pastry. Place palms of hands, fingers spread out, on top of pastry and roll back and forth with 4 or 5 quick movements, moving hands outwards along pastry as you roll. Roll up to end of pastry, then unroll carefully. Turn pastry round 180°, dust again with flour and roll again. The advantage of this method is that pastry can be rolled very thinly, and it is good for stretching fillo pastry; the disadvantage is that the centre can become much thinner than the edges and often is creased in the process. I call this the 'rock and roll' method — this might give you an indication of the kind of movement involved.

In special recipes, I refer to the chemist or druggist fold as it gives an interesting finish to individual, fillo-wrapped packages (Arnaki se Fillo, page 56 and Talaş Kebap, page 140).

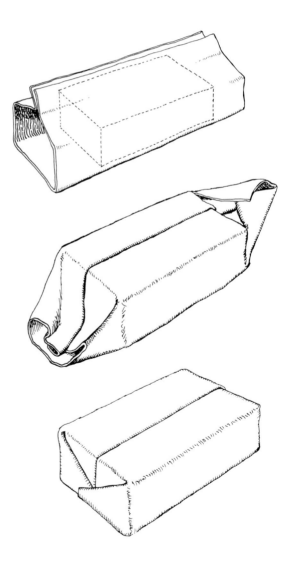

Cutting and Shaping Techniques

Many recipes refer to cutting foods in diamond shapes for serving. This can be done whether the dish is round, square or rectangular.

The shaping of pastries in triangles or rolls, though described in recipes, is perhaps clarified with diagrams.

SYRUPS

Syrups are widely used for fruit preserves, pastries and cakes. Recipes are self-explanatory but it is helpful to know the basics.

Use a heavy pan and dissolve sugar in water over medium heat, stirring occasionally. Boiling should begin only after all sugar crystals have been dissolved. Once boiling, do not stir, as the syrup will become cloudy or even crystallize. When a thick syrup is required, you can usually judge this by the nature of the bubbling. As the syrup boils, the bubbles become smaller and the sound of the bubbling changes; the sides of the pan become peppered with minute drops of syrup.

If you have a candy thermometer, the temperature of a thin syrup should be 105°C (220°F); for thick syrup, 110°C (230°F).

Experienced cooks have their own favourite methods of determining when a syrup is right: putting a drop on the thumbnail or a cold saucer — drop does not spread when syrup is thick enough; dropping it off the end of a spoon — when thick enough the last drop clings to the end of the spoon; spooning a tablespoon of syrup onto a saucer and cooling it quickly by spooning it up with a small spoon and dropping it back until cool.

When testing thickness, remove syrup from heat, for if thickness of syrup is right, you must not risk the syrup overcooking.

BACLAWA 'BE'AJ' (Nut Pastries) *recipe page 218.*

THE FOOD PROCESSOR

If there is one appliance which is tailor-made for Middle East cooking, then the food processor must be it. Though the container might not be large in capacity, preparation time is so abbreviated that even if processing food in separate portions is necessary, you are still way ahead. Where applicable, recipes give details on using both the food processor and the blender as well as the conventional method.

Use your food processor for chopping and grinding nuts to whatever degree required, coarsely chopped to finely ground; for crumbing bread; for chopping large amounts of herbs and onions; for grating cheese and vegetables; for grinding or chopping meat; for grinding pulses, whether soaked and still raw, or cooked; and for puréeing anything that requires puréeing.

The food processor makes the best Taramosalata, the finest Baba Ghannouj or Melitzanosalata, the creamiest tahini and tarator sauces, and is a great time and effort saver when making kibbi. Anyone tackling Middle East cookery should consider equipping their kitchen with this whizz of an appliance.

YOGHURT

To the Middle Eastern cook the making of yoghurt is a necessary part of daily routine. Because it is made so frequently and the art is so developed, each batch is as good as the last; the traditional method always produces a good yoghurt in the Middle Eastern kitchen.

As the Western cook might not use yoghurt as frequently I have given a second method which ensures a constant good result, minimizing the varied results obtainable if following traditional methods in the Western kitchen.

YOGHURT I (Yaourti, yogurt, madzoon, laban, mast, maust, yurt, leben hamid)

Combine 6 cups whole milk with ¾ cup full-cream milk powder or skim milk powder and bring to the boil. Remove from heat and leave to cool down until a little above blood heat. The favoured method for testing temperature is to insert a little finger into the milk for a count of 10 before the sting of the heat is felt. It is wise to check with a thermometer — 45°C (115°F) is the desired temperature.

Blend ¼ cup of the warm milk with ¼ cup starter (fresh, commercially made yoghurt). Gently stir starter into milk and pour into a casserole dish or deep bowl. Cover with lid or plate, then wrap in thick towels or a blanket. Leave undisturbed for at least 6 hours at room temperature and away from draughts. Remove covers and test. Yoghurt is ready when it is set like a junket. For a more tart flavour yoghurt may be left in its wraps for up to 12 hours.

Remove wraps, place covered container in refrigerator and chill for 2 hours before using.

If using this yoghurt as a starter for a new batch, then the starter should be used within 3 days, otherwise the balance of the bacteria in the culture alters, causing variable results.

YOGHURT II

Equipment required

Large jar, 6-cup capacity; 6 sterilized jars of 1-cup capacity or 3 of 2-cup capacity; preserving pan or large pot; thermometer; blanket or thick towels.

Blend ¾ cup full-cream milk powder or skim milk powder into 6 cups whole milk, preferably homogenized. Pour into clean 6-cup jar, cover with lid and stand in a pan of water. Heat water until milk temperature is 80°C (180°F). Remove jar from hot water bath and cool to 45°C (115°F). Remove ¼ cup of the warm milk and blend with ¼ cup fresh, commercial yoghurt. Stir into milk in jar, then pour into smaller jars. Seal jars with lids and stand in preserving pan. Add water to pan to come up to necks of jars. Heat until water temperature is 50°C (120°F) and remove from heat. Cover pan with lid, then wrap in thick towels or a blanket. Leave undisturbed for 3 hours. Remove jars, screw lids on tightly and store in refrigerator.

Yoghurt made this way will keep in good condition for 7 to 10 days, with little change in the balance of the culture. Use some of this for your next yoghurt. After making 3 or 4 batches, it is advisable to begin with a fresh starter.

A thermostatically controlled yoghurt maker is a good investment for those who make yoghurt frequently as it is so simple to use and ensures good results.

LOW-FAT YOGHURT

Use skimmed milk and skim milk powder instead of whole milk and full-cream powdered milk. Follow directions given in either Yoghurt I or II.

DRAINED YOGHURT

Recipes often call for drained yoghurt. Simply place yoghurt in a cheese cloth or doubled piece of butter muslin, tie with string and suspend from a fixed object over a receptacle to collect draining liquid. Leave for 2-4 hours depending on initial thickness of yoghurt. When drained, yoghurt should have the consistency of softened cream cheese.

STERILIZING JARS

Pickles, preserves and spoon sweets should be packed into sterilized jars to ensure good keeping qualities. Wash jars well in hot suds, rinse and drain. Stand upright on a baking sheet and place in cold oven. Close door and set oven temperature on 140°C (275°F). Once this temperature is reached, switch off oven and leave jars in oven until required for filling. As a general rule, pack hot foods in hot jars, cooled foods in cooled jars, in order to prevent breakage.

GREECE

Having cut my first tooth on a paximathi and coped with many a childhood illness fortified with bowls of Avgolemono Soupa, I had taken Greek cooking for granted. When friends returned from a visit to Greece with a grand passion for Greek cooking, I began to look at it through the eyes of my non-Greek friends. And what did I see? I saw a cuisine shaped through over 3,000 years of history; through the geography and climate of a country lolling in azure blue seas; through sloping mountains thrusting upwards to the heavens where man and nature vie for control; through the people of the land whose joy for life is evident every evening at the quaysides, in the tavernas, in town squares, at the kafenia.

Such vast differences in geography and climate have given Greek cookery an infinite variety, but there are still some dishes that are universally prepared and loved: Avgolemono, the delightfully tangy egg and lemon combination used in sauces to bathe meats, fish and vegetables, and as a soup with chicken, lamb or fish stock, recognized as the crowning glory of Greek cooking; Taramosalata, the caviare of Greece, so symbolic of the sea and its importance to the Greek; Moussaka, the marrying of eggplant, lamb and a cheese-topped sauce, echoing the Oriental influence in Greek cooking; octopus and squid, regarded in horror by those who have not dared to taste them and relished by those who have; Spanakopita, a delightful combination of spinach, herbs, eggs and cheese, but with regional variations and adaptations; and many, many more.

While there are no taboos regarding any particular food, fasting is an important part of the Orthodox faith, and after the fasting, there is feasting! During periods of fasting no animal products — meat, butter, cheese, milk or eggs —may be taken, so Greek cuisine offers many dishes for those who prefer to lessen the amounts of such foods in their diet.

Spanakopita is a most popular, very typically Greek pie, and not to be denied its enjoyment when fasting, it is prepared similarly to the Spanakopita Peloponnisos recipe, though its final shape could be a roll, smaller rolls or a flat pie, depending on the mood of the cook. This is a favourite of Chantal Countouri, a well-known Greek-Australian actress whose family came from southern Peloponnese. Chantal frequently adds eggs and feta cheese, then it becomes yet another variation of Spinach Pie.

FASSOULATHA (Bean Soup) *recipe page 37.*

The permutations and combinations of Greek cooking are endless. If any recipe seems to be omitted, the basic recipe could be included under anothér name. For example, if you have tried Trigona in Greece, a sweet pastry filled with walnuts, then it is a simple matter to adapt the Baklava recipe. Just cut the pastry into strips, butter, put on some of the filling and fold into triangles. Baking is quicker and the cooled syrup is poured on the hot pastries. If you prefer Floyeres (Almond Pipes), use almonds instead of walnuts, and roll the strips into cylinders. Actually Floyeres are similar to the Sariği Burma in the chapter on Turkey, using the alternative shaping at the end of that recipe. Indeed any other Greek recipe you might be looking for could be in Turkey, Cyprus or Armenia.

THE FLAVOURS OF GREEK FOOD

The flavours of Greek foods tend to be subtle rather than overpowering. Favourite herbs are parsley, always the flat leaf variety, rosemary, dill, fennel, bay leaves, mint, rigani (a wild marjoram not to be confused with oregano) and celery leaves. Basil always grows in Greek gardens but was seldom used in cooking, though its addition to the Greek cooking pot is increasing of late. It is of religious significance as the Greeks claim that basil grew on the site of the Cross. A sprig is always handed to a visitor on his departure as a gesture of goodwill.

Of the spices, cinnamon, cloves, nutmeg, masticha and mahlepi (mahleb, the kernel of the black cherry stone, imported from Syria) are the most frequently used; all but masticha and mahlepi feature in both savoury and sweet dishes.

For sweet preserves, the leaf of the rose geranium imparts a particular fragrance and often replaces cinnamon and lemon rind.

Amongst the fruits, the lemon reigns supreme. A Greek garden without a lemon tree is unthinkable. Seafoods and vegetables without lemon? Well, almost never. Even lamb is not spared. The rind makes a superb sweet preserve and is used in most other preserves, together with the juice to prevent the sugar crystallizing. Then of course there would be no Avgolemono without the lemon — nothing can substitute for it, though it is believed that the sour sauce of Ancient Greece used the juice of the citron, since lemon was not introduced until much later.

On second thoughts, the lemon does not reign alone, for without the olive, would there be a Greece? For countless centuries the olive tree has been symbolic of Greek life, enduring against all adversities. The fragrant oil, from earliest history, has sustained the people, has been used in trade and has given Greek cooking its essence.

MEALS GREEK STYLE

Greece is a country established in the European cultural traditions, and with a lifestyle similar to that of most countries bordering the Mediterranean; eating is a very social occasion, reminiscent of the symposiums of Ancient Greece.

To the Greek, having food is incidental. What is important is enjoying the company of friends, discussing a wide variety of topics with much gesticulating — with the occasional pause to dip a piece of bread into Taramosalata or pop an olive into the mouth and sip an ouzo or a beer. From midday on this scene is enacted in a wide variety of locations. It could be at an outdoor restaurant, in the town square, in the colourful Plaka in the old part of Athens, or at any waterfront taverna anywhere in Greece. Such occasions can extend far into the early hours of the morning. This basically is how the Greek regards eating, as just part of the happy business of living.

The main meal of the day is taken at midday and the food is served in a Western manner, that is at a table spread with a cloth, with china, cutlery and glassware. The food is placed in its dishes on the table at the beginning of the meal. There could be a roast leg of lamb with potatoes that were cooked in the same dish to absorb the flavours of the meat with its rigani, lemon and butter. A Greek salad, a mixture of sweet red tomatoes, crisp cucumbers and sweet peppers, feta cheese, olives and perhaps lettuce, would accompany the meat course. Bread is served with every meal and is used to soak up the salad dressing or meat juices. A wine, more often than not a retsina, accompanies the meal. Quite often other dishes could be served, such as one of the vegetable stews for which the Greeks are famous.

Dessert is seldom served; if it is, it could be a simple bowl of yoghurt or rizagolo (creamed rice). Fresh fruit and cheese complete the meal. In summer lunch is taken outdoors on the terrace, patio or balcony or in the garden.

After lunch it is time for siesta, and even if there is a guest present he is offered pyjamas and a bed. Very hospitable! After siesta is the time when the exotic sweets and pastries are likely to be eaten, if not at home then at the local zaharoplastio, similar to the French *pâtisserie*.

Early evening sees a repeat of the symposium-type gathering described earlier, which often suffices as the evening meal, as the variety of mezethakia served in Greece is limited only by the imagination of the cook and the availability of ingredients.

Where an evening meal is served it could be taken at any time from 8 to 11 p.m. and this is generally a lighter meal. More often than not, particularly in the summer months, it is taken at a restaurant or taverna. Early bedtime for children during summer vacation is seldom demanded and even more seldom obeyed — there is too much living to do.

COOKING METHODS

Greece is more Western than Eastern, and even the humble village home has a modern stove. Even so, it is still a practice in cities as well as rural and island villages to take the midday meal, ready prepared in its *tapsi* (round baking dish) or *tsoukali* (casserole dish), to the local bakery so that the kitchen will not become hot from the heat of the stove — a very popular practice during the summer months. Women who hold a job also take advantage of the baker's oven and deliver the prepared food on their way to work, to be col-

lected at midday. The baker tends, checks, stirs and turns the food. After the early morning's bake, the food cooks slowly in the heat left in the oven — a marvellous service for little cost. Slow cookers will never take on in Greece while the baker is so obliging.

Kitchen equipment is as modern as any, though you'll find traditional items such as the pestle and mortar, a *briki* for making coffee, *tapsi* and *tsoukalia* (mentioned previously), *saganaki* (two-handled frying pan), a long piece of wooden dowel used as a rolling pin for pastry, and perhaps a *kakavi,* a large copper pot once hung over the hearth for cooking, now seldom used except for ornamentation.

INGREDIENTS FOR GREEK COOKING

Fortunately you can buy anything you might need at your usual market, and any particularly Greek ingredient is available at Greek, Armenian and Middle Eastern food stores. Rigani is a must, with feta cheese, olive oil, fillo pastry, macaroni, dried beans and peas. But why list them? The recipes are self explanatory and the introductory chapters and glossary will fill in the gaps. What I am trying to say is that you do not need to chase around for the ingredients for Greek cooking — you probably use most of them anyway.

PRONUNCIATION

Recipe names have been transliterated from the Greek. Pronounce each syllable with equal emphasis, for example to-ma-tes, with 'o' as in *ought,* 'a' as in *past,* and 'es' as in *esteem.*

Pronounce 'e' as in *egg,* 'ou' as in *soup,* 'i' as in *sit* and 'y' as in 'i' when between consonants, and as in *yes* or *your* when followed by a vowel.

TOMATA PELTES
TOMATO PASTE

Makes approximately 1 kg (2 lb)

5 kg (10 lb) tomatoes
2 tablespoons salt

1. Choose ripe, sound tomatoes. Do not use any with signs of decay. Wash well, core out stem end and slice into a large preserving pan.
2. Cover and heat gently until tomatoes are soft. Rub through a sieve.
3. Return juice to pan and leave on moderately low heat, uncovered, until reduced by half (tomato purée at this stage).
4. Pour into 2 large dishes (baking dishes will do) and place in the sun; protect with a covering of gauze.
5. Dry in the sun for 2-4 days, stirring paste now and then. Alternatively place dishes in a cool oven, 100°C (200°F) and let purée evaporate; this will take 4-6 hours.
6. When paste is the consistency of that available commercially (a soft paste), stir in salt and place in sterilized jars. Put a layer of oil on top of paste and seal. Store in a cool place, but once paste is in use, store in refrigerator.

SALTSA AVGOLEMONO
EGG AND LEMON SAUCE

Makes 2½ cups
Cooking time: 10 minutes

1½ cups stock
1 tablespoon cornflour (corn starch)
3 eggs, separated
juice of one lemon
salt
freshly ground white pepper

1. Bring stock to the boil.
2. Mix cornflour to a paste with a little cold water and add to stock, stirring until thickened and bubbling. Let it boil for 1 minute.
3. In a bowl beat egg whites until stiff, add egg yolks and continue beating until light and fluffy. Add lemon juice gradually, beating constantly.
4. Gradually pour in boiling, thickened stock, beating constantly.
5. Return sauce to pan and cook, stirring constantly, over low heat for 1-2 minutes to cook the egg. Do not allow sauce to boil. Remove from heat and continue to stir for 1 minute. Season to taste.
6. Serve immediately with poached fish, boiled or steamed vegetables, meat and chicken dishes.

Note: Use stock to complement dish with which it is to be served: fish stock for poached fish, chicken stock for boiled or steamed vegetables — or use cooking liquid from the dish with which it is to be served.

MAYONNEZA
MAYONNAISE

Makes 1½ cups

2 egg yolks
1 small clove garlic, crushed
½ teaspoon dry mustard
½ teaspoon sugar
salt
freshly ground white pepper
¼ cup lemon juice
1 cup olive oil
1 tablespoon boiling water

1. Use a small mixing bowl and a wooden spoon or balloon whisk, or the small bowl on an electric mixer.
2. Remove all traces of egg white from yolks using a piece of egg shell. Place in bowl and stir yolks well with garlic, mustard, sugar, about ½ teaspoon salt and some pepper. Beat until light and smooth.
3. Add 2 teaspoons of the lemon juice and about a quarter of the oil, a drop at a time. Blend in remainder of the lemon juice and oil alternately, this time pouring oil in a thin trickle.
4. When mayonnaise is thick, adjust flavour and seasoning with more lemon juice, salt and pepper if necessary.
5. Finally beat in the boiling water so that mayonnaise will not separate if it is to be stored for a while before use. Serve with steamed fish, cooked lobster and prawns or as directed in recipes.

Note: Should mayonnaise curdle, begin again with an egg yolk beaten in a clean bowl. Gradually add curdled mayonnaise and mixture will begin to emulsify immediately.

MIZITHRA
COTTAGE CHEESE

Makes about 600 g (1¼ lb)

10 cups whole milk, not homogenized
3 teaspoons salt
2 rennet (junket) tablets
1 tablespoon cold water

Given modern-day packaging and health concerns regarding fat content, whole, unhomogenized milk could be difficult to obtain. Homogenized milk may be used instead, as can fortified milk with a low-fat content. If using either of these alternatives, double the amount of rennet to 4 tablets. Skim milk which has not been fortified with skim milk powder is not recommended.

1. Heat milk in a heavy pan until lukewarm and stir in salt. Remove from heat.
2. Crush rennet tablets in a small bowl, add cold water and stir until dissolved.
3. Slowly pour rennet liquid into milk, stirring milk gently. Cover pan with lid and leave at side of stove, undisturbed, for 30 minutes.
4. When set, break up curds by stirring with a whisk or spoon. Let curds settle.
5. Line a colander or large sieve with a double layer of muslin or cheesecloth. Ladle curds into this. Collect whey in a bowl if required (see end of recipe).
6. Let curd drain for a while, then scrape down cheese on sides of cloth and tie ends of cloth together. Suspend from a fixed object and leave to drain for another 6 hours at room temperature, then suspend from a shelf in the refrigerator with a dish to gather remaining whey. Leave for another 12 hours to drain thoroughly.
7. Turn out of cloth and store in a sealed container in refrigerator. It will keep for 4-5 days.

Note: The whey may be used for making a whey cheese such as Anari, a Cyprus cheese normally made after the making of Haloumi cheese. The Syrians also make a whey cheese called Kareeshee bi Limoun. See Index for these recipes. Another use for whey is for storing feta cheese in the home. The glossary entry on Feta cheese gives details.

MELITZANOSALATA
EGGPLANT DIP

Makes 2 cups
Cooking time: 30-50 minutes
Oven temperature: 180°C (350°F)

1 large or 2 medium oval eggplants
    (aubergines), about 500 g (1 lb) in all
1 clove garlic
salt
¾ cup soft white breadcrumbs
¼ cup lemon juice
½ cup olive oil
1 small onion, grated
¼ cup chopped parsley
freshly ground black pepper

1. Place whole, unpeeled eggplant on a baking sheet and cook in a moderate oven for 30-50 minutes, depending on size, until soft to the touch. While hot remove skin and chop flesh roughly. Drain off excess moisture.
2. Have garlic clove crushed with ½ teaspoon salt in a mortar. Gradually add warm eggplant to mortar alternately with crumbs.
3. Add lemon juice and olive oil alternately, working mixture thoroughly with pestle. Mix in onion, parsley, additional salt to taste, and pepper.
4. Place in a bowl and chill well. Mixture thickens when thoroughly chilled.
5. Garnish with black olives and serve with crackers, toast fingers or crusty bread.

To make in blender or food processor: Place all ingredients except oil in blender or food processor. Process until smooth and gradually add olive oil; this makes a smoother purée.

Variation: Peel and chop 1 large, ripe tomato and add to mixture with eggplant.

Note: Eggplant discolours quickly once exposed to air, so mixing quickly with other ingredients is important.

TIROPITA
CHEESE PIE

Serves: 6 as a light meal, 12 as an appetizer
Oven temperature: 200°C (400°F)
Cooking time: 30 minutes

2 cups milk
½ cup fine semolina
2 tablespoons butter
1 cup coarsely grated sharp cheddar cheese
1 cup crumbled feta cheese
⅓ cup grated kefalotiri or parmesan cheese
3 eggs
¼ teaspoon ground nutmeg
2 tablespoons finely chopped parsley, optional
salt
white pepper to taste
10 sheets fillo pastry
½ cup melted butter

1. Combine milk and semolina in heavy-based pan, add butter and stir constantly over heat until thickened and bubbling. Reduce heat and let mixture boil gently for 2 minutes.
2. Add cheeses and stir until well blended. Remove from heat and cool. Stir occasionally while cooling.
3. Beat eggs well and stir into cheese sauce. Add nutmeg, parsley, and salt and pepper to taste.
4. Butter a 25 x 30 cm (10 x 12 inch) baking dish and line with 5 fillo pastry sheets, brushing each sheet with butter.
5. Spread filling in dish and top with remaining pastry sheets, again brushing each with butter. Brush top with remaining butter and tuck edges under to hold in filling.
6. Score top sheets in squares or diamonds according to servings required — small for appetizers and snacks, larger for a light meal or first course.
7. Sprinkle top lightly with cold water to prevent pastry curling and bake in a hot oven for 30 minutes or until puffed and golden.
8. Cool in dish for 10 minutes. Cut into portions and serve hot or warm.

Note: Short crust pastry or home-made Fillo Pastry (page 15) may be used instead of fillo pastry sheets.

SPANAKOPITA PELOPONNISOS
PELOPONNESE SPINACH ROLLS

Serves: 6-8
Oven temperature: 180°C (350°F)
Cooking time: 50 minutes

1 kg (2 lb) spinach
1 medium-sized onion, chopped
1 leek, chopped
1 cup chopped spring onions
⅓ cup olive oil
½ cup chopped parsley
3 teaspoons chopped dill or fennel
¼ teaspoon ground nutmeg
salt
freshly ground black pepper
8 sheets fillo pastry
olive oil or butter for assembling rolls

1. Wash spinach well and cut off any coarse stems. Chop coarsely and put into a large pan. Cover and place over heat for 7-8 minutes shaking pan now and then or turning spinach with a fork. Heat just long enough to wilt spinach so that juices can run out freely. Drain well in a colander, pressing occasionally with a spoon.
2. Gently fry onion in olive oil for 10 minutes, add chopped leek and spring onions and fry gently for further 5 minutes until transparent.
3. Place well-drained spinach in a mixing bowl and add oil and onion mixture, herbs and nutmeg. Blend thoroughly, adding salt and pepper to taste.
4. Place a sheet of fillo pastry on work surface and brush lightly with olive oil. Top with 3 more sheets of pastry, brushing each with oil.
5. Brush top layer lightly with oil and place half the spinach mixture along the length of the pastry towards one edge and leaving 4 cm (1½ inches) clear on each side.
6. Fold bottom edge of pastry over filling, roll once, fold in sides then roll up. Place a hand at each end of roll and push it in gently like a concertina. Repeat with remaining pastry and filling.
7. Place rolls in an oiled baking dish leaving space between rolls. Brush tops lightly with oil and bake in a moderate oven for 30 minutes until golden. Serve hot cut in portions.

SPANAKOPITA
SPINACH PIE

Serves: 8 as a first course, 4 as a light meal
Oven temperature: 180°C (350°F)
Cooking time: 1 hour

1 kg (2 lb) spinach
1 medium-sized onion, chopped
½ cup olive oil
1 cup chopped spring onions (scallions)
½ cup chopped parsley
2 teaspoons chopped dill or fennel
¼ teaspoon ground nutmeg
½ cup mizithra or cottage cheese
1 cup well-crumbled feta cheese
¼ cup finely grated kefalotiri or
    parmesan cheese
4 eggs, lightly beaten
salt
freshly ground black pepper
10 sheets fillo pastry
melted butter for assembling pie

1. Prepare spinach as directed in Step 1 of Spanakopita Peloponnisos recipe (above).
2. Gently fry onion in oil for 10 minutes, add spring onion and fry for further 5 minutes.
3. Place drained spinach with onion-oil mixture in a large mixing bowl. Add herbs, nutmeg, cheeses and eggs and stir to combine. Check saltiness of mixture, then add salt and pepper to taste.
4. Brush a 25 x 30 cm (10 x 12 inch) baking dish with butter and line with a sheet of fillo pastry. Top with another 4 sheets, brushing each with butter.
5. Spread filling in pastry-lined dish and top with remaining fillo, brushing each sheet again with butter. Trim edges if necessary and tuck pastry in on all sides.
6. Brush top lightly with butter and score top layer of pastry lightly into squares using a sharp knife or razor blade. Sprinkle a little cold water on top to prevent pastry curling up.
7. Bake in a moderate oven for 45 minutes until puffed and golden brown. Remove from oven and leave for 5 minutes before cutting into portions for serving.

SPANAKOPITES APO TI SAMOS
SPINACH PIES FROM SAMOS

Makes 20
Oven temperature: 190°C (375°F)
Cooking time: 40 minutes

750 g (1½ lb) fresh spinach or 2 x 250 g (8 oz)
   packages frozen leaf spinach
1 cup finely chopped spring onions
¼ cup olive oil
2 cups crumbled feta cheese
¼ cup finely chopped dill or fennel
2 eggs, beaten
¼ teaspoon ground nutmeg
salt
freshly ground pepper

To finish:
10 sheets fillo pastry
½ cup olive oil

1. Prepare spinach as directed for Spanakopita Peloponnisos, Step 1. If using frozen spinach, defrost, drain well and chop. Place in a mixing bowl.
2. Heat oil in a frying pan and gently fry spring onion until soft.
3. Add oil and onion to spinach with cheese, herbs, eggs and nutmeg. Mix well to combine, then add salt and pepper to taste.
4. Open out fillo pastry sheets and cut in half, giving pieces approximately 20 x 30 cm (8 x 12 inches) in size. Stack and cover with cloth.
5. Take a sheet and brush lightly with oil. Fold in half to make a strip about 10 cm (4 inches) wide. Brush again with oil and spread about 2 tablespoons of filling across one long edge, leaving sides clear of filling. Fold in sides, then roll up firmly. Bend roll round into a coil and place in an oiled baking dish. Repeat with remaining ingredients, placing in one layer in the baking dish.
6. Brush tops lightly with oil and bake in a moderately hot oven for 25 minutes until golden brown. Serve hot or cold as an appetizer or light meal. If serving cold, use butter instead of olive oil unless your oil is of high quality.

AGINARES ME ANITHO
ARTICHOKES WITH DILL

Serves: 4 as a light meal, 8 as a first course
Cooking time: 45-50 minutes

12 medium-sized globe artichokes
   (see page 9 for preparation)
½ cup chopped spring onions, white part only
¼ cup olive or other oil
juice of 1 lemon
3 cups water
salt
freshly ground white pepper
2 tablespoons finely chopped dill
3 teaspoons cornflour
cold water
2 eggs
additional chopped dill to garnish

1. Prepare artichokes as directed for artichoke hearts and cut each in half.
2. In a large pan gently fry spring onion in oil until soft. Add juice of ½ lemon, water, about 2 teaspoons salt and a good grinding of pepper. Bring to the boil.
3. Drain prepared artichokes and add to pan with dill. Return to a slow simmer, cover and simmer gently for 30 minutes or until artichokes are tender.
4. Strain cooking liquid into a pan and boil until reduced to half original quantity (about 1½ cups). Keep artichokes hot in a slow oven.
5. Mix cornflour to a paste with a little cold water and stir into simmering liquid. Stir until thickened and bubbling and leave to simmer gently.
6. Beat eggs in a mixing bowl until light and frothy and gradually add remaining lemon juice. Gradually pour in simmering stock, beating constantly. Return to pan and stir over low heat for a minute or 2 to cook the egg.
7. Pile artichokes on a warm platter, pour sauce on top and sprinkle with chopped dill. Serve as a light meal or as a first course.

SPANAKOPITES APO TI SAMOS (Spinach Pies from Samos) *recipe above.*

AGINARES ME AVGOLEMONO
ARTICHOKES WITH EGG AND LEMON SAUCE

Serves: 6
Cooking time: 40 minutes

6 globe artichokes
juice of 1 lemon
1 tablespoon olive oil
Egg and Lemon Sauce (page 26)
chopped fresh dill or parsley for garnish

1. Prepare whole artichokes (see page 9). Cook in boiling, salted water, with lemon juice and oil added, for 30 minutes or until tender. Test by pulling a leaf — if it comes away easily they are done.
2. Lift out with a slotted spoon and invert to drain. Place in a serving dish and keep hot.
3. Make Egg and Lemon Sauce using chicken stock or half stock and half cooking liquid from artichokes. Pour over artichokes and sprinkle with chopped dill or parsley if desired. Serve as a first course.

Variations: Substitute asparagus, broccoli, Brussels sprouts or celery hearts for globe artichokes. Steam or boil according to vegetable used and make sauce with chicken stock.

AVGOTARAHO
DRIED MULLET ROE (BOTARGO)

One of my most persistent childhood memories is of my mother preparing avgotaraho. For the uninitiated this is the salted and dried roe of the mullet, rich amber in colour and a delight to eat, though its one annoying characteristic is that it rather clings to the teeth. At least the taste lingers for longer!

First of all you need to be on good terms with your fishmonger, particularly if he has a large Greek clientele. Cultivate the friendship so that it is ripe by early autumn or fall, wherever you happen to live. This is when the mullet is about to spawn and some of the catch will yield trembling pairs of yellow roe. Now a good fishmonger knows how to gut the fish so as not to cut into the roe: doing so will lessen his profit and the number of satisfied customers into the bargain.

My mother was fortunate; she did not have much competition as there were very few Greeks in our town. Fortunate for Dad too! (The fishmonger was Greek anyway.)

fresh mullet roe in pairs
good quality cooking salt (powdered not
   crystals)
bees' or paraffin wax, optional

1. Remove red veins on each roe by carefully scraping with the back edge of a spoon or a coin. Spoon edge should not be sharp as this could break the fine skin. Leave roe in pairs.
2. Arrange side by side in a flat dish, sprinkle thickly with salt and place another layer of roe on top if you have a good supply. Top with another lot of salt, adding enough to completely mask the roe. Leave for 6 hours.
3. Have a large bowl of cold water ready and dip each pair of roe into the water, lift out immediately and place flat on a rack. Smooth roe with fingers and drain for 10 minutes.
4. When drained, place flat on a clean wooden board and carefully place another board on top. Weigh down top board with a heavy object if board is not very heavy. Leave for 30 minutes.
5. Remove roe to a rack (stainless steel or chrome plated) and dry in an airy, shaded place for 1 week, turning roe once each day. Cover lightly with muslin to protect them. After drying, roe will be firm and an amber shade, varying in depth according to the original colour.
6. Store roe in a cool place — not in a sealed container. The longer they are stored, the firmer they become, and they will keep for up to 6 months. To store for longer, roe may be dipped in melted bees' or paraffin wax, placed on flat trays and left until set. This protects the roe more, but it does not dry out as much as the uncoated roe. Connoisseurs prefer very firm roe.
7. To eat, remove wax coating if present and fine skin, and slice thinly. Excellent with crusty bread and butter as an appetizer. The dried roe may be used to make Taramosalata. Grate amount required and blend well with a little lemon juice until softened. Follow recipe directions to complete the Taramosalata (page 34).

TIROPITAKIA
CHEESE TRIANGLES

Makes about 5 dozen
Oven temperature: 190°C (375°F)
Cooking time: 20 minutes

Cheese Filling:
375 g (12 oz) feta cheese
1 cup ricotta cheese or Mizithra (page 27)
¼ cup finely chopped parsley
2 teaspoons finely chopped mint, optional
freshly ground black pepper
2-3 eggs

To finish:
500 g (1 lb) fillo pastry
¾ cup melted butter

1. Crumble feta cheese into a bowl, combine with ricotta or mizithra cheese, then mash finely with a fork to blend thoroughly. Add parsley, mint if used and pepper to taste.
2. Lightly beat 2 eggs and stir into cheese. Mixture should be soft but still hold its shape. If too stiff, add another egg.
3. Cut each fillo pastry sheet into 3 strips, each about 13 x 30 cm (5 x 12 inches) in size. Stack on a cloth and cover with another folded, dry cloth. Place a moistened cloth on top.
4. Take a strip of fillo and brush lightly with butter. Fold in half lengthwise and brush again with butter. Place a generous teaspoon of the cheese mixture towards bottom edge of strip and fold end of strip diagonally over filling so that bottom edge is in line with folded edge, forming a triangle. Fold up once, then fold diagonally to opposite side. Continue to fold in a triangle to end. of strip. Repeat with remaining ingredients.
5. Place finished triangles on lightly greased baking sheets and brush tops lightly with butter. Bake in a moderately hot oven for 20 minutes or until puffed and golden. Serve hot.

BOUREKAKIA APO TIRI
CHEESE ROLLS

Use ingredients as for Tiropitakia recipe. Cut pastry sheets in half, giving strips of fillo about 25 x 30 cm (10 x 12 inches) in size. Butter and fold in half lengthwise. Brush again with butter. Spread about a tablespoon of filling along bottom edge, keeping sides clear. Turn end of pastry over filling and fold in sides along the length of the strip to contain filling. Roll up firmly and place fold side down on greased baking sheets. Bake for 20-25 minutes until golden brown and puffed.

Note: Filling used for Tiropita, page 28, may be used instead of the cheese filling given. Use 2 eggs so that filling is firmer and easier to work with.

SPANAKOPITAKIA
SPINACH PASTRIES

Use half quantity of the spinach filling given in the recipe for Spanakopita, page 29. Shape in triangles or rolls as directed in Cheese Triangles and Rolls.

To freeze cheese and spinach pastries: Prepare pastries ready for baking, placing them on foil-lined baking sheets. Brush tops lightly with butter and place in freezer only until firmly frozen. Remove carefully and pack into freezer containers, placing plastic film between layers. Seal and store in freezer. When required for serving, remove pastries to greased baking sheets and bake in a moderately hot oven for 20-25 minutes until golden brown and puffed.

TARAMOSALATA
FISH ROE PUREE

Tarama is the salted roe of the grey mullet or cod, the basis of this popular and delicious Greek meze. As there are various types available, you might have to experiment to find one to your liking, and adjust the recipe accordingly.

The best tarama to my mind is the one imported from Greece. Usually available in bulk or in jars, it is a very firm dusty pink paste. Sometimes a retailer 'improves' it by softening the tarama (with what I do not know) and brightening it with food colouring. Avoid this one.

Small cans of locally produced tarama are more widely available and handy to have in the refrigerator. This is a firm, orange coloured paste and just a little bitter to my taste, though this lessens considerably if the taramosalata is refrigerated a day or two before serving.

Avgotaraho, salted, dried, amber coloured roe, is often available at fishmongers and delicatessens. This makes an excellent taramosalata, but choose one which is not too hard. See recipe for making your own avgotaraho, page 32.

The strong-flavoured tarama must be broken down with crustless stale white bread, preferably from a Greek or continental-style loaf. Equal proportions by weight of these two ingredients is a good rule of thumb. Some cooks add mashed potato instead of the bread, or a combination of the two, to the detriment of the final taramosalata.

Makes about 2½ cups

125 g (4 oz) tarama
4-5 thick slices crustless stale white bread
cold water
1 small clove garlic, crushed
½ small onion, finely grated or ground
about ¼ cup lemon juice, strained
1 egg yolk or 1 whole egg
½-¾ cup olive oil

For serving:
black olive to garnish
crusty bread
radishes, celery and cucumber sticks

1. Turn tarama into bowl of electric mixer and beat until softened.
2. Soak bread in cold water, squeeze dry and crumble finely. Gradually add to tarama with crushed garlic and finely grated onion. Beat until smoothly combined, adding half of the lemon juice while beating.
3. When smooth, add egg yolk, beat well, then slowly add ½ cup oil. Taste and add more lemon juice if mixture is salty. Add remaining olive oil gradually until taramosalata is light and creamy. If very stiff, add egg white and beat in well. (Some taramas will take the egg white, while others have a satisfactory consistency without it.)
4. When completed tarama should hold its shape; chilling will thicken it further. Store in a sealed container in the refrigerator until required.
5. To serve, pile tarama in a deep bowl and garnish with a black olive. Serve with crusty bread, assorted crackers and a dish of crisp celery pieces, radishes and firm sticks of cucumber. The vegetable accompaniment is not traditional, but a joy to eat with the taramosalata spread onto the pieces.

Food processor or blender method: The former appliance is perfect for making taramosalata. Just put in the ingredients — the tarama, soaked, squeezed bread, whole or chopped garlic clove, roughly chopped onion and half the lemon juice. Process until smooth, then add egg yolk and gradually pour in oil through feeder tube. Adjust flavour and consistency as in Step 3 above. With the blender follow similarly, but be cautious as over-blending heats up the mixture, altering the consistency.

TARAMOSALATA (Fish Roe Purée) *recipe above.*

PSOMI
GREEK BREAD

This is the crusty, torpedo-shaped bread available at Greek and continental delicatessens. The moist atmosphere in the oven, and the spraying of the bread with water produces a thick, crisp crust.

Makes 2 loaves
Oven temperature: 190°C (375°F)
Cooking time: 35-40 minutes

6 cups plain flour
1 sachet active dry yeast
2 cups warm water
2 teaspoons salt
3 teaspoons sugar
1 tablespoon melted warm butter or oil
1 tablespoon fine semolina
water

1. Sift flour into a mixing bowl and warm in a low oven.
2. Dissolve yeast in ¼ cup warm water, stir in remaining water, salt and sugar.
3. Remove about 2 cups flour from bowl and keep aside. Make a well in the remaining flour and pour in yeast liquid.
4. Stir in a little of the flour until liquid is thick, cover and leave in a warm place until frothy — about 10 minutes.
5. Stir rest of flour into liquid, adding butter or oil gradually. Beat with wooden spoon or hand until smooth for 10 minutes, or on electric mixer with dough hook for 5 minutes.
6. Gradually knead in reserved flour in bowl or on a board. Only knead in enough to stop dough sticking. Dough is ready when it is satiny and surface has wrinkled texture. Shape into a ball.
7. Oil bowl, put in dough smooth side down then turn over so that top is oiled. Cover bowl with plastic wrap and place in a warm place for 1-1½ hours until doubled in bulk.
8. Punch down and divide into 2. Turn onto floured board and form each into a torpedo-shaped loaf.
9. Grease a baking sheet and sprinkle with semolina. Place loaves well apart on sheet and make 4 diagonal slashes across top of each loaf. Cover with a cloth and leave in a warm place until doubled — about 1 hour. Pre-heat oven.
10. Place a dish of boiling water on floor or lowest shelf of oven. Spray bread lightly with water and bake in moderately hot oven for 35-40 minutes. After first 15 minutes, spray loaves again with water, then again 10 minutes later.
11. Cool on a rack near an open window.

SPANAKORIZO
SPINACH PILAF

Serves: 6
Cooking time: 25 minutes

750 g (1½ lb) spinach
½ cup olive oil
1 cup chopped spring onions
1 leek, chopped, optional
2 cups short grain rice
¼ cup lemon juice
2 tablespoons chopped parsley
1 teaspoon chopped dill
3 cups water
salt
freshly ground black pepper

1. Remove roots and damaged leaves from spinach. Wash spinach well in several changes of water. Drain, tear leaves into pieces and chop stalks.
2. In a deep pan heat oil and gently fry onion and leek if used until soft.
3. Wash rice, drain well and add to onion. Cook for 5 minutes, stirring frequently.
4. Add remaining ingredients and bring to the boil. When boiling add prepared spinach, stir well and cover tightly with lid. Reduce heat and simmer gently on low heat for 15 minutes.
5. Remove from heat, leave tightly covered and allow to stand for 5-10 minutes before serving. Serve hot as an accompaniment to main meals, particularly with grilled meats and fish. Also good served cold.

Note: Silverbeet (Swiss chard) may be used instead of spinach. Remove stalks, wash better stalks and chop finely. Parboil for 5 minutes in salted water, drain and add to rice with chopped leaves.

AVGOLEMONO SOUPA
EGG AND LEMON SOUP

Serves: 6
Cooking time: 25 minutes

6 cups chicken or fish stock
⅓ cup short grain rice or small soup noodles
salt to taste
3 eggs, separated
juice of 1 large lemon
white pepper

1. Bring stock to the boil and add rice or noodles and salt to taste. Stir until stock returns to a slow boil, cover and simmer gently for 20 minutes or until rice or noodles are tender. Skim during cooking if necessary.
2. In a bowl beat egg whites until stiff, add yolks and beat until light and creamy. Gradually beat in lemon juice.
3. Ladle about a quarter of the simmering soup into the eggs, whisking constantly.
4. Gradually add egg mixture to soup, stirring vigorously. Remove soup from heat. Keep stirring for 1 minute and adjust seasoning with salt and white pepper. Serve immediately.

Note: This soup does not reheat satisfactorily so must be prepared just before serving. Only the stock can be prepared beforehand. Rice or noodles must be cooked in the stock just before it is required for serving.

FASSOULATHA
BEAN SOUP

Serves: 6-8
Cooking time: 2½-3 hours

2 cups dried haricot (navy), cannellini, lima or
   black eyed beans
8 cups water
1 large onion, finely chopped
1½ cups chopped, peeled tomatoes
2 tablespoons tomato paste
1 cup chopped celery, including leaves
1 cup diced carrot
¼ cup chopped parsley
⅓ cup olive oil
freshly ground black pepper
½ teaspoon sugar
salt

For serving:
chopped parsley

1. Wash beans well in several changes of water. Place in a large pot with the 8 cups water and bring to the boil. Boil for 2 minutes, remove from heat and leave pan covered until beans become plump. Time varies according to beans, with the smaller beans plumping in 1 hour; larger beans take about 2 hours.
2. Add remaining ingredients except salt and bring to the boil. Cover pan and boil gently for 1½ hours. Add salt to taste and cook for further 30-60 minutes until beans are tender. Again time depends on beans.
3. Serve hot in soup plates, sprinkling chopped parsley on each serve. Crusty bread, black olives, cheese and wine can accompany fassoulatha for a complete meal.

MAYERITSA
EASTER SOUP

The Paschal lamb, so much a part of the Greek Easter Sunday celebrations, usually comes with head and edible innards. The head is left on and it secures the lamb to the spit more successfully. The innards are either used for making Mayeritsa, or for making Kokoretsi tis Souvlas (page 60). Often extra ingredients are obtained for making both.

A bowl of Mayeritsa is the first meal served after the Lenten fast and follows immediately after the Saturday midnight service of the Resurrection.

As you are unlikely to purchase a lamb with all its spare parts, the recipe is given with ingredients and amounts easily obtained from your meat retailer.

Serves: 6-8
Cooking time: 3½-4 hours

500 g (1 lb) lamb tripe
water
2 lamb lungs
1 lamb heart
1 lamb liver
juice of 1 lemon
¼ cup butter
2 cups chopped spring onions
2 tablespoons chopped parsley
2 teaspoons chopped fresh dill
salt
freshly ground white pepper
⅓ cup short grain rice

To finish:
3 eggs
juice of 1 lemon (about ¼ cup)

1. Rinse tripe well, put in a pan and cover with cold water. Bring to the boil, then drain.
2. Rinse lungs, heart and liver, cover with cold water and add juice of 1 lemon. Soak for 30 minutes, then drain.
3. Put scalded tripe in a deep pan and add 8 cups cold water. Bring to the boil, then simmer, covered, for 1 hour. Add lungs, heart and liver and simmer gently, uncovered, for further 10 minutes, skimming as required.
4. Lift out all meats and cut into very small pieces, discarding any tubes, etc, from heart and liver. Reserve stock.
5. In a separate pan gently fry onion in butter until transparent. Add chopped meats and stir over medium heat for 5 minutes. Put pan contents into stock.
6. Add parsley, dill and salt and pepper to taste, cover and simmer gently for 2 hours or until meats are tender. Add washed rice and boil, uncovered, for further 20 minutes, adding a little more water if necessary.
7. Beat eggs in a bowl until foamy and gradually beat in lemon juice. Ladle about 2 cups boiling stock into egg mixture, beating constantly. Pour into soup and stir over low heat for a minute or two to cook the egg. Do not let soup boil again. Remove pan from heat and keep stirring for a further minute so that the heat of the pan will not curdle the egg. Serve immediately.

Note: The soup may be prepared up to Step 6 and removed from heat before the rice is added. When required for serving add rice and complete the cooking.

BAMYES TIGANITES
FRIED OKRA

Serves: 6
Cooking time: 20 minutes

500 g (1 lb) bamyes (okra, for preparation see page 9)
¼ cup olive oil
salt to taste
lemon wedges for serving

1. Prepare okra as directed. Dry very well with paper towels or a cloth.
2. Heat oil in a large frying pan with lid to fit. Add prepared okra and fry over medium heat, turning okra carefully with blunt-ended tongs to brown evenly.
3. When lightly browned, reduce heat to low, cover pan with lid and cook on low heat for 10 minutes or until okra are tender. Sprinkle lightly with salt.
4. Serve hot as a vegetable accompaniment with lemon wedges for squeezing onto okra. Cooked this way, okra tastes like asparagus.

AVGOLEMONO SOUPA (Egg and Lemon Soup) *recipe page 37.*

TOMATES YEMISTES
STUFFED TOMATOES

Serves: 6
Cooking time: 45 minutes
Oven temperature: 180°C (350°F)

12 medium-sized ripe tomatoes
sugar
salt
freshly ground black pepper
½ cup olive oil
1 large onion, chopped
¼ cup pine nuts, optional
1½ cups short grain rice
½ cup currants
1½ cups hot water
2 tablespoons chopped parsley
2 tablespoons chopped mint
water or dry white wine

1. Slice tops from tomatoes and reserve. Scoop out pulp and sprinkle cavities with a little sugar. Keep aside.
2. Put pulp in a saucepan with salt, pepper and ½ teaspoon sugar and simmer until soft. Press through a sieve and reserve pulp.
3. Gently fry onion in half of the oil until transparent. Add pine nuts (if used) and cook for further 5 minutes.
4. Stir in rice, currants, hot water, parsley, mint and season to taste. Bring to the boil, cover and simmer gently for 10 minutes until liquid is absorbed.
5. Fill tomatoes, allowing room for rice to swell. Replace tops and stand in an oven dish.
6. Pour puréed tomato pulp and an equal quantity of water or white wine into dish. Spoon remaining oil over tomatoes and cook, uncovered, in a moderate oven for 30 minutes. Serve hot or cold.

Note: This makes a pleasant luncheon dish or an attractive accompaniment to main meals.

BRIAMI
VEGETABLE CASSEROLE

Serves: 6
Cooking time: 1½ hours
Oven temperature: 180°C (350°F)

1 kg (2 lb) zucchini (courgettes)
500 g (1 lb) potatoes
2 green sweet peppers
2 cloves garlic, crushed
2 cups chopped, peeled tomatoes
½ teaspoon sugar
2 onions, sliced
salt
freshly ground black pepper
2 tablespoons chopped parsley
2 teaspoons chopped fresh dill or fennel
½ cup olive oil
chopped parsley, dill or fennel to garnish

1. Cut zucchini and potatoes into 1 cm (½ inch) slices. Remove seeds and white membrane from peppers and slice. Mix together crushed garlic, tomatoes and sugar.
2. Oil an oven dish and arrange some sliced onion on base. Add a layer of zucchini, potatoes and peppers combined, and top with some tomato mixture. Season with salt and pepper and sprinkle on some of the herbs and olive oil. Repeat until all ingredients are used, 3 to 4 layers according to size of dish, finishing with herbs and oil.
3. Cover and cook in a moderate oven for 1-1½ hours until vegetables are tender, removing cover for last 15 minutes.
4. Garnish with additional chopped herbs and serve immediately as a course on its own or as an accompaniment to roast and grilled meats, fish or meat patties.

Variation: Reduce zucchini to 500 g (1 lb) and add equal quantity of eggplant (aubergine) sliced thickly and salted for 30 minutes. Rinse and dry before using.

AGINARES ALA POLITA
BRAISED ARTICHOKES

Serves: 6
Cooking time: 30 minutes

12 globe artichoke hearts
½ cup chopped spring onions
500 g (1 lb) baby carrots, scraped
12 button onions, peeled
12 small new potatoes, scraped
juice of 1 lemon
¾ cup olive oil
water or chicken stock
salt
freshly ground black pepper
fresh dill or parsley, chopped
4 teaspoons cornflour

1. Prepare artichoke hearts (see page 9).
2. Line a wide-based pan with spring onions. Arrange carrots on top with whole onions, potatoes and artichoke hearts.
3. Add lemon juice, olive oil and enough water or chicken stock to barely cover. Season to taste with salt and pepper and sprinkle 1 tablespoon dill or parsley over vegetables.
4. Cover and cook over gentle heat for 30 minutes or until vegetables are tender.
5. Remove large vegetables to a heated platter with a slotted spoon, arranging them attractively. Keep hot.
6. Mix cornflour to a paste with a little cold water and thicken liquid in pan — let it boil gently for 2 minutes. Pour sauce over vegetables and garnish with additional chopped herb.

KOUKIA TIGANITA
FRIED BROAD BEANS

Serves: 6
Cooking time: 15 minutes

500 g (1 lb) very young broad beans
boiling, salted water
flour for coating
olive oil for frying
lemon wedges for serving

1. Wash broad beans well. Remove tops and tails, pulling off strings as they are removed. Leave whole.
2. Drop into boiling salted water and boil rapidly for 5 minutes. Remove and drain well. Leave until dry.
3. Roll beans in flour to coat. Heat enough oil in frying pan to coat base and shallow fry beans over medium high heat until golden brown, turning to brown evenly. Serve hot with lemon wedges for squeezing onto beans.

SALATES
SALADS

To the Greek a salad ranges from the puréed Taramosalata and Melitzanosalata, through the variety of boiled vegetable salads simply dressed with olive oil and lemon juice and usually served lukewarm, and finally to the traditional concept of salads using raw ingredients.

The cooked and raw vegetable salads require dressings and these are given with serving suggestions. Use them for Cyprus cooking as well.

LATHOXITHO
OIL AND VINEGAR DRESSING

Substitute wine vinegar for lemon juice and add ½ teaspoon dry mustard. Prepare as for Latholemono (page 42) and serve with any raw vegetable salad, or cooked dried bean, potato and beetroot salads.

LATHOLEMONO
OIL AND LEMON DRESSING

½ cup olive oil
¼ cup lemon juice
2 teaspoons chopped fresh oregano or parsley,
    optional
1 clove garlic, crushed, optional
½ teaspoon salt
freshly ground black pepper

1. Combine ingredients in a bowl and beat well with a fork or put in a screw top jar, seal and shake well.
2. Beat or shake again just before using.

Uses: Pour onto hot, boiled vegetables such as green beans, endive, zucchini or courgettes (particularly good if their blossom is still attached), broccoli, globe artichokes, cauliflower, cabbage, spinach, silverbeet (Swiss chard), wild greens such as dandelion and amaranth (vlita). Serve hot or let the vegetable cool to room temperature. Use the dressing also for brushing onto fish, shellfish, lamb or chicken when grilling. Excellent served with lobster and prawns.

SALATA HORIATIKO
VILLAGE SALAD

Serves: 6

4 medium-sized tomatoes
2 slender, young green cucumbers
1 sweet green pepper
2 medium-sized onions, sliced
125 g (4 oz) feta cheese
½ cup black olives
1 quantity Lathoxitho (page 41)

1. If peeled tomatoes are desired, pour boiling water over them and leave for 10 seconds. Drain and peel. Cut tomatoes into wedges.
2. Peel cucumber thinly and halve lengthwise. Cut in 1 cm (½ inch) slices.
3. Wash, core and seed pepper and remove white membrane. Halve and cut into thick strips. Separate onion slices into rings.
4. Place prepared ingredients in a bowl, dice the feta cheese and put on top with the olives. Pour on dressing just before serving.

SALATA ELINIKI
GREEK SALAD

Which ingredients are used and in what quantities is up to the cook. The greens, feta and olives are mandatory, and many would not regard it as a Greek salad without the anchovies. The combination depends on what is available and the meal it is to accompany — a plainer salad for rich meals, a salad with a variety of ingredients for plain meals such as grilled meats, chicken and fish.

salad greens such as cos (romaine), imperial or
    iceberg lettuce, endive, chicory etc.
onion rings or chopped spring onions
sliced radishes
tomato wedges
cucumber slices
sweet pepper strips
sliced celery
feta cheese
black olives
anchovy fillets
chopped, fresh dill or parsley
pickled capers
Lathoxitho (page 41)

1. Wash greens well, shake off excess moisture and wrap in a tea towel. Place in a refrigerator for 1-2 hours to dry the greens and make them crisp. Break up greens, or shred coarsely using a very sharp knife (the Greek method and a good one as the greens are less likely to be bruised).
2. Place greens in a bowl and add any other ingredients required. Sprinkle on herb, add dressing just before serving and toss at the table.

SALATA ELINIKI (Greek Salad) *recipe above.*

OKTAPOTHI TOURSI
PICKLED OCTOPUS

Serves: 6-8
Cooking time: 45-60 minutes

1 octopus, about 1 kg (2 lb)
1 clove garlic, crushed
½ cup olive oil
½ cup vinegar
salt and pepper to taste

1. To clean octopus, pull off tentacles, remove intestines and ink sac. Cut out eyes and beak. Remove skin and rinse well.
2. Place body and tentacles in a pan without any liquid. Cover and simmer octopus in its own juices over low heat until it turns deep pink and is tender (about 45–60 minutes).
3. Drain and when cool enough to handle strip off suckers from tentacles if desired. Cut head and tentacles into bite-sized pieces and place in a bowl.
4. Add garlic, olive oil, vinegar, salt if necessary and pepper to taste. Mix well, cover and leave to marinate in refrigerator for 12 hours before using. Stir occasionally.
5. To serve, lift out of marinade, pile into a dish, garnish with lemon wedges and parsley. Supply cocktail picks for your guests' convenience.

OKTAPOTHI KRASATO
OCTOPUS IN RED WINE

Serves: 5-6
Cooking time: 2 hours

1 octopus, about 1 kg (2 lb)
⅓ cup olive oil
1 large onion, chopped
2 cloves garlic, crushed
½ cup dry red wine
ink from octopus, optional
1½ cups chopped, peeled tomatoes
salt
freshly ground black pepper
2 tablespoons finely chopped parsley

1. Clean octopus as directed in Step 1 of Oktapothi Toursi, above. Reserve ink sac if desired.
2. Place in a pan without any liquid, cover and simmer for 15 minutes. Octopus will exude its own juice. Drain and cool a little.
3. Cut body and tentacles into small pieces, stripping off suckers if desired.
4. Heat oil in pan and gently fry onion until transparent. Add garlic and octopus pieces and stir over heat for 5 minutes longer. Add wine and let it cook until most of wine has evaported.
5. Reduce heat and add ink from sac if used, tomatoes and salt and pepper to taste. Cover and simmer gently on low heat for 1½ hours or until octopus is tender. Add water during cooking if necessary, only adding it if mixture looks like scorching.
6. Add most of parsley, cook for further minute, then serve hot with boiled pasta or rice. Sprinkle remaining parsley on top.

Note: The ink from octopus may be sizzled in olive oil in a frying pan, combined with lemon juice and used as a bread dip. Delicious!

SOUPIES ME SPANAKI
CUTTLEFISH WITH SPINACH

Soupies (cuttlefish) as distinct from kalamaria (squid) are preferred for this dish, though either may be used. Cleaning cuttlefish can be a rather messy business as these marine molluscs have an ink sac from which the pigment sepia is obtained. The sac ruptures easily and is usually ruptured by the time you purchase them, so don't be put off by their colour – the ink rinses off easily.

Serves: 6
Cooking time: 1¼ hours

750 g (1½ lb) cuttlefish or squid
⅓ cup olive oil
water
salt
freshly ground black pepper
750 g (1½ lb) spinach
1 cup chopped spring onions
juice of ½ lemon

1. Rinse cuttlefish or squid and remove head, attached tentacles and intestines; discard intestines. Pull out cuttle bone or fine transparent bone if squid is being prepared. Pull off fine skin and rinse. Remove eyes and beak from head, leave head attached to tentacles and pull or rub off skin from tentacles, or as much skin as will easily come off.
2. Slice hood or body into strips. If squid are large, slice head and tentacles — cuttlefish tentacles are usually small and these are left intact.
3. Place prepared cuttlefish or squid in a pan and set on medium heat. Cover and cook for 15 minutes in its own juice.
4. Add half the oil, just enough water to cover, and salt and pepper to taste, cover and simmer gently for 45 minutes or until tender.
5. Meanwhile trim spinach and wash thoroughly. Drain well and chop leaves and stalks coarsely.
6. Heat remaining oil in a separate pan and gently fry spring onion until soft, add spinach and stir over heat until it wilts.
7. Add spinach mixture to cuttlefish or squid with lemon juice and adjust seasoning with salt and pepper. Cover and simmer for further 10-15 minutes. Serve hot.

GARITHES YIOUVETSI
BAKED PRAWNS

Serves: 6
Oven temperature: 250°C (500°F)
Cooking time: 50 minutes

1 kg (2 lb) large uncooked prawns (shrimp)
1 medium-sized onion, finely chopped
½ cup olive oil
1 cup chopped spring onions (scallions)
2 cloves garlic, crushed
2 cups chopped, peeled tomatoes
½ cup dry white wine
¼ cup chopped parsley
½ teaspoon dried rigani or oregano
salt
freshly ground black pepper
125 g (4 oz) feta cheese

1. Shell prawns, leaving last segment of shell and the tail intact. De-vein and rinse. Drain and dry with paper towels and refrigerate until required.
2. In a pan gently fry onion in oil until transparent, add spring onion and garlic and cook 2 minutes longer. Add tomatoes, wine, most of the parsley, rigani, and salt and pepper to taste. Cover and simmer gently for 30 minutes until thick.
3. Spoon half of the tomato sauce into 6 individual oven dishes or 1 large oven dish. Add prawns and spoon remaining sauce over them. Coarsely crumble feta cheese and sprinkle on top.
4. Cook in a very hot oven for 10-12 minutes until prawns are pink and the feta melted and lightly browned. Sprinkle with remaining parsley and serve immediately as a first course with crusty bread.

PILAFI ME MYTHIA
MUSSEL PILAF

Serves: 6
Cooking time: 45 minutes

1.5 kg (3 lb) fresh mussels
water
salt
¼ cup olive oil
¼ cup butter
1 large onion, finely chopped
½ cup dry white wine
freshly ground black pepper
2 cups short grain rice
¼ cup chopped parsley
parsley sprigs and lemon wedges to garnish

1. Scrub mussels with a stiff brush, scraping shells with a knife blade to clean them thoroughly. Tug beard towards pointed end to remove. Place in a bowl of lukewarm salted water until mussels open. If any are open to begin with, tap shell — if mussel does not close, then discard it. While mussels are open, run lukewarm water into the bowl so that any sand can be expelled from the mussels. Drain.
2. Heat oil and butter in a deep pan and add onion. Fry gently until transparent. Add mussels, cover pan and cook for 5 minutes until shells open. If any do not open, then discard them.
3. Add 3 cups cold water, wine, 1½ teaspoons salt and pepper to taste. Cover pan and bring to a slow simmer. Simmer gently for 10 minutes, then remove mussels with a slotted spoon.
4. Wash rice until water runs clear, then add to liquid in pan with the parsley. Bring to the boil, stirring occasionally. Reduce heat, cover pan tightly and cook over low heat for 15 minutes.
5. While rice is cooking scoop mussels from shells and reserve. Keep 6 mussels in the shell for garnish.
6. Put shelled mussels on top of rice. Place two paper towels over rim of pan and fit lid on firmly. Leave on low heat for further 5 minutes, then remove pan to side of stove and leave for 10 minutes.
7. Blend mussels through rice with a fork and pile pilafi in a dish. Garnish with reserved mussels, parsley sprigs and lemon wedges.

Note: ½ cup tomato purée (not paste) may replace ½ cup water for a different flavour.

PILAFI ME GARITHES
PRAWN PILAF

Follow basic ingredients and method for Pilafi me Mythia, replacing mussels with 1 kg (2 lb) uncooked prawns (shrimp). Rinse well and cook gently in their shells until prawns turn pink (Steps 2 and 3). Shell prawns and devein them, reserving 6 in their shells for garnish. Follow remainder of method, adding shelled prawns to rice at Step 6. Tomato purée may also replace some of the water for this pilaf.

GARITHES YIOUVETSI (Baked Prawns with Feta) *recipes page 45.*

HINA YEMISTI ME KASTANA
ROAST GOOSE WITH CHESTNUT STUFFING

Serves: 8-10
Cooking time: 3½ hours
Oven temperature: 180°C (350°F)

1 goose, about 4 kg (8 lb)
½ lemon
salt and pepper
apples and chestnuts to garnish

Chestnut Stuffing:
250 g (8 oz) chestnuts (page 387)
1 small onion, chopped
¼ cup butter
4 cooking apples, peeled and diced

1. Remove fat from cavity of goose. Dry well inside and out and sprinkle cavity with salt and pepper.
2. Fill with stuffing (directions follow), secure opening and truss. Rub goose with cut lemon, season well and place on a rack in a roasting pan.
3. Roast in a moderate oven for 3½ hours or until tender.
4. Place goose on a warm platter and leave in a warm place for 20 minutes.
5. Skim fat from pan juices and dilute with a little white wine. Reheat, adjust seasoning and strain into a sauce boat.
6. Garnish goose with apple slices and whole chestnuts fried gently in butter.

To prepare stuffing: Shell and peel chestnuts and break in half. Fry onion slowly in butter until soft, add chestnuts and cook for a few minutes longer. Remove from heat and add prepared apples. Mix well and fill bird.

KOTOPOULO KAPAMA
BRAISED CHICKEN

Serves: 6
Cooking time: 1½ hours

1 chicken, about 2 kg (4 lb)
¼ cup butter
1 onion, finely chopped
1 clove garlic, crushed
1½ cups chopped, peeled tomatoes
1 tablespoon tomato paste
½ cup dry white wine
1 bay leaf
2 pieces cinnamon bark
½ teaspoon sugar
salt
freshly ground black pepper

1. Cut chicken into serving pieces and wipe dry. Melt butter in a heavy saucepan or flameproof casserole and brown chicken on all sides. Remove to a plate when browned.
2. Reduce heat and add onion and garlic. Fry gently until onion is transparent and add remaining ingredients. Cover and simmer for 20 minutes.
3. Return chicken to pan, cover and simmer gently for 45 minutes or until chicken is tender.
4. Remove bay leaf and cinnamon bark and serve Kapama with boiled macaroni or spaghetti and grated cheese.

Note: Braised Chicken may also be cooked in a moderately slow oven, 160°C (325°F) for 1-1½ hours.

KOTOPOULO STIFATHO
CHICKEN WITH ONIONS

Follow Kotopoulo Kapama recipe (above). Add 750 g (1½ lb) small whole onions (peeled with root ends cross-cut to prevent centres popping) and 3 whole cloves to sauce with the browned chicken pieces (Step 3). Cook for 45 minutes to 1 hour. Remove cloves. Serve with mashed potatoes and a boiled green vegetable or a tossed salad.

KOTOPOULO ME BAMYES
CHICKEN WITH OKRA

Proceed as for Kotopoulo Kapama (page 48). Lightly brown 500 g (1 lb) prepared okra (see page 9) in a little butter. Add to chicken 20 minutes before end of cooking time (Step 3). Serve with whole boiled or mashed potatoes.

LAMBRATIS ANDROS
EASTER LAMB OR KID ANDROS STYLE

The major problem with preparing this Easter lamb speciality from the lovely island of Andros is having an oven large enough for the lamb. Perhaps an obliging restaurateur or baker in your area might let you use his oven at a convenient time.

In Andros they use a special cover made of baked clay to keep the lamb moist and succulent. Foil is a reasonable substitute, but has to be removed to give the browning effect naturally produced with the traditional covering.

Serves: 20
Oven temperature: 180°C (350°F)
Cooking time: 4-5 hours

1 baby lamb or kid about 10-12 kg (20-25 lb)
salt
freshly ground black pepper
2 lemons
¼ cup melted butter
¼ cup olive oil

Spinach and Feta Stuffing:
2.5 kg (5 lb) spinach
3 cups chopped spring onions
¾ cup olive oil
1 cup short grain rice
1.5 kg (3 lb) feta cheese
¼ cup chopped fresh dill
¼ cup chopped fresh mint
salt
freshly ground black pepper

1. Wipe lamb inside and out with a damp cloth. Rub cavity and outside of lamb with lemon juice, salt and pepper. Cover and leave aside until stuffing is prepared.
2. Trim roots from spinach and remove discoloured and damaged leaves. Wash spinach in several changes of water, drain well and chop coarsely.
3. In a large deep pan (not aluminium) gently fry spring onions in oil until soft, add spinach and stir over heat until it wilts. Stir in washed rice, cover pan and cook on low heat for 10 minutes until most of liquid is absorbed. Remove from heat and cool.
4. Break up feta into small chunks and add to spinach mixture with herbs. Mix well, taste, then add salt if necessary and a generous grinding of pepper. Blend thoroughly.
5. Partly sew up cavity with white string, pack stuffing in through opening and finish sewing up the cavity.
6. Push foreshanks back towards body and tie in position, passing string over back of carcase. Tie back legs, leaving them a little apart — tying will prevent them splaying outwards.
7. Rub outside again with lemon juice, salt and pepper and place on a rack set in a large catering-size baking dish.
8. Combine melted butter with olive oil and brush half of this over the lamb or kid. Cover dish with large sheets of foil, sealing joins with double folds. Press foil under edges of dish to seal completely.
9. Bake in moderate oven for 4-5 hours. After 2 hours lift foil and brush meat with butter-oil mixture. Cook for further 1½-2 hours, remove foil, brush again and cook uncovered for 30 minutes or until meat is cooked through and browned.
10. Remove from oven, cover with the foil and a thick cloth and leave to rest for 30 minutes before carving.
11. Lift lamb or kid onto a large wooden board, remove string and spoon stuffing onto a platter. Turn the carcase onto its back and chop along backbone from the inside with a cleaver. Then chop each half into chunks and pile onto platters. Meat on the legs may be carved into slices.

PASTITSO
MACARONI AND MEAT PIE

Serves: 12 as a first course; 6-8 as a main course
Cooking time: 1½ hours
Oven temperature: 180°C (350°F)

500 g (1 lb) long macaroni
4 tablespoons butter
¾ cup grated kefalotiri or parmesan cheese
¼ teaspoon nutmeg
salt and pepper
3 eggs, lightly beaten

Meat Sauce:
1 large onion, chopped
1 clove garlic, crushed
2 tablespoons butter
750 g (1½ lb) ground beef
¼ cup tomato paste
½ cup dry red or white wine
½ cup stock
2 tablespoons chopped parsley
½ teaspoon sugar
salt and pepper

Cream Sauce:
⅓ cup butter
½ cup flour
3 cups milk
¼ teaspoon nutmeg
salt and pepper
1 egg, lightly beaten

1. Cook macaroni in boiling, salted water until just tender. Drain and return to pan.
2. Melt butter until golden brown and pour over macaroni. Add ½ cup of the cheese, the nutmeg, salt and pepper to taste and toss well. Leave until cool, add eggs and toss again. Keep aside.
3. Make meat sauce. Gently fry onion and garlic in butter until onion is soft, increase heat and add ground beef. Stir well and cook until meat begins to brown.
4. Add remaining meat sauce ingredients, cover and simmer over gentle heat for 20 minutes.
5. Make cream sauce. Melt butter in a saucepan, stir in flour and cook gently for 2 minutes. Add milk all at once and bring to the boil, stirring constantly. Boil gently for 1 minute.
6. Add nutmeg, salt and pepper to taste and cool a little before stirring in beaten egg.
7. Add ½ cup of this sauce to the cooked meat sauce.
8. To assemble Pastitso, butter a 33 x 23 x 8 cm (13 x 9 x 3 inch) oven dish. Spoon half of the prepared macaroni evenly in the base and top with the meat sauce. Cover with remaining macaroni, levelling top.
9. Pour on cream sauce and spread to completely cover macaroni. Sprinkle remaining cheese on top and cook in a moderate oven for 50 minutes until golden brown.
10. Let it stand for 10 minutes before cutting into squares to serve.

KEFTETHES
MEAT PATTIES

Serves: 6

2 eggs
4-5 slices stale white bread
water
1 large onion, grated
juice of 1 lemon
2 tablespoons chopped parsley
1-2 teaspoons chopped mint, optional
2 tablespoons grated kefalotiri or parmesan
   cheese
2 teaspoons salt
freshly ground black pepper
1 kg (2 lb) finely ground beef or lamb
flour for coating
oil for frying

1. Beat eggs lightly in a deep mixing bowl. Remove crusts from bread and discard, soak bread in cold water and squeeze dry. Crumble into eggs and add onion, lemon juice, herbs, cheese and seasonings. Leave for 10 minutes.
2. Add meat and blend lightly and thoroughly, mixing with hands if necessary. Cover and refrigerate for 1 hour.
3. With moistened hands shape into balls about the size of a small egg. Roll in flour and flatten each to a thick patty.
4. Shallow fry in hot oil until nicely browned (3-4 minutes each side). Lift out and drain on absorbent paper.
5. Place in serving dish as they are cooked and drained, and keep hot until all patties are done. Serve hot with a boiled green vegetable and mashed potatoes or with a tossed salad and fried potatoes.

Note: Make Tomato Sauce (page 82) omitting cinnamon and pour over keftethes before serving.

PASTITSO (Macaroni and Meat Pie) *recipe above*

KEFTETHAKIA
COCKTAIL MEAT BALLS

Follow recipe for Keftethes (page 50) substituting 1 tablespoon ouzo for lemon juice. Shape into meat balls the size of a small walnut, coat with flour and deep fry in hot oil, a few at a time. Drain and serve hot or cold as an appetizer. Garnish with lemon wedges and parsley and supply cocktail picks for your guests' convenience.

KEFTETHES APO TON PONTOS
MEAT PATTIES FROM PONTI

Serves: 5-6
Cooking time: 8-10 minutes

500 g (1 lb) veal stew meat
250 g (8 oz) pork stew meat
3 thick slices stale bread, crusts removed
1 onion, finely chopped
1 clove garlic, finely chopped
3 tablespoons chopped parsley
1 teaspoon chopped mint
1 teaspoon chopped basil
1 medium-sized tomato, peeled and chopped
1 egg
1 tablespoon vinegar
1 teaspoon bicarbonate of soda
1½ teaspoons salt
freshly ground black pepper
flour to coat
oil for frying

1. Finely grind veal and pork, leaving some fat on pork. Combine meats.
2. Soak bread in cold water. Squeeze dry and crumble into a mixing bowl.
3. Add onion, garlic, herbs, tomato, egg and vinegar; blend in soda, salt and pepper.
4. Add meat and blend in lightly and thoroughly, using hand if necessary. Chill for 1 hour.
5. Taking about 2 tablespoons of the mixture at a time, roll into balls. Moisten hands occasionally.
6. Roll balls in flour and flatten into rounds 5 cm (2 inches) in diameter.
7. Shallow fry in hot oil for 4-5 minutes each side. Patties will puff up. Turn carefully with spatula or tongs.
8. Drain on paper towels and serve immediately with fried potatoes and vegetables or salad.

PSITO KATSAROLAS LEMONATO
POT ROAST WITH LEMON

Serves: 6
Cooking time: 3 hours

1 boned shoulder of lamb or veal, about
    1.5 kg (3 lb)
⅓ cup lemon juice
salt
freshly ground black pepper
2 teaspoons rigani or oregano
3 tablespoons olive oil
2 cloves garlic, crushed

1. If lamb is used, trim excess fat. Open out shoulder and rub flesh with some of the lemon juice. Sprinkle with salt and pepper and about ½ teaspoon of the rigani. Roll up and tie securely with white string.
2. Rub outside of meat with more lemon juice, salt, pepper and rigani.
3. Heat oil in a heavy-based pan and brown meat on all sides. Reduce heat and add remaining lemon juice, garlic and remaining rigani.
4. Cover tightly and simmer over low heat for 2½ hours or till meat is tender. Turn meat occasionally during cooking.
5. Remove string and slice roast to serve. Pour juices into a bowl and serve separately.

Note: 750 g (1½ lb) small peeled potatoes, browned in a little oil, may be added to roast 1 hour before end of cooking time.

STIFATHO
BRAISED BEEF AND ONIONS

Serves: 5-6
Oven temperature: 160°C (325°F)
Cooking time: 2-2½ hours

1 kg (2 lb) braising beef
¼ cup butter or oil
1 medium onion, finely chopped
2 cloves garlic, crushed
1 cup tamato purée (not paste)
½ cup red wine
2 tablespoons wine vinegar
1 bay leaf
2 pieces cimmanon bark
4 whole cloves
1 teaspoon sugar
salt
freshly ground black pepper
750 g (1½ lb) small onions
2 tablespoons currants, optional

1. Cut beef into 3 cm (1¼ inch) cubes. Heat half the butter in a frying pan and brown meat, placing one layer of meat in pan at a time. Transfer to a casserole dish when browned.
2. Add chopped onion and garlic to pan with remaining butter and fry gently until onion is soft.
3. Add tomato purée, wine and wine vinegar and stir to lift pan juices. Pour over meat in casserole.
4. Add bay leaf, spices, sugar and season to taste. Cover and cook in a moderately slow oven for 1 hour.
5. While meat cooks, remove tops and roots from small onions and place in a bowl. Cross-cut root ends to prevent centres popping out during cooking. Cover with boiling water, leave 2 minutes and drain. Skins will slip off easily.
6. Add onions to casserole with currants (if used) and continue to cook for further 1-1½ hours until meat and onions are tender and sauce is thick. Remove cinnamon bark and serve with mashed potatoes or pilaf.

Note: This dish may be cooked slowly on top of the stove.

MELITZANES MOUSSAKA
EGGPLANT MOUSSAKA

Serves: 6-8
Cooking time: 2 hours
Oven temperature: 180°C (350°F)

1 kg (2 lb) eggplant (aubergine)
oil

Meat Sauce:
1 large onion, chopped
2 cloves garlic, crushed
2 tablespoons oil
1 kg (2 lb) ground beef or lamb
1 cup chopped, peeled tomatoes
2 tablespoons tomato paste
½ cup white wine
2 tablespoons chopped parsley
1 teaspoon sugar
¼ teaspoon cinnamon
salt and pepper

Cream Sauce:
¼ cup butter
⅓ cup flour
2 cups milk
⅛ teaspoon nutmeg or cinnamon
¼ cup grated kefalotiri or
    parmesan cheese
salt and pepper
1 egg, lightly beaten

1. Cut eggplant into 5 mm (¼ inch) slices with skin on. Sprinkle slices with salt and leave for 1 hour. Dry with paper towels.
2. Oil the base of a baking dish, add a layer of eggplant and brush with oil. Lightly brown under a hot grill, turn, brush again with oil and brown other side. Alternatively, eggplant may be shallow-fried in oil. Stack on a plate when cooked.
3. Gently fry onion and garlic in oil for 10 minutes. Add meat and brown over high heat, stirring well. Add remaining meat sauce ingredients, seasoning to taste. Cover and simmer gently for 30 minutes.
4. Melt butter in a saucepan, stir in flour and cook gently for 2 minutes. Add milk all at once and bring to the boil, stirring constantly. Let sauce bubble gently for 1 minute.
5. Remove from heat, stir in nutmeg or cinnamon, 1 tablespoon of the cheese, and salt and pepper to taste. Cover top of sauce with buttered paper if not required immediately.
6. Grease an oven dish, 33 x 23 x 5 cm (13 x 9 x 2 inches) and place a layer of eggplant slices in the base. Top with half of the meat sauce, add another layer of eggplant, remainder of meat and finish with eggplant.
7. Stir beaten egg into sauce and spread on top. Sprinkle with remaining cheese. Bake in a moderate oven for 1 hour. Let stand 10 minutes before cutting into squares to serve.

ARNI FRICASSE
LAMB FRICASSEE

Serves: 4-6
Cooking time: 1¾ -2 hours

1 large onion, chopped
2 tablespoons butter
1 kg (2 lb) lean boneless lamb, cubed
1 cup hot water
2 tablespoons chopped parsley
1 teaspoon chopped dill or fennel, optional
salt and pepper
prepared vegetable (see end of Method)
Egg and Lemon Sauce (page 26)
chopped parsley or dill for garnish

1. In a heavy-based saucepan or Dutch oven gently fry onion in butter until transparent.
2. Increase heat and add cubed lamb. Cook, stirring constantly, until meat juices evaporate. Meat should not brown.
3. Reduce heat and add hot water, herbs and salt and pepper to taste. Cover and simmer gently for 1-1½ hours.
4. Add prepared vegetable and continue to cook until lamb and vegetable are tender.
5. Carefully drain liquid from pan into a measuring jug and make up to 1½ cups with hot water or stock. Keep pan contents hot.
6. Make Egg and Lemon Sauce according to directions. Pour over lamb and vegetable, cover and leave at the side of the stove for 5 minutes.
7. Arrange lamb and vegetable on a serving dish and sprinkle with chopped herb. Serve immediately with crusty bread and a chilled white wine.

Add any one of the following vegetables:
8-12 small globe artichoke hearts (see Globe Artichokes, page 9). Add to meat after 1 hour and cook for further 30-45 minutes.
500 g (1 lb) celery stalks cut into 8 cm (3 inch) lengths and blanched in boiling, salted water for 5 minutes. Drain, add to meat after 1 hour and cook for further 45 minutes. Pork can be used instead of lamb with this vegetable.
4 heads endive, washed well and trimmed of any coarse leaves. Slit heads in half lengthways and blanch in boiling salted water for 2 minutes. Drain, add to meat after 1½ hours and cook for further 15 minutes.
4 small firm heads lettuce, washed well and quartered. Place in a colander and scald with boiling water. Add after 1½ hours and cook for further 15 minutes.

ARNI LEMONATO
ROAST LEMON LAMB

Serves: 6-8
Oven temperature: 180°C (350°F)
Cooking time: 2½ hours

1 leg of lamb, about 2 kg (4 lb)
2-3 cloves garlic
juice of 2 lemons
salt
freshly ground black pepper
1 teaspoon dried rigani or oregano
2 tablespoons butter or margarine
1 cup hot water

1. Wipe leg with a damp cloth. Cut small slits over surface of lamb. Cut garlic cloves into slivers and insert in slits.
2. Rub entire surface with lemon juice and season with salt and pepper. Sprinkle with herb and place in a roasting pan.
3. Cook in a moderate oven for 1 hour. Drain off fat and add hot water to pan. Spread butter on lamb and return to oven.
4. Cook for further 1½ hours or until lamb is cooked to taste. Turn during cooking to brown evenly.
5. Allow lamb to rest in a warm place for 15-20 minutes before carving. Skim off excess fat from pan juices, reduce if necessary and serve with the lamb.

Note: 1 kg (2 lb) potatoes, peeled and quartered, may be cooked with the lamb during the last hour. Sprinkle with additional lemon juice, herb, salt and pepper.

AGINARES ME AVGOLEMONO (Artichokes with Egg and Lemon Sauce) *recipe page 32.*

ARNAKI SE FILLO
LAMB IN FILLO

This is one of the ways in which a basic Greek recipe can be revamped to produce a really superb dish. Basically it is Arni Palikari (Lamb Bandit Style). Traditionally the food was wrapped in paper before cooking so that the cooking aromas would not betray the presence of the bandits. Nowadays aluminium foil has replaced the paper. This recipe goes one step further and makes the individual package totally edible by using fillo pastry. Many Greek restaurateurs make use of fillo in this way in similar recipes.

Serves: 6
Oven temperature: 200°C (400°F)
Cooking time: 25-30 minutes

6 boneless lamb leg steaks, about 2 cm
  (¾ inch) thick
freshly ground black pepper
2 tablespoons butter or oil
2 medium-sized onions, sliced
1 clove garlic, crushed
12 sheets fillo pastry
½ cup melted butter
salt
3 medium-sized tomatoes, peeled
1 teaspoon rigani or oregano
125 g (4 oz) feta cheese cut into 6 slices

1. Trim steaks of most of the fat and shape neatly — trimmings can be used in a ground lamb dish. Season with pepper.
2. Heat butter or oil in a frying pan and brown steaks quickly on each side — do not cook through. Lift out onto a dish and leave until cool.
3. Add onion to pan and fry gently until transparent, add garlic and remove from heat.
4. Brush a sheet of fillo pastry with melted butter and place another sheet on top, brushing again with butter. Fold in half to make almost a square of fillo. Put aside and cover with a dry tea towel, then one dampened with warm water. Repeat with remaining fillo to give 6 prepared squares.
5. Take one square and brush top with butter — leave remaining pastry covered.
6. Place a lamb steak in the centre and season lightly with salt. Top with onion-garlic mixture and cover with 2 slices of tomato. Sprinkle with a little rigani, salt and pepper and place a slice of feta cheese on top.
7. Bring up ends of fillo pastry and double-fold over top. Fold in ends as you would a package then tuck ends underneath. This is known as the chemist's (druggist's) fold. Place on a buttered baking tray. Repeat with remaining ingredients.
8. Brush tops and sides of packages lightly with melted butter and bake in a pre-heated hot oven for 15 minutes. Serve immediately if possible, though they will survive in the oven with heat turned off for about 10 minutes. Garnish with parsley sprigs and serve with boiled green beans or zucchini dressed with olive oil and lemon juice.

Note: Medallions of lamb cut from a trimmed loin can be used instead of the steaks. You will require 12, and place 2 in each package.

SKEMBE YAHNI
TRIPE STEW

Serves: 4-5
Cooking time: 2¼ hours

750 g (1½ lb) tripe
juice of 1 lemon
water
2 tablespoons butter
1 large onion, chopped
¼ cup chopped parsley
¼ cup tomato paste
1 cup water
½ cup dry white wine
salt
freshly ground black pepper
chopped parsley to garnish

1. Wash tripe well, drain and cut into small squares or fingers. Place in a dish, add lemon juice, stir and leave for 1 hour.
2. Place tripe in pan, add water to cover and bring to the boil. Drain off water and remove tripe to a plate.
3. Clean pan and add butter. Melt over medium heat and add onion. Fry gently until transparent.
4. Stir in parsley, fry 1 minute, then add tomato paste, water, wine and salt and pepper to taste. Bring to a slow simmer.
5. Return tripe to pan, cover and simmer gently for 2 hours or until tripe is tender. To test for tenderness, take out a piece and pull. If it breaks apart easily, tripe is cooked.
6. Place in serving dish, garnish with parsley and serve hot with pilaf and a tossed salad.

YEMISTA ME LAHANO
STUFFED CABBAGE LEAVES

Serves: 6
Cooking time: 1½ hours

1 large onion, finely chopped
1 tablespoon olive oil
1 kg (2 1b) ground beef or lamb
⅓ cup short grain rice
1 tomato, peeled and chopped
2 tablespoons chopped parsley
1 teaspoon chopped dill or mint
⅛ teaspoon ground cinnamon
freshly ground black pepper
24 cabbage leaves
salted water
1 tablespoon butter
2 cups hot stock or water
salt
1 tablespoon cornflour
2 eggs, separated
juice of 1 lemon
chopped dill or parsley to garnish

1. Gently fry onion in oil until soft. Mix into meat with rice, tomato, herbs and cinnamon, seasoning to taste with salt and pepper. Divide into 24 portions.
2. Blanch cabbage leaves in boiling, salted water for 5 minutes until softened. Drain and cut out thick centre of larger leaves (very large leaves may be cut in half).
3. Place one portion of stuffing on base of leaf, turn up base, fold in sides and wrap firmly into a neat roll. Repeat with remaining ingredients.
4. Pack rolls close together, seam sides down, in a deep pan lined with trimmings from cabbage leaves. Add stock or water, butter, salt and pepper to taste.
5. Invert a heavy plate on top of rolls and cover pan tightly. Simmer gently for 1½ hours.
6. When cooked, drain off stock carefully into a small saucepan. Reduce to 1½ cups over heat and thicken with cornflour mixed to a paste with a little cold water. Let it boil 1 minute.
7. Beat egg whites in a bowl until stiff, add yolks and beat thoroughly. Gradually beat in lemon juice, then boiling stock.
8. Return sauce to small pan, place over low heat and stir constantly until egg is cooked — do not boil.
9. Arrange rolls on a heated serving dish and spoon some of the sauce over them. Garnish with chopped dill or parsley and serve remaining sauce separately. Serve with mashed potatoes.

Note: Grape vine leaves may be used instead of cabbage — about 40 will be required since they take less filling.

KOLOKITHAKIA YEMISTA
STUFFED ZUCCHINI

Follow recipe for Yemista me Lahano, substituting 24 medium-sized zucchini (courgettes) for cabbage leaves. Cut off stems, wash zucchini and cut 1 cm (½ inch) off stem end. Reserve ends. Scoop out centres with a small spoon or special zucchini corer. Fill with meat mixture. Make corks from reserved ends and press one in each opening. Place in layers in a pan and finish as for Yemista me Lahano.

ARNI SOUVLAKI
SKEWERED LAMB

Serves: 6-8
Cooking time: 15 minutes

1 leg lamb, about 2 kg (4 lb), boned
½ cup olive oil
½ cup dry white wine
juice of 1 lemon
2 teaspoons dried rigani or oregano
2 cloves garlic, crushed or chopped
3-4 bay leaves, broken in pieces
salt and pepper

1. Cut lamb into 4 cm (1½ inch) cubes and place in a glass or earthenware dish. Add remaining ingredients to lamb, mix well to coat meat, and cover. Leave in refrigerator to marinate for 12-24 hours, stirring meat occasionally.
2. Lift lamb out of marinade and thread onto metal skewers. Pieces of bay leaf may be placed between lamb cubes.
3. Cook under a hot grill or over glowing charcoal, turning and basting frequently with marinade. Grill for 15 minutes or until cooked to taste. Place on a platter and garnish with parsley and lemon wedges. Serve hot.

YAHNI ME KOUKIA
MEAT STEW WITH BROAD BEANS

Serves: 5-6
Cooking time: 2-2½ hours

1 kg (2 lb) beef or boneless lamb stew meat
2 tablespoons oil or butter
1 large onion, finely chopped
2 cloves garlic, crushed
½ cup chopped celery
1 medium-sized carrot, sliced
1 cup chopped, peeled tomatoes
¼ cup tomato paste
¼ cup dry red wine
1 cup water
3 cloves
1 bay leaf
¼ cup chopped parsley
salt
freshly ground black pepper
½ teaspoon sugar
500 g (1 lb) very young broad beans

1. Trim meat and cut into 3 cm (1¼ inch) cubes.
2. Heat half the oil or butter in a heavy pan and brown meat quickly on each side, adding a single layer of meat to pan at a time. Remove to a plate when browned.
3. Reduce heat, add remaining oil and onion and fry onion gently until transparent. Add garlic, celery and carrot and fry for a few minutes longer.
4. Add tomato, tomato paste, wine, water, cloves, bay leaf and most of parsley. Return meat to pan and add salt and pepper to taste and the sugar. Cover and simmer gently for 45 minutes for lamb, 1¼ hours for beef.
5. Wash broad beans well, top and tail, pulling off strings at the same time. Cut into 8 cm (3 inch) lengths. Add to yahni, cover pan and simmer for further 30-45 minutes or until meat is tender.
6. Put yahni in a serving dish and sprinkle with remaining parsley. Serve hot with a tossed salad and crusty bread.

Note: Other vegetables may replace the broad beans; use same quantity unless otherwise specified.
Green beans: Top, tail and string if necessary. Slit down centre.
Green peas: Shell 1 kg (2 lb) green peas and add; 2 cups frozen peas may be used instead of fresh peas.
Celery: Omit celery from basic recipe. Cut ½ bunch celery into 8 cm (3 inch) lengths and blanch in boiling, salted water for 5 minutes. Drain and add.
Zucchini (courgettes): Top and tail and cut into 1 cm (½ inch) slices.
Cauliflower: Break 1 small head cauliflower into florets, soak in salted water, drain, rinse and add.
Potatoes: Peel 750 g (1½ lb) medium-sized potatoes, quarter and add.
Okra: Prepare as directed on page 9, then add to yahni.

PAITHAKIA ALA HASAPIKO
LAMB CHOPS BUTCHER'S STYLE

Serves: 6
Oven temperature: 180°C (350°F)
Cooking time: 1½ hours

1 kg (2 lb) lamb shoulder chops
¼ cup olive or other cooking oil
salt
freshly ground black pepper
½ teaspoon rigani or oregano
2 onions, sliced
4 tomatoes, peeled and sliced
500 g (1 lb) potatoes, peeled and sliced

1. Trim excess fat from lamb chops.
2. Brush a baking dish with 1 tablespoon of the oil and place chops in a single layer in dish. Season with salt and pepper and sprinkle on rigani or oregano.
3. Place onions on top of chops, and cover with a layer of sliced tomatoes. Season tomatoes lightly.
4. Pour on remaining oil and bake in a moderate oven for 1 hour. Top with potatoes, season lightly and brush with a little more oil, return to oven and cook for further 30 minutes. Serve hot with a green vegetable, salad and bread.

Variation: Add a sliced carrot to pan with onions, and a cup of shelled peas with potatoes for a complete one-dish main course.

ARNI SOUVLAKI (Skewered Lamb) *recipe page 57.*

KOKORETSI TIS SOUVLAS
SKEWERED VARIETY MEATS

Serves: 6, more as an appetizer
Cooking time: 15-20 minutes

250 g (8 oz) lamb sweetbreads
water
1½ lemons
500 g (1 lb) lamb liver
2 lamb hearts
2 lamb kidneys

Marinade:
1 small onion, grated
juice of 2 lemons
½ cup olive oil
3 bay leaves, each broken in 3 pieces
1 teaspoon dried rigani or oregano
2 tablespoons chopped parsley
1 teaspoon salt
freshly ground black pepper

To finish:
sausage casings

1. Rinse sweetbreads, place in a pan and cover with water. Add juice of ½ lemon. Bring to the boil, then drain.
2. Put liver, heart and halved kidneys in a bowl with cold water to cover and add the juice of 1 lemon. Soak for 30 minutes, then drain. Remove skin from liver and trim larger tubes from liver and heart; cut out fatty core from kidneys.
3. Cut meats and sweetbreads into 3 cm (1¼ inch) pieces and place in a glass or ceramic bowl.
4. Blend marinade ingredients and pour over prepared meats. Cover and leave in refrigerator to marinate for at least 2 hours. Put sausage casings in cold water and leave to soak during this time.
5. Thread meats alternately on 6 skewers, adding 2 pieces of bay leaf to each skewer among meats. Drain sausage casings and wind a length of casing around meats on each skewer, tucking ends in to keep casings in place.
6. Grill slowly over glowing charcoal, turning skewers frequently and brushing kokoretsi occasionally with marinade. Cook for 15-20 minutes, adjusting height of grid, or moving skewers to cooler part of fire so that kokoretsi cooks slowly. Serve hot.

KREATOPITA
LAMB PIE

Serves: 6
Oven temperature: 200°C (400°F)
Cooking time: 1½ hours

Pastry:
3 cups plain flour
pinch salt
½ cup butter
¾ cup cold water

Lamb Filling:
1 kg (2 lb) lean boneless lamb from leg
¼ cup butter
1 large onion, finely chopped
1 cup water
salt
freshly ground black pepper
1 cup mizithra or ricotta cheese
½ cup crumbled feta cheese
¼ cup chopped parsley
1 teaspoon chopped dill

To finish:
1 small egg
1 tablespoon milk
sesame seeds

1. Sift flour and salt into a bowl and rub in butter with fingertips until mixture resembles fine crumbs. Sprinkle in water and mix to a soft, workable dough. Knead until smooth, cover and leave to rest until filling is ready.
2. Cut lamb into 2 cm (¾ inch) cubes.
3. Melt butter in a pan and fry onion gently until transparent. Increase heat, add lamb and stir over high heat for 5 minutes until lamb loses red colour. Reduce heat to low.
4. Add water and salt and pepper to taste. Cover and simmer gently for 45 minutes. There should be little liquid left. Reduce if necessary.
5. Turn lamb into a bowl and blend in cheeses, herbs, and adjust seasoning with salt and pepper.
6. Divide pastry in two portions, one slightly larger than the other. Roll out larger piece and line a 23 cm (9 inch) pie plate. Spread filling in pastry.
7. Roll out remainder of pastry to fit top. Moisten edges of pastry in dish with water and lift top in position. Press edges to seal, trim pastry and crimp edge.
8. Beat egg with milk and glaze top of pie. Sprinkle with sesame seeds and bake in a hot oven for 30 minutes until golden brown. Serve hot, cut in wedges.

MELOPITA
HONEY PIE

*Oven temperature: (200°C (400°F) reducing to
170°C (325°F)*
Cooking time: 45 minutes

Pastry:
1½ cups plain flour
pinch of salt
1 tablespoon caster sugar
⅓ cup butter
1 egg, separated
2 teaspoons lemon juice
2 tablespoons cold water

Filling:
500 g (1 lb) mizithra or ricotta cheese
½ cup honey
1 tablespoon caster sugar
pinch of salt
3 eggs
2 teaspoons lemon juice
2 teaspoons ground cinnamon

1. Sift flour, salt and sugar into mixing bowl. Cut in butter with 2 knives, then rub with fingertips until mixture resembles fine crumbs. Beat egg yolk with lemon juice and cold water and blend in, using a knife. When dough clings together knead lightly until smooth, cover and rest for 30 minutes.
2. Beat cheese until smooth, gradually beat in honey and sugar. Beat in eggs, lemon juice and 1 teaspoon cinnamon.
3. Roll out pastry on a lightly floured board to a 30 cm (12 inch) circle. Line a greased 25 cm (10 inch) springform tin or pie plate with the pastry. Lightly beat egg white and brush some of this over pastry.
4. Pour cheese mixture into pastry case and smooth top.
5. Bake in a hot oven for 15 minutes, reduce to moderately slow and bake a further 30 minutes until set. Switch off heat and open oven door slightly. Leave pie in oven until cool. Dust with remaining cinnamon and serve cut in wedges or in traditional diamond-shaped pieces.

Note: Store honey pie in covered container in refrigerator. Bring to room temperature before serving.

GALATOBOUREKO
CUSTARD PIE

Serves: 12
Cooking time: 1 hour
Oven temperature: 180°C (350°F)

4 cups milk
¾ cup sugar
¾ cup fine semolina
¼ cup butter
grated rind of ½ lemon
piece of cinnamon bark
pinch of salt
5 eggs, lightly beaten
1 teaspoon vanilla essence
10 sheets fillo pastry
¾ cup melted, unsalted butter

Syrup:
1 cup sugar
¾ cup water
piece of cinnamon bark
2 teaspoons lemon juice

1. Mix milk, sugar, semolina, butter, lemon rind, cinnamon bark and salt in a heavy-based saucepan and heat until thickened, stirring constantly. Let custard bubble gently over low heat for 5 minutes.
2. Take from heat and remove cinnamon. Cover with a piece of buttered paper to prevent skin forming. When cool, blend in eggs and vanilla.
3. Butter a 33 x 23 cm (13 x 9 inch) oven dish. Place half of the fillo pastry sheets in the dish, brushing each sheet with the melted butter.
4. Pour in custard and top with remaining sheets, again brushing each with butter as it is placed in position. Brush top with remaining butter and score through top three sheets of fillo in 8 cm (3 inch) squares or diamonds. Sprinkle top lightly with water.
5. Trim edges and bake in a moderate oven for 45 minutes until pastry is golden brown and custard is set when tested with a knife. Remove from oven and cool thoroughly in the dish.
6. Dissolve sugar in water over low heat, increase heat to medium and bring to the boil. Add cinnamon bark and lemon juice and boil for 10 minutes.
7. Cool syrup to lukewarm before straining and pouring over the cool pie. Leave until cold before serving.

KATAIFI ME KREMA I
SHREDDED PASTRY WITH CUSTARD I

Oven temperature: 190°C (375°F)
Cooking time: 1 hour

Custard Filling:
4 cups milk
¾ cup cornflour
4 eggs, beaten
pinch salt
½ cup sugar
1 teaspoon vanilla essence

Kataifi Crust:
500 g (1 lb) kataifi (shredded pastry)
¾ cup melted, unsalted butter

Syrup:
2 cups sugar
1½ cups water
thin strip lemon rind
piece of cinnamon bark
3 teaspoons lemon juice

1. Combine milk and cornflour in a heavy pan. Blend in beaten eggs and add salt and sugar. Place over medium heat and stir constantly until thickened and bubbling. Remove from heat, stir in vanilla essence and cover top of custard with buttered paper to prevent a skin forming.
2. Place kataifi in a large bowl and gently separate strands with fingers.
3. Grease a 20 x 28 cm (8 x 11 inch) oven dish with some of the butter. Put half the kataifi in the base, pressing it down to make it compact. Drizzle ¼ cup butter evenly over it.
4. Pour custard filling over kataifi, spreading it evenly. Top with remaining kataifi. Spread evenly and pat down gently. Pour remaining melted butter evenly over top.
5. Bake in a moderately hot oven for 45 minutes until golden brown. Remove from oven and leave until cool.
6. Dissolve sugar in water over medium heat, add lemon rind and cinnamon bark and bring to the boil. Add lemon juice and boil over medium heat for 15 minutes, skimming when necessary. Do not stir once syrup is boiling.
7. Strain hot syrup over cooled pastry. Leave until cold and cut into diamond shapes to serve.

KATAIFI ME KREMA II
SHREDDED PASTRY WITH CUSTARD II

The previous recipe is the traditional way in which this dessert is made. As the custard and syrup soften the kataifi, many good cooks use the following method for a crisp finish.

1. Prepare syrup and leave until cool (Step 7).
2. Place the kataifi in a bowl and loosen strands. Pour on ½ cup melted, unsalted butter and mix with fingers to coat strands.
3. Spread kataifi in two buttered 20 x 28 cm (8 x 11 inch) straight-sided oven dishes and press down to make it compact.
4. Bake in a moderately hot oven for 20-25 minutes until golden — take care that it does not become too brown.
5. Remove from oven and pour cool syrup evenly over hot kataifi in each dish. Cover each dish with a tea towel so that kataifi softens slightly, otherwise it will be difficult to cut.
6. Make custard as directed in previous recipe (Step 1) and pour while hot onto kataifi in one dish. Invert other dish of kataifi on top of the custard. Leave uncovered until cool, then cut into diamond shapes to serve.

KOURABIETHES (Shortbread Cookies) *recipe page 64.*

KOURABIETHES
SHORTBREAD COOKIES

Makes 40
Cooking time: 20 minutes
Oven temperature: 160°C (325°F)

1 cup unsalted butter
3 tablespoons icing (confectioner's) sugar, sifted
1 egg yolk
1 tablespoon brandy
½ cup finely chopped toasted almonds, optional
2½ cups plain flour
1 teaspoon baking powder
whole cloves
2 cups icing (confectioner's) sugar

1. Melt butter until bubbles subside and sediment is golden brown — do not burn. Pour oiled butter and sediment into mixing bowl.
2. When butter has solidified add first quantity of icing sugar and beat on electric mixer until light and fluffy. Add egg yolk and brandy and beat well.
3. Remove bowl from mixer and stir in almonds if used. Sift flour and baking powder twice and mix lightly into butter mixture. Knead by hand until smooth.
4. Break off small pieces the size of a large walnut. Shape into crescents, or roll into balls, place on a flat surface and pinch tops twice, making 4 indentations and at the same time flattening them slightly.
5. Insert a clove in the top of each cookie, and place on ungreased baking sheets.
6. Bake in a moderately slow oven for 20 minutes until lightly coloured. Do not brown. Leave to cool on tray for 10 minutes.
7. Sift icing sugar over waxed paper and lift warm cookies onto this. Sift more icing sugar on top and sides.
8. When cool, place in a container and sift remaining sugar on top of cookies. Seal and store for 2 days before using to improve the flavour.
9. When serving, place each in a small paper cup cake container.

Note: The melting and light browning of the butter is not traditional but it does give a delightful flavour to the cookies. Many excellent Greek cooks use this method, but omit this step if you wish.

KOULOURAKIA
SESAME COOKIES

Makes 70
Cooking time: 15-20 minutes
Oven temperature: 190°C (375°F)

1 cup butter
1 cup caster sugar
1 teaspoon vanilla essence
3 eggs
5 cups plain flour
3 teaspoons baking powder
½ teaspoon ground cinnamon
¼ teaspoon ground cloves
¼ cup milk
½ cup toasted sesame seeds

1. Cream butter and sugar with vanilla essence until light and fluffy.
2. Beat eggs, reserve 1 tablespoon for glazing and add remainder gradually to butter mixture, beating well.
3. Sift dry ingredients twice. Stir into creamed mixture alternately with milk to form a soft dough. Knead lightly until smooth. If dough is sticky, chill for 1 hour.
4. Scatter some sesame seeds lightly on one side of pastry board. Shape pieces of dough into thick pencil shapes and roll onto the sesame seeds to coat lightly or according to taste.
5. Double over rolled dough and twist, or form into rings, figure eights or coils. Place on greased baking sheets and glaze with reserved egg beaten with a little milk.
6. Bake in a moderate oven for 15-20 minutes until golden brown. Cool on a wire rack and store in an airtight container.

Variation: Roll dough in granulated sugar instead of sesame seeds. Glaze lightly with milk.

MELOMAKARONA
HONEY DIPPED COOKIES

Makes 60
Cooking time: 25-30 minutes
Oven temperature: 180°C (350°F)

1 cup butter
¾ cup caster sugar
grated rind of 1 orange
¾ cup corn or peanut oil
6 cups plain flour
4 teaspoons baking powder
¾ cup orange juice

Nut Filling, optional:
1 tablespoon honey
1-2 teaspoons orange juice
1½ teaspoons ground cinnamon
1½ cups finely chopped walnuts
2 drops almond essence

Honey Syrup:
1 cup sugar
1 cup water
¼ cup honey
piece of cinnamon bark
2 teaspoons lemon juice

1. Beat butter and sugar with orange rind until creamy. Gradually add oil and continue beating until mixture is very light and fluffy.
2. Sift flour with baking powder and stir in alternately with orange juice. Knead dough lightly with hands for 1 minute.
3. To make nut filling, thin honey down with orange juice and blend into remaining ingredients.
4. Take a scant tablespoon of dough and flatten it a little. Place a teaspoon of the nut filling in the centre and fold dough over to enclose filling. Shape into ovals, pinching ends to a point.
5. Decorate tops with tines of a fork or by crimping cookies diagonally across top in four rows with special crimper (see end of Method).
6. Place on lightly greased baking sheets and bake in a moderate oven for 25-30 minutes until golden. Cool on wire racks.
7. To make honey syrup, combine sugar, water and honey in a saucepan and stir over heat until dissolved. Bring to the boil, add cinnamon bark and lemon juice and boil for 10 minutes over medium heat.
8. Dip cookies into boiling syrup, four at a time, turning cookies once. Leave in syrup 10 seconds in all, longer if well-soaked cookies are preferred. Lift out onto a rack and leave until cool. During dipping syrup becomes thick after a while. Thin down with a little water.
9. If no nut filling is used, sprinkle tops with crushed walnuts or toasted sesame seeds and cinnamon. Only those which are to be served should be dipped; store remainder in an airtight container and dip when required.

Crimper: Icing crimpers will be familiar to many pastry cooks and cake decorators who work with icing. If you do not own a crimper (or have never seen one), have the family handyman cut a piece of tin or aluminium plate about 2.5 x 10 cm (1 x 4 inches). Bend metal in half over a thin rod and cut 6 to 8 evenly spaced saw-like teeth on the narrow edges. Curl the 'teeth' slightly inwards.

KATAIFI
SHREDDED NUT PASTRIES

Makes 40 pieces
Oven temperature: 180°C (350°F)
Cooking time: 50-55 minutes

500 g (1 lb) kataifi pastry (see Glossary)
1 cup melted unsalted butter

Nut Filling:
1 cup coarsely ground walnuts
1 cup coarsely ground almonds
½ cup caster sugar
1 teaspoon ground cinnamon
¼ teaspoon ground cloves
1 egg white, lightly beaten
1 tablespoon brandy

Syrup:
2 cups sugar
1½ cups water
1 teaspoon lemon juice
thin strip of lemon rind
4 cloves
1 piece cinnamon bark
1 tablespoon honey

1. Take an eighth of the pastry strands and spread out on a board to a 18 x 25 cm (7 x 10 inch) rectangle with strands running roughly lengthwise.
2. Using a pastry brush, dab some butter over strands.
3. Combine nut filling ingredients and spread about 2 tablespoons of filling along one narrow edge.
4. Roll up firmly into a neat roll. Repeat with remaining ingredients.
5. Place rolls close together in a 20 x 30 cm (8 x 12 inch) slab cake pan or baking dish. Brush top with remaining butter.
6. Bake in a moderate oven, one shelf above centre, for 50-55 minutes until golden brown.
7. Meanwhile dissolve sugar in water over heat, add lemon juice and rind, cloves and cinnamon. Bring to the boil and boil over medium heat for 10 minutes. Stir in honey, strain and cool.
8. Pour cooled syrup over hot pastries and place a folded cloth on top. Leave until cool.
9. Cut each roll into 5 pieces diagonally if preferred.

Alternative shaping: Take a small handful of pastry strands and spread out fairly compactly on board. Have strands running towards you as much as is possible and dab with butter. Mould a tablespoon of nut filling into a short sausage shape and place on one end. Roll up firmly into a neat roll and place in baking dish. Repeat with remaining ingredients. Make about 30 rolls each about 5 cm (2 inches) long. Continue from Step 6.

VASILOPITA
NEW YEAR BREAD

New Year Bread is traditionally cut at midnight on New Year's Eve. After baking, a coin is inserted through a slit in the base. The person who finds the coin will have luck in the New Year. Long ago the coin used to be a gold one, then later a silver coin was used. These could be incorporated into the dough before baking. Nowadays because of the nickel content of coins it is undesirable to bake a coin in the cake.

Cooking time: 45 minutes
Oven temperature: 190°C (375°F)

1 sachet active dry yeast
¾ cup lukewarm milk
3 eggs, beaten
1½ teaspoons grated orange rind
¾ cup caster sugar
4½ cups plain flour
¼ teaspoon salt
½ teaspoon ground cinnamon
¼ teaspoon ground masticha
½ cup melted butter
egg for glazing
blanched split almonds

1. Follow mixing, kneading and proving directions in Easter Bread recipe (page 68, Steps 1 to 4).
2. When doubled in bulk punch down and turn on to lightly floured surface. Knead lightly and shape into a round loaf.
3. Place on a large greased baking sheet or in a greased 25 cm (10 inch) deep cake tin. Cover and let rise in a warm place until doubled — about 1½-2 hours.
4. Glaze with well-beaten egg and arrange blanched almonds in numbers to denote the New Year, pressing in lightly.
5. Bake in a moderately hot oven for 45 minutes until golden brown and cooked when tested. If bread browns too quickly place a piece of greased brown paper on top. Cool on a wire rack.

KATAIFI (Shredded Nut Pastries) *recipe above.*

TSOUREKI TOU PASKA
EASTER BREAD

Cooking time: 30 minutes
Oven temperature: 190°C (375°F)

1 sachet active dry yeast
½ cup warm milk
2 eggs, beaten
1 teaspoon grated lemon rind
½ cup caster sugar
3½ cups plain flour
¼ teaspoon salt
1 teaspoon ground mahlepi or allspice
½ cup melted butter
1 egg for glazing
sesame seeds

1. Dissolve yeast in ¼ cup of the milk. Add remainder of milk, eggs, lemon rind and sugar.
2. Sift 3 cups flour, salt and spice into a warm bowl and make a well in the centre. Pour in yeast mixture and stir to blend in flour, gradually adding warm melted butter.
3. Mix dough with hands until it comes away from sides. Turn on to a floured surface and knead until smooth and elastic, adding remaining flour as required. Knead for 10 minutes.
4. Place ball of dough in a clean bowl brushed with melted butter. Turn dough over to coat top with butter and cover bowl with a cloth or plastic wrap. Leave to prove (rise) in a warm place until doubled in bulk.
5. Punch down dough and turn on to a floured surface. Knead lightly and tear into three equal portions. Roll each into a rope 30 cm (12 inches) long.
6. Press ends together and plait (braid) loosely; press ends together and tuck under loaf. Place on a greased baking tray, cover with a cloth and leave to rise until doubled — about 1-2 hours depending on warmth.
7. Glaze top with well-beaten egg and sprinkle with sesame seeds.
8. Bake in a moderately hot oven for 30 minutes until golden brown and cooked when tested (tap base — it will sound hollow when cooked).

Variation: Proceed as above but make each rope 50 cm (20 inches) long. Plait and shape into a ring, pressing the two ends together. Place on a greased baking tray and press four Paskalina Avga (red-dyed eggs, below) at intervals into braid. Prove, glaze and cook as directed — sesame seeds may be omitted.

PASKALINA AVGA
RED-DYED EASTER EGGS

Dyeing eggs is a ritual in every Greek and Cypriot Greek Orthodox household on the day before Good Friday. This is performed without great attention to detail by many cooks, and the eggs can end up cracked, rendering them useless for the ritual game on Easter Sunday morning of who can crack whose eggs, a game children delight in. Also uneven dyeing frequently occurs with the usual method of boiling the eggs in the dye bath, so I suggest hard-boiling first then a brief boil in the dye.

12 eggs
water
½ teaspoon (1 packet) powdered red dye
   (from Greek food stores)
½ cup white vinegar
oil for finishing

1. Put eggs carefully into a pan and cover with cold water. Set on gentle heat and bring slowly to the boil so that eggs will not crack. Leave to boil uncovered on medium heat for 15 minutes. Eggs should be turned gently early in cooking to centre the yolks.
2. Put 4 cups water in another pan which will accommodate eggs in a single layer. Bring to the boil and add ½ cup hot water from pan to dye placed in a bowl. Dissolve dye and add to water with the vinegar. Return to the boil and let dye boil until eggs are ready.
3. Lift hot eggs from first pan into the dye bath. Increase heat and let eggs boil steadily for 2 minutes, stirring gently now and then so that the dye will take evenly.
4. Lift eggs out with a slotted spoon and place on folded paper towels to dry. Cool a little, then rub with an oil-soaked cloth to give eggs a pleasant sheen.
5. Another 6 eggs may be dyed in the same dye bath. Add about 2 tablespoons more vinegar.

BAKLAVA
BAKLAVA

Makes 30 pieces
Oven temperature: 160°C (325°F)
Cooking time: 1 hour

20 sheets fillo pastry
¾ cup melted, unsalted butter
2 cups finely chopped walnuts
1 cup finely chopped almonds
¼ cup caster sugar
2 teaspoons ground cinnamon
⅛ teaspoon ground cloves

Syrup:
1½ cups sugar
1½ cups water
¼ cup honey
thinly peeled strip of lemon rind
small piece cinnamon bark
3 cloves
2 teaspoons lemon juice

1. Butter base and sides of 33 x 23 x 5 cm (13 x 9 x 2 inch) oven dish and place nine sheets of fillo separately into dish, brushing each with melted butter.
2. Mix nuts, sugar and spices and spread half of this mixture over fillo. Top with another two sheets of fillo, brushing each with butter.
3. Spread remaining nuts on top and finish with remaining fillo, brushing each sheet as before.
4. Trim edges and brush top with butter. Cut baklava with a sharp knife into diamond shapes. Sprinkle lightly with water to prevent top layers curling upwards.
5. Bake on centre shelf in a moderately slow oven for 30 minutes. Move up one shelf and cook for further 30 minutes. Cover with greased brown paper or foil if top colours too quickly. Pastry must be allowed to cook thoroughly.
6. When baklava goes into the oven, make the syrup. Place sugar, water and honey in a heavy pan and stir over medium heat until sugar is dissolved. Add remaining syrup ingredients, bring to the boil and boil for 15 minutes. Strain and cool.
7. Spoon syrup evenly over hot baklava. Leave for several hours before cutting again into serving portions.

THIPLES
FRIED ROSETTES

Makes 30
Cooking time: about 45 seconds each pastry

3 eggs
1 tablespoon caster sugar
pinch of salt
1½ cups plain flour
peanut or corn oil for frying
warmed honey
toasted sesame seeds
ground cinnamon

1. Beat eggs until frothy, then add sugar and salt and beat until thick.
2. Sift flour and gradually stir into eggs with a wooden spoon. Dough should be slightly sticky.
3. Turn dough onto a lightly floured board, dust with flour and knead lightly. Divide into 2 balls.
4. Place one ball of dough on floured surface, dust top with flour and roll out thinly as instructed on page 16.
5. Using pastry wheel or sharp knife, cut into strips 2 cm (¾ inch) wide and about 50 cm (20 inches) long.
6. Have oil for deep frying heating to 200°C (400°F).
7. Take a strip of pastry and pinch the sides together at 2 cm (¾ inch) intervals to form little boat-shaped depressions. On a flat surface, shape strip into a flat coil, beginning at centre. Shape coil loosely and pinch pastry strip firmly together at intervals to hold shape.
8. Repeat with 4 more strips, then fry rosettes 2 at a time in hot oil. Turn to cook evenly. Pastries should be a light golden colour when cooked. Drain on paper towels. Repeat with remaining pastry.
9. When all are cooked, place a layer of pastries on a platter and drizzle warmed honey into depressions, letting honey fall off the end of a fork. Sprinkle with toasted sesame seeds and dust with cinnamon. Pile more pastries on top, finishing each layer with honey, sesame seeds and cinnamon. Serve warm or cold. Store remaining pastries in a sealed container at room temperature.

HALVAS FOURNO
SEMOLINA CAKE

Oven temperature: 180°C (350°F)
Cooking time: 50 minutes

125 g (4 oz) butter
¾ cup caster sugar
grated rind of 1 lemon
3 eggs
1½ cups fine semolina
1 cup plain flour
4 teaspoons baking powder
½ cup milk
½ cup finely chopped, toasted almonds
blanched split almonds

Syrup:
2½ cups sugar
3 cups water
2 tablespoons lemon juice

1. Cream butter, sugar and lemon rind until light and fluffy. Add eggs one at a time and beat in well.
2. Sift semolina, flour and baking powder twice and fold into butter mixture alternately with milk. Blend in chopped almonds.
3. Spread into a buttered 18 x 28 cm (7 x 11 inch) slab cake tin. Arrange split almonds in rows on top of batter.
4. Bake in a moderate oven for 50 minutes until cake is golden and shrinks slightly from sides of tin.
5. Meanwhile dissolve sugar in water over heat, add lemon juice and bring to the boil. Boil over medium heat for 20 minutes and leave until cool.
6. When cake is cooked, pour cooled syrup over hot cake. Syrup penetrates more evenly if cake surface is pricked with a fine skewer before pouring on syrup.
7. Leave in tin until cool, then cut into squares or diamond shapes for serving.

KARITHOPITA
WALNUT CAKE

Cooking time: 45 minutes
Oven temperature: 180°C (350°F)

125 g (4 oz) butter
¾ cup caster sugar
4 eggs, separated
1½ cups plain flour
4 teaspoons baking powder
1 teaspoon ground cinnamon
pinch of salt
2 cups finely chopped walnuts

Syrup:
1½ cups sugar
1½ cups water
1 piece cinnamon bark
1 teaspoon lemon juice
1 tablespoon brandy

1. Cream butter and sugar until light and fluffy, add egg yolks and beat in well.
2. Sift flour, baking powder, cinnamon and salt twice.
3. Beat egg whites until stiff.
4. Fold sifted flour into creamed mixture, then mix in about a third of the beaten egg whites.
5. Fold in ground walnuts and lastly fold in remaining egg whites, using a metal spoon to blend mixture evenly and quickly.
6. Spread evenly into a buttered 23 x 30 cm (9 x 12 inch) baking dish and bake in a moderate oven for 45 minutes or until cake is cooked when tested.
7. Meanwhile dissolve sugar in water over heat, add cinnamon bark and lemon juice and bring to the boil. Boil for 10 minutes, remove from heat, stir in brandy, cool, and strain into a jug.
8. Pour cold syrup evenly over hot cake and leave cake until cool. Cut into squares or diamond-shaped pieces to serve. Delicious served with whipped, unsweetened cream.

KOPENHAI
COPENHAGEN ALMOND TORTE

Makes 28-30 pieces
*Oven temperature : 190°C (375°F) reducing to 180°C
(350°F)*
Cooking time: 1 hour

Pastry:
¾ cup butter
¼ cup caster sugar
grated rind of 1 orange
2 egg yolks
2½ cups flour
pinch of salt

Almond Filling:
6 eggs, separated
½ cup caster sugar
¼ teaspoon almond essence
¼ cup plain flour
½ teaspoon baking powder
2 cups ground almonds
pinch of salt

To finish torte:
8 sheets fillo pastry
¼ cup melted unsalted butter
2 cups granulated sugar
1 cup water
thin strip orange rind
thin strip lemon rind
2 teaspoons lemon juice
2 pieces cinnamon bark

1. Cream butter and sugar with grated orange rind until light and fluffy; beat in egg yolks. Sift flour and salt and stir into butter mixture to form a soft dough.
2. Lightly grease a round 20 cm (12 inch) dish (a *tapsi*) or a 25 x 30 cm (10 x 12 inch) baking dish. Roll out pastry on floured board and place in dish. As pastry moulds easily any tears can be pressed together. An alternative is to put pastry in dish without rolling, and press it over base and sides with fingers. Even out by rolling with a straight-sided glass.
3. Bake in a moderately hot oven for 15-20 minutes until lightly coloured. Remove and cool.
4. To make almond filling, beat egg yolks, sugar and almond essence until thick and light.
5. Sift flour with baking powder and combine with ground almonds. Fold this lightly into beaten egg yolks.
6. Beat egg whites with salt until stiff but not dry and fold lightly into almond mixture. Pour into pastry-lined dish.
7. On a flat surface butter a fillo pastry sheet, top with another and butter. Continue until all sheets are used. Leave top sheet unbuttered.
8. Lift onto top of almond filling and trim edges of fillo in line with pastry crust, using kitchen scissors.
9. Brush top with remaining butter. With a sharp knife or razor blade make slits through top 2 or 3 sheets running the length of the dish and spacing them 4 cm (1½ inches) apart.
10. Bake in a moderate oven for 45 minutes until top is golden and filling set.
11. Meanwhile dissolve sugar in water over medium heat, add fruit rinds, lemon juice and cinnamon bark and bring to the boil. Boil for 10 minutes, strain and cool.
12. When torte is cooked, cut through slits in pastry down to the bottom crust. Pour cooled syrup over hot torte, leave until cool. Cut diagonally to give diamond-shaped pieces for serving.

PASTELLI
SESAME AND HONEY CANDIES

Makes 30
Cooking time: 35-40 minutes

1 cup sugar
¼ cup water
1 cup honey
2 cups sesame seeds

1. Combine sugar, water and honey in a heavy pan. Stir occasionally over low heat until sugar dissolves.
2. Increase heat to medium and bring to the boil. Boil for about 15 minutes to the soft ball stage. (When a little is dropped into cold water it forms a soft ball.) If you have a candy thermometer, cook to 115°C (240°F).
3. Stir in sesame seeds and return to the boil. Boil for 15 minutes until seeds turn golden and a little of the syrup dropped into water forms a hard ball, 130°C (265°F). Take care not to overcook as the sesame seeds will brown too much, spoiling the flavour.
4. Pour into an oiled 18 x 28 cm (7 x 11 inch) slab cake pan, or on to an oiled marble slab, shaping it into a rectangle of that size with a spatula.
5. When almost cool, cut into squares, triangles or fingers. Cut again when completely cold and wrap pieces in waxed paper or cellophane.

TAHINOPITA
TAHINI CAKE

This cake is frequently made during Lent as it contains no animal products. Peanut butter, the smooth, creamy variety, may be used instead of tahina.

Oven temperature: 180°C (350°F)
Cooking time: 45-60 minutes

1 tablespoon vegetable margarine or peanut
    oil
1 cup tahina
1 cup caster sugar
grated rind of 1 orange
¾ cup strained orange juice
2¼ cups plain flour
pinch salt
3 teaspoons baking powder
½ teaspoon bicarbonate of soda
½ teaspoon ground allspice
½ cup finely chopped walnuts
½ cup sultanas (white raisins)

1. Grease a 20 cm (8 inch) tube pan or a 20 x 30 cm (8 x 12 inch) slab cake pan with melted margarine or oil. Chill in refrigerator until required.
2. Beat tahina, sugar and orange rind for 10 minutes, then gradually beat in orange juice.
3. Sift dry ingredients twice and fold into tahina mixture. Blend in walnuts and sultanas.
4. Dust chilled cake pan with flour and turn batter into pan. Spread evenly and knock base of pan on table top to settle batter.
5. Bake in a moderate oven for 55-60 minutes for tube pan, 45 minutes or so for slab cake. When cooked, invert cake in its pan onto cake rack and leave for 2-3 minutes before lifting pan from cake. Cool cake and cut in slices or squares to serve. Store cake in a sealed container.

FINIKIA
SEMOLINA HONEY COOKIES

Makes 60
Oven temperature: 180°C (350°F)
Cooking time: 25 minutes

125 g (4 oz) butter
½ cup caster sugar
grated rind of 1 orange
½ cup corn or peanut oil
2½ cups plain flour
4 teaspoons baking powder
1½ cups fine semolina
1 teaspoon ground cinnamon
pinch ground cloves
½ cup orange juice
toasted sesame seeds or chopped walnuts for
    serving

Syrup:
1 cup water
1 cup sugar
½ cup honey
piece of cinnamon bark
2 teaspoons lemon juice

1. Cream butter, sugar and orange rind until light and fluffy. Gradually add oil and continue to beat on high speed until mixture thickens to whipped cream consistency.
2. Sift flour and baking powder twice and combine with semolina and spices. Gradually add to creamed mixture alternately with orange juice. When combined knead with hand to form a firm dough.
3. Shape tablespoonfuls of dough into ovals, place on ungreased baking sheets and pinch ends to form torpedo shape.
4. Bake in a moderate oven for 25 minutes until golden brown and crisp. Cool on baking sheets.
5. In a pan stir water and sugar over heat until sugar dissolves. Add honey, cinnamon bark and lemon juice and bring to the boil. Boil over medium heat for 10 minutes and remove cinnamon.
6. While syrup is boiling, dip cookies in 3 at a time, turn over in syrup, then remove to a rack placed over a dish. Repeat with number required for serving. Store remainder in a sealed container for later dipping.
7. Sprinkle dipped cookies with sesame seeds or chopped walnuts and serve.

AMIGTHALOTA
ALMOND PEARS

Amigthalota are a speciality from the island of Ithra (Hydra). Flavouring these almond delicacies with rose or orange flower water is a matter of taste. If you like these scented flavours then omit lemon rind from recipe. Whatever flavouring is used, Amigthalota make an excellent accompaniment to after-dinner coffee. Serve in petit-four cases.

Makes 30
Cooking time: 20 minutes
Oven temperature: 160°C (325°F)

3 cups ground almonds
½ cup icing (confectioner's) sugar, sifted
¼ cup egg whites (about 2)
½ teaspoon grated lemon rind, optional
2 drops almond essence
whole cloves
additional icing sugar
rose or orange flower water, optional

1. Blend ground almonds with icing sugar measured after sifting.
2. Add lightly beaten egg whites with lemon rind if used and almond essence. Mix to a firm dough with hands.
3. Clean hands and rub with a little butter to prevent dough sticking while shaping. Break off small pieces of dough the size of a walnut and form into pear shapes.
4. Insert a whole clove in the top of each to resemble a stem and place upright on a buttered and floured baking sheet.
5. Bake in a moderately slow oven for 20 minutes, covering with brown paper if tops begin to brown.
6. Sift 2 cups icing sugar into a bowl and dip hot Amigthalota into it. If desired, a little rose or orange flower water may be brushed onto Amigthalota before dipping into icing sugar. Place on a wire rack to cool.
7. Sift remaining sugar from bowl into base of a container and arrange cooled Almond Pears upright in a single layer.
8. Sift more sugar thickly over tops and sides, seal and store for a day or two before using.

KYTHONOPASTO
QUINCE PASTE

Cooking time: 45-50 minutes

pulp from Kythoni Peltes (page 74)
granulated sugar
water
bay leaves
caster sugar

1. Purée quince pulp by pressing through a sieve or process in food processor.
2. Measure purée into a heavy pan. Add 1 cup sugar and ¼ cup water to each cup of pulp.
3. Set over medium low heat and stir occasionally until sugar is dissolved.
4. Bring to the boil, then boil steadily for 40-45 minutes, stirring occasionally so that paste cooks evenly. As paste is thick, it has a tendency to scorch, so watch carefully.
5. When cooked, paste comes away from sides of pan and is dark red in colour. Spread while hot into an oiled slab cake pan so that it is 2 cm (¾ inch) thick. Leave in pan at room temperature for 2-3 days, lightly covered with muslin.
6. When dry and firm, cut into small diamond shapes with an oiled knife. Lift out and place in a container with bay leaves between layers. Seal tightly.
7. When serving, dip tops lightly into caster sugar to give pieces a fine coating. Kythonopasto keeps indefinitely stored at room temperature and is traditionally served in place of a spoon sweet, accompanied with a glass of iced water.

KYTHONI PELTES
QUINCE JELLY

This method might seem complicated. Peels and cores are boiled separately to extract the pectin which is necessary for setting. Of course, you can cook the quince together with peels and cores with a lot less fuss, but the Greeks waste nothing: the pulp left after making the jelly makes a delightful confection, Kythonopasto (Quince Paste), so it is worthwhile keeping the pulp free of peels and cores for this purpose.

Cooking time: 2 hours

1 kg (2 lb) quinces
4 cups water
granulated sugar
2 teaspoons lemon juice
2 rose geranium leaves

1. Wash quinces well to remove the fuzz. Peel and core. Slice quinces into preserving pan and add 2 cups water. Leave aside and do not be concerned if quince discolours.
2. Place peels and cores into a pan with remaining water and boil for 30 minutes. Strain and make liquid up to 2 cups with water.
3. Add liquid from peels to sliced quinces in pan. Bring to the boil and simmer gently for 1 hour until quince flesh is very tender.
4. Scald a large piece of cheese cloth or doubled butter muslin, wring out and drape over a deep bowl.
5. Pour quince and liquid into cloth and gather up ends. Tie with string and suspend over bowl. Secure to a fixed object so that juice can drip slowly into bowl. Leave for 24 hours. Do not squeeze bag to hasten dripping as this will make jelly cloudy.
6. Measure juice into clean preserving pan. For each cup of juice add 1 cup sugar. Stir over heat till sugar dissolves, add lemon juice and washed geranium leaves and bring to the boil.
7. Boil rapidly for 25 minutes, skimming frequently. Test a teaspoonful on a cold saucer. Leave to cool. Run finger across jelly in saucer — setting point is reached when surface wrinkles. It is advisable to remove pan from heat while jelly is being tested as you could overcook the jelly.
8. Remove leaves and ladle hot jelly into hot sterilized jars. Seal when cold.

KYTHONI XYSTO
GRATED QUINCE PRESERVE

Cooking time: 1½ hours

4 quinces, about 1 kg (2 lb)
3 cups water
4 cups sugar
2 strips thinly peeled lemon rind
1 piece cinnamon bark or 2 rose geranium
   leaves
¼ cup blanched split almonds, toasted
2 tablespoons lemon juice

1. Wash quinces well and rub off all fuzz. Peel, quarter and remove core.
2. Place peels and cores in a pan with 2 cups water and boil for 20 minutes.
3. Grate quince quarters and place in a heavy preserving pan with remaining water. Leave aside until peels are boiled. Do not be concerned if quince discolours.
4. Strain liquid from peels into a measuring jug and make up to 2 cups with water. Add this to grated quince with the sugar, lemon rind and cinnamon bark or washed geranium leaves.
5. Place over medium heat and stir occasionally with a wooden spoon until sugar is dissolved.
6. Bring to the boil and boil fairly rapidly for 1 hour or until it gels when tested on a cold saucer.
7. Stir in almonds and lemon juice and boil 1 minute longer. Ladle into hot, sterilized jars and seal when cold.

Note: As the peel and core contain pectin, the setting ingredient for jellies and preserves, it is advisable that these be boiled to extract the pectin.

KYTHONI XYSTO (Grated Quince Paste) *recipe above*;
KYTHONI PELTES (Quince Jelly) *recipe above*;
KYTHONOPASTO (Quince Paste) *recipe page 73.*

GLYKO KARPOUZI
WATERMELON RIND PRESERVE

Cooking time: 1½-1¾ hours

1 kg (2 lb) watermelon rind
water
3 cups sugar
2 small pieces cinnamon bark
1 thinly peeled strip of lemon peel
2 tablespoons lemon juice
¼ cup honey
½ cup split blanched almonds, toasted

1. Remove all traces of pink from watermelon rind. Peel off green skin. Cut firm white flesh into 2 cm (¾ inch) cubes.
2. Place cubes in a preserving pan and cover with cold water. Bring to the boil and simmer for 1 hour or until rind is translucent. Drain.
3. Place 3 cups water in pan with sugar, cinnamon bark, lemon peel, 1 tablespoon lemon juice and honey. Stir over heat till sugar dissolves and bring to the boil, skimming when necessary.
4. Add drained watermelon rind, return to the boil and boil gently for 15 minutes. Remove from heat, cover and leave for 12 hours or overnight.
5. Return to the boil over medium heat and boil until syrup is thick when tested on a cold saucer. Remove cinnamon and lemon peel.
6. Add remaining lemon juice and toasted almonds, boil 1 minute, then ladle into warm, sterilized jars. Seal when cold.

GLYKO PORTOKALI
PRESERVED ORANGE ROLLS

6 large, thick-skinned oranges
water
3 cups sugar
1 tablespoon lemon juice

1. Lightly grate entire surface of each orange. Score peel deeply from stem end to base into 6 segments and remove peel carefully.
2. Tightly roll up peel, passing a needle and long thread through each roll, tying on first roll. When 12 rolls are threaded, tie ends together to form a circle of rolls.
3. Put rolls into a pan of cold water, bring to the boil and drain immediately. Repeat boiling and draining process twice more to remove bitterness from peel.
4. Cover rolls with cold water again and bring to the boil. Boil gently for 45-60 minutes until tender. Drain and place on paper towels to dry.
5. In a clean pan dissolve sugar in 3 cups water over heat and bring to the boil. Add lemon juice and boil syrup for 5 minutes.
6. Add strings of orange rolls and boil for 10 minutes, timed from when preserve returns to the boil. Skim when necessary. Remove from heat, cover and leave overnight.
7. Next day bring pan contents to the boil and cook gently for 15-20 minutes or until syrup is thick when tested on a cold saucer.
8. Cool a little, remove threads and place rolls and syrup into sterilized jars. Seal when cold and store in a cool place.

FRAPA GLYKO
PRESERVED GRAPEFRUIT ROLLS

Substitute 4 thick-skinned grapefruit for oranges in Glyko Portokali recipe (above) . After grating, cut peel into sixths or eighths, depending on size of fruit. Follow instructions, except that the rolls must be boiled 4 times instead of 3 (see Step 3).

LEMONI GLYKO
PRESERVED LEMON PEEL

Again follow recipe for Glyko Portokali, substituting 6 thick-skinned lemons for oranges. Cut peel into quarters after grating, then cut each quarter in half, giving 8 triangles of peel from each lemon. Do not roll and thread — just follow on from Step 3. Alternatively, rolls can be made — leave quarters as they are peeled from the fruit, boil and drain as in Step 3. They will then be soft enough to roll up and thread. Continue on from Step 4.

PORTOKALI GLACE
GLACE ORANGE PEEL

4 large thick-skinned oranges
4 cups granulated sugar
2 cups water
2 tablespoons liquid glucose or ¼ cup light corn syrup

1. Prepare orange peel by following Steps 1 to 4 in Glyko Portokali recipe (page 76).
2. Dissolve sugar in the 2 cups water over medium heat. Add glucose or corn syrup and bring to the boil. Add strings of rolls and return to the boil.
3. Boil gently for 10 minutes, skimming when necessary. Transfer to a bowl and leave for 24 hours so that peel can absorb sugar.
4. Drain syrup back into pan, bring to the boil over medium heat and boil for 10 minutes.
5. Remove threads from rolls and pour syrup over rolls in bowl. Invert a plate onto the rolls to keep them submerged in the syrup and leave for further 24 hours.
6. Drain syrup back into pan, bring to the boil and boil for 5 minutes. Add rolls, return to the boil and boil for further 5 minutes. Return to bowl, submerging rolls as before and leave for 24 hours.
7. Place wire rack over a dish and place rolls on rack to drain. Leave to dry in a warm place for 48 hours. When dry store in a sealed container.

LEMONI GLACE
GLACE LEMON PEEL

Follow directions given for Portokali Glace using 4-6 thick-skinned lemons, depending on size. Leave in triangular segments as instructed in Lemoni Glyko (page 77).

FRAPA GLACE
GLACE GRAPEFRUIT ROLLS

Follow directions given for Portokali Glace, using 3 grapefruit. Boil and change water 4 times before boiling peel until tender. Continue from Step 2.

CYPRUS

With my parents hailing from the Greek island of Kythera, I have always felt an affinity with the people of Cyprus, as both Kythera and Cyprus, through legend, lay claim to the goddess Aphrodite. Legend has it that Aphrodite rose from the sea and went to Kythera, and then to Cyprus. The Cypriots tell it differently. For the romantic amongst you, Cyprus is regarded as the Island of Aphrodite, and for an island so endowed with beauty, there could hardly be a more appropriate symbol.

Before I visited Cyprus, I was under the mistaken impression that Cypriot and Greek cooking were much the same. I was proved wrong and pleasantly surprised.

One of Cyprus's most interesting dishes would have to be Afelia. The basic food can be either pork, new potatoes, mushrooms or globe artichoke hearts, and it is cooked with crushed coriander seeds and red wine. Irrespective of the food used in the dish, it is still called Afelia, so I have numbered the variations and depend on the English translation to distinguish between them.

I was also pleased to find that stuffed vine leaf rolls were not called dolmathakia as they are in Greece. They go under the delightful name of

Koupepia — meaning little cigars.

Cyprus cooking seems to be a happy mixture of Greek, Lebanese-Syrian and Turkish cuisines with an unmistakable mark that makes it Cypriot. Naturally with my heritage, Greek cooking is the best known to me and I was happy to be able to add more Greek recipes through the pages of Cyprus, though both Greece and Cyprus have a great variety of dishes, perhaps because of their history and proximity to Europe. Nevertheless the recipes in this chapter are very much Cypriot in execution as they have a great passion for certain ingredients such as cinnamon and coriander.

Perhaps to really experience the Cypriot cuisine and its adaptation of recipes from other countries, a visit to a taverna best proves the point. One we visited in Nicosia only serves mezethakia — twenty-five in all. They came in steady procession throughout the course of the evening. Koupepia, Koupes, feta and haloumy cheese, olives, Tabouleh, Hummus, Tahinosalata, Talattouri, Souvlakia, Miala, lounza (grilled and topped with melting haloumy), Stifatho, Tavas, marides (fried small fish), Panjaria Salata, raw artichoke hearts, celery sticks, cucumber, tomato, octopus in wine . . . We were informed that we could have a grilled fillet steak afterwards! You will find recipes for most of these in various chapters as well as that following. The description given should suffice for the remainder.

A trip to the local market in Nicosia gave me further insight into the uniqueness of Cypriot food. Our guide, though claiming that she was not a good cook, filled me in on the preparation of vegetables, one which particularly intrigued me being kolokassi. More about that in the recipe section.

The Cypriot fondness for pork is evident in their meat markets. They make a ham called hiromeri, very similar to the Italian prosciutto, and lounza, cured, smoked pork fillet. My description of lounza with haloumy cheese previously mentioned is virtually the recipe itself, and lounza is available at Greek and Cypriot food stores.

In the little village of Kakopetria I was told how to make Cypriot sausages. The village method calls for days of soaking the pork and spices in red wine — at room temperature! With regard to your health, the recipe I have given is one used by Cypriot butchers which you can prepare with confidence.

The same cook gave me her recipe for making green walnut preserves. The process involved is lengthy, but well worth trying. A friend of ours recalls his boyhood days in Cyprus when he and his friends would be commandeered to peel the walnuts. They thought it great fun to go round for days with blackened hands. It happened to me — but I did not regard it as fun! Rubber gloves are strongly advocated.

The breads of Cyprus, though similar to Greek breads, have some interesting variations. Haloumopsomi is filled with chunks of haloumy cheese. This cheese can be made in the home and I have given you a recipe for making your own, but it is also readily available at Greek and Cypriot food stores, as well as specialist cheese shops. The same cheese is combined with cheddam and other ingredients and used as a filling for Flaounes (Easter cheese pies), the pie crust being a yeast dough. Elioti is another typically Cypriot bread with onions and black olives baked in it. Both Haloumopsomi and Elioti may be prepared with frozen bread dough — the recipes give details.

THE FLAVOUR OF CYPRIOT FOODS

While olive oil is almost as widely used as in Greece, the Cypriot cook prefers corn oil for the preparation of many dishes. Butter is considered somewhat of a luxury and is used only in the making of Greek pastries and cakes. Typical Cypriot cakes and cookies often use lard or corn oil, for example the Lokoumia Parayemista cookie, similar to the Ma'amoul of Lebanon, which is made in huge quantities especially for pre-wedding festivities. In Cyprus these are made with lard but expatriate Cypriots prefer to use butter, and so do I.

While cassia bark is widely used in Greece instead of cinnamon, in Cyprus the more delicately flavoured cinnamon bark is preferred. This is sold in sticks or quills, the kind generally used in Western cooking. A good Cypriot cook prefers to pound the bark to a powder rather than buy it already ground.

Coriander, native to southern Europe, is a most popular flavour ingredient. Both the leaves and the dried seeds are used extensively.

The Cypriots take pride in being self-sufficient and in rural areas they prepare their own pourgouri (burghul) and haloumy and anari cheese, ham and a pasta called trahana. The latter is made with soured milk and ground wheat. It is a lengthy process and ends up as small, square noodles. Trahana forms the basis of winter soups, cooked in chicken broth with perhaps a little tomato to flavour it and with cubes of haloumy cheese stirred in just before it is removed from the fire. Trahana is also made in Greece, with semolina (farina) used instead of the ground wheat. Trahana is readily available at Greek and Cypriot stores.

EATING CYPRIOT STYLE

With such a history it is natural for the Cypriots to take their meals in a Western manner, though it is not served in separate courses. A meat, fish or poultry dish will form the basis of the meal, perhaps preceded by a soup. When fasting, a vegetable dish such as Polypikilo, Louvana or Louvia Mavromatika me Lahana could replace the meat or poultry. A salad, either a cooked green vegetable with an oil and lemon dressing or a combination of raw vegetables, would be served as an accompaniment. Olives, cheese, pickles, bread, fresh fruit and wine complete the meal.

The Cypriot lifestyle is very similar to that of Greece and Turkey, which is what one would expect. One delightful custom practised both in Cyprus and Greece is the serving of glyko (spoon sweets). These delightful fruit preserves are lovingly prepared by Greek and Cypriot women, using fruits in season. When a visitor calls, the glyko is served in small glass or silver dishes with a spoon. It is accompanied by a glass of iced water — certainly necessary as they are very sweet — and after this formality coffee with perhaps a selection of pastries is served.

COOKING METHODS

For Cypriot cooking, a Western kitchen needs little extra in the way of equipment, as any pot, pan or casserole can be used. In Cyprus the kitchen can be as up-to-date as your own, or a farm-style kitchen with an open hearth where sausages and hams can be smoked in the chimney; large pots for preparing Zalatina and Haloumi cheese, and *talaria,* woven baskets for draining the curds. In rural areas where they make their own pickles, breads, trahana, sweet preserves and cured olives every kitchen would be equipped with large utensils and large storage jars, usually of glazed or unglazed pottery, depending on their use.

The *tapsi,* a round baking dish, is used for roasting meats and baking sweets; a *tava,* an unglazed terracotta casserole for preparing a dish by the same name; a *saganaki,* a two-handled frying pan for cooking *mezes* to be taken directly to the table. Any baking dish, casserole or frying pan can do in their stead.

For rolling pastry, a long length of dowel is a definite advantage, as the Cypriot cook prepares pastries in great quantities, and a dowel makes the process so much simpler.

INGREDIENTS FOR CYPRIOT COOKING

The recipes are self explanatory and ingredients used are readily available. Burghul, rice, pulses, pastas, semolina and cinnamon, coriander leaves and seeds and haloumy cheese are necessary ingredients. You can see that it would not be difficult to prepare Cypriot food in your kitchen.

HALOUMI
HALOUMY CHEESE

Haloumi is a favourite cheese in Cyprus, Greece and Lebanon. In Cyprus it is frequently made in the home when plenty of milk is available. Sheep's milk is traditionally used, but cow's milk gives a satisfactory result.

The Cyprus home cheese maker uses reed baskets called talaria for draining the curds. A colander lined with butter muslin works just as well.

Quantity produced with amount of milk used in the following recipe is quite small for the effort entailed; however if you have copious amounts of milk available, use 1 rennet tablet to each litre of milk, 4 tablets to each Imperial or US gallon.

For Lebanese-style haloumi, sprinkle cheese after salting with black cumin seeds instead of dried mint.

Makes 250 g (8 oz)

3 rennet (junket) tablets
2 tablespoons cold water
8 cups whole milk
good quality cooking salt
1 tablespoon dried mint

1. Crush rennet tablets in a small bowl, add cold water and stir to dissolve.
2. Place milk in a large pot and warm to blood heat or no more than 38°C (100°F). Add dissolved rennet and stir gently for a few seconds only. Cover pot and leave in a warm place for 30 minutes until set.
3. Using a straw or wire whisk, stir set milk to break up curds. Leave until curds settle.
4. Line a colander with a doubled piece of butter muslin and set colander over a deep basin or pot. Ladle curds into colander, collecting whey in receptacle.
5. When well drained, lift cloth with curds onto a clean chopping board set on sink top. Shape curds with hand into a square about 2 cm (¾ inch) thick, fold cloth over top and press gently with hand. Raise one end of board so that remaining whey can drain. Leave for 1½-2 hours.
6. Return collected whey to original pot and put on to boil.
7. When curds are well drained and compact, cut into 4 and carefully put pieces into boiling whey. Cook until cheese floats, remove from heat and leave for 5 minutes.
8. Have ready about ¼ cup salt on a plate and crumble the mint to coarse flakes.
9. Lift out each piece of cheese with an egg slice and place on a board. While hot, press pieces with hand to flatten a little. Dab dry with paper towels. Dip pieces on each side in the salt, sprinkle some mint on one side, fold in three to enclose mint and press with hand to keep cheese in shape. This step must be carried out while cheese is warm and pliable.
10. Pack cooled cheese into a sterilized jar. Dissolve 2 tablespoons salt in 2 cups whey and pour over cheese. Seal and store in a cool place. Cheese may be eaten when freshly made, or allowed to mature in the salty whey for 6 weeks.

ANARI
COTTAGE CHEESE

Anari is a whey cheese similar to the Italian ricotta. When haloumi is made in the Cyprus household, the whey is used for making anari before the haloumi is completed.

whey from haloumi cheese
4 cups whole milk
4 teaspoons lemon juice, strained

1. Before whey is used for cooking haloumi (Step 6 of Haloumi recipe, above), bring to boil and add milk and lemon juice.
2. Return to the boil, stirring constantly with whisk. Curds will form on top of whey. If milk does not curd, add a little more strained lemon juice. Remove from heat and leave aside for 10 minutes.
3. Strain through a colander lined with a doubled piece of butter muslin, collecting whey in another receptacle.
4. When most of whey has drained out, scrape down curds from sides of cloth, gather ends and tie cloth with string. Hang over sink for 2 hours or more to drain completely.
5. When well drained, turn anari into a bowl, cover and refrigerate. Use within 2 to 3 days.
6. Return reserved whey to pot and proceed with Haloumi recipe. It may be necessary to skim fine milky curds from top of whey after making anari and before haloumi is returned to it.

SKORTHALIA
GARLIC SAUCE

Makes 1½ cups

4-5 cloves garlic
¼ cup white vinegar
salt
125 g (4 oz) crustless stale white bread
½ cup ground almonds
½ cup olive oil
1 tablespoon lemon juice
freshly ground white pepper

1. Soak halved garlic cloves in vinegar for 10 minutes. Remove garlic to a mortar, add ½ teaspoon salt and pound to a paste.
2. Soak bread in cold water and squeeze dry. Crumble into small particles and gradually blend into garlic, adding a little vinegar to smooth the mixture.
3. When well pounded and smooth, transfer to a bowl if mortar is small. Gradually beat in ground almonds and olive oil alternately with remaining vinegar. Beat in lemon juice and add salt to taste. If mixture is very thick, beat in a little more oil or lemon juice, depending on flavour balance. Mixture should be the consistency of stiff mayonnaise.
4. Turn into a serving bowl and serve with fried fish, squid, fried or boiled vegetables or as directed in recipes.

Food processor or blender method: Soak garlic as above. Place all ingredients except oil in container and process or blend until smooth. Gradually beat in oil. Adjust seasoning, flavour and consistency as above and blend until smooth. Do not over-beat as mixture could heat and curdle.

SALTSA TOMATA
TOMATO SAUCE

Makes about 2 cups
Cooking time: 40 minutes

1 large onion, finely chopped
¼ cup corn oil or butter
1 cup chopped, peeled tomatoes
½ cup tomato paste
1 cup stock or water
1 bay leaf
large piece cinnamon bark
1 teaspoon sugar
salt
freshly ground black pepper

1. Gently fry onion in oil or butter in a heavy pan. When transparent add tomatoes and fry until soft.
2. Add tomato paste, stock or water, bay leaf, cinnamon bark, sugar and salt and pepper to taste. Bring to a gentle simmer, cover and simmer gently for 30 minutes, removing lid for last 10 minutes so that moisture can evaporate to thicken sauce.
3. Remove bay leaf and cinnamon bark and serve on boiled spaghetti or as directed in recipes.

AGINARES OMA
RAW ARTICHOKES

In Cyprus the globe artichoke is enjoyed more often raw than cooked. Use young artichokes and remove 3 or 4 layers of leaves to expose the hearts. Cut off the top section of the leaves and trim carefully around base to neaten. Cut into quarters and remove choke with a spoon. Drop into a bowl of water to which the juice of 2 lemons has been added. When ready to serve, drain well and serve with crisp celery sticks as a *meze*. Lemon wedges can be added for squeezing to individual taste, or the artichokes may be dipped into Tahinosalata (see page 182).

A selection of appetizers: AGINARES OMA (Raw Artichokes) *recipe above*, with celery and cucumber; KOUPEPIA (Stuffed Grape Vine Leaves) *recipe page 84;* PANJARIA SALATA (Beetroot Salad) *recipe page 95;* LOUKANIKA (Pork Sausages) *recipe page 104;* ELIES TSAKISTES (Cracked Green Olives) *recipe page 85.*

MIALA ME LEMONI
MARINATED BRAINS

Serves: 6
Cooking time: 20 minutes

6 sets lamb brains
water
salt
white vinegar
1 clove garlic

Dressing:
juice of 1 lemon
⅓ cup olive oil
salt
freshly ground white pepper
2 tablespoons finely chopped parsley

1. Place brains in a bowl and cover with cold water. Add 1 tablespoon each vinegar and salt. Soak for 15 minutes.
2. Drain and remove skin if possible. This is difficult if brains have been frozen. Any veins should be removed.
3. Place in a pan with fresh water to cover, add 1 teaspoon salt, 1 tablespoon vinegar and whole, peeled garlic clove. Bring to a slow simmer, cover pan and simmer gently for 15 minutes until tender. Do not boil.
4. Drain well, cut into cubes and place in a bowl.
5. Beat dressing ingredients together and pour over brains. Cover and leave to marinate in refrigerator for 2 hours or longer. Serve in the dressing as a *meze*.

KOUPEPIA
STUFFED GRAPE VINE LEAVES

Serves: 8 for first course, 6 for main course
Cooking time: 1½ hours

375 g (12 oz) preserved vine leaves or 60 fresh
    leaves
1 medium-sized onion, finely chopped
2 tablespoons corn oil
500 g (1 lb) finely ground lamb
250 g (8 oz) finely ground veal
½ cup rice
2 tablespoons finely chopped parsley
2 teaspoons finely chopped mint
1½ teaspoons salt
freshly ground black pepper
2 tablespoons lemon juice
1 tablespoon butter
2 cups light stock

Egg and Lemon Sauce:
2 tablespoons butter
2 tablespoons flour
1½ cups chicken or lamb stock
2 eggs
1-2 tablespoons lemon juice
salt
freshly ground white pepper

1. Rinse grape vine leaves (fresh or preserved) in cold water and blanch in boiling water for 3 minutes in 3 or 4 lots. Remove to basin of cold water with slotted spoon, then into a colander to drain.
2. Gently fry onion in oil until soft. Lightly mix lamb, veal, rice, onion and oil, herbs, salt and pepper until well combined.
3. To shape Koupepia place a vine leaf, shiny side down, on work surface. Snip off stem if necessary. Place about a tablespoon of meat mixture near stem end, fold end and sides over stuffing and roll up firmly. Stuffing is sufficient for about 4 dozen rolls.
4. Line base of a heavy pan with 6 leaves (use damaged ones) and pack Koupepia close together in layers. Sprinkle each layer with a little of the lemon juice.
5. Cover top of rolls with remaining grape vine leaves. Add the butter and 2 cups stock to pan with any remaining lemon juice. Invert a heavy plate on top to keep rolls in shape during cooking.
6. Cover pan with lid and place over medium heat. Bring to a slow simmer, then simmer gently over low heat for 1½ hours.
7.   To make sauce, melt butter in a small saucepan and stir in flour. Cook 2 minutes without browning and stir in the 1½ cups stock. Stir constantly until sauce thickens and bubbles.
8. Beat eggs in a bowl until frothy and beat in 1 tablespoon lemon juice. Pour the hot sauce into the eggs gradually, beating constantly. Return sauce to pan and stir over gentle heat for 2 minutes to cook the egg. Care must be taken as sauce could curdle. If this happens, sprinkle a little cold water into sauce and beat with egg whisk.
9. Drain cooked rolls and arrange on a hot serving dish. Garnish with parsley and lemon slices. Serve egg and lemon sauce in a separate sauce boat.

Note: Koupepia may be served cold without the sauce as an appetizer. Serve with a bowl of yoghurt on the side.

ELIES TSAKISTES
CRACKED GREEN OLIVES

fresh green olives
water
rock salt
grape vine leaves
lemon slices

For serving:
juice of 1 lemon
1 clove garlic, crushed
¼ cup coriander seeds
¼ cup olive oil

1. Crack olives by hitting each separately with a mallet or smooth stone. Only the flesh has to be cracked; do not hit too hard as the seed should remain intact.
2. Place cracked olives in a large jar (or jars) and cover with cold water. Keep olives submerged with a small heavy plate or clean flat stone. Change water every 24 hours; do this 4 times in all.
3. Measure last amount of water poured from the olives before discarding. Now measure the same amount of fresh water into a large pot and add ⅓ cup rock salt to each 4 cups water. Stir over low heat until dissolved. (When cool you can check the strength of the brine with a fresh egg. The right strength is reached when egg floats with an area about 2.5 cm (1 inch) in diameter breaking the surface.)
4. Pour brine over olives in jar, place washed grape vine leaves and lemon slices on top and seal. Leave in a dark, cool place for at least 3 weeks; they may be kept like this for a few months.
5. When required for serving take out about 2 cups olives. Any growth on top is of no importance so long as the olives are not soft, showing signs of decay. If they are soft, discard them — it may be that only olives at the top are affected. Remove fungus.
6. Rinse olives under cold water, drain well and place in a bowl. Squeeze on lemon juice. Add crushed garlic, coarsely pounded coriander seeds and olive oil. Stir well and leave for 1-2 hours before serving as an appetizer with bread or as an accompaniment to meals.

KOUPES
CIGARS OR BURGHUL SHELLS WITH GROUND MEAT FILLING

Makes about 35
Cooking time: 6-8 minutes each lot

2 cups fine pourgouri (burghul)
1½ cups boiling water

Filling:
250 g (8 oz) ground lamb or beef
1 large onion, finely chopped
1 tablespoon corn oil
¼ cup finely chopped parsley
pinch ground cinnamon
salt
freshly ground black pepper

To finish:
oil for deep frying

1. It is not necessary to wash pourgouri, but do so if you wish. If washed, drain well in a fine sieve, pressing with the back of a spoon to extract all moisture.
2. Put dry or moist pourgouri in a bowl and add boiling water. Stir well, cover and leave aside for 2-3 hours.
3. Meanwhile make filling. Put lamb, onion and oil in a frying pan and stir over high heat until juices evaporate and meat begins to brown. Add parsley, cinnamon, and salt and pepper to taste. Remove from heat and cool.
4. Knead pourgouri well to form a coarse-textured dough. Break off a piece about the size of a small walnut and mould in moistened hand, squeezing dough to form an oval, cigar shape. Wet forefinger and push into one end of oval, to make a hole. Work other hand around outside of dough to make the wall of the koupa as thin as possible. A long forefinger is a definite advantage.
5. Fill hollow with about a teaspoon of meat filling and close the opening, moistening dough with a little water to seal. Any breaks can be sealed by dabbing with water. Smooth koupa with moistened hands and put on a tray. Repeat with remaining ingredients.
6. Deep fry 6 or 8 at a time in hot oil. Let them fry for a minute or so before turning. Keep frying and turning for 6-8 minutes or until deep golden brown and crisp. Drain on paper towels and serve hot as an appetizer.

TALATTOURI
YOGHURT AND CUCUMBER SALAD

Serves: 6

2 cups drained yoghurt (page 21)
2 slender green cucumbers
salt
2 cloves garlic, crushed
2-3 teaspoons dried mint
1-2 tablespoons olive oil
mint sprigs to garnish

1. Drain 2½ cups yoghurt as directed for 1 hour only—this should give 2 cups thick yoghurt.
2. Peel cucumbers and cut into quarters lengthwise. Slice thinly and place in a bowl. Mix in about 3 teaspoons salt and leave to stand for 1 hour. Drain well in a colander.
3. Blend cucumbers into yoghurt with garlic and finely crushed mint to taste. Add salt to taste if necessary.
4. Blend in olive oil a little at a time, adding as much as the talattouri will take to make a thick, creamy mixture. Chill well and serve in a deep bowl garnished with mint sprigs. Serve as a *meze* with raw artichokes, crisp celery sticks, fried smelts and sardines and crusty bread. Talattouri also makes an excellent sauce for fried fish.

SAGANAKI HALOUMI
FRIED HALOUMY CHEESE

Serves: 4
Cooking time: 2 minutes

250 g (8 oz) haloumy cheese
flour for coating
olive or corn oil for frying
1 lemon

1. Cut cheese into 5 mm (¼ inch) slices and coat with flour if desired.
2. Heat enough oil in a small, 2-handled frying pan (*saganaki*) to cover base to a depth of 5 mm (¼ inch) and fry cheese for about 1 minute each side. Squeeze lemon juice to taste onto cheese.
3. Place pan on a heat-proof plate and take immediately to the table. Serve with additional lemon wedges and eat with crusty bread which is dipped into the lemon-flavoured oil in the pan. A very quick to prepare and tasty *meze*.

SAGANAKI ALA PEREA
FRIED PRAWNS AND ARTICHOKES

Years ago I tried this delicious combination at the White Towers Restaurant in London, run by Mr John Stais, a Greek Cypriot. This version is very close to the White Towers', if my memory serves me well.

Serves: 2
Cooking time: 25 minutes

4 globe artichoke bases (for preparation
    see page 9)
salted water
¼ cup olive oil
250 g (8 oz) uncooked prawns (shrimp)
125 g (4 oz) small mushrooms
1 tablespoon lemon juice
salt
freshly ground black pepper
¼ cup dry sherry
1 tablespoon finely chopped parsley

1. Prepare artichoke bases as directed and cut each in half. Cook until tender in boiling, salted water — about 15 minutes. Drain well and leave until dry.
2. Shell prawns and devein. Rinse and dry. Wipe and trim mushrooms and leave whole.
3. Heat oil in a small, two-handled frying pan (*saganaki*) and add artichokes. Fry quickly until lightly browned on each side, push to one side and add prawns, mushrooms and lemon juice. Fry on medium high heat, stirring continually, until prawns turn pink — do not overcook.
4. Stir artichokes into prawn and mushroom mixture and add sherry. Reduce heat to low, add salt and pepper to taste and simmer gently for 1 minute. Sprinkle with parsley and serve at once, taking pan to the table on a heat-proof plate. Serve with crusty bread as a first course.

Note: To serve more than 2, use a large frying pan to accommodate larger quantity of ingredients. When cooked, divide into heated individual ramekin dishes and place on heat-proof plates.

LOUVIA MAVROMATIKA ME LAHANA (Black-eyed Beans with Silverbeet) *recipe page 92.*

MIALA TIGANITA
FRIED BRAINS

Serves: 6
Cooking time: 30 minutes

Prepare brains as for Miala Me Lemoni (page 84) up to and including Step 3. Drain, dry well with paper towels and cut into 1 cm (½ inch) slices. Dip in flour to coat and shallow fry in hot corn oil or butter until golden brown. Serve hot with lemon wedges as a *meze*.

FLAOUNES
EASTER CHEESE PIES

These pleasant cheese pies are prepared in enormous quantities to be eaten on Easter Sunday morning. The recipe given to me by a good Cypriot cook began with 6 pounds cheddam, 3 pounds haloumy cheese and 3 or 4 dozen eggs. You can imagine the proportions of the rest of the recipe! She has a large family, and would certainly need some helpers to prepare the pies. I have scaled the recipe down considerably.

Cypriot cooks in Australia find that cheddam cheese, a combination of cheddar and edam cheeses, is a good substitute for the cheese used in Cyprus. Should this not be available, try the Greek kasseri cheese, or use a mild flavoured cheddar combined with edam.

The flavouring of the cheese mixture varies also. Some cooks use the easily available dried mint, others insist on fresh mint, and still others substitute sultanas for the mint. I prefer the mint flavour.

Makes about 30
Oven temperature: 220°C (425°F)
Cooking time: 12-15 minutes

Yeast Dough:
6 cups plain flour
1 sachet active dry yeast
1 cup warm water
1 cup warm milk
1 teaspoon salt
2 teaspoons sugar
¼ cup corn oil
1 tablespoon melted butter

Cheese Filling:
250 g (8 oz) cheddam cheese
125 g (4 oz) haloumy cheese (page 81)
4 teaspoons fine semolina (farina)
1 teaspoon baking powder
4 teaspoons crushed dried mint or 2
    tablespoons finely chopped fresh mint
4 eggs, lightly beaten

To finish:
1 egg, beaten
sesame seeds

1. Sift flour into a mixing bowl and warm in a low oven.
2. Dissolve yeast in ¼ cup warm water, add remaining water, milk, salt and sugar and stir well.
3. Remove about 2 cups flour from bowl and keep aside. Pour yeast mixture into centre of flour and stir in a little flour to thicken liquid. Cover and leave for about 10 minutes until frothy.
4. Gradually stir in flour, then slowly add oil combined with melted butter. Beat by hand or with dough hook on electric mixer for 10 minutes, adding half the reserved flour gradually.
5. Sprinkle board with more flour and turn dough out. Knead for 5-10 minutes, using as much flour as dough will take. When smooth and satiny, shape into a ball.
6. Oil bowl lightly, put in dough and turn to coat with oil. Stretch a piece of plastic film over bowl and leave in a warm place until doubled in bulk — about 1-1½ hours.
7. While dough is rising, make cheese filling. Coarsely grate cheeses into a bowl and add semolina sifted with baking powder. Work with wooden spoon to soften cheese and blend ingredients to a thick paste.
8. Gradually blend in eggs and mint, and mix to a fairly stiff paste. It may be necessary to hold back a little egg as cheeses vary in moistness and mixture must hold its shape.
9. Punch down dough and turn out on to a lightly floured board. Divide into two and shape into balls. Roll out each ball of dough until 5 mm (¼ inch) thick and cut into 10 cm (4 inch) rounds. Place rounds on a cloth and keep covered until all dough is shaped.
10. Place a generous tablespoon of filling in centre of a round of dough, spreading it slightly. Pull dough up at 3 points to make a triangle, or 4 points to make a square. About 2 cm (¾ inch) of dough should overlap filling all round. Press points of triangles or squares to seal edges. Use fingers or tines of fork.
11. Brush dough overlap with beaten egg and sprinkle with sesame seeds. Place flaounes on greased baking sheets and bake in a hot oven for 12-15 minutes until cheese filling is puffed and flaounes are golden. Serve warm or cold.

KOLOKETES
PUMPKIN PIES

Makes 30
Oven temperature: 200°C (400°F) reducing to
   180°C (350°F)
Cooking time: 30 minutes

Pumpkin Filling:
3 cups diced butternut pumpkin squash
2 tablespoons pourgouri (coarse burghul)
1 medium-sized onion, chopped
¼ cup peanut or corn oil
½ teaspoon ground cinnamon
pinch ground cloves
1½ teaspoons salt
freshly ground black pepper

Pastry:
4 cups plain flour
pinch of salt
¾ cup peanut or corn oil
½ cup cold water
3 teaspoons lemon juice
beaten egg and milk for glazing

1. Peel pumpkin, remove seeds and cut into 5 mm (¼ inch) dice. Measure and place diced pumpkin into a bowl. Add remaining filling ingredients, stir to combine, cover and leave for 12 hours or overnight.
2. Sift flour and salt into a mixing bowl, add oil and rub in with fingertips until distributed evenly.
3. Add water and lemon juice and mix to a firm dough. Knead lightly, cover and leave to rest for 30 minutes.
4. Roll out dough thinly (about the thickness of a normal pie crust) and cut into 15 cm (6 inch) rounds.
5. Take a round of pastry and moisten edge with a little water. Place a good tablespoonful of filling in centre, fold over and press edges to seal well. Flute edge with fingers or press with tines of fork.
6. Place finished pies on lightly greased baking trays and glaze tops with an egg beaten with a little milk.
7. Bake in a hot oven for 10 minutes, reduce to moderate and bake for further 20 minutes. Serve hot or cold.

MOUNGRA
PICKLED CAULIFLOWER

1 sachet active dry yeast
1 cup warm water
1½ cups plain flour
1 teaspoon salt
1 cauliflower, about 1.5 kg (3 lb)
salt
water
8-9 cups water
¼ cup white mustard seed

1. Dissolve yeast in ¼ cup of the warm water, add remaining water and add to flour and salt in a large mixing bowl. Stir until combined and beat till smooth. Cover bowl with plastic food wrap and leave for 3 days to ferment.
2. Separate cauliflower into florets and soak in cold salted water for 10 minutes. Drain.
3. Half fill a large pot with water, add 1 tablespoon salt and bring to the boil. Add half the cauliflower, return to the boil then lift cauliflower out with a perforated spoon. Place immediately into a bowl of cold water and drain in colander. Repeat with remaining cauliflower.
4. Bring 8-9 cups water to the boil. Cool a little, then pour gradually into the fermented dough, stirring well to form a thin, milky liquid.
5. Pound mustard seeds just enough to crack them and sprinkle a little in the base of a large stone crock or sterilized glass jar. Place some cauliflower in jar and sprinkle with mustard. Repeat till ingredients are used.
6. Pour milky liquid over contents, covering cauliflower completely. Cover with lid or plastic film.
7. Each day turn cauliflower pieces with your hand (wash hand and forearm well before doing this). Do this for 8 days. Cauliflower is then ready for eating. Moungra will keep for 1 month providing cauliflower is turned every 2 days.

KOULOURA
BREAD RING

Makes 1 loaf
Oven temperature: 190°C (375°F)
Cooking time: 30 minutes

3 cups plain flour
1 sachet active dry yeast
½ cup warm water
½ cup warm milk
1 teaspoon salt
2 teaspoons sugar
2 tablespoons oil
water
sesame seeds

1. Sift flour into a bowl and warm in a slow oven.
2. Dissolve yeast in ¼ cup warm water, add remaining water, milk, salt and sugar.
3. Remove about 1 cup flour from bowl and reserve. Pour yeast mixture into centre, and stir in enough flour to thicken liquid. Cover and leave in a warm place until frothy.
4. Stir in rest of flour in bowl, adding oil gradually, then beat with hand or wooden spoon for 10 minutes, or on electric mixer with dough hook for 5 minutes.
5. Knead in reserved flour by hand either in bowl or on a board. Only knead in enough to stop dough sticking and knead until smooth and satiny — about 10 minutes. Shape into a ball.
6. Oil bowl, put in dough smooth side down and turn over so top is oiled. Cover bowl with plastic wrap and leave in warm place to rise until doubled in bulk.
7. Punch down and turn onto a lightly floured board. Flatten out into a circle then roll up firmly. Roll back and forth with palms of hands so that it forms a thick rope 50 cm (20 inches) long, tapering in at each end.
8. Lift onto a greased baking sheet and form into a ring, overlap ends and tuck under loaf. Cover with a cloth and leave to rise in a warm place. Preheat oven.
9. Brush bread with water and sprinkle with sesame seeds. Bake in a moderately hot oven for 30 minutes until golden brown and cooked. Cool on a rack.

Note: This is also a popular Greek bread.

ELIOTI
OLIVE BREAD

During periods of fasting according to religious traditions, meat, eggs and dairy products should not be eaten. One way of adding interest to meals is to serve olive bread. It is so delicious you will want to make and serve it often, whether fasting or not — unless you are fasting to reduce weight.

As many cooks may not feel confident about making their own bread, frozen bread dough may be used. Defrost according to package directions and follow on from Step 2. The olive mixture is sufficient for 2 loaves frozen bread dough.

Makes 1 loaf
Oven temperature: 190°C (375°F)
Cooking time: 35-45 minutes

1 quantity Kouloura dough (above)
1 medium-sized onion, finely chopped
1 tablespoon olive oil
1 cup black olives
oil for glazing

1. Make dough according to directions, replacing milk in recipe with warm water if necessary. Leave to prove in a warm place.
2. Gently fry onion in oil until transparent. Halve olives and remove seeds. Combine onions and olives and leave until cool.
3. Punch down dough and turn onto a lightly floured board. Press out to a rectangle about 1 cm (½ inch) thick. If using frozen dough, press out to shape when thawed, putting one loaf on top of the other to make 1 large loaf.
4. Spread onion and olive mixture over dough, leaving sides clear. Roll up firmly from longer side and shape into a loaf. Press ends to seal.
5. Place on a greased baking sheet and make 4 shallow diagonal slashes across top. Cover with a cloth and leave in a warm place until doubled in bulk. Preheat oven.
6. Brush top lightly with oil and bake in a moderate oven for 35-40 minutes or until golden. Serve warm or cold.

HALOUMOPSOMI (Haloumy Cheese Bread) *recipe page 92;*
ELIOTI (Olive Bread) *recipe above;*
FLAOUNES (Easter Cheese Pies) *recipe page 88.*

HALOUMOPSOMI
HALOUMY CHEESE BREAD

Makes 1 loaf
Oven temperature: 190°C (375°F)
Cooking time: 35-40 minutes

1 quantity Kouloura dough (page 90)
250 g (8 oz) haloumy cheese
milk or egg for glazing
sesame seeds

1. Make dough according to directions, cover and leave to rise in a warm place until doubled in bulk.
2. Cut cheese into 1 cm (½ inch) dice.
3. Punch down dough and turn onto lightly floured board. Press out to a rectangle 1 cm (½ inch) thick.
4. Place cheese cubes over dough, leaving sides clear. Roll up firmly from longer side and press ends to seal, forming loaf into an oval shape.
5. Grease a baking sheet and place loaf carefully on it. Make 4 shallow, diagonal slashes on top with a sharp knife. Cover with a cloth and leave in a warm place until doubled. Preheat oven.
6. Brush top and sides lightly with milk or egg beaten with a little water. Sprinkle with sesame seeds.
7. Bake in a moderately hot oven for 35-40 minutes until golden and cooked. Cool on a rack and serve warm or cold.

LOUVIA MAVROMATIKA ME LAHANA
BLACK-EYED BEANS WITH SILVERBEET

Though a relatively simple dish, the combination of black-eyed beans and silverbeet is delicious. Dressed with olive oil and lemon juice, it is often enjoyed as a main meal, served with crusty bread, some cheese and a glass of wine.

Serves: 6
Cooking time: 2½ hours

2 cups louvia mavromatika (black-eyed beans)
6 cups water
1 kg (2 lb) silverbeet (Swiss chard)
salt
2 cloves garlic, optional
½ cup olive oil
juice of 1 lemon
lemon wedges for serving

1. Wash dried beans well, place in a pan and cover with the 6 cups water. Bring to the boil, boil uncovered for 2 minutes and remove from heat. Cover pan and leave for 2 hours or until plump.
2. Return to heat and bring to a slow simmer. Simmer covered for 1½ hours or until just tender.
3. Wash silverbeet in several changes of water. Cut off stems and trim them. Cut stems in 1 cm (½ inch) pieces and add to beans with salt to taste. Cover and cook for further 10 minutes.
4. Shred silverbeet leaves coarsely and add to beans. Cover and cook for further 15 minutes or until beans and silverbeet are tender. Drain well and turn into a deep bowl.
5. Crush garlic with a little salt if used. Blend into olive oil with lemon juice and pour over hot vegetables. Toss well and serve with lemon wedges so that flavour may be adjusted to individual taste. Serve hot or warm.

POURGOURI PILAFI
BURGHUL PILAF

Serves: 6
Cooking time: 1 hour

1 medium-sized onion, finely chopped
¼ cup corn oil or butter
3¼ cups chicken stock or water
2 cups pourgouri (coarse burghul)
salt
yoghurt for serving

1. In a deep pan gently fry onion in oil until transparent. Add chicken stock or water and bring to the boil.
2. Place pourgouri in a sieve and wash quickly under cold running water. Pour into boiling liquid and add salt to taste.
3. Stir until boiling again, reduce heat, cover and simmer gently for 20 minutes until liquid is absorbed.
4. Remove pan from heat, place a cloth or 2 paper towels over the rim of the pan and replace lid. Leave for 15 minutes, then serve with yoghurt as an accompaniment to Afelia, mixed vegetable dishes, Keftethes or any dish normally served with rice pilaf.

Note: Often vermicelli is added to the pourgouri for variety. Add ½ cup crumbled vermicelli noodles to pan with the onion and fry until golden. Add 1 additional cup stock or water and proceed from Step 2.

PATCHA
LAMB'S HEAD SOUP

Patcha is not only a Cyprus dish: Turkey, Iraq and the Gulf States all have their versions, but they all use lamb's feet. As these are not readily available in Western countries for reasons of hygiene, only the Cyprus version is given. Again the head is not always available, so the recipe has been modified to overcome this marketing problem, with the result similar to the traditional dish.

Serves: 6
Cooking time: 2½ hours

1 kg (2 lb) lamb soup bones
water
6 lamb tongues
salt
3 sets lamb brains
¼ cup vinegar

To finish:
¼ cup butter
¼ cup plain flour
1 small garlic clove, crushed
lamb stock from above
2 eggs
2 tablespoons lemon juice
white vinegar
6 slices dry toast

1. Put lamb bones in a large pot and cover with cold water. Scrub tongues and add to pot, set on medium heat and bring to the boil, skimming when necessary.
2. When well skimmed and boiling, add salt to taste, cover and simmer gently for 1½ hours or until tongues are tender. Test with a skewer inserted at root end of tongue.
3. Meanwhile soak brains in vinegar with cold water to cover for 30 minutes. Drain and remove skin if possible (not possible if brains were frozen) and any dark veins.
4. When tongues are tender add brains to pan, cover and simmer very gently for 15 minutes until cooked. Do not boil.
5. Lift tongues and brains from lamb stock. Skin tongues and remove gristle and bone from root end. Cut tongues and brains in thick slices, place in a dish and spoon on a little stock to keep them moist. Cover dish and keep warm.
6. Strain 2 cups lamb stock into measuring jug. Strain remaining stock into a small pan and keep hot.
7. Melt butter in a saucepan and stir in flour. Cook for 2 minutes without allowing roux to colour. Add garlic, cook for a few seconds, then pour in lamb stock from jug, stirring constantly. Keep stirring until sauce boils and thickens. Reduce heat and let sauce bubble gently while preparing eggs.
8. Beat eggs in a bowl until foamy and gradually beat in lemon juice. Pour the thickened stock onto the eggs, beating constantly. Return to pan and heat for 2-3 minutes until sauce begins to bubble. The flour will prevent sauce curdling.
9. Place a slice of toast in each of 6 deep plates and sprinkle with 1 teaspoon vinegar. Pour ¼ cup reserved hot lamb stock onto each slice of toast. Arrange sliced tongue and brains on toast and pour hot egg and lemon sauce on top. Serve immediately.

YOURVARLAKIA AVGOLEMONO
MEAT BALL SOUP

Serves: 6
Cooking time: 1 hour

500 g (1 lb) finely ground lamb
1 small onion, finely chopped
1 egg, beaten
⅓ cup short grain rice
2 tablespoons finely chopped parsley
1 teaspoon finely chopped mint, optional
salt
freshly ground black pepper
flour for coating
5 cups light stock
1 tablespoon butter
2 eggs
juice of 1 lemon
chopped parsley to garnish

1. Mix lamb with onion, egg, rice, parsley, mint if used and salt and pepper to taste. Shape into meat balls the size of a small walnut and coat lightly with flour.
2. Bring stock to the boil in a soup pot, season if necessary and drop in prepared meat balls; add the butter. Cover and simmer gently for 1 hour.
3. In a mixing bowl beat eggs until light and foamy and gradually beat in lemon juice. Slowly add about 2 cups of the simmering stock, beating constantly.
4. Pour egg mixture into soup and stir constantly over low heat for 2 minutes to cook the egg, then remove from heat and stir for a further minute so that heat of pot will not cause the egg to curdle.
5. Ladle soup into deep soup plates and sprinkle with a little chopped parsley. Serve with crusty bread.

LOUVANA
SPLIT PEA PUREE

Serves: 6
Cooking time: 2 hours

2 cups yellow split peas
5 cups water
2 medium-sized potatoes
2 medium-sized onions, sliced
¼ cup olive oil
salt

To serve:
lemon wedges
olive oil
black olives
bread

1. Pick over split peas, discarding any that are discoloured. Wash in several changes of cold water. Place in a deep, heavy pan and add 5 cups cold water.
2. Put on medium heat and bring to the boil, skimming when necessary. When boiling, reduce heat to low, cover pan and simmer gently for 1 hour without stirring.
3. Peel potatoes and cut into small dice. In a small pan fry onion in oil until lightly flecked with brown. Add potatoes, onion and oil to the split peas, cover and simmer for further hour or until peas and potatoes are very soft. Do not stir during cooking as this causes scorching.
4. When cooked, stir in salt to taste and beat until puréed. Soup may be processed in blender or food processor in small lots and returned to pan to reheat.
5. Serve in deep plates with lemon wedges to be added to individual taste. Additional olive oil is usually poured onto the purée. Serve with black olives and bread. Often a salad of tomatoes, cucumber, sweet peppers and onion is served on the side.

FAKES XITHATI
SOUR LENTIL SOUP

Serves: 6
Cooking time: 1½ hours

2 cups brown lentils
8 cups water
1 cup finely chopped spring onions
1 clove garlic, crushed, optional
¼ cup finely chopped coriander leaves or
   parsley
⅓ cup olive oil
¼ cup cold water
1 tablespoon flour
¼ cup vinegar or to taste
salt
freshly ground black pepper

1. Wash lentils in several changes of cold water, or place in a sieve and run water through them. Drain.
2. Put lentils in a large pot with 8 cups water, spring onion, garlic if used, oil and coriander or parsley (or a combination of the two if preferred).
3. Bring to the boil, cover pan and simmer on low heat for 1 hour or until lentils are soft.
4. Put water and flour in a screw top jar, seal and shake until thoroughly combined. This prevents lumps forming. Pour this gradually into boiling soup, stirring constantly, until thickened slightly. Add vinegar and salt and pepper to taste. Return to the boil, boil gently for 5 minutes, then serve hot.

PSAROSOUPA AVGOLEMONO
EGG AND LEMON FISH SOUP

Serves: 6
Cooking time: 2½ hours

2 kg (4 lb) fish heads, backbones and
   trimmings
water
2 small onions
4 small carrots, scraped and quartered
½ cup chopped celery, including leaves
¼ cup coarsely chopped parsley
salt
freshly ground black pepper
⅓ cup short grain rice
3 eggs
juice of 1 lemon

1. Wash fish heads and trimmings in cold water and place in a large pot. Add 8 cups water and bring to the boil, skimming when required.
2. Add whole, peeled onions, carrots, celery, parsley, about 2 teaspoons salt and pepper to taste. Cover and simmer gently for 1½ hours.
3. Strain stock into a bowl and discard all flavouring ingredients. Return stock to cleaned pot, adjust seasoning and bring to the boil. Add washed and drained rice and boil, uncovered, for 20 minutes or until rice is tender.
4. Beat eggs in a bowl until foamy and gradually beat in lemon juice. Ladle about 2 cups boiling stock into bowl, beating constantly, then stir into gently boiling stock. Keep stirring over heat for 1 minute, remove pot from heat and stir for further minute so that heat of pan will not curdle the eggs. Serve immediately.

PANJARIA SALATA
BEETROOT SALAD

Serves: 6-8
Cooking time: 35-50 minutes

6 medium-sized beetroot (beets) with tops
water
salt
Skorthalia (page 82)

Dressing (optional):
⅓ cup olive oil
2 tablespoons vinegar
1 tablespoon finely chopped coriander leaves,
   optional

1. Wash beetroot well, cut off tops, leaving about 3 cm (1¼ inches) on beetroot. Select the tender, undamaged leaves of the beetroot, discarding remainder.
2. Boil beetroot in salted water to cover until tender — about 30-45 minutes. Boil tops separately in salted water for 15 minutes.
3. Peel beetroot and slice or cube into a bowl. Drain tops and add to bowl if desired, or leave in a separate bowl.
4. Either serve at room temperature with Skorthalia, or mix dressing ingredients, pour over hot beetroot and leaves and allow to cool before serving.

POLYPIKILO
VEGETABLE POTPOURRI

Serves: 6
Oven temperature: 170°C (325°F)
Cooking time: 1½ hours

2 medium-sized eggplants (aubergines)
salt
500 g (1 lb) potatoes
500 g (1 lb) zucchini (courgettes)
6 medium-sized ripe tomatoes
¾ cup corn oil
½ cup soft white breadcrumbs
3 cloves garlic, finely chopped
½ cup finely chopped parsley
freshly ground black pepper
½ cup water

1. Wash eggplants, remove stems and cut into 1 cm (½ inch) slices. Sprinkle with salt and leave for 30 minutes. Rinse and dry well with paper towels.
2. Peel and slice potatoes thinly. Cut zucchini in 1 cm (½ inch) slices. Peel tomatoes and slice thinly.
3. Pour a little oil in the base of a large oven dish and add half the breadcrumbs, garlic and parsley.
4. Layer the eggplant, potatoes, zucchini and tomatoes in the dish, seasoning lightly with salt and pepper. Repeat layers, finishing with tomatoes.
5. Pour remaining oil over vegetables and add the water. Season tomatoes with salt and pepper and sprinkle remaining garlic, parsley and breadcrumbs on top.
6. Bake in a moderately slow oven for 1½ hours or until vegetables are tender. Check during latter part of cooking and add a little water if necessary — polypikilo should be fairly moist. Serve hot or at room temperature.

AFELIA I
POTATOES WITH CORIANDER

The next three recipes are all called Afelia, though the vegetable used differs in each one. Afelia is a Cypriot style of cooking vegetables or pork with coriander seeds and red wine. More detail in the Meats section of this chapter, page 106.

Serves: 6
Cooking time: 35-40 minutes

1 kg (2 lb) small new potatoes
¼ cup corn oil
½ cup dry red wine
salt
freshly ground black pepper
3 teaspoons crushed coriander seeds

1. Choose even-sized potatoes. Wash well and dry with paper towels. Crack potatoes by hitting each one sharply with a mallet.
2. Heat oil in a large frying pan with lid to fit. Add potatoes and fry over high heat to brown them lightly, turning potatoes frequently by shaking pan.
3. Reduce heat, and when potatoes are cooking less vigorously, add red wine and salt and pepper to taste. Cover tightly and simmer gently on low heat for 20-25 minutes or until potatoes are tender. Shake pan occasionally.
4. Sprinkle crushed coriander seeds over potatoes, cover and simmer for 2 minutes longer. Serve hot as a vegetable accompaniment to grilled or roast lamb, pork, veal or chicken.

AFELIA II
MUSHROOMS WITH CORIANDER

Follow above recipe, substituting 500 g (1 lb) medium-sized mushrooms for potatoes. Trim and wipe clean with a dry cloth — do not wash. Leave whole and fry in oil until juices evaporate. Reduce heat, add red wine and salt and pepper to taste. Cover and simmer for 10 minutes. Add crushed coriander seeds, cook for further 2 minutes and serve.

AFELIA III
ARTICHOKE HEARTS WITH CORIANDER

Substitute 12 artichoke hearts for potatoes, preparing them as instructed on page 9.

Drain and dry well after preparation and cut each heart into quarters. Fry in oil until lightly browned. Reduce heat, add wine, salt and pepper, cover and simmer for 15-20 minutes until tender. Add coriander seeds, cook a little longer and serve hot.

YEMISTA
STUFFED VEGETABLES

Serves: 6
Oven temperature: 180°C (350°F)
Cooking time: 1½ hours

6 medium-sized sweet green peppers
6 medium-sized tomatoes
6 medium-sized long eggplants (aubergines)

Stuffing:
1 large onion, finely chopped
2 tablespoons corn oil
1 kg (2 lb) finely ground lamb or beef
½ cup tomato purée
½ cup short grain rice
2 tablespoons chopped parsley
1 teaspoon dried mint, optional
salt
freshly ground black pepper

To finish:
pulp from tomatoes
½ cup tomato purée
small piece cinnamon bark
½ cup water
¼ cup corn oil or butter
½ teaspoon sugar
salt
freshly ground black pepper

1. Prepare vegetables as directed in Step 1 in Armenian recipe for Stuffed Vegetables, page 174.
2. In a large frying pan gently fry onion in oil until transparent. Add meat and stir constantly over high heat until crumbly and colour changes.
3. Reduce heat, add remaining stuffing ingredients and simmer, covered, until liquid is absorbed.
4. Fill vegetables, leaving a little room for filling to expand. Replace tops. Arrange in rows in a baking dish.
5. Cook tomato pulp until soft, blend in remaining sauce ingredients and pour over vegetables in dish.
6. Cover dish with foil and bake for 30 minutes in a moderate oven. Remove foil and baste vegetables with sauce. Bake for further 15-20 minutes until vegetables are tender.
7. Serve hot with crusty bread and salad.

Other vegetables suitable for stuffing: Zucchini, silver beet (Swiss chard) leaves, blanched cabbage leaves or artichokes may all be prepared and filled with the meat stuffing mixture. The zucchini may be oven baked, but the other vegetables are best cooked in a large pan on top of the stove in a light stock instead of the tomato sauce. When prepared this way, the tomato purée in the stuffing mixture should be omitted and a little lemon juice added instead. Finish with an Egg and Lemon Sauce, following directions given in Koupepia recipe, page 84.

KALAMARIA PARAYEMISTA
STUFFED SQUID

Serves: 5-6 as an appetizer
Cooking time: 1½ hours

1 kg (2 lb) small squid
½ cup corn oil
1 medium-sized onion, finely chopped
½ cup short grain rice
½ cup tomato purée
¼ cup water
small piece cinnamon bark
2 cloves
salt
freshly ground black pepper
½ cup dry white wine

1. Select squid with hoods about 10-12 cm (4-5 inches) long.
2. To clean squid, pull off head and attached tentacles. Cut out eyes and beak and discard. Clean dark skin from head and tentacles by pulling it off or rubbing off with a cloth dipped in coarse salt. Rinse, chop 3 or 4 into small pieces and keep aside. Remainder may be stored and fried later.
3. Clean out hood (body) and remove transparent backbone from inside. Pull or rub off skin. Rinse well, drain and dry.
4. Heat 1 tablespoon oil in a pan and gently fry onion until transparent. Stir in rice and stir over heat for 2 minutes. Add tomato purée, water, cinnamon bark, cloves, chopped squid, and salt and pepper to taste. Cover and simmer over low heat for 10 minutes or until liquid is absorbed. Remove cinnamon bark and cloves.
5. Fill hoods with rice mixture, packing it in loosely as rice expands and hoods contract during cooking. Close top with wooden cocktail picks or sew with strong thread.
6. Heat remaining oil in a deep pan and fry squid hoods until lightly coloured, turning them frequently. Reduce heat, add wine, cover and simmer gently on low heat for 1 hour or until squid is tender. Add a little water to pan if necessary during cooking. Serve hot or warm as a mezethaki (appetizer).

OKTAPOTHI STIFATHO
BRAISED OCTOPUS AND ONIONS

Serves: 6
Cooking time: 2 hours

1 octopus, about 1 kg (2 lb)
¼ cup corn oil
1 medium-sized onion, chopped
2 cloves garlic, finely chopped
1 cup tomato purée
¼ cup dry red wine
¼ cup wine vinegar
salt
freshly ground black pepper
2 cloves
1 large piece cinnamon bark
750 g (1½ lb) small onions

1. Pull tentacles from octopus and keep aside. Remove intestines, ink sac, eyes and beak and discard. Wash head and tentacles and pull skin off head.
2. Place head and tentacles in a pan, cover and let octopus cook on medium heat for 10 minutes until its juices are exuded. Drain, cool and cut into small pieces.
3. Heat oil in a heavy pan and gently fry chopped onion until transparent. Add garlic and prepared octopus and fry over medium heat for 5 minutes.
4. Add tomato purée, wine, vinegar, salt and pepper to taste, cloves and cinnamon. Cover and simmer over low heat for 30 minutes.
5. Peel small onions and cut a cross in the root end of each onion to prevent centres popping during cooking. Add to pan, cover and cook for further hour or until octopus is tender. If desired, peeled onions may be blanched in boiling water for 5 minutes, drained and then added to octopus.
6. Remove cloves and cinnamon bark, adjust seasoning and serve stifatho with a plain rice pilaf.

PSARI TIGANITO
FRIED FISH

In both Cyprus and the Greek islands, an abundance of fish is prepared with vinegar based sauces used as a marinade to preserve fried fish for a few days. Psari Savoro has a simple sauce of garlic, rosemary, vinegar and wine; Psari Marinato adds the ubiquitous tomato plus a few more herbs. Both sauces are well worth trying.

KALAMARIA PARAYEMISTA (Stuffed Squid) *recipe above.*

PSARI SAVORO
FRIED FISH WITH ROSEMARY AND VINEGAR

Serves: 6
Cooking time: 15-20 minutes

1 kg (2 lb) small whole fish, fish fillets or
    steaks suitable for frying
salt
plain flour
olive or corn oil for shallow frying
3 cloves garlic, finely chopped
1 teaspoon fresh or dried resemary spikes
¼ cup brown vinegar
¼ cup dry white wine
freshly ground black pepper

1. Clean and scale fish if necessary. Rinse and pat dry. Sprinkle fish with salt, cover and leave for 20 minutes.
2. Coat fish with flour and shallow fry in hot oil until golden brown and cooked through. Drain and place fish in a dish.
3. Pour all but ¼ cup oil from pan. Add garlic and rosemary to pan and cook for a few seconds. Sprinkle in 3 teaspoons flour and stir over medium heat until lightly coloured.
4. Remove pan from heat and pour in vinegar. Take care as vinegar sizzles. Stir in wine and return to heat, stirring sauce until bubbling. Add salt and pepper to taste and pour over fish. Serve hot or store, covered, in a cool place, preferably the refrigerator, and serve cold.

PSARI MARINATO
FISH WITH TOMATO-HERB SAUCE

Ingredients as for Psari Savoro

Additional ingredients:
1 bay leaf
2 tablespoons finely chopped parsley
½ cup tomato purée (not paste)
1 cup water
½ teaspoon sugar

1. Prepare and fry fish as for Psari Savoro. Keep fish hot in dish. Drain oil from pan and clean pan.
2. Return ¼ cup oil to pan, adding more if necessary. Add garlic and 2 tablespoons flour and stir over medium heat until flour colours.
3. Stir in vinegar, wine, rosemary, bay leaf, parsley, tomato purée and water. Bring to the boil, stirring constantly. Let sauce bubble gently on low heat for 5 minutes or so.
4. Adjust seasoning with salt and pepper and add sugar. Pour over fish and serve hot or cold.

PSARI STO FOURNO
BAKED FISH

Serves: 6
Oven temperature: 180°C (350°F)
Cooking time: 35-40 minutes

2 whole baking fish, each about 1.5 kg (3 lb)
juice of 1 lemon
salt
freshly ground black pepper
½ cup corn or olive oil
½ cup soft white breadcrumbs
3 cloves garlic, finely chopped
½ cup finely chopped parsley
3 large tomatoes, peeled
2 large potatoes, peeled

1. Clean and scale fish if necessary. Wipe dry and rub inside and out with lemon juice, salt and pepper. Cover and refrigerate for 1-2 hours.
2. Take a baking dish large enough to accommodate fish and brush with oil. Sprinkle breadcrumbs over base and top with the chopped garlic and most of the parsley.
3. Place fish in the dish and pour on a little of the oil. Slice tomatoes and arrange over the fish.
4. Cut potatoes into thick finger lengths (chips) and place in dish around and between fish. Season tomatoes and potatoes with salt and pepper and pour remaining oil over all ingredients in dish.
5. Bake in a moderate oven for 35-40 minutes, covering dish for first 15 minutes. Remove cover and bake until fish and potatoes are cooked. Sprinkle with remaining parsley and serve hot.

GALLOS YEMISTOS
ROAST STUFFED TURKEY

Serves: 8-10
Cooking time: 4½ hours
Oven temperature: 180°C (350°F)

1 turkey, about 4 kg (8 lb)
1 lemon
salt
freshly ground black pepper
½ cup corn oil or melted butter
½ cup water
2 small pieces cinnamon bark

Stuffing:
1 onion, finely chopped
½ cup chopped celery
2 tablespoons butter
250 g (8 oz) ground veal
turkey liver, chopped
1 cup short grain rice
½ cup dry white wine
1 cup stock made from remaining giblets
½ cup currants
½ cup slivered, blanched almonds
½-1 teaspoon ground cinnamon
salt
freshly ground black pepper

1. Wipe turkey inside and out with paper towels. Cut lemon into quarters and rub cavities with cut lemon. Sprinkle lightly with salt and pepper.
2. Fill neck and body cavities with stuffing (see end of Method). Secure openings and truss.
3. Rub skin with cut lemon, then salt and pepper. Place in a roasting dish and pour on oil or butter. Add water and cinnamon bark to dish.
4. Cook in a moderate oven for 4 hours, basting every 30 minutes with pan juices. Cover turkey with a piece of foil for first three hours of cooking, remove to brown during last hour.
5. When cooked, remove to a warm platter, skim pan juices and strain into a sauceboat.

To make stuffing: Fry onion and celery gently in butter for 10 minutes. Add veal and liver and stir over heat for 5 minutes. Stir in rice, wine and stock, cover pan and cook for 10 minutes. Remove from heat, mix in remaining ingredients and season to taste.

HIRINO ME MELITZANES
PORK WITH EGGPLANT

Serves: 5-6
Oven temperature: 170°C (325°F)
Cooking time: 3 hours

1 kg (2 lb) pork stew meat, from shoulder
1 large onion, chopped
1 clove garlic, crushed
¼ cup corn or peanut oil
2 cups chopped, peeled tomatoes
salt
freshly ground black pepper
2 medium-sized eggplants
finely chopped parsley for garnish

1. Trim pork and cut into fairly large cubes.
2. Grease a heated frying pan with some trimmed pork fat and brown pork on all sides. Transfer to casserole dish. Drain off fat.
3. Add onion and garlic to pan with 1 tablespoon of the oil and fry gently until onion is transparent.
4. Add tomatoes, salt and pepper to taste, stir well to lift browned sediment and bring to the boil. Pour over pork in dish.
5. Cover dish with lid and cook in a moderately slow oven for 1½ hours.
6. Meanwhile wash eggplant, remove stem and cut lengthwise into quarters. Place in a colander and sprinkle cut surfaces liberally with salt. Leave for 30 minutes. Rinse and dry with paper towels.
7. Heat remaining oil in clean frying pan and brown eggplant pieces on all sides.
8. Skim fat from casserole and place eggplant on top of pork. Cover, return to oven and cook for further 1 hour.
9. Sprinkle with finely chopped parsley and serve from the casserole. Serve with mashed or fried potatoes and a tossed salad.

ARNI PSITO
ROAST LAMB

Serves: 6
Oven temperature: 180°C (350°F)
Cooking time: 2½ hours

1 leg lamb, about 2 kg (4 lb)
2 cloves garlic
salt
freshly ground black pepper
1 kg (2 lb) medium-sized potatoes
lemon juice
2 large onions, sliced
1½ cups chopped, peeled tomatoes
½ cup stock or water
¼ cup red or white wine
1 bay leaf
small piece cinnamon bark
2 tablespoons butter

1. Wipe leg with paper towels and cut slits in surface. Cut garlic into slivers and insert into slits.
2. Season lamb with salt and pepper and place in roasting dish. Cook in a moderate oven for 1 hour. Drain off fat.
3. Peel potatoes, halve lengthwise and cut part way down through rounded side of each half. Place rounded side up around lamb and sprinkle with lemon juice, salt and pepper.
4. Top potatoes with onion slices and tomatoes. Add bay leaf and cinnamon, dot with butter and add liquid to dish.
5. Return to oven and cook for further 1½ hours, turning lamb occasionally to brown evenly.
6. Remove lamb to carving platter and keep warm.
7. Skim excess fat from dish contents. (Reserve this fat for mixing through hot spaghetti.)
8. Carve lamb and serve with potatoes, the tomato-onion sauce and a side salad or green vegetable.

TAVAS
LAMB AND CUMIN CASSEROLE

This dish is named after the pot in which it is cooked. A tava *is made of unglazed terracotta with a snug-fitting lid. Before the advent of the home oven, the* tava *was placed on glowing embers in a hole in the ground with earth packed around and on top of the pot. The lamb cooked slowly to mouthwatering tenderness. Though you might not find a Cypriot* tava, *there are numerous terracotta casseroles now available.*

In Cyprus the tava *is never washed in suds – just wiped clean, rinsed with hot water, dried and left to air in the cupboard until next time. Only this particular dish is prepared in the* tava.

Serves: 6
Oven temperature: 150°C (300°F)
Cooking time: 2½-3 hours

1.5 kg (3 lb) boneless lamb shoulder or leg
3 large onions, sliced
3 cups chopped, peeled tomatoes
2 teaspoons artisha (cumin seed)
salt
freshly ground black pepper
½ cup water

For serving:
additional cumin seed
Pourgouri Pilafi (page 93)

1. Cut lamb into 3 cm (1¼ inch) cubes. Place in a deep casserole dish, preferably unglazed terracotta. Add sliced onions and chopped tomatoes.
2. Crush cumin seeds with pestle and mortar and sprinkle into dish with salt and pepper to taste. Stir well, then add water. Cover tightly and cook in a slow oven for 2½-3 hours until lamb is tender.
3. Check after 1½ hours and add more water, though this should not be necessary. It depends on how tightly the lid fits.
4. When lamb is tender and sauce thick, serve at the table in the dish. Pound additional cumin seed and place in a bowl so that it may be added to individual taste. Serve with Pourgouri Pilafi.

ARNI PSITO (Baked Lamb) *recipe above*

KANELLONIA
MEAT FILLED PANCAKES

Serves: 6-8
Oven temperature: 180°C (350°F)
Cooking time: 1½ hours

Pancakes:
1 cup plain flour
¼ teaspoon salt
4 eggs
1½ cups milk

Meat Filling:
1 small onion, finely chopped
2 tablespoons butter
500 g (1 lb) finely ground beef or veal
1 tablespoon finely chopped parsley
½ teaspoon ground cinnamon
½ cup water
salt
freshly ground black pepper
1 tablespoon flour
½ cup milk
1 egg

To finish:
1 cup Saltsa Tomata (page 82)
¼ cup grated haloumy cheese or kefalotiri

1. Sift flour and salt into a mixing bowl, break eggs into the centre and gradually stir flour into the eggs. When half the flour is blended in, add half the milk. Mix to a smooth batter and beat with a wooden spoon for a few minutes. Stir in remainder of milk, cover bowl and leave batter to stand for 30 minutes.
2. Meanwhile gently fry onion in half the butter in a pan until soft. Increase heat, add ground meat and stir over high heat until juices evaporate and meat is crumbly.
3. Reduce heat and add parsley, cinnamon, water and salt and pepper to taste. Cover and simmer gently for 20 minutes or until liquid evaporates. Set aside.
4. Melt remaining tablespoon butter in a small saucepan and add flour. Stir over medium heat for 2 minutes without allowing flour to colour, then pour in milk, stirring constantly until thickened and bubbling. Stir into ground meat mixture, leave to cool a little, then blend in beaten egg.
5. Heat a 15 cm (6 inch) frying pan or pancake pan and grease with a wad of paper towel dipped in oil. Using a jug, pour in 2-3 tablespoons batter and tilt pan to coat base evenly. Cook until browned on the bottom, turn and cook for further minute. Remove to a plate. Cook remaining pancakes and stack on plate.
6. Place about 2 tablespoons meat filling along centre of each pancake and roll up. Place in rows in a greased baking dish and pour Saltsa Tomata on top. Sprinkle with grated cheese and bake in a moderate oven for 15-20 minutes. Serve as a first course or as a light meal.

LOUKANIKA
PORK SAUSAGES

Makes about 1 kg (2 lb)

1 kg (2 lb) boneless pork from shoulder
¼ cup port wine
1 teaspoon whole black peppercorns
½ teaspoon ground black pepper
1½ teaspoons ground coriander
¼ teaspoon ground cinnamon
¼ teaspoon whole cumin seeds
2 teaspoons salt
2 cloves garlic
grated rind of 1 orange
sausage casings

1. Pork should have about 20 per cent fat. If purchased with skin (rind), have a little more than amount specified as skin must be removed.
2. Chop pork finely or pass through meat grinder using coarse screen.
3. Place pork in a glass or ceramic mixing bowl and add port wine, spices, salt, garlic and orange rind. Blend until thoroughly combined.
4. Cover and leave in refrigerator for 1 day, stirring mixture occasionally.
5. Place sausage casings in cold water so that they may be loosened. Remove a length as required.
6. Fill casings using meat grinder and a special attachment, or use a large funnel with a long nozzle, pushing skin onto nozzle and easing it off as it fills. Push meat through with the handle of a wooden spoon. End of skin should be knotted just as meat begins to come through nozzle.
7. When filled, twist sausages into 15 cm (6 inch) lengths, twisting the first one way, the second in the opposite direction and so on. Knot other end.
8. Store loosely covered in refrigerator until required. To serve, fry in a little pork fat until cooked through. Cut into small pieces when serving as an appetizer.

ZALATINA
BRAWN

Traditionally this is made with pig's head. As this part of the animal is not often available, and if it is, the thought of cooking one is intolerable, you can make a perfectly good brawn with other parts of the carcase. Trotters or veal shanks will supply the necessary gelatinous properties, as will the rind (skin) and bones of the pork shoulder.

Cooking time: 4 hours

2 veal shanks, cracked
2 pig's trotters (knuckles), cracked
1 kg (2 lb) fresh pork shoulder cut in 4-5 pieces
2-3 pig or lamb tongues
cold water
1 teaspoon cracked black peppercorns
large piece cinnamon bark
2-3 fresh or dried hot chilis
salt
⅓ cup white vinegar
½ cup lemon juice

1. Wash meats, place in a pot and cover with cold water. Bring slowly to the boil, skimming when necessary. When well-skimmed and boiling, add peppercorns, cinnamon bark, chilis and about 3 teaspoons salt, cover and simmer gently for 3 hours or until meat is very tender.
2. Remove pieces and trim off meat. Discard bones, fat and skin. Cut meat into small cubes and keep aside. Skin tongues and cube.
3. Reduce stock by boiling until about 6 cups remain, skimming as required. Strain through a muslin-lined sieve into a clean pan and add cubed meat and tongue to stock.
4. Add vinegar and lemon juice, then adjust seasoning with salt and pepper. Bring back to the boil, then pour into 2 loaf pans or moulds. Refrigerate until set.
5. Serve Zalatina cut into slices as an appetizer or part of a cold buffet.

To garnish Zalatina: Bay leaves, fresh herb sprigs, sliced hard-boiled eggs, blanched sweet red and green pepper strips or sliced olives, alone or in combination, may be used as a garnish. Pour a little of the cooled stock into the base of each mould, set in a dish of iced water. When thickened, arrange selected garnish in a pleasing pattern and spoon a little more stock on top. Leave in iced water until set, then carefully fill with cooled Zalatina. When set, dip moulds into fairly hot water for a few seconds. Run a knife around sides to loosen Zalatina, place a flat plate over mould, invert and shake downwards to free Zalatina.

SHEFTALIA
BARBECUED SAUSAGES

The essential ingredient for these tasty sausages is panna, the caul fat from pig (the outer covering of the paunch). When purchased, caul fat looks like long strips of creamy pink pork fat. Opened out it is attractively patterned with lacy threads of fat on very fine tissue, finer than sausage casings. The simply flavoured meat mixture is wrapped in pieces of panna, forming small sausages.

Sheftalia must be cooked over glowing charcoal — once cooked the only evidence of the covering is the delicious flavour imparted on the contents.

Makes 50

500 g (1 lb) finely ground fatty pork
500 g (1 lb) finely ground veal or lamb
1 large onion, finely chopped or grated
½ cup finely chopped parsley
2 teaspoons salt
freshly ground black pepper
250 g (8 oz) panna (caul fat from pig)

1. Combine pork with veal or lamb, onion, parsley, salt and a generous grinding of black pepper.
2. Dip panna into a bowl of warm water for a minute or two, remove and carefully open out a piece at a time, laying it flat on work surface. Cut with kitchen scissors into pieces about 10 cm (4 inches) square.
3. Take a good tablespoonful of meat mixture and shape into a thick sausage about 5 cm (2 inches) long. Place towards one edge of piece of panna, fold end and sides over meat and roll up firmly. Repeat with remaining ingredients.
4. Thread sausages on flat sword-like skewers, leaving space between them. Number on each skewer depends on their length.
5. Cook over glowing charcoal, turning frequently. Do not place too close to heat as sheftalia must cook fairly slowly so that the inside is well cooked and the outside nicely browned without being burnt. The panna melts during cooking, keeping the meat moist and adding flavour. Excessive flaring of fire can be controlled with a sprinkle of water on the coals. Serve sheftalia as an appetizer or main course.

AFELIA

The Cypriots say if a dish has coriander seeds in it, then it is Cypriot. There are many who would argue this point, nevertheless the Cypriots are inordinately fond of this spice. Coriander is native to southern Europe and the Mediterranean region, its use going back to 1552 B.C. More detail in the Glossary.

Afelia is a name applied to pork and vegetable dishes which feature the cracked seeds. Whether it is pork with coriander, mushrooms with coriander or a combination, the dish is still called Afelia. Pork Afelias follow; you will find vegetable Afelias in that section. To Cypriot tastes, I might be a little conservative with my quantities of coriander — add more if you so desire.

AFELIA I
FRIED PORK WITH CORIANDER

Serves: 4
Cooking time: 15-20 minutes

750 g (1½ lb) boneless pork shoulder, leg or
  loin
1 cup dry red wine
1 teaspoon salt
freshly ground black pepper
2 tablespoons corn oil or butter
2-3 teaspoons crushed coriander seeds
Pourgouri Pilafi (page 93) for serving

1. Cut pork into 2 cm (¾ inch) cubes, removing any skin if present, but leaving fat on the pieces. Place in a glass or ceramic bowl and add wine, salt and a good grinding of black pepper. Stir to blend flavours, cover and marinate in refrigerator for several hours, turning pork occasionally.
2. Drain pork, reserving marinade. Heat oil or butter in a heavy frying pan, add pork and fry over high heat, stirring frequently, until browned and just cooked through. Remove to a plate.
3. Add marinade to pan and reduce until about ¼ cup remains. Return pork and sprinkle with coriander. Toss over heat long enough to heat pork and serve immediately with pourgouri pilafi and a tossed salad or green vegetable.

AFELIA II
BRAISED PORK WITH CORIANDER

Serves: 4-5
Cooking time: 1¼ hours

750 g (1½ lb) pork fillet, leg or loin pork
¼ cup butter
500 g (1 lb) new potatoes, peeled
250 g (8 oz) small mushrooms
1 cup red wine
salt
freshly ground black pepper
2 teaspoons crushed coriander seeds

1. Cut pork into approximately 3 cm (1¼ inch) pieces leaving some fat on meat as this is desirable.
2. Heat half the butter in a heavy based pan and brown potatoes. Remove and keep aside.
3. Add remaining butter and brown pork on each side, push to side of pan.
4. Trim and clean mushrooms and fry quickly in pan next to meat. Stir to combine. Reduce heat to low.
5. Pour in wine, add salt and pepper to taste and place potatoes on top.
6. Sprinkle with coriander seeds, cover pan with lid and simmer over low heat for 45 minutes or until pork and potatoes are tender.
7. Serve with a tossed green salad.

TAVAS (Lamb and Cumin Casserole) *recipe page 102.*

RAVIOLES
BOILED CHEESE-FILLED PASTA

It could well be that Ravioles and Kaloyrka are Venetian legacies to Cyprus from their occupation of the island (1489-1571). Then again somewhat similar pasta dishes are to be found in Armenia, Iran and Afghanistan.

The origin of pasta is shrouded by history, but can be traced back to China. My money is on the Mongol influence (in 13th and 14th centuries) which could have filtered down from Persia or the Caucasus. The name, Ravioles, could well be modern Italian influence in Cyprus as elsewhere, but the dish is as much a part of Cyprus cookery today as Afelia, Koloketes and so on.

Serves: 6
Cooking time: 1-1¼ hours
Dough:
3 cups plain flour
1 teaspoon salt
2 eggs, lightly beaten
½ cup cold water

Cheese Filling:
1½ cups grated haloumy cheese
1 cup Anari (page 81) or ricotta cheese
2 eggs
1-2 teaspoons dried mint

To finish:
boiling salted water
½ cup melted butter
grated haloumy or kefalotiri, or a mixture of
    both

1. Sift flour and salt into a bowl, add eggs and most of the water. Mix to a soft dough, adding more water if necessary. Turn onto a floured board and knead for 10 minutes until elastic and smooth, adding a little flour if dough still sticks. Cover and rest for 1 hour.
2. Meanwhile thoroughly combine cheese filling ingredients, adding crushed mint to taste. Mixture should be fairly stiff.
3. Divide dough in two equal portions and roll out thinly as described on page 16.
4. Cut dough into strips 8 cm (3 inches) wide. Spread a strip on work surface and place a teaspoon of cheese filling at 4 cm (1½ inch) intervals on one side of the centre of the strip.
5. Using a pastry brush dipped in water, lightly moisten pastry around one side of filling with a scalloped effect. Fold pastry over filling, pressing well between the mounds of filling and along the edge.
6. Cut ravioles in crescents with a 5 cm (2 inch) biscuit cutter. Press edges again with the tines of a fork to seal well, place on a cloth and cover. Repeat with remaining ingredients, rolling out pastry trimmings as well.
7. Cook 15 ravioles at a time in a large pot of boiling, salted water for 15-20 minutes or until tender. Remove with a slotted spoon to a colander set over simmering water.
8. When all are cooked, turn into a dish and pour on melted butter. Sprinkle with grated cheese and serve hot.

Note: Cooked ravioles may be refrigerated in a sealed container and heated in a colander over boiling water when required for serving.

KALOYRKA
BOILED MEAT-FILLED PASTA

Serves: 6
Cooking time: 1½-2 hours

1 quantity dough, see Ravioles (above)

Meat Filling:
500 g (1 lb) finely ground beef or lamb
1 large onion, finely chopped
2 tablespoons corn oil
¼ cup finely chopped parsley
salt
freshly ground black pepper
1 cup water

To finish:
boiling, salted water
1 quantity Saltsa Tomata (page 82)

1. Prepare dough as directed in Ravioles recipe, Steps 1 and 3.
2. Heat a frying pan and add ground meat, onion and oil. Stir over high heat until meat changes colour and is crumbly. Reduce heat, add parsley, salt and pepper to taste and water. Cover and simmer for 30 minutes or until moisture evaporates. Cool.
3. Roll dough, cut, fill and shape Kaloyrka as directed for Ravioles, Steps 3, 4, 5 and 6.
4. Cook in boiling salted water, 15 at a time, for 15-20 minutes or until tender. Remove to a colander set over simmering water, using a slotted spoon. Cook remaining Kaloyrka.
5. Turn into serving dish and cover with hot Saltsa Tomata. Serve immediately. Grated cheese may be served on the side if desired.

HIRINO ME KOLOKASSI
PORK WITH TARO

When I was introduced to kolokassi in Cyprus I did not recognize it. The locals informed me it was Cyprus sweet potato and only available there – and indeed it does look like a very large sweet potato. As it turned out the Egyptians use it also, but it is unknown elsewhere in the region.

The preparation of kolokassi is accompanied with a certain amount of ritual. Scrub root, dry well, peel, do not wet once peeled – if you happen to do so, dry it well again. Chip off pieces – do not chop into it. To chip, slice into the root at an upwards angle, then break piece off as wedge thins. As the root is rather large in circumference, work your way around it, thus ending up with pieces rather like apple wedges. All this is to prevent the vegetable from becoming slimy during cooking. The whole matter of the kolokassi intrigued me, until I found out that it was the taro (Colocasia esculenta) native to the Pacific Islands – a long way from home!

Serves: 6
Cooking time: 1½ hours

1 kg (2 lb) boneless stewing pork
¼ cup corn oil
1 large onion, chopped
1½ cups thickly sliced celery
1 cup tomato purée
salt
freshly ground black pepper
1 kg (2 lb) kolokassi (taro)
juice of ½ lemon

1. Cut pork into 2 cm (¾ inch) cubes, leaving some fat on the meat.
2. Heat half the oil in a heavy pan and brown pork cubes, transferring to a plate when browned.
3. Reduce heat, add remaining oil, onion and celery and fry gently until onion is transparent. Add tomato purée and bring to the boil, stirring to lift browned juices.
4. Return pork to pan and add about 2 teaspoons salt and pepper to taste. Cover and simmer for 45 minutes.
5. Scrub kolokassi, dry well with paper towels and peel. If kolokassi is soiled during peeling, rinse and dry well. Chip off pieces as described in introduction to recipe.
6. When meat is half-cooked place kolokassi on top of meat in pan and sprinkle lemon juice over the top. Tilt pan so that liquid runs over the kolokassi, adding a little water if necessary. Cover tightly and simmer for further 30-45 minutes or until pork and kolokassi are tender. Do not stir once kolokassi is added.
7. Tilt pan and skim off excess fat. Adjust seasoning and serve.

KOLOKASSI VRASTO
BOILED TARO

The large kolokassi root is also scrubbed and boiled in its skin until tender. When cooked, peel off skin, cube the flesh and combine with sliced celery, lemon juice, olive oil, salt and pepper. Serve warm.

POULLES TIGANITES
FRIED TARO SHOOTS

While on the subject of kolokassi, the vegetable as it is grown in Cyprus produces small torpedo-shaped offshoots. These are simply scrubbed and peeled, again keeping the root dry, except for a final rub with lemon juice, then fried slowly in hot oil until golden brown and tender. Lemon juice and salt are sprinkled on at the table. Delicious served with Skorthalia (Garlic Sauce, page 82), and often served alongside boiled beetroot.

YIOUVETSI
LAMB CASSEROLE WITH PASTA

Serves: 6
Oven temperature: 180°C (350°F)
Cooking time: 2 hours

6 lamb leg or shoulder chops, thickly cut
¼ cup butter or corn oil
1 large onion, finely chopped
1 cup tomato puree
1 cup chopped, peeled tomatoes
3 cloves
large piece cinnamon bark
salt
freshly ground black pepper
4-5 cups boiling water or stock
2 cups orzo or kritharaki (rice-shaped pasta)
¼ cup grated kefalotiri or parmesan cheese
½ cup diced haloumy or feta cheese

1. Have meat retailer cut chops about 4 cm (1¼ inches) thick. Alternatively purchase a leg of lamb and have it cut into 6 pieces.
2. Place lamb in a baking dish and spread or pour oil or butter on top. Bake in a moderate oven for 20 minutes.
3. Add onion to dish and return to oven for further 10 minutes.
4. Add tomato puree, chopped tomatoes, cloves, cinnamon bark and salt and pepper to taste. Baste meat with liquid and cook for further hour until meat is tender, adding a little of the water or stock if necessary.
5. When meat is cooked add water or stock and stir in pasta. Cook for further 20 minutes, stirring occasionally, and adding a little more liquid if mixture looks dry.
6. When pasta is tender, sprinkle cheese over pasta and return to oven for 5 minutes. Serve immediately.

Note: This is a popular restaurant dish in Greece, Cyprus and Egypt. The pieces of meat are placed in individual casserole dishes after the initial cooking, and the sauce, pasta and water or stock added to each dish, then cooking is completed. In the home I suggest dividing the meat and pasta after it is cooked and just before adding the cheese. Return to oven for cheese to melt.

THAKTILA KYRION
LADIES' FINGERS

Makes about 4 dozen
Cooking time: 1-2 minutes each lot

Pastry:
3 cups plain flour
¼ teaspoon salt
¼ cup corn or peanut oil
¾ cup cold water

Nut Filling:
1 cup finely chopped almonds
2 tablespoons caster sugar
½ teaspoon ground cinnamon

Syrup:
1½ cups sugar
¾ cup water
2 teaspoons lemon juice
2 tablespoons honey
1 teaspoon orange flower water, optional

To finish:
corn or peanut oil for frying
chopped almonds for serving

1. Sift flour and salt into mixing bowl, add oil and stir into flour, then rub mixture with fingertips to distribute oil evenly. Add water and mix to a soft dough. Knead until smooth, cover bowl and leave pastry to rest for 1 hour.
2. Combine nut filling ingredients.
3. Make syrup: In a pan dissolve sugar in water over heat, add lemon juice and honey and bring to the boil. Boil 5 minutes, stir in orange flower water if used, leave syrup to cool.
4. Knead pastry lightly on floured board, divide in three. Take one lot and roll out very thinly. Cut into 8 cm (3 inch) squares.
5. Place a teaspoon of nut filling along one edge, keeping filling away from sides. Fold over three times, press join and each end firmly to seal. Press ends with a fork. Place finished pastries on a cloth-lined tray and keep covered. Roll out remainder of pastry, fill and finish as above.
6. Place about 2 cups oil in a medium-sized pan and heat. Deep fry a few pastry fingers at a time for about 1-2 minutes, turning them to brown evenly. Cook until golden, lift out with a slotted spoon and place immediately into cold syrup. Turn pastries in syrup, leave for 1 minute, then lift out onto rack to drain. Repeat with remaining pastries.
7. When cold, sprinkle with chopped toasted almonds. Pastries keep well in a sealed container.

BOUREKIA TIS ANARIS (Fried Cheese Pastries) *recipe page 112.*

BOUREKIA TIS ANARIS
FRIED CHEESE PASTRIES

Makes about 6 dozen
Cooking time: 2 minutes each lot

Pastry:
3 cups plain flour
¼ teaspoon salt
¼ cup corn or peanut oil
¾ cup cold water

Cheese Filling:
1½ cups soft curd cottage cheese (anari,
    mizithra or ricotta)
¼ cup caster sugar
1 egg, lightly beaten
1½ teaspoons ground cinnamon

To finish:
corn oil for deep frying
icing (confectioner's) sugar for serving

1. Sift flour and salt into a mixing bowl. Pour oil into centre, then gradually work in flour till mixture is crumbly. Use fingertips to rub oil evenly into flour. Mix to a soft dough with the water, knead lightly, cover and leave to rest for 1 hour.
2. Cream cottage cheese with sugar and gradually blend in beaten egg and cinnamon.
3. Roll out half the pastry as thinly as possible. Use a rolling pin, or better still a 60 cm (2 foot) length of wooden dowelling (a popular and very effective Cypriot and Greek method.)
4. Cut pastry into 8 cm (3 inch) rounds with a pastry cutter. Roll and cut remainder of pastry and trimmings, stack and cover with cloth.
5. Moisten edge of pastry round with water. Place a teaspoon of cheese filling in the centre, fold over and press edge with fork to seal. Place finished pastries on a cloth-lined tray.
6. Heat oil to 190°C (375°F) or until a cube of bread turns golden in 30 seconds. Fry pastries a few at a time, turning to brown evenly — they should cook in about 2 minutes. Lift out with a slotted spoon and drain on paper towels.
7. Serve warm, sprinkled with sifted icing sugar. Any not required for immediate serving should be stored in refrigerator and heated in a moderate oven for 5 minutes before serving.

LOKOUMIA PARAYEMISTA
NUT-FILLED SEMOLINA COOKIES

Makes about 45
Oven temperature: 200°C (400°F)
Cooking time: 20-25 minutes

4½ cups fine semolina
1½ cups melted butter, either salted or
    unsalted
1 cup water
large piece cinnamon bark
2 teaspoons orange flower water

Nut Filling:
1½ cups coarsely ground almonds
¼ cup caster sugar
1½ teaspoons ground cinnamon

To finish:
¼ cup orange flower water
icing (confectioner's) sugar

1. Put semolina in a mixing bowl, add melted butter and mix well with a wooden spoon until butter is distributed evenly. Cover bowl with a piece of plastic film stretched on top and leave for 6-8 hours or overnight.
2. Put water and cinnamon bark in a small pan and bring to the boil. Remove cinnamon and pour boiling water onto semolina. Add orange flower water and mix until well blended. Leave for a few minutes to cool down, then knead until smooth. Dough should be firm; if crumbly add a little more water.
3. Combine nut filling ingredients.
4. Break off pieces of dough the size of a large walnut and mould into an oval shape. Make a hole with your forefinger through the centre from one end and enlarge hole by turning dough in hand and working finger inside dough. Fill with a generous teaspoon of filling and close end. Alternatively press dough flat in the palm of your hand, put filling in the centre and close dough around filling. Remould dough into an oval shape.
5. Place lokoumia on an ungreased baking sheet and bake in a hot oven for 20-25 minutes until cooked and only lightly coloured.
6. As hot lokoumia are removed from oven, brush with orange flower water.
7. Sift icing sugar on a large piece of waxed paper and place hot lokoumia on sugar. Sift icing sugar thickly on tops and sides and leave until cold. Store when cold in a sealed container. When serving, sift more icing sugar on top to give a smooth finish.

GLYKO KARITHI
GREEN WALNUT PRESERVE

*First requirement for this preserve is a walnut tree.
Though the preparation is lengthy, the preserve is well
worth trying as it is superb. Incidentally, a similar
preserve, but flavoured with cardamon, is made in
Iran, where it is called Morabaye Gerdu.*

*The walnuts must be picked very early in summer
when the green fruit are not yet full size and the inner
shell is still soft. Test a nut by pricking it deeply in
several places with a darning needle, paying particular
attention to the long crease on one side; this indicates the
join of the forming shell and is the part of the shell
which hardens first. If there is no hint of resistance, cut
the nut in half to check again. You will see the thick
outer green covering progressing to white. The actual nut
meat should be apparent – if it is clear and gelatinous,
then the nuts are ready for the preserving pan. If the nut
meat is not visible try again in a few days.*

2 kg (4 lb) green walnuts (50 nuts)
cold water
½ cup slake lime
6 cups granulated sugar
1½ cups water
thinly peeled rind of 1 lemon
large piece cinnamon bark
3 cloves
¼ cup lemon juice
¼ cup honey

1. To prepare walnuts it is advisable to wear rubber gloves as the iodine present stains the hands black — a stain impossible to remove, though it does wear off entually. Peel walnuts thinly with a sharp knife, placing peeled nuts in cold water.
2. Leave in cold water to cover for 8 days; change water daily.
3. Put lime in 2 cups water and stir to dissolve. When dissolved, add walnuts and sufficient cold water to cover. Stir, then leave for 4 hours.
4. Drain walnuts and rinse well in several changes of cold water. Tip into a colander and run cold water through them as well to remove all traces of lime. This treatment firms the outer covering on the nut, otherwise it would disintegrate during cooking.
5. Place walnuts in a preserving pan and cover with cold water. Bring to the boil and boil gently, uncovered, until tender — about 1-1½ hours. Test with a needle.
6. Drain walnuts, then, wearing rubber gloves for protection, pierce each walnut in several places so that syrup can penetrate.
7. Place walnuts in a clean pan in layers, sprinkling 1 cup sugar over each layer. Pour on water and leave for 2 hours, so that sugar can dissolve slowly.
8. Put onto heat, adding lemon rind, cinnamon bark and cloves to pan. Heat gently, shaking pan contents to help dissolve remaining sugar crystals. When syrup begins to boil, add lemon juice and boil for 5 minutes. Remove from heat, cover and leave for 24 hours.
9. Add honey to pan contents and return to the boil. Boil on medium heat for 10 minutes without stirring. Skim when necessary.
10. When syrup is very thick — the consistency of honey when a little is cooled on a cold saucer — the preserve is ready. Remove lemon rind, cinnamon and cloves. Ladle into hot sterilized jars and leave until cold before sealing. Store at room temperature.

KAFES
COFFEE

Somehow precise measures sound odd for the Cypriot and Greek way of making coffee, so I have departed from my usual style.

You will require a *briki* (a long-handled coffee pot, wide at the base and tapering in at the top), or a small saucepan.

To each demitasse cup of cold water measured into the pot, add 1 heaped teaspoon of powdered (not instant) coffee and sugar to taste.

For sweet coffee *(glykos)* add the same amount of sugar; for moderately sweet coffee *(metrios)* add a level teaspoon of sugar; or no sugar, if that is your preference *(sketos)*.

Stir over heat only until sugar is dissolved and bring to the boil. The coffee forms a creamy froth on top called kaimak. As the froth turns in from the sides and the coffee begins to rise in the pot, remove from heat at once and pour a little into each cup to distribute the froth, then fill cups.

TURKEY

Istanbul stands majestically astride Europe and Asia, symbolic of the nature of Turkish cuisine. A single bridge straddling the Bosphorus links two culinary heritages, though each has in itself evolved through centuries of history.

In the 1920s Ataturk determined to Westernize all that is Turkey, including her cuisine. I am so glad that he did not complete this part of his project, though fried pastries using a choux pastry base and Dondurmas (water ices) certainly look as though he made some attempt.

A tour of the Topkapi Palace in Istanbul, once home of sultans, princes, their wives and concubines, gives a further insight into Turkish cooking. Just a look at the names of the recipes emphasizes the romantic, exotic era when Turkey's cuisine was being developed: Hünkâr Beğendi (Sultan's Delight), Kadin Göbeği (Ladies' Navels), Kadin Budu (Ladies' Thighs), Dilber Dudaği (Sweet Lips), Hanim Parmaği (Dainty Fingers), İmam Bayildi (Swooning Imam) — the latter certainly not because of any of the former, I assure you.

In Turkey the sea and its gifts plays a large part in the lifestyle and the food. One favourite dish, Kiliç Sis (Skewered Swordfish), is a Turkish delicacy long remembered by visitors. The aroma of fish cooking over glowing charcoal or by other means permeates the air around the shores of the Bosphorus — Sardalya Sarmasi, Midye Dolmasi, Balik Plaki and many more. A favourite sauce served with many seafoods is Tarator, a delectable combination of ground nuts, garlic, olive oil and vinegar. Though hazelnuts are generally used, almonds, pine nuts and walnuts are sometimes substituted.

DONER KEBAP

This famous Turkish speciality is found throughout Turkey and other countries of the region, though it is definitely Turkish in origin. As it is impractical for home preparation, a description will have to suffice.

Even-sized rounds of boneless lamb, taken from a whole carcase, are marinated for 24 hours in a mixture of olive oil, vinegar, onion, parsley, thyme, oregano or other combinations of herbs. A long, very heavy spit is loaded with the meat, layers interspersed with slices of fat from the tail of the lamb. The bottom of the spit is fitted with a disc to keep the meat in place and the top is finished with a whole green pepper and a tomato for colour. The loaded spit is then placed before a vertical fire of charcoal or electrically heated elements. It is motor-driven so that the Kebap revolves to cook evenly. As the lamb cooks on the outside it is deftly sliced off into a special pan and served immediately in pide (flat bread) with salad. The Doner Kebap is now prepared in many Western cities with ethnic groups, since it is as popular in Lebanon, Syria, Greece and Iraq as it is in its native Turkey. It is called Chawarma in Lebanon and Syria, Grass in Iraq and Gyros in Greece.

THE FLAVOUR OF TURKISH FOOD

Turkey's cuisine, coloured by its history, is a mixture of Oriental and Byzantine influences, with the subtlety of Western cuisine softening the impact. Yoghurt would have to be one of the most important elements, its use stretching back into pre-history. While mostly enjoyed in its simplest form, with perhaps a dash of salt or a sprinkling of sugar, it is married into soups, becomes a sauce with little effort and imparts a delicious flavour to cakes and desserts.

Perhaps the next pillar of Turkish cooking would be its Pilavlar, renowned in world cuisine and worthy of their place. In researching, writing and testing the recipes I became aware that no matter how they were formulated there would be some cooks who would agree and others who would strongly disagree with my methods. This is the beauty of Turkish cooking: a dish is a reflection of the cook, her love of food, and her dedication to its preparation for the pleasure of her family.

Herbs are subtly used in Turkish cooking, predominantly parsley, dill, mint, bay leaves and to a lesser extent thyme and oregano. In spicing, pepper, bahar (allspice), cinnamon and paprika are the most widely used. A favourite Turkish garnish to foods is paprika steeped in oil. Cerkes Tavüğü goes one step further: a dedicated cook will painstakingly extract the oil from walnuts to blend with paprika for the garnish. This, by the way, would be without doubt one of the most delicious chicken dishes I have ever tasted.

Turkey produces a wide variety of fruit and vegetables, all excellent in their season, but tomatoes in summer are a special joy. A good Turkish cook would prefer to use fresh tomatoes rather than tomato paste, but certainly uses the latter when tomatoes are out of season.

The lemon is almost as popular in Turkey as it is in Greece and Cyprus; indeed many Turkish recipes using lemon juice are similar to Greek recipes, particularly when combined with egg.

Terbiye, Terbiyeli Tavuk Suyu, and Terbiyeli Kofte are similar to the Egg and Lemon Sauce, Soup, and Meat Ball Soup of Greece and Cyprus.

Olive oil and butter are favoured for cooking above all other oils and fats, though peanut or corn oil can be used for general frying, particularly for pastries. Olive oil is essential for vegetable dishes, not only for its flavour, but because such dishes are often eaten cold and other oils coagulate on cooling.

EATING TURKISH STYLE

The early days of the Ottoman Empire saw Istanbul (then called Constantinople) as a cosmopolitan city of Turks, Greeks, Armenians, Bulgars, Circassians, Venetians, Genoese, Jews, Serbs and Arabs. With such a beginning, is it any wonder that confusion exists as to what is Turkish and what is not?

The point is that Turkish cuisine, as with most cuisines, has been shaped by its history, but the people of the country through ensuing generations have marked it indelibly so that it is now a cuisine with its own national character.

Perhaps Istanbul today is the epitome of all that is Turkish. Her streets are thronged with vendors selling Sis Kebaps and Kofte in pide (the Turkish flat bread) with crisp cucumbers, sweet peppers and tomatoes or simit, crusty bread rings smothered with sesame seeds; with lemonade and visine (sour cherry drink) vendors, laden with highly-polished glass tanks with brass ornamentation strapped to their backs or slung across their bodies; and with the typical Turkish coffee vendor, a gleaming brass urn on his back, a pile of handle-less cups in his hand which he continually flings up and down, their jingling and his cry heralding his presence.

If a Turk wants refreshment, whether bought from an itinerant vendor or from a shop or store, the opportunity is ever present.

The coffee house is a favourite meeting place, a predominantly male domain, with coffee drinking an extremely popular pastime. Coffee was introduced to Turkey by the Arabs and in turn Turkey introduced it to Europe.

The pastry shops are a delight to the eye and a threat to the waistline. Lokum (Turkish Delight) is made in huge quantities with an unbelievable assortment of flavours varying from the typical pink coloured and rose water flavoured confection to one so filled with chopped nuts and dried fruit that the Lokum in the mixture just serves to hold the gelatinous mass together.

One feature of entertaining in a Turkish home is the serving of an assortment of *mezes*. These are placed en masse on a table and so served. It is called a *raki* table. Of course raki, a potent aniseed-flavoured spirit of Turkey, is always served at such a gathering. And though the occasion might appear at first to resemble a Western cocktail party, it could continue until the early hours of the morning, with an ever-changing assortment of hot and cold *mezes* being served.

While the serving of Turkish meals differs from house to house and between the city and rural dweller, it is basically the same. Meals are served Western style at a table, with all the dishes for the meal placed on the table at the same time. Meat or chicken is generally combined with vegetables for a Güveç or Türlü, or Plaki. If Kebap or Kofte is prepared, a separate vegetable accompaniment would be served. A salad, either an elaborate assortment or a simple combination of one or two ingredients, plus pickles and yoghurt and the inevitable pilav, are always present. Cheese, bread and fresh fruit complete the meal. The beverage is usually ayran (yoghurt drink), particularly in summer.

When a Turk wishes to entertain in a grand manner, the range of recipes is such that a banquet to delight any gourmet can be prepared. It is not unusual to find Turks entertaining in such a way, particularly those who have a high social status.

COOKING METHODS

While the household might have a modern stove, cooking on a charcoal fire is still very much preferred. The Western barbecue, of whatever type, will serve you most satisfactorily. For food preparation the pestle and mortar is an essential item of kitchen equipment. Cooking pots and pans are either tin-lined copper or aluminium, with a variety of pottery dishes for oven cooking. Any Western cooking utensil can be used for Turkish cooking with the addition of a food processor or blender to replace the pestle and mortar, though using the latter does give the cook a great deal of satisfaction.

For making Turkish coffee a small, long-handled coffee pot, called a *jezve,* is essential and these are readily available at Middle Eastern stores. A small saucepan really does not give the same results.

INGREDIENTS FOR TURKISH COOKING

There are few, if any, ingredients used in Turkish cooking which are difficult to obtain. Cosmopolitan influences have been felt in most Western countries and such foods are commonplace. One vegetable, the eggplant (aubergine), which is so much a part of Turkish cooking, is now widely known; however recipes using this vegetable detail the Turkish methods for its preparation. The preferred variety of eggplant is the long purple fruit but as this particular one is only available during the summer you will have to choose the smallest possible oval eggplants at other times to produce dishes such as Imam Bayildi. The introductory chapters and glossary give further details on foods for Turkish cooking and the recipes are self explanatory.

PRONUNCIATION

Turkey changed from the Arabic script in the 1920s. Her written language now includes accents and a guide is given to assist you with pronunciation of recipe names.

Â/â as in *past* (used only in words originating from the Ottoman Turkish)

A/a as in *past*

E/e as in *egg*

I/ı as the second vowel in *valid*

İ/i as in *pit*

O/ö as the vowel in *err*

O/o as in *over*

U/ü as in *unit*

U/u as in *put*

Ç/ç as 'ch' in *chair*

S/s as 'sh' in *ship*

G/ğ is a soft, slightly aspirate 'g', always between vowels

The Turkish alphabet contains no Q, W or X.

YOGURT SALÇASI
YOGHURT SAUCE

1-2 cloves garlic
½ teaspoon salt
1 cup yoghurt

1. Pound garlic with salt in a mortar. Alternatively use a garlic press and blend with salt.
2. Combine with yoghurt, cover and chill until required. Serve with fried vegetables, kebabs and as specified in recipes.

TARATOR
HAZELNUT SAUCE

Makes 2 cups

1 cup shelled hazelnuts
1 cup soft white breadcrumbs
3 cloves garlic, crushed
1 tablespoon water
1 cup olive oil
½ cup white vinegar
1 teaspoon salt

1. Blanch hazelnuts if desired. Place in a bowl, cover with boiling water and leave for 5 minutes. Drain and peel off skins. This is not necessary, but I find it improves the flavour and appearance of the sauce.
2. Grind hazelnuts in blender, food processor or nut grinder, or pound in a mortar. If using grinder or mortar place nuts in a bowl when pulverized.
3. Add breadcrumbs, garlic and water and process or beat by hand while adding oil in a thin stream. Gradually add vinegar, beat well until smooth. Stir in salt. The blender gives the smoothest sauce; other methods give a textured sauce.
4. Transfer to serving bowl and chill. Serve with seafoods, fried vegetables and plain cooked vegetable salads, or according to recipe directions.

Note: Though the true Turkish tarator is almost always prepared with hazelnuts, walnuts are sometimes used. Blanched almonds or pine nuts are also used, in which case add lemon juice instead of vinegar.

HAMOUR
SHORTCRUST PASTRY

2½ cups plain flour
½ teaspoon salt
½ cup firm butter
⅓ cup cold water
1 egg yolk

1. Sift flour and salt into mixing bowl. Cut butter into small pieces and rub into flour, using fingertips until mixture resembles fine crumbs.
2. Beat egg yolk lightly and add to flour mixture with water. Mix to a soft dough, knead lightly until smooth, cover and leave to rest for 20-30 minutes before using as directed.

PATLICAN KIZARTMASI
EGGPLANT FRITTERS

Serves: 6
Cooking time: about 20 minutes

3 long eggplants (aubergines), each about
    250 g (8 oz)
salt
1 quantity beer batter (page 137)
oil for shallow frying

For Serving:
Yoğurt Salçası (page 117)
OR Tarator (page 117)

1. Remove stems from eggplants and wash well. Peel off 1 cm (½ inch) strips lengthwise to give a striped effect. Cut into 5 mm (¼ inch) slices and spread on a tray. Sprinkle liberally with salt and leave for 30 minutes. Dry with paper towels.
2. Make batter according to directions, Step 1.
3. Dip each eggplant slice into batter and shallow-fry in hot oil until tender and golden brown on both sides. Slices cook in about 3 minutes. Drain on paper towels.
4. Serve hot with Yoğurt Salçası or Tarator as an appetizer or as a side dish to main meals.

HAVUÇ KIZARTMASI
CARROT FRITTERS

Substitute 750 g (1½ lb) large carrots for eggplants in Patlıcan Kızartması. Scrape and slice diagonally in 1 mm (¼ inch) pieces. Cook in boiling, salted water for 5 minutes until just tender, drain and dry, and continue from Step 2.

KABAK KIZARTMASI
ZUCCHINI FRITTERS

In place of eggplant in Patlıcan Kızartması recipe, use 750 g (1½ lb) medium-sized zucchini (courgettes). Trim and cut in 1 mm (¼ inch) slices lengthwise or diagonally, depending on how they are to be served. Salt if you like, but this softens them and they are better if slightly firm when cooked.

BÖREKLER
SAVOURY PASTRIES

These delicate pastries are filled and shaped in various ways. Though you might like to try your hand at making your own pastry, the readily available fillo pastry (yufka in Turkish) is the ideal pastry as nothing can match its crisp, light flakiness. However you will need home-made pastry for certain böreks.

Fillings are listed separately from the final shaping, as the shape of the börek, rather than the filling, determines the name.

The role of the börek in Turkish cuisine is not merely as an appetizer or first course: they are often served as an accompaniment to light soups, and the more substantial versions containing meat or chicken fillings are served as main courses. You will find the latter in the Meat and Poultry sections of this chapter.

KIYMA
GROUND MEAT FILLING

1 large onion, finely chopped
2 tablespoons butter
500 g (1 lb) finely ground lamb or beef
½ cup finely chopped parsley
salt
freshly ground black pepper

1. In a frying pan gently fry onion in butter until transparent.
2. Increase heat, add ground meat and stir frequently until meat is crumbly. Fry until juices evaporate and meat begins to brown.
3. Remove pan from heat, add parsley and salt and pepper to taste. Use as required.

BEYAZ PEYNİR
WHITE CHEESE FILLING

250 g (8 oz) beyaz peynir (feta cheese)
1 egg
½ cup finely chopped parsley
freshly ground black pepper

1. Crumble cheese in a bowl using fingers or a fork.
2. Beat egg lightly and blend into cheese with parsley and a good grinding of black pepper. Use as required.

ISPANAK
SPINACH FILLING

750 g (1½ lb) fresh spinach or 250 g (8 oz) package frozen chopped spinach
1 medium-sized onion, finely chopped
2 tablespoons olive oil
½ cup crumbled beyaz peynir (feta cheese)
1 egg, beaten
¼ cup finely chopped parsley
salt
freshly ground black pepper

1. Clean fresh spinach well, removing discoloured leaves, roots and any coarse or damaged stems. Wash well in several changes of water and shake leaves to remove excess moisture. Chop coarsely. If using frozen spinach defrost according to package directions.
2. Place fresh spinach in a large pan, cover and put over medium heat for 7-8 minutes, tossing occasionally. Cook only until wilted.
3. Place fresh wilted or frozen defrosted spinach in a sieve and press with back of a spoon to extract moisture. Transfer to a bowl.
4. Gently fry onion in olive oil until transparent and add onion and oil to spinach with cheese, egg and parsley. Combine ingredients thoroughly, seasoning to taste with salt and pepper. Use as required.

BURMA BÖREK
BAKED PASTRY ROLLS

Makes 30
Oven temperature: 190°C (375°F)
Cooking time: 20 minutes

10 sheets yufka (fillo) pastry
½ cup melted butter
1 quantity meat, cheese or spinach filling (above)

1. Open out pastry sheets and cut each sheet into strips as for Sigara Böreği (page 120). Stack and cover with cloth.
2. Take a strip of pastry and brush lightly with melted butter. Spread a generous tablespoon of filling towards narrow edge, keeping filling clear of sides. Fold in sides and roll up. Place seam side down on a buttered baking sheet. Repeat with remaining ingredients.
3. Brush rolls lightly with butter and bake in a moderately hot oven for 20 minutes until golden. Serve hot.

Note: Smaller cocktail-sized Burma Börekler may be made by cutting pasty sheets in quarters. Use less filling; yield is greater.

PIRASAPİDE
LEEK PIE

Serves: 6-8
Oven temperature: 200-220°C (400-425°F)
Cooking time: 30 minutes

1 quantity Hamour pastry (page 117)
4-5 leeks
salt
1 cup crumbled beyaz peynir (feta cheese)
¼ cup finely chopped parsley
¼ teaspoon hot chili pepper
⅓ cup olive oil
4 eggs

1. Make pastry according to directions, cover and leave aside.
2. Remove roots and discoloured leaves from leeks. Cut off most of green tops, leaving about 8 cm (3 inches). Halve leeks lengthwise and wash well to remove soil between leaves.
3. Cut out root core, then slice leeks fairly finely. If leeks are small, measure, as you will require 6-7 cups sliced leeks. Prepare more if necessary.
4. Place in a colander and wash again to ensure all soil has been removed. Drain well, then sprinkle with 1 tablespoon salt, rubbing it through the leeks with your hands. Leave for 15-20 minutes until leeks are limp, then press leeks well so that moisture drains out.
5. Combine leeks in a bowl with crumbled feta, parsley, chili pepper and oil. Beat eggs, put 2 teaspoons of egg aside and add remainder to leeks. Stir well to blend.
6. Divide pastry in two with one piece slightly larger than the other. Roll out larger piece on a floured board and place in a 30 cm (12 inch) round baking dish or a 30 x 25 cm (12 x 10 inch) baking dish.
7. Spread leek filling in pastry-lined dish and moisten pastry edge with water. Roll out remaining pastry and place in position over top. Press pastry to seal well, trim and crimp edge.
8. Beat reserved egg with a little milk and brush top of pastry. Cut small slits over surface with the point of a knife.
9. Bake in a hot oven for 30 minutes until golden brown. Let pie stand for 10 minutes before cutting in serving portions.

Note: Yufka (fillo) pastry sheets may be used instead of the Hamour pastry. You will require 10 sheets in all. Line dish with 5 sheets, brushing each with melted butter. Put filling in and top with remaining sheets, again brushing each with butter. Trim edges and butter top sheet. Score top layers lightly in serving portions using a sharp knife or razor blade. Sprinkle top lightly with water to prevent pastry curling.

SIGARA BÖREĞI
FRIED CIGARETTE PASTRIES

Makes 75
Cooking time: About 60-75 seconds each lot

20 sheets yufka (fillo) pastry
1 quantity meat, cheese or spinach filling
   (page 119)
water for sealing
oil for deep frying

1. Open out pastry sheets and cut each sheet into 3 strips, about 12 cm (5 inches) wide and 30 cm (12 inches) long. Stack on a tea towel, folding towel over top.
2. Take a strip of pastry and place on work surface with narrow edge towards you. Thinly spread 2 teaspoons of filling towards edge, keeping 2 cm (¾ inch) in from sides of pastry.
3. Turn end of pastry over filling then fold in sides, pressing fold along length of pastry. Brush folded sides and top edge of pastry lightly with water. Roll up firmly so that finished pastry is as slender as possible. Place seam-side down on a cloth-lined tray and repeat until ingredients are used.
4. Deep fry pastries a few at a time in hot oil, turning to brown evenly. Lift out with a slotted spoon and drain on paper towels. Serve hot as an appetizer or as an accompaniment to light soups.

Note: Finished pastries may be reheated in a moderate oven if necessary.

SARDALYA SARMASI
SARDINES IN GRAPE VINE LEAVES

Serves: 6
Cooking time: 4-6 minutes

24 fresh sardines
salt
24 grape vine leaves, fresh or preserved
⅓ cup olive oil
freshly ground black pepper
lemon wedges for serving

1. Twist head off sardines, gut them and rinse under cold running water. Drain and dry on paper towels.
2. Spread out on a dish and sprinkle each side with salt. Cover and leave for 20-30 minutes.
3. Rinse fresh or preserved vine leaves in cold water, drain and pat dry with paper towels. Remove stems if present.
4. Spread a vine leaf on work surface and brush shiny side with olive oil. Put a sardine across base of leaf, sprinkle sardine with pepper and dab with oil. Roll up firmly and place on hinged barbecue grid. Assemble remaining ingredients.
5. Close grid and brush outside of rolls with oil. Cook over glowing charcoal for 2-3 minutes each side, or cook under a hot grill. If no hinged grid is available secure leaves with wooden cocktail picks previously soaked in cold water for 30 minutes.
6. Serve immediately on a plate with plenty of lemon wedges. The sardine is unwrapped and lemon juice squeezed on to taste. The vine leaves are not eaten — they are used to impart a pleasing and unusual flavour to the fish.

CİĞER TAVASI
FRIED LIVER BITS

Serves: 10-12
Cooking time: 3-4 minutes each lot

500 g (1 lb) lamb or calf liver
water
salt
plain flour
olive oil for frying
freshly ground black pepper
½ cup chopped spring onion
¼ cup finely chopped parsley

1. Soak liver in salted water to cover for 30 minutes. Remove fine skin and larger tubes and cut liver into 2 cm (¾ inch) cubes. Drain well.
2. Toss liver cubes in flour to coat.
3. Place oil to a depth of 5 mm (¼ inch) in a frying pan and heat well. Fry liver quickly, browning on all sides. Add only a single layer of cubes to pan at a time and turn liver with tongs. Take care not to overcook liver.
4. Remove to a serving dish with a slotted spoon, then sprinkle with salt and pepper to taste. Top hot liver with chopped spring onions and parsley and serve immediately, providing cocktail picks for your guests' convenience.

PİLAV
PILAF

The pilavlar of Turkey have an established place in world cuisine; even so we have only been exposed to a few variations. The possible permutations and combinations of the pilav are endless. The recipes given here are indicative of the various ways in which pilav is prepared; once you have mastered pilav cooking you can devise your own variations.

The Turkish cook soaks her rice in hot, salted water for 10-30 minutes. With the rices available today this is unnecessary. However washing is necessary if you are to achieve the right result. Place in a bowl, add cold water and stir. Pour it off and add fresh water. Do this until water runs clear. Another method is to place rice in a sieve. Move the grains constantly with fingers so that the starch is released as the cold water runs through.

As rice grains vary in hardness according to the variety, you may find the directions given need slight modification for the type you are using. Perhaps you might require more or less liquid, and the cooking time may need to be extended or reduced. Make a note of any alterations necessary for that particular brand of rice.

To serve pilav, either fluff up with fork and pile on serving dish or press hot pilav into an oiled mould and turn out onto serving dish. A little of the sauce from the accompanying food may be spooned on top as additional garnish.

İÇ PİLAV
LIVER PILAF

Serves: 6
Cooking time: 50 minutes

2 cups long grain rice
250 g (8 oz) chicken or goose livers
⅓ cup butter
¼ cup pine nuts
1 cup chopped spring onions, white part only
¼ teaspoon ground allspice
¼ cup currants
3 cups chicken stock
salt
freshly ground black pepper
¼ cup finely chopped parsley or dill

1. Wash rice until water runs clear, then leave to drain well in a sieve.
2. Clean livers and slice finely or dice.
3. Heat half the butter in a small pan and fry pine nuts until golden. Remove to a plate using a slotted spoon.
4. To same butter in pan, add spring onion and fry gently until transparent, add prepared liver and stir over medium heat until colour changes; do not overcook. Stir in allspice and keep aside in pan.
5. In a deep, heavy pan heat remaining butter, add drained rice and stir over medium heat until grains change from translucent to opaque without colouring. Stir in currants, then add chicken stock, about 2 teaspoons salt and pepper to taste. Stir occasionally until boiling, reduce heat to low, cover and simmer for 15 minutes.
6. Remove lid and add reserved pine nuts, spring onion and liver mixture and parsley or dill. Stir gently through the rice with a wooden spoon.
7. Place two paper towels over the rim of the pan and fit lid on tightly. Cook on low heat for further 20 minutes, remove from heat and leave aside for 10 minutes before serving. An excellent accompaniment for roast poultry or lamb.

PATLICANLI PİLAV
EGGPLANT PILAF

Serves: 6
Cooking time: 50 minutes

2 oval eggplants (aubergines), about 500 g
  (1 lb) in all
salt
1 large onion
⅓ cup olive oil
2 cups chopped, peeled tomatoes
1½ teaspoons salt
freshly ground black pepper
2 tablespoons chopped parsley
2 teaspoons chopped fresh mint
2 cups long grain rice
2½ cups light stock or water
yoghurt for serving

1. Cut eggplants into large cubes with skin on. Place in a colander and sprinkle liberally with salt. Leave for 30 minutes. Rinse and dry with paper towels.
2. Halve onion lengthwise and slice.
3. Heat ¼ cup oil in a heavy-based pan and fry eggplant cubes until lightly browned. Remove and keep aside.
4. Add remaining oil to pan and gently fry onion until transparent. Add tomatoes, seasoning, herbs and fried eggplant. Bring to the boil.
5. Wash rice until water runs clear. Drain and place on top of eggplant mixture. Add stock or water.
6. Bring to the boil without stirring. Reduce heat, cover pan and leave to simmer gently for 30 minutes. Turn off heat, place a cloth or 2 paper towels over the rim of the pan and replace lid. Let pilav stand for 10 minutes.
7. Stir gently and turn onto a heated dish. Serve with yoghurt.

PATLICANLI PILAV (Eggplant Pilaf) *recipe above.*

TÜRKİSTAN PİLAVI
TURKISTAN CARROT PILAF

Serves: 5-6
Cooking time: 30 minutes

2 cups long grain rice
¼ cup butter
2 cups coarsely grated carrots
½ teaspoon whole black peppercorns
1 teaspoon sugar
3½ cups chicken stock
salt

1. Wash rice until water runs clear. Drain well.
2. Heat butter in a heavy pan, add grated carrot and peppercorns and fry over medium heat for 3 minutes, stirring often. Sprinkle in sugar towards end of frying.
3. Add rice and fry for further 2 minutes, stirring constantly.
4. Pour in stock and add salt to taste. Stir until boiling, then reduce heat to low. Cover with lid and cook over low heat for 25-30 minutes. Remove from heat and place a cloth or 2 paper towels under lid and leave covered for 10 minutes before serving. Excellent with roast chicken or Tavuk Yufka İçinde.

BEYAZ PİLAV
WHITE PILAF

Serves: 6
Cooking time: 35 minutes plus 10 minutes to rest

2 cups long grain rice
¼ cup butter
3½ cups chicken stock
salt to taste

1. Wash rice until water runs clear. Drain well.
2. Heat butter in a heavy pan and add drained rice. Stir over medium heat for 5 minutes.
3. Add stock and salt to taste, stir occasionally until boiling. Reduce heat, cover with lid and simmer for 25-30 minutes. Test grain to gauge when cooked — grain should be firm to the bite but evenly tender.
4. Turn off heat, place a cloth or 2 paper towels over the rim of the pan and replace lid. Leave for at least 10 minutes before removing cover. It may be left for as long as 30 minutes without spoiling, depending of course on the quality of the grain.
5. Fluff up with fork and serve, or spoon into an oiled mould, press firmly and unmould on to serving dish.

DÜĞÜN PİLAV
WEDDING PILAF

Ingredients as for Beyaz Pilav, with the addition of ¼ cup pine nuts or blanched pistachio nuts, and substituting meat stock for chicken. Fry nuts with rice and continue on from Step 3.

DOMATESLI PİLAV
TOMATO PILAF

Ingredients and method as for Beyaz Pilav with the addition of 1½ cups chopped, peeled tomatoes half-way through frying the rice. Chicken or meat stock may be used, reducing quantity to 2½ cups if canned tomatoes have been used. Add pepper to taste as well as salt.

124

YUFKALI PİLAV
PILAF IN PASTRY

Serves: 8-10
Oven temperature: 190°C (375°F)
Cooking time: 1½ hours

½ cup split or slivered almonds
¼ cup butter
1 large onion, finely chopped
1 cup coarsely grated carrot
250 g (8 oz) lean boneless lamb cut in 1 cm
   (½ inch) cubes
1 cup chopped dried apricots
1 teaspoon ground allspice
1½ teaspoons salt
freshly ground black pepper
3½ cups water or light stock
1 cup crumbled vermicelli noodles
2 cups long grain rice

To finish:
6-8 sheets yufka (fillo) pastry or 1 quantity
   Hamour pastry (page 117)
⅓-½ cup melted butter

1. Fry almonds in half the butter in a deep pan. When golden, remove with slotted spoon to a plate. Keep aside.
2. Add remaining butter to pan with onion and fry gently until transparent. Add carrot and fry 5 minutes longer.
3. Increase heat and add lamb cubes. Stir until lamb changes colour, add apricots, allspice, salt and a good grinding of pepper. Stir in 1 cup water or stock, reduce heat, cover and simmer gently for 15 minutes.
4. Add remaining liquid and return to the boil, then stir in vermicelli and well-washed rice. Bring back to the boil over medium heat, stirring occasionally. Cover and reduce heat to low. Cook slowly for 20 minutes until liquid is absorbed and rice is just tender. Leave aside with lid on.
5. Preheat oven. Have ready an 8-cup pudding basin or square casserole dish brushed with melted butter.
6. Brush a sheet of yufka pastry with melted butter and place another on top. Put aside and butter remaining pastry sheets in pairs in the same way. You will require 3 pairs of buttered sheets for a pudding basin, 4 for a casserole dish.
7. Place one pair of pastry sheets in prepared dish, positioning it across the base and up the sides with end hanging well over the edge. Butter pastry in dish then arrange remaining pastry in the same way so that dish is covered with pastry with generous overlap. If you are using hamour pastry, roll it out to fit utensil with enough overlap to cover finished pie.
8. Stir almonds through pilav and place into dish, spreading top evenly. Pour ¼ cup melted butter over pilav then fold pastry across top to cover, buttering top of each layer as it is put into place. Brush top with butter.
9. Bake in a moderately hot oven for 30 minutes. Invert onto serving platter and cut pie into wedges. Serve as a light meal, as part of a buffet, or as a first course.

FASULYE PLAKİSİ
WHITE BEAN STEW

Serves: 6-8
Cooking time: 2-2½ hours

2 cups dried haricot (navy) beans or other
   small white beans
6 cups water
2 large onions, chopped
½ cup olive oil
2 cloves garlic, chopped
1 cup diced carrot
1 cup sliced celery including leaves
¼ cup tomato paste
½ teaspoon sugar
pinch hot chili pepper
juice of ½ lemon
salt
¼ cup chopped parsley

1. Wash beans in several changes of cold water and place in a large pan. Cover with 6 cups cold water and bring to the boil. Boil for 2 minutes, remove from heat, cover and leave for 2 hours or until beans are plump.
2. In a frying pan heat oil and fry onion until transparent. Add garlic, carrot and celery and fry for 5 minutes, stirring often. Set aside.
3. Return beans to the boil and boil gently, covered, for 30 minutes. Add fried vegetables, tomato paste, sugar and chili pepper, cover and simmer for 1½ hours or until beans are tender without being broken.
4. Add lemon juice, salt to taste and half of the parsley. Cook for 10 minutes longer. Serve in a deep dish sprinkled with remaining parsley. May be served hot or cold.

ISPANAKLI YUMURTA
SPINACH AND EGGS

Serves: 2 as a luncheon dish, 4 as a first course
Cooking time: 20-25 minutes

750 g (1½ lb) spinach or 1 packet frozen
    spinach
1 medium-sized onion, finely chopped
2 tablespoons butter
⅓ cup coarsely crumbled beyaz peynir or
    feta cheese
salt
freshly ground black pepper
4 eggs

1. Clean spinach, removing roots and coarse stems. Wash leaves well, shake off excess water and shred. If using frozen spinach follow directions in Step 3.
2. Gently fry onion in butter in a frying pan with lid to fit. Cook until transparent.
3. Add shredded spinach and stir over medium heat until leaves wilt and liquid runs. Continue to cook until just enough liquid to cover base of pan remains. Frozen spinach may be placed in pan, pan covered and left on low heat. Turn spinach occasionally until thawed, combine with onions then bring to a simmer.
4. Season with salt and pepper and stir in crumbled cheese.
5. Make 4 depressions in spinach and break in 4 eggs. Cover pan and cook over medium heat until eggs set. Serve immediately.

Note: To serve attractively as a first course, divide spinach mixture into 4 individual ovenproof dishes and heat in a moderate oven. Add eggs, drizzle a little melted butter over each and bake until set.

MENEMEN
VEGETABLE OMELET

Serves: 4
Cooking time: 20-25 minutes

1 sweet green pepper
1 sweet red pepper
1 large onion
¼ cup butter or oil
1 cup chopped, peeled tomatoes
salt
freshly ground black pepper
6 eggs
½ cup crumbled beyaz peynir or feta cheese
¼ cup chopped parsley

1. Halve peppers, remove stem, seeds and white membrane. Cut into short strips. Halve onion lengthwise and slice in semi-circles.
2. Heat butter or oil in a large frying pan, add peppers and onion and fry over medium heat until onion is transparent. Stir often.
3. Add tomatoes, salt and pepper and bring to the boil. Simmer gently for a few minutes until vegetables are soft.
4. Beat eggs lightly and pour into pan, stir gently into vegetables until creamy.
5. Combine cheese with all but 1 tablespoon parsley, add to eggs and fold in gently. Serve immediately with remaining parsley sprinkled on top.

SIGARA BÖREGI (Fried Cigarette Pastries) *recipe page 120.*

İSKEMBE ÇORBASI
TRIPE SOUP

Serves: 5-6
Cooking time: 2¼ hours

500 g (1 lb) tripe
water
1 small onion, quartered
salt
white pepper
¼ cup butter
¼ cup plain flour
½ cup milk
2 egg yolks
2 tablespoons lemon juice
2 teaspoons paprika
1 tablespoon oil
3-4 cloves garlic, crushed
⅓ cup white vinegar

1. Wash tripe, cover with cold water and bring to the boil. Pour off water, add 5 cups cold water and onion and return to heat. Add 2 teaspoons salt and white pepper to taste. Cover and simmer gently for 2 hours until tender.
2. Remove onion and discard. Lift out tripe and cut into small strips. Reserve liquid.
3. Melt butter in a small saucepan and stir in flour. Cook for 1 minute without allowing flour to colour. Stir in milk and 3 cups liquid from tripe. Stir constantly until thickened and bubbling, then leave over low heat to simmer gently.
4. Beat egg yolks in a mixing bowl and beat in lemon juice. Pour in thickened liquid, stirring constantly.
5. Return tripe strips to tripe liquid remaining in pan and pour in egg mixture, stirring constantly. Still stirring, cook over gentle heat until soup bubbles gently. Adjust seasoning and remove from heat.
6. Blend paprika into oil and set aside.
7. Combine garlic and vinegar, put into a small bowl and place on the table.
8. Serve soup in bowls with a little paprika oil floated on top as garnish. Garlic-vinegar mixture is added according to individual taste.

DÜĞÜN ÇORBASI
WEDDING SOUP

Serves: 6-8
Cooking time: 2-2¼ hours

500 g (1 lb) boneless lamb stew meat
500 g (1 lb) lamb soup bones
8 cups water
1 onion, quartered
1 carrot, quartered
salt
freshly ground black pepper
⅓ cup butter
½ cup flour
3 egg yolks
2-3 tablespoons lemon juice
2 tablespoons melted butter
2 teaspoons paprika

1. Place lamb meat and soup bones in a large pot and add water, onion and carrot. Bring to a slow simmer, skimming when necessary. Add salt and pepper to taste, cover and simmer gently for 1½ hours until lamb meat is tender.
2. Remove bones and discard. Lift out meat and cut into small pieces. Strain stock, return to pot and let it simmer gently.
3. In a large pan melt butter and stir in flour. Cook gently for 2 minutes without allowing it to colour. Gradually add the hot stock, stirring constantly. When smooth and bubbling, let it simmer gently.
4. Beat egg yolks in a bowl and gradually add lemon juice, holding back a little. Gradually beat in about 2 cups thickened stock, then pour into soup. Stir over gentle heat and return lamb pieces to soup. Heat gently, still stirring, until egg is cooked. Adjust flavour with lemon juice and add more salt if necessary. Remove from heat.
5. Combine melted butter and paprika. Serve soup in deep bowls and pour a little butter-paprika mixture into centre of each as garnish.

PİYAZ
WHITE BEAN SALAD

Serves: 6-8
Cooking time: 2-2½ hours

2 cups dried haricot (navy) or other white
   beans
6 cups cold water
salt
1 clove garlic
2 small onions
¼ cup lemon juice
1 tablespoon white vinegar
¼ cup olive oil
¼ cup good salad oil
¼ cup chopped parsley
1 teaspoon chopped fresh mint
2 teaspoons chopped dill

To finish:
1 sweet green pepper
3 hard-boiled eggs

1. Wash beans very well, cover with cold water and put on to boil. When boiling, remove from heat and leave aside until plump. Alternatively beans may be soaked in cold water overnight, in the refrigerator if weather is warm.
2. Return (or bring) beans to the boil in their soaking water, cover and simmer gently over low heat until tender but still intact. Cooking time will vary according to bean used, but about 2 hours cooking time should be sufficient. Add salt to taste after 1½ hours cooking. When tender, drain well and turn into a bowl.
3. Crush garlic with a little salt. Halve onions lengthwise then slice thinly into semicircles. Add to hot beans with lemon juice, vinegar and combined oils. Leave until cool.
4. Gently mix in chopped herbs and chill salad for 1-2 hours.
5. Serve in a deep bowl garnished with sliced green pepper and sliced or quartered hard-boiled eggs.

HÜNKÂR BEĞENDİ
SULTAN'S DELIGHT

Serves: 6
Cooking time: 40-50 minutes

500 g (1 lb) small eggplants (aubergines)
1 tablespoon lemon juice
¼ cup butter
¼ cup flour
¾ cup milk
salt
freshly ground black pepper
½ cup soft white breadcrumbs, optional
½ cup grated kashkaval, kasseri or coon
   cheese
finely chopped parsley
Tas Kebap for serving (page 138)

1. Grill eggplant over glowing charcoal or impale on a fork and hold over a gas flame. Alternatively place on electric hotplate set on medium heat. Turn frequently until soft to the touch and skin is charred to a certain degree. Another alternative is to char skin only, then cook in a moderate oven for 10-20 minutes depending on size of eggplant.
2. Rinse off any burnt skin under cold water, then peel off remaining skin. Purée in blender or food processor, adding lemon juice to keep eggplant light in colour.
3. Melt butter in a heavy-based pan and stir in flour. Cook gently for 2 minutes without allowing flour to colour, then add milk, stirring constantly until thickened and bubbling.
4. Add eggplant purée and leave over gentle heat till reduced a little and very thick — about 20 minutes. Stir occasionally. If desired, fine breadcrumbs may be stirred into purée to thicken it further. Remove from heat.
5. Stir in cheese and beat well until smooth, then add salt and pepper to taste.
6. Pile purée around edge of serving dish and sprinkle with chopped parsley. Fill centre with Tas Kebap or serve hot with roast lamb or chicken dishes.

Note: If you have a microwave oven, char eggplant as described in Step 1, pierce skin in several places with a fine skewer and cook in microwave for 3-5 minutes, depending on size.

DOMATES SALATASI
TOMATO SALAD

Serves: 6-8

4 medium-sized, firm tomatoes
2 long, young cucumbers
¼ cup lemon juice
1 tablespoon white vinegar
¼ cup olive oil
1 teaspoon finely chopped fresh mint
1 tablespoon finely chopped parsley
salt
freshly ground black pepper
black olives
parsley sprigs to garnish

1. Peel tomatoes if desired. Slice fairly thinly and arrange in two rows on an oval platter.
2. Peel cucumbers and score with tines of a fork. Slice thinly and arrange on one side of the tomatoes.
3. Beat together lemon juice, vinegar, oil and herbs and add salt and pepper to taste. Pour over tomatoes and cucumbers. Cover and chill until required.
4. Just before serving, place drained olives on other side of tomatoes and garnish platter with parsley sprigs. This salad accompanies most meals, particularly in summer when tomatoes are at their best.

İMAM BAYILDI
SWOONING IMAM

The story of the Imam swooning over this dish has been told so often that I shan't tell it again. Little did the man know that he would be immortalized through this most famous of eggplant dishes.

There are versions of this dish in countries from Greece to Iran. It has always featured in Greek cuisine, with the claim that a Greek cook prepared it for the Imam while he lived in Greece. The truth will never be known!

Serves: 4-8
Cooking time: 1¼ hours

8 long eggplants of medium size
salted water
3 medium-sized onions
½ cup olive oil
4 cloves garlic, chopped
3 medium-sized tomatoes, peeled
¼ cup chopped parsley
salt
freshly ground black pepper
2 tablespoons lemon juice
pinch of sugar
½ cup water

1. Remove stems from eggplants. Peel off 1 cm (½ inch) strips of skin lengthwise at intervals to give a striped effect. Cut a deep slit on one side of each eggplant lengthwise, stopping short of top and base. Place in a bowl of cold, well-salted water and leave for 30 minutes. Drain, squeeze out moisture and dry with paper towels.
2. Slice onions lengthwise then cut into slender wedges. In a heavy pan heat half the oil and fry onion gently until transparent. Add garlic, cook 1 minute, then combine in a bowl with chopped tomatoes, parsley and salt and pepper to taste.
3. Place remaining oil in pan and fry eggplants over high heat until lightly browned but still rather firm. Remove pan from heat and turn eggplants so that slit faces up.
4. Spoon vegetable mixture into slits, forcing in as much filling as possible. Spread remaining filling on top. Add lemon juice, sugar and water and cover pan tightly. Cook over gentle heat for 45 minutes until tender. Add more water only if necessary as eggplants release a lot of moisture.
5. Leave to cool to room temperature and serve as an appetizer or as a light meal with bread, or chill and serve as a salad accompaniment.

PIYAZ (White Bean Salad) recipe page 129.

GÜVEÇ or TÜRLÜ
VEGETABLE CASSEROLE

There is some confusion about the name of this dish. To the Turks, Türlü is a lamb or chicken and vegetable casserole. Yet in other countries of the region Türlü is prepared as an all-vegetable casserole, with cooks admitting to it being a Turkish dish. Güveç on the other hand is a casserole of meat or poultry and vegetables, or vegetables on their own.

Serves: 6
Oven temperature: 180°C (350°F)
Cooking time: 1½-2 hours

2 long eggplants or 1 medium-sized oval
   eggplant
salt
4 small zucchini
3 small sweet green peppers
250 g (8 oz) okra (see page 9), optional
250 g (8 oz) green beans
4-5 small ripe tomatoes, peeled
½ cup olive oil
3 small onions, sliced
2 cloves garlic, crushed
¼ cup chopped parsley
freshly ground black pepper
½ cup water

1. Remove stem from eggplant, wash well then peel off 1 cm (½ inch) strips of skin lengthwise at intervals giving a striped effect. Cut long eggplants in 1 cm (½ inch) slices; oval eggplant should be quartered lengthwise, then cut into chunky pieces. Spread eggplant on a tray and sprinkle liberally with salt. Leave for 30 minutes, then pat dry with paper towels.
2. Trim zucchini and cut into 4 cm (1½ inch) pieces. Remove stem and seeds from peppers and quarter. Prepare okra as directed. String beans if necessary and slit in half (French cut). Slice tomatoes.
3. Heat half the oil in a frying pan and fry eggplant until lightly browned. Remove to a plate — do not drain.
4. Add remaining oil to pan, add sliced onions and fry gently until transparent. Stir in garlic, cook 1 minute, then remove pan from heat.
5. Place a layer of eggplant in the base of a casserole dish. Top with some of the zucchini, peppers and beans. Spread some onion mixture on top and cover with tomato slices. Sprinkle with salt, pepper and some of the parsley. Repeat until all ingredients are used, reserving some tomato slices and parsley.
6. Place prepared okra on top if used and cover with last of tomato. Sprinkle with parsley, salt and pepper and add water and oil drained from eggplant.
7. Cover casserole and cook in a moderate oven for 1-1½ hours until vegetables are tender. Serve from casserole as an accompaniment to roast or grilled meats and poultry. Often this is served as a light meal on its own; bread and peynir (feta) cheese are then served with it.

KARNIBAHAR KIZARTMASI
FRIED CAULIFLOWER

Serves: 6
Cooking time: 25-30 minutes

1 medium-sized cauliflower
water
salt
juice of ½ lemon
2 eggs
freshly ground white pepper
fine dry breadcrumbs
oil for deep frying

For serving:
Yoğurt Salçasi (page 117)
OR Tarator (page 117)

1. Break cauliflower into florets and soak in salted water to cover, to release any insects. Rinse well.
2. Bring 6 cups water to the boil with the lemon juice and 2 teaspoons salt. Drop in florets and boil rapidly, uncovered, for 8-10 minutes until just tender.
3. Drain in colander and spread out on paper towels to dry.
4. Beat eggs and add white pepper and salt to taste. Dip florets in egg, then roll in breadcrumbs to coat completely. Place on tray until all florets are prepared.
5. Deep fry a few at a time in hot oil, turning to brown evenly. Lift out with slotted spoon and drain on paper towels.
6. Serve hot as a vegetable accompaniment or as an appetizer with Yoğurt Salçasi or Tarator.

ZEYTİNYAĞLİ PIRASA
BRAISED LEEKS

Serves: 6
Cooking time: 35-40 minutes

6 medium-sized leeks
1 medium-sized onion, sliced
½ cup olive oil
2 tablespoons tomato paste
½ cup water or light stock
¼ cup finely chopped parsley
½ teaspoon sugar
salt
freshly ground black pepper
juice of ½ lemon
1 teaspoon chopped dill
parsley or dill sprigs and lemon slices to
   garnish

1. Remove coarse outer leaves from leeks and trim off root even with base. Cut off most of green tops. Halve lengthwise and wash well to remove all traces of soil. Drain.
2. In a deep frying pan gently fry onion in oil until transparent. Add tomato paste mixed with water or stock, half the chopped parsley, sugar, and salt and pepper to taste. Bring to the boil, cover pan and simmer on low heat for 10 minutes.
3. Add leeks and lemon juice and spoon liquid over leeks. Cover and simmer gently for 15-20 minutes or until tender.
4. Remove to a serving dish and sprinkle with remaining parsley and the chopped dill. Serve at room temperature or chilled, garnishing with herb sprigs and lemon slices.

HAVUC PLAKİSİ
BRAISED CARROTS

Serves: 6
Cooking time: 35-40 minutes

750 g (1½ lb) medium-sized carrots
2 medium-sized onions
¼ cup olive oil
1 cup water
¼ cup finely chopped parsley
1 teaspoon sugar
salt
freshly ground black pepper
1 teaspoon lemon juice

1. Wash and scrape carrots. Cut diagonally in 5 mm (¼ inch) slices. Cut onions in half lengthwise, then slice into semicircles.
2. Heat oil in a pan and add onions. Fry gently on medium heat until transparent. Add carrots and fry for further 5 minutes, stirring frequently.
3. Add water, half the parsley and sugar. Season with salt and pepper to taste, cover pan tightly and simmer on low heat for 15-20 minutes until tender. Add lemon juice and turn into dish.
4. Leave to cool at room temperature or chill if preferred and serve sprinkled with remaining parsley. Serve as a vegetable accompaniment.

BALIK PLAKİ
BAKED FISH

Serves: 6
Oven temperature: 180°C (350°F)
Cooking time: 1 hour

6 fish steaks
salt
freshly ground black pepper
2 medium-sized onions
⅓ cup olive oil
2 cloves garlic, finely chopped
½ cup chopped celery, including leaves
½ cup thinly sliced carrot
1½ cups chopped, peeled tomatoes
½ cup water
lemon slices and chopped parsley for serving

1. Season fish with salt and pepper. Cover and leave aside while preparing sauce.
2. Halve onions lengthwise, then slice into semicircles. In a frying pan heat oil and gently fry onion with garlic, celery and carrot until onion is transparent. Add tomatoes and water and season to taste with salt and pepper. Cover and simmer gently for 20 minutes.
3. Spoon some of the sauce into the base of an oven dish. Add fish steaks and top with remaining sauce. Bake in a moderate oven for 30 minutes or until fish flakes easily with a fork. Serve hot or cold.

KILIÇ ŞIŞ
SKEWERED SWORDFISH

Swordfish is highly esteemed in Turkey and is caught in the Black Sea as well as the Mediterranean. It is also readily available outside this region. If, however, swordfish is not sold by your supplier, use another firm-fleshed fish such as halibut.

Serves: 6
Cooking time: 10-12 minutes

1 kg (2 lb) swordfish

Marinade:
¼ cup lemon juice
2 tablespoons olive oil
1 small onion, sliced
1 teaspoon paprika
1 teaspoon salt
freshly ground black pepper
2 bay leaves, crumbled

Limon Salçası:
¼ cup olive oil
¼ cup lemon juice
¼ cup finely chopped parsley
salt
freshly ground black pepper

1. Have swordfish cut 3 cm (1¼ inches) thick when purchasing. Remove skin if present and cut fish into 3 cm (1¼ inch) cubes.
2. Combine marinade ingredients in a glass or ceramic bowl. Add fish, turn to coat with marinade, cover and refrigerate for 3-4 hours, turning fish occasionally.
3. Thread fish onto 6 skewers and cook over glowing charcoal for 10-12 minutes, turning skewers frequently and brushing occasionally with marinade.
4. Combine Limon Salçası ingredients in a screw top jar, seal and shake.
5. Serve hot skewered fish with Beyaz Pilav and the lemon sauce served separately.

Note: Limon Salçası (Lemon Sauce) is used as a dressing for grilled, fried, boiled and baked fish, salads and vegetables.

BALIK KÖFTESI
FISH BALLS

Serves: 8-10 as an appetizer
Cooking time: 6-8 minutes each lot

Fish Balls:
750 g (11/2 lb) white fish fillets
1/2 cup chopped spring onions
1/4 cup chopped parsley
1 teaspoon chopped fresh dill
11/2 cups soft white breadcrumbs
1 egg
salt
freshly ground black pepper

To finish:
plain flour for coating
oil for deep frying
lemon wedges for serving

1. Skin fillets and remove any bones. Chop roughly and combine with onion, parsley and dill.
2. Put fish mixture through food grinder using fine screen, or process to a paste in food processor in 2 lots.
3. Turn into a bowl and add crumbs, egg, about 1 teaspoon salt and pepper to taste. Mix to a firm paste, adding a few more breadcrumbs if necessary as quantity depends on type of fish used.
4. With moistened hands shape into balls the size of a walnut. Chill to firm if time allows.
5. Coat balls with flour and deep fry 8 at a time in hot oil for 6-8 minutes, turning to brown evenly. Drain on paper towels and serve hot with lemon wedges.

IMAM BAYILDI (Swooning Imam) *recipe page 130.*

MİDYE DOLMASI
STUFFED MUSSELS

Serves: 8-10
Cooking time: 1 hour

Filling:
1 large onion, finely chopped
⅓ cup olive oil
¼ cup pine nuts
⅔ cup long grain rice, washed
2 tablespoons chopped parsley
½ teaspoon ground allspice
1 cup chopped peeled tomatoes
1 cup water or fish stock
salt
freshly ground black pepper

To finish:
40 large mussels
1 cup water or fish stock

For serving:
lemon slices or wedges
parsley sprigs
Tarator (page 117)

1. Gently fry onion in oil until transparent, add pine nuts and fry 2 minutes. Stir in rice, parsley, spice, tomatoes and liquid and add salt and pepper to taste. Cover and simmer gently for 15 minutes until liquid is absorbed.
2. Prepare mussels as directed below.
3. Place a generous teaspoon or 2 of filling in each mussel and close the shell as much as possible. Arrange in a heavy pan in even layers. Invert a heavy plate on top to keep mussels closed.
4. Add water or stock to pan, bring to a simmer, cover and simmer gently for 30 minutes. Turn off heat and leave in pan until cool.
5. Lift out mussels and wipe with paper towels. Shells may be lightly oiled for a more attractive appearance. Arrange on serving dish and garnish with lemon and parsley sprigs. Serve with Tarator. If not required for immediate use, place mussels in refrigerator. They can be served chilled or at room temperature.

To prepare mussels: Scrub mussels well with a stiff brush, scraping shell with a knife to remove any marine growth. Tug beard towards pointed end to remove. To open easily, place scrubbed mussels in warm salted water. As they open, insert point of knife between the 2 shells and slide it towards pointed end to sever the closing mechanism. For stuffing, do not separate shells; shells may be separated if removing mussel meat for other recipes.

HAMSİ KIZARTMASI
FRIED BRISLINGS OR SPRATS

Serves: 6 as an appetizer
Cooking time: 2 minutes each lot

500 g (1 lb) brislings, sprats or other tiny fish
salt
plain flour
1 cup oil for frying

For serving:
parsley sprigs and lemon slices to garnish
Limon Salçasi (see Kiliç Şiş, page 134)

1. Wash and drain fish; no need to clean insides unless you prefer to do so. Leave fish intact. Drain, sprinkle with salt and leave for 10 minutes.
2. Coat fish with flour. Take 4 or 5 fish, moisten tails with water and press tails together to form a fan, dusting tails again with flour.
3. Heat oil in a frying pan and fry fish until golden brown and crisp — about 1 minute each side.
4. Drain on paper towels. Serve hot, garnished with parsley and lemon slices and with a bowl of Limon Salçasi on the side.

MİDYE TAVASI
FRIED MUSSELS

Traditionally mussels are rolled in flour, then dipped in beer. The modern Turk has combined the two to make this crisp, light batter — so much simpler and less messy — and the result is delicious. Islam forbids the drinking of wine or its use in cooking. No directive was given on the use of beer and spirits.

Serves: 6
Cooking time: 15-20 minutes in all

Beer Batter:
1 cup flour
1 teaspoon salt
about ¾ cup beer

To finish:
40 mussels (see page 136)
flour for coating
oil for deep frying

For serving:
lemon wedges
parsley sprigs
Tarator (page 117)

1. Sift flour and salt into a mixing bowl. Pour in beer and mix to a smooth batter, adding a little more beer if necessary.
2. If mussels are in their shells, prepare as directed in Midye Dolması recipe (page 136), and release mussels from shells with the point of a knife. Drain mussels on paper towels.
3. Toss mussels in flour to coat lightly. Dip in batter and deep fry a few at a time in hot oil, turning to brown evenly. Remove with slotted spoon and drain on paper towels.
4. Serve hot, garnishing platter with lemon and parsley. Have Tarator in a bowl and provide cocktail picks.

TAVUK YUFKA İÇİNDE
CHICKEN IN PASTRY

Serves: 6
Oven temperature: 190°C (375°F)
Cooking time: 45 minutes

4 whole chicken breasts or 1 kg (2 lb) boneless
   chicken breasts
⅓ cup butter
4 small onions
1 large ripe tomato, peeled
salt
freshly ground black pepper
¾ cup water

To finish:
12 sheets yufka (fillo) pastry
⅓ cup melted butter
parsley sprigs for garnish

1. If whole breasts are used, bone out and remove skin. Cut each breast in half.
2. Heat half the butter in a frying pan and brown chicken over medium heat, turning frequently. Cook for 10 minutes until just cooked through. Remove to a plate.
3. Cut onions lengthwise and slice thinly into semicircles. Add to pan with remaining butter and fry gently until transparent. Chop tomato and add with salt and pepper to taste. Stir in water and cook gently until moisture evaporates. Mixture should look oily.
4. Cut chicken breasts in strips about 5 cm (2 inches) long and stir gently into pan contents. Remove from heat.
5. Brush a sheet of yufka pastry with melted butter, top with another sheet, butter it then fold in half to form almost a square shape. Brush again with butter.
6. Place a sixth of the filling towards the centre and slightly towards one corner. Fold this corner over filling, fold adjacent corners on top and finish like a parcel, tucking last corner underneath package. Place on lightly buttered baking sheet. Repeat with remaining ingredients.
7. Brush top of each lightly with butter and bake in a moderately hot oven for 15 minutes until golden. Serve immediately, garnishing with parsley sprigs. Türkistan Pilavı is a good accompaniment.

ÇERKES TAVÜGÜ
CIRCASSIAN CHICKEN

Serves: 6
Cooking time: 2 hours

1 chicken, about 1.5 kg (3 lb)
1 large onion, quartered
1 carrot, quartered
2 sprigs parsley
3 cups cold water
salt
freshly ground white pepper
3 slices stale white bread, crusts removed
1½ cups finely ground walnuts
½ teaspoon paprika
1 clove garlic, crushed, optional

For serving:
1 tablespoon walnut oil (see Note)
½ teaspoon paprika
finely chopped parsley, optional

1. Place chicken in a medium-sized pan with onion, carrot, parsley and water. Bring to a slow simmer, skimming when necessary. Add 1½ teaspoons salt and pepper to taste. Cover and simmer gently for 1½ hours — do not boil as this makes flesh stringy.
2. Cool a little, then remove chicken to a plate. Strip off flesh, returning skin and bones to a pan. Boil stock with bones and skin until reduced by half. Strain and reserve stock.
3. Cut chicken meat into 5 cm (2 inch) strips and place in a bowl. Moisten with 2 tablespoons stock, cover and chill.
4. Soak bread in a little chicken stock, squeeze and crumble into a bowl. Add walnuts, paprika and garlic if used. Combine and pass through food grinder using fine screen, or process in food processor or blender.
5. Slowly beat in 1 cup warm chicken stock, adding a little more if necessary to make a smooth, thick sauce. Adjust seasoning with salt and pepper.
6. Mix a third of the walnut sauce gently into chicken. Shape chicken mixture into an attractive mound on a shallow dish and spread remaining sauce over it. Cover lightly with plastic wrap and chill.
7. Steep paprika in walnut oil for 10 minutes or longer and drizzle over the top just before serving. Garnish with chopped parsley if desired. Serve cold with salad accompaniments.

Note: Walnut oil is obtainable from some health food stores and is usually very expensive. See Glossary for preparation.

TAS KEBAP
BRAISED LAMB

Serves: 6
Cooking time: 2 hours

1 kg (2 lb) boneless lamb stew meat
¼ cup butter
2 medium-sized onions, finely chopped
¼ cup chopped sweet green pepper, optional
1½ cups chopped, peeled tomatoes or ¼ cup tomato paste
1-1½ cups water
½ teaspoon ground allspice
salt
freshly ground black pepper
¼ cup chopped parsley

For serving:
Hünkâr Beğendi (page 129)
or Beyaz Pilav (page 124)

1. Trim meat and cut into 2 cm (¾ inch) cubes.
2. Heat half the butter in a heavy pan and brown meat quickly on each side, transferring to a plate as it browns.
3. Add remaining butter to pan and add onion and green pepper if used. Fry gently until onion is transparent.
4. Add tomatoes or tomato paste and 1 cup water if using tomatoes, more if using paste. Stir well to lift browned sediment and add allspice, salt and pepper to taste, and most of parsley.
5. Return lamb to pan, cover and simmer gently for 1½ hours or until lamb is tender and sauce thickened.
6. Pile in centre of Hünkâr Beğendi. If serving with Beyaz Pilav press cooked pilav into an oiled ring mould and unmould onto serving platter. Spoon some of the sauce over the rice and place meat in centre of ring.
7. Sprinkle meat with reserved chopped parsley and serve hot.

BALIK KÖFTESI (Fish Balls) *recipe page 134.*

TALAŞ KEBAP
LAMB IN PASTRY

Serves: 4
Oven temperature: 180-190°C (350-375°F)
Cooking time: 1½ hours

750 g (1½ lb) boneless lamb from shoulder
2 tablespoons butter
1 small onion, finely chopped
1 cup chopped peeled tomatoes
2 tablespoons chopped parsley
salt
freshly ground black pepper
8 sheets yufka (fillo) pastry
⅓ cup melted butter

1. Trim lamb and cut into 1 cm (½ inch) cubes.
2. Heat butter in a pan, add lamb and brown over high heat, stirring often. Reduce heat to medium.
3. Add onion and cook with lamb for 10 minutes, stirring occasionally.
4. Stir in tomatoes and parsley and add salt and pepper to taste. Cover and simmer gently for 1 hour. Increase heat to reduce liquid to a thick sauce if necessary. Remove from heat.
5. Spread out one sheet fillo pastry, brush with melted butter and place another sheet on top. Brush top with butter and fold pastry in half to give almost a square shape. Cover with cloth and assemble remainder of pastry similarly.
6. Take one lot of pastry and brush top with butter. Spread a quarter of the lamb mixture towards one end, leaving sides clear. Fold end of pastry over filling, roll once, fold sides in, then roll up. Place seam-side down on a buttered baking sheet. Repeat with remaining pastry and lamb.
7. Brush top of pastries with butter and bake in a pre-heated moderate oven for 25-30 minutes until puffed and golden. Serve immediately.

Note: Commercial puff pastry may be used instead of fillo: 375 g (12 oz) is sufficient. Roll out thinly, cut into 4 rectangles 15 x 20 cm (6 x 8 inches). Moisten sides and press to seal, instead of folding sides over filling. Bake in a hot oven 230°C (450°F) for 10 minutes, then reduce to moderate.

DÜĞÜN ETİ
WEDDING MEAT

Another wedding feast dish. Ingredient quantities have been scaled down considerably – even the Turks don't wait for a wedding just to prepare this spicy lamb dish.

Serves: 6
Cooking time: 2 hours

6 lamb shoulder chops cut 4 cm (1½ inches) thick
¼ cup butter
2 medium-sized onions, chopped
1½ cups chopped, peeled tomatoes
1 cup water
1½ teaspoons ground cinnamon
½ teaspoon whole allspice, crushed
3 cloves
salt
freshly ground black pepper

For serving:
grilled tomato slices
Düğün Pilav (page 124)

1. Trim chops if necessary. Heat half the butter in a heavy pan and brown meat on each side. Remove to a plate.
2. Add remaining butter and gently fry onion until soft. Add tomatoes, water and spices and stir well to lift browned juices. Bring to the boil, then reduce heat.
3. Return lamb to pan and add salt and pepper to taste. Cover pan and simmer over low heat for 1½ hours or until meat is tender. Remove cloves if desired.
4. Arrange lamb on a warm platter and place grilled tomato slices around lamb. Pour sauce over meat. Serve with Düğün Pilav.

KADIN BUDU
'LADIES' THIGHS' CROQUETTES

The Turks' appreciation of the fair sex is apparent even in the naming of recipes. Form the meat mixture with a certain voluptuousness to an elongated egg shape. Don't make them too plump — we all like to be flattered, don't we?

Serves: 6
Cooking time: about 20-25 minutes in all

750 g (1½ lb) finely ground lean lamb or beef
1 cup boiled rice
1 medium-sized onion, finely chopped
½ cup crumbled beyaz peynir (feta cheese)
¼ cup finely chopped parsley
1 teaspoon finely chopped dill
salt
freshly ground black pepper
2 large eggs
plain flour for coating
oil for shallow frying

1. Combine meat, boiled rice, onion and cheese, then pass through meat grinder using fine screen.
2. Add herbs, salt and pepper to taste and 1 lightly beaten egg. Mix by hand to a smooth paste.
3. Take a generous tablespoon of the mixture and form into an elongated egg shape, wider at one end than the other, or into simpler torpedo shape. Moisten hand with water to facilitate handling. Place kadın budu into a baking dish side by side as they are finished.
4. Beat remaining egg well and pour over kadın budu, then turn them over in dish to coat them evenly with a film of egg.
5. Place about ½ cup flour in a plate and roll budu in flour, one at a time, placing them into a frying pan of heated oil as they are coated. Use one hand for rolling them in the flour, keep other hand dry for moving them to the pan.
6. Fry over high heat until golden brown, turning them frequently with tongs so that they keep their shape.
7. Drain on paper towels and serve hot with vegetable or salad accompaniment.

İZMİR KÖFTESİ
MEATBALLS IN TOMATO SAUCE

Serves: 5-6
Cooking time: 1½ hours

750 g (1½ lb) finely ground beef or lamb
1 clove garlic, crushed
1 small onion, finely grated
2 thick slices stale white bread
water
1 egg
1 teaspoon ground cumin
2 tablespoons finely chopped parsley
salt
freshly ground black pepper
flour for coating
¼ cup butter or oil

Tomato Sauce:
1½ cups chopped, peeled tomatoes
½ cup finely chopped sweet green pepper
½ teaspoon sugar
salt
freshly ground black pepper
½ cup water

1. In a mixing bowl combine meat with garlic and onion. Soak bread in cold water, squeeze dry and crumble into bowl. Add egg, cumin, parsley and salt and pepper to taste. Blend thoroughly to a smooth paste.
2. With moistened hands shape tablespoons of the meat mixture into oval, sausage-like shapes. Coat lightly with flour.
3. Heat butter in a deep pan and fry meatballs until lightly browned on all sides. Remove to a plate when browned.
4. Add tomatoes and chopped pepper to pan and stir over medium heat for 5 minutes. Add sugar and salt and pepper to taste, then stir in water. Bring to the boil and return meatballs to pan. Bring to a slow simmer.
5. Cover and simmer gently for 1 hour, until meatballs are tender and sauce is thick. Serve with pilaf.

SIS KEBAP
SKEWERED LAMB AND VEGETABLES

Serves: 6
Cooking time: 10-12 minutes

1 kg (2 lb) boneless lamb from leg
juice of 1 large lemon
¼ cup olive oil
1 onion, thinly sliced
freshly ground black pepper
1 bay leaf, crumbled
½ teaspoon dried thyme

To finish:
12 small onions
boiling salted water
1 sweet red pepper
1 sweet green pepper
salt

For serving:
Beyaz Pilav (page 124)

1. Cut lamb into 3 cm (1¼ inch) cubes and place in a glass or ceramic bowl. Add lemon juice, olive oil, onion slices, pepper, bay leaf and thyme. Salt should not be added until after cooking as it tends to draw out meat juices. Cover and marinate in refrigerator for 4-6 hours, turning meat occasionally. Leave for longer if desired.
2. Peel onions and par-boil in salted water for 5 minutes. Drain.
3. Wash peppers and remove core, seeds and white membrane. Cut into 3 cm (1¼ inch) squares.
4. Lift lamb from marinade and thread onto 6 long skewers, alternating cubes of meat with onions and pepper pieces.
5. Cook over glowing charcoal for 10-12 minutes, turning frequently and brushing with marinade when required. After sealing the meat, remove skewers to cooler part of fire or raise the grid, otherwise the vegetables will burn.
6. Serve hot on a bed of Beyaz Pilav. The rice may be coloured with ½ teaspoon turmeric, added when frying the rice in the butter.

KESKÜL
ALMOND CUSTARD

Serves: 6
Cooking time: 45 minutes

¾ cup whole blanched almonds (1 cup
    ground almonds)
4 cups milk
¼ cup ground rice
¼ teaspoon salt
¼ cup sugar
4 drops almond essence
chopped pistachio nuts or toasted slivered
    almonds
pomegranate seeds, optional

1. Grind almonds finely in food processor or blender, or pass through grinder 2 or 3 times using fine screen.
2. Place in bowl, knead with hand to a firm paste.
3. Heat 1 cup milk to boiling point, pour onto almonds and stir with wooden spoon until well blended. Leave aside to steep.
4. Blend ¼ cup cold milk with ground rice in a large bowl. Heat remaining milk in a heavy pan, preferably one with a non-stick coating. When boiling pour onto ground rice mixture, stirring constantly, then return mixture to pan.
5. Bring to the boil, add salt and boil gently for 10 minutes, stirring occasionally.
6. Strain almond milk through a fine sieve, pressing almonds with back of spoon. Pour almond milk into pan, stir well to blend and add sugar. Boil gently for a further 10 minutes.
7. Stir in almond essence and pour into individual dessert bowls. Serve garnished with chopped pistachio nuts or almonds and pomegranate seeds if available.

MİDYE DOLMASI (Stuffed Mussels) *recipe page 136*

KADIN GÖBEĞI
LADIES' NAVELS

The name and the finished dish are colourfully Turkish, while the basic dough is very definitely French. Though the ingredient proportions differ from the traditional formula, it is choux pastry nonetheless, prepared in the Turkish manner.

Makes about 20

Syrup:
2 cups granulated sugar
1½ cups water
strained juice of ½ lemon

Choux Pastry:
1 cup plain flour
¼ teaspoon salt
1 cup water
¼ cup butter
2 large eggs, lightly beaten
⅛ teaspoon almond essence

To finish:
oil for shaping and frying
whipped cream or kaymak (clotted cream, see Ushta, page 213)
¼ cup finely chopped, blanched pistachio nuts

1. In a heavy pan dissolve sugar in water over medium heat, stirring occasionally. Bring to the boil, add lemon juice and boil rapidly, without stirring, for 15 minutes. Leave syrup in pan to cool.
2. Sift flour and salt onto a square of stiff paper.
3. In another heavy pan heat water and butter until boiling. Pour in flour all at once, stirring constantly with a wooden spoon or balloon whisk. Keep stirring until mixture leaves sides of pan, then cook on low heat, stirring occasionally, for further 5 minutes.
4. Remove roux from heat and turn into a bowl. Cool for 2 minutes then gradually beat in eggs. Add almond essence and beat until smooth and satiny. A balloon whisk will break up lumps, a wooden spoon is better for beating to a smooth finish, so utilize the two for Steps 3 and 4.
5. Oil hands and take pieces of dough the size of a walnut. Roll into smooth balls and place on an oiled tray. Flatten into rounds about 5 cm (2 inches) in diameter and press oiled forefinger into centre of each to make a hole. Keep hands oiled during shaping so that dough will not stick.
6. Place enough oil in a large electric frypan to come to a depth of 1 cm (½ inch). Heat until just warm and place half of the prepared göbeği into oil.
7. Increase heat to 200°C (400°F) as soon as they are added. When göbeği rise to the surface and are puffed, turn them over. Fry them for 15 minutes in all, timed from when the göbeği are first placed into pan. Turn frequently during last half of cooking time so that they brown evenly.
8. When cooked, remove from oil with a slotted spoon and drain briefly on paper towels. Put into syrup, turn them and leave for 5 minutes before removing to a plate.
9. Turn off frypan and allow oil to cool down before adding second lot.
10. To serve, arrange göbeği on a flat platter and place a dollop of whipped cream or kaymak in the centre. Sprinkle with pistachio nuts.

Note: If you have no electric frypan, use a large frying pan set on a thermostatically controlled hot plate or burner. Otherwise use an ordinary burner, start at low and increase heat to midway between medium and high settings.

DİLBER DUDAĞI
LIPS OF THE BEAUTY

Follow Kadın Göbeği recipe to Step 4.
  Oil hands and take pieces of dough the size of a walnut. Roll into balls. Flatten a ball of dough in your hand to a 6 cm (2½ inch) round and fold dough over so that pastry resembles lips on curved edge.
  Place on an oiled tray until all are shaped. Fry and finish as for Kadın Göbeği, Steps 6 to 9. Serve plain or with whipped cream or kaymak.

HANIM PARMAĞI
DAINTY FINGERS

Follow Kadın Göbeği recipe to Step 4. At Step 5, shape about 2 teaspoons of dough into finger lengths about 8 cm (3 inches) long. Keep hands oiled, and place finished parmaği on an oiled tray.

Heat oil for deep frying to 200°C (400°F) and deep fry 8 to 10 at a time for 10 minutes, turning to brown evenly. Drain briefly on paper towels and place into prepared syrup. Leave for 5 minutes to soak, then lift out and serve while warm piled on a platter. Sprinkle with finely chopped walnuts or pistachio nuts if desired.

LOKUM
TURKISH DELIGHT

Cooking time: 1½ hours
Makes about 1 kg (2 lb)

4 cups granulated sugar
4½ cups water
1 teaspoon lemon juice
1 cup cornflour
1 teaspoon cream of tartar
1-2 tablespoons rose water
red food colouring
½ cup chopped, toasted almonds, unblanched
¾ cup icing (confectioner's) sugar
additional ¼ cup cornflour

1. Combine sugar, 1½ cups water and lemon juice in a thick-based pan. Stir over low heat until sugar dissolves, brushing sugar crystals off side of pan with a bristle brush dipped in cold water.
2. Bring to the boil and boil to soft ball stage, 115°C (240°F) on a candy thermometer. Remove from heat.
3. In another thick-based pan blend cornflour, cream of tartar and 1 cup cold water until smooth. Boil remaining 2 cups water and stir into cornflour mixture, then place over heat. Stir constantly until mixture thickens and bubbles. Use a balloon whisk if lumps form.
4. Pour hot syrup gradually into cornflour mixture, stirring constantly. Bring to the boil and boil gently for 1¼ hours. Stir occasionally with a wooden spoon and cook until mixture is a pale golden colour. Stirring is essential.
5. Stir in rose water to taste and a few drops of red food colouring to tinge it a pale pink. Blend in nuts if used, and remove from heat.
6. Pour into an oiled 23 cm (9 inch) square cake tin and leave for 12 hours to set.
7. Combine icing sugar and the ¼ cup cornflour in a flat dish.
8. Cut Turkish Delight into squares with an oiled knife and toss in sugar mixture. Store in a sealed container with remaining sugar mixture sprinkled between layers.

Variations:
Crème de Menthe Lokum: Replace rose water and red food colouring with 2 tablespoons Creme de Menthe liqueur and a little green food colouring. Omit nuts.

Orange Lokum: Use 1-2 tablespoons orange flower water instead of rose water; use orange food colouring.

Vanilla Lokum: Use 2 teaspoons vanilla essence instead of rose water and colouring, and stir in ½ cup toasted chopped almonds or chopped walnuts. Do not blanch almonds.

KUSYUVASI
BIRD'S NEST PASTRIES

Makes 20
Oven temperature: 180°C (350°F) reducing to
  150°C (300°F)
Cooking time: 35 minutes

Syrup:
2½ cups sugar
1½ cups water
thinly peeled rind of ½ lemon
strained juice of ½ lemon

Nut Filling:
1½ cups finely chopped, blanched almonds
½ cup finely chopped, blanched pistachio
  nuts
2 tablespoons caster sugar

To finish:
20 sheets yufka (fillo) pastry
¾ cup melted, unsalted butter

1. Put sugar and water into a heavy pan and dissolve over medium heat, stirring occasionally. Bring to the boil, add lemon rind and juice and boil, without stirring, for 15 minutes. Cool and strain into a jug. Chill until required.
2. Combine almonds and pistachio nuts, put about a third of the mixture aside and stir sugar into remainder.
3. Open out yufka sheets and place between two dry tea towels. Cover top with a lightly dampened tea towel to prevent pastry drying.
4. Take 1 sheet yufka and spread out on work surface. Brush with melted butter and fold in half lengthwise. Brush again with butter and sprinkle 1 tablespoon nut filling near folded edge. Turn pastry over filling, fold in 1 cm (½ inch) on each side, and roll up to within 4 cm (1½ inches) of other edge.
5. Lift pastry up by rolled edge with the flap hanging towards you and twirl into a ring, curling it away from you. Tuck loose pastry under, into centre of ring, to form a nest. Repeat with remaining ingredients.
6. Place pastries in a buttered baking dish and brush tops lightly with butter.
7. Bake in a moderate oven for 20 minutes, reduce to slow and bake for further 15 minutes so that pastry cooks through without over-browning.
8. Pour half the cold syrup over the hot pastries. Leave until cool, then sprinkle some of the reserved nuts in the centre of each pastry. Remove to serving platter and serve remaining syrup in a jug for adding to individual taste.

İNCİR COMPOSTU
FIGS IN SYRUP

Serves: 6-8
Cooking time: 45 minutes

500 g (1 lb) dried figs
4 cups cold water
blanched almonds
¾ cup granulated sugar
thin strip lemon rind
juice of 1 lemon
¼ cup honey

For serving:
chopped almonds, pistachios or walnuts
whipped cream or yoghurt

1. Wash figs well and cover with the cold water. Leave for 8 hours until plump. Drain off water into a heavy pan.
2. Insert an almond into each fig from the base. Set aside.
3. Add sugar to water in pan and heat, stirring occasionally, until sugar is dissolved. Add lemon rind, juice and honey and bring to the boil.
4. Add prepared figs and return to the boil. Boil gently, uncovered, for 30 minutes, until figs are tender and syrup is thick. Remove lemon rind.
5. Arrange figs upright in a bowl. Pour syrup over figs, cool, cover and chill.
6. Sprinkle with chopped nuts and serve with whipped cream or yoghurt.

DOMATES SALATASI (Tomato Salad) *recipe page 130.*

AŞURE
NOAH'S PUDDING

The credit for this dish goes back a long, long way. Of course it is pure assumption, but it illustrates the romantic nature of the Turks. It is said that on the last day on the Ark, the women used up all the remaining foods and came up with Aşure.

In Turkey today this pudding is prepared with great ceremony during the month of Muharrem, also known as the Month of Aşure. Usually a vast quantity is made so that some may be given to friends and relatives. It is considered impolite not to give any to any person who may catch the cooking aroma.

As the right wheat for Aşure is difficult to find outside of the Middle East, the recipe is usually made with coarse burghul elsewhere.

Serves: 12-16
Cooking time: 4½ hours

½ cup chick peas
½ cup dried haricot (navy) beans
1 cup coarse bulgar (burghul)
½ cup short grain rice
water
1½ cups granulated sugar
½ teaspoon salt
1½ cups milk
¾ cup sultanas (white raisins)
¼ cup currants
½ cup chopped dried apricots
½ cup chopped dried figs
½ cup chopped blanched almonds
½ cup chopped walnuts
¼ cup pine nuts
¼ cup rose water
pomegranate seeds, almonds or pistachio nuts
    to garnish

1. Wash chick peas and beans well and place in separate bowls. Cover each with 1½ cups cold water and leave overnight.
2. Rinse burghul and rice and place in separate bowls with 4 cups cold water in the burghul; 1 cup water on the rice. Leave overnight.
3. Next day put chick peas and beans with their soaking water in separate pans and cook for 1½-2½ hours until tender. Chick peas will take longer to cook than the beans.
4. Put burghul with its soaking water and an additional 3 cups water in a large heavy pot. Drain rice and add. Put on low heat and cook gently, uncovered, for 40-50 minutes until very soft and porridge-like in consistency.
5. Add drained cooked chick peas and beans and another cup of water. Leave on low heat, uncovered, for 30 minutes, stirring occasionally until liquid is well reduced and Aşure is thick.
6. Add sugar, salt and milk and cook for 15 minutes longer. Stir in prepared fruits and nuts and remove from heat. Add rose water, stir well and pour into 1 large bowl or individual sweet bowls.
7. Cool to room temperature and serve as it is or cover and chill in refrigerator. Serve decorated with pomegranate seeds if available, otherwise decorate with blanched almonds or pistachio nuts.

SARIĞI BURMA
SULTAN'S TURBANS

Sarığı Burma is also prepared in Lebanon and Syria where it goes under the delightful name of Zind es Sitt (Ladies' Wrists). It is important to have very fresh, pliable fillo pastry sheets as the roll has to be crumpled up. Brittle pastry breaks. If you find early attempts fail, then shape the remainder of the ingredients as directed at the end of the method. For handling fillo sheets, see page 15.

Makes 24
Oven temperature: 180°C (350°F)
Cooking time: 30 minutes

Syrup:
2 cups granulated sugar
1½ cups water
1 tablespoon lemon juice
small piece cinnamon bark
2 cloves

Nut Filling:
2 cups finely ground almonds or walnuts
¼ cup caster sugar
1 teaspoon ground cinnamon

To finish:
24 sheets yufka (fillo) pastry
¾ cup warm, melted, unsalted butter

1. Dissolve sugar in water in a heavy pan over medium heat, stirring occasionally. Bring to the boil. When dissolved, add lemon juice, cinnamon and cloves and boil for 15 minutes without stirring. Skim if required. Strain and cool.
2. Combine nut filling ingredients. Have a length of wooden dowelling on hand, 5 mm (¼ inch) in diameter and 50 cm (20 inches) long.
3. Spread a sheet of pastry on work surface with longer edge towards you. Brush lightly and evenly with warm melted butter. Sprinkle 2 tablespoons of almond filling evenly across lower third of pastry, keeping 3 cm (1¼ inches) clear of base and just a little in from sides. Fold bottom edge over filling and place wooden dowelling along edge. Roll pastry with filling firmly over dowelling to end of sheet. Make sure end of pastry sticks on firmly; if not, brush again with a little warm melted butter.
4. Grip dowelling at each end of pastry and push hands gradually towards one another, crumpling up pastry evenly as you push. When evenly crumpled and with the roll less than half its original length, slip roll off dowelling onto work surface. Trim ends, then twist into a flat snail-like coil.
5. Repeat with remaining ingredients taking care that pastry does not dry out, otherwise shaping will be difficult. To keep butter warm, set container in a pan of hot water.
6. Place completed burma close together in a buttered baking dish. Brush lightly with melted butter and bake in a moderate oven for 25-30 minutes, until light golden brown. When cooked, pour cooled thick syrup over hot burma. Leave in dish until cold before serving or store in a sealed container at room temperature.

Alternative Shaping: Assemble and roll on dowel (Step 3) then slide pastry off onto work surface. Cut roll with a sharp knife in 10 cm (4 inch) lengths. Complete, following on from Step 5.

DONDURMA ÇİLEKLİ
STRAWBERRY WATER ICE

Serves: 6-8

Syrup:
2 cups water
1 cup sugar
2 teaspoons lemon juice

To finish:
2 cups strawberry purée
1 teaspoon strained lemon juice
¼ cup milk
red food colouring

1. In a heavy pan combine water and sugar and stir over heat until sugar is dissolved. Add lemon juice and bring to the boil. Boil for 5 minutes, skimming when necessary, and leave until cool.
2. To make strawberry purée rub washed and hulled strawberries through a fine sieve. (A generous 3 cups whole strawberries should yield 2 cups purée.)
3. Combine purée with cooled syrup, lemon juice and milk and stir in a few drops of food colouring. Pour into a freezer tray or loaf cake pan and freeze.
4. Spoon into chilled dessert glasses and serve immediately. If desired, ice can be broken up with a fork before placing in glasses.

DONDURMA LİMONLU
LEMON WATER ICE

Serves: 6-8

4 lemons
3 cups water
1 cup granulated sugar
1 egg white
lemon food colouring, optional

1. Wash lemons well. Peel rind thinly from lemons so that there is little or no pith left on the rind.
2. Put rind in a pan with the water and bring slowly to the boil. Boil uncovered for 10 minutes. Strain into a measuring jug and discard rind. If necessary make up liquid to 2 cups with water and return to pan.
3. Add sugar to pan and dissolve over medium heat, stirring occasionally. Bring to the boil and boil on medium heat for 5 minutes. Leave until cool.
4. Juice the lemons and strain. Measure ¾ cup juice and add to the cooled syrup. Pour into a bowl and place in freezer. Leave until half frozen, then stir well to break up ice crystals.
5. Beat egg white until stiff. Blend thoroughly into half frozen syrup with a little lemon food colouring if desired. Return to freezer and leave until just firm.
6. Remove from freezer and beat well until smooth and light.
7. Pour into a loaf cake pan, cover with foil and freeze until very firm — about 3 hours or longer.
8. To serve, draw a metal spoon across the dondurma and place the flaky curls into chilled sweet glasses. Alternatively scoop out with an ice cream scoop.

DONDURMA PORTAKAL
ORANGE WATER ICE

Serves: 6-8

thinly peeled rind of 2 oranges
thinly peeled rind of 1 lemon
3 cups water
1 cup granulated sugar
1 cup orange juice
¼ cup lemon juice

1. Boil orange and lemon rinds in water, strain and measure as in Step 2 of Dondurma Limonlu recipe, and make syrup as in Step 3.
2. Add orange and lemon juice to syrup and pour into a bowl. Freeze for 3 hours until firm. Flake with a fork and pile flakes into chilled sweet glasses.

Note: Orange food colouring may be added to syrup if desired.

DONDURMA KIRAZ
CHERRY WATER ICE

Follow ingredients and method as for Dondurma Çilekli, substituting 2 cups cherry purée for the strawberry purée. To make cherry purée, wash and pit about 3 cups cherries and purée in food processor or blender. Measure and add to syrup with lemon juice, milk and red food colouring if necessary. Freeze and serve in chilled sweet glasses.

DONDURMA (Water Ices): strawberry, *recipe page 149*;
orange, *recipe above*; lemon, *recipe above*.

YOĞURT TATLISI
YOGHURT CAKE

Oven temperature: 180°C (350°F)
Cooking time: 50-55 minutes

¾ cup butter
1 cup caster sugar
grated rind of 1 lemon
5 eggs, separated
1 cup yoghurt
2¼ cups plain flour
2 teaspoons baking powder
pinch salt
½ teaspoon bicarbonate of soda

Syrup:
1 cup granulated sugar
¾ cup cold water
thin strip lemon rind
1 tablespoon strained lemon juice

1. Cream butter, lemon rind and sugar until fluffy, add egg yolks separately, beating well after each addition, then blend in yoghurt.
2. Sift dry ingredients and fold into creamed mixture.
3. Beat egg whites until stiff and fold into batter. Turn into a greased and floured 20 cm (8 inch) tube pan.
4. Bake in a moderate oven for 50 to 55 minutes.
5. Meanwhile, make syrup. Combine sugar and water in a pan, stirring over medium heat until dissolved. Bring to the boil, add lemon rind and juice and boil on medium heat, without stirring, for 10 minutes. Remove lemon rind and cool syrup.
6. Cool cake in tin for 5 minutes, then turn onto a serving dish.
7. Spoon cold syrup over cake, letting it seep slowly into cake. Serve warm, cut in thick slices with whipped cream or kaymak.

KAYISI REÇELİ
APRICOT JAM

2 cups dried apricots
3 cups cold water
juice of 1 lemon
3 cups granulated sugar
½ cup blanched, split almonds, optional

1. Wash apricots very well in cold water. Chop in small pieces and place in a bowl with the 3 cups water. Leave to soak for 12 hours.
2. Put fruit and water in which they were soaked in a preserving pan. Add lemon juice and bring to the boil. Boil gently, covered, for 30 minutes or until apricots are very soft.
3. Add sugar and stir to dissolve. Return to the boil and boil quickly, stirring often. Boil for 15 minutes then test a little on a cold saucer. Draw finger across surface of cooled jam — it is right when surface wrinkles. Remember to remove jam from heat while testing. Return to heat if necessary and test again after 5 minutes.
4. Stir in almonds if used and pour jam into hot, sterilized jars. Seal when cold. Store in a cool place.

ÇİLEK REÇELİ
STRAWBERRY JAM

1 kg (2 lb) strawberries
juice of 2 lemons
3½ cups granulated sugar

1. Wash and hull strawberries. Halve fruit and place in a preserving pan with the lemon juice.
2. Set on medium heat, cover pan and bring to the boil. Reduce heat to low and simmer gently for 20-30 minutes until fruit is very soft.
3. Remove pan from heat and add sugar. Stir to combine, then return to medium heat, stirring again to dissolve sugar.
4. Bring to the boil and boil on medium heat for 15 minutes or until jam sets when a little is tested on a cold saucer. See Kayısı Reçeli recipe, Step 3, for more detail on testing.
5. Cool jam a little, then ladle into hot, sterilized jars. Seal when cold and store in a cool place.

GŪL REÇELİ
ROSE PETAL JAM

4 cups fragrant rose petals
3 cups granulated sugar
2 cups water
juice of ½ lemon

1. Snip off white base of each petal with kitchen scissors and discard. Wash petals gently in cold water and drain.
2. Layer petals in a bowl, sprinkling 2 tablespoon of the sugar on each layer. Leave overnight.
3. Next day put remaining sugar and the water in a heavy pan and set over medium heat. Stir occasionally until sugar is dissolved then bring to the boil. Add lemon juice and boil for 5 minutes without stirring. Remove syrup from heat and cool to lukewarm.
4. Stir rose petals and their liquid into the syrup and return pan to heat. Bring slowly to the boil and boil gently for 15 minutes or until syrup is thick when tested on a cold saucer. Ladle into warm, sterilized jars and seal when cool.

TÜRK KAHVESİ
TURKISH COFFEE

The coffee is prepared in a small, long-handled pot tapering in at the top, and called a *jezve*. The purist (and they all are in Turkey when it comes to making coffee) would grind the beans to a fine powder just before brewing. Turkish brass coffee mills are sold throughout the Middle East.

When offered a cup, you will be asked if you like it *sade* (unsweetened), *orta* (moderately sweetened) or *şekerli* (very sweet).

Turkish coffee ideally is made one cup at a time, or three at the most. Measure one demitasse cup cold water into jezve and add 1 heaped teaspoon powdered Turkish coffee and sugar if desired — a level teaspoon for orta, a heaped teaspoon or more for şekerli. Stir and put on medium-low heat. When coffee rises in pot remove from heat immediately, and spoon froth into cup. Return pot to heat and cook until coffee rises again. Remove, fill cup. Some prefer to heat coffee 3 times in all, though twice is sufficient, particularly if only making 1 cup. With the repeated heating method, a little froth is spooned into each cup each time it is removed from the heat, as a good cup of kahve must have a creamy foam floating on top.

ARMENIA

Proclaimed as a Soviet Republic in 1920, Armenia regained its nationhood in 1991, after the collapse of the Soviet Union. During the years of oppression, the nationalistic spirit lived on, both in the people of the Armenian SSR and in those who, through the events of history, found a home elsewhere. They have shown that while adversity altered their fate, it has never altered their spirit. It is to their credit that in spite of insurmountable odds, Armenians have preserved their language, religion, customs and traditions.

To really understand the evolvement of a cuisine, one must know something of a country's history. I doubt if there ever has been a country which has undergone such upheavals as Armenia and about which the world knows so little. Perhaps knowing something of Armenia's history will shed light on many aspects of Near and Middle East cooking previously subject to controversy.

Tradition has it that the kingdom of Armenia was founded by Haig, a descendant of Noah, in the Near East region of Lake Van. For centuries it was ruled by Haig's successors. There followed invasions by Assyrians, Medes and Persians; it was conquered by Alexander the Great and passed on to the ancient Syrian King, Seleucus I, with independence finally declared in 189 B.C. This was short-lived however, and Armenia was even-

tually made a protectorate of Rome. Nero confirmed a Parthian prince as King of Armenia in A.D. 66. With Christianity eventually introduced, Armenia has the distinction of being the oldest Christian State. Peace reigned for the next 300 years or so. A succession of invasions followed for the next 1,500 years, with brief periods of independence.

While Byzantium was in its zenith, Armenian Orthodox church leaders and many Armenians were centred in Constantinople, as were numbers of Greeks, and it was during this era, the pre-Ottoman era, that the exotic cuisine of Byzantium was developed, influencing Armenian and Greek cooking and eventually Turkish. It must also be noted that the Armenian boundaries through history have expanded and contracted considerably, accounting for so many similarities to Turkish dishes.

Mongol hordes swept across India, Afghanistan, Persia and Armenia into Russia in the thirteenth century, and though their mission was not one of goodwill, it is believed that they introduced pasta and noodles, almost a hundred years before Marco Polo's return from China. An Armenian noodle-type dish called Mante also features in Russian cooking in slightly varied form; it is a speciality of Uzbrek on the eastern side of the Caspian Sea, and both areas were once under Mongol influence. In Turkish cooking

Mante is known as Tartar Boreği (the Mongols in their surge, were joined by other peoples and became known collectively as Tartars). It is only through similar clues that one might hope to piece together the jigsaw of culinary origins.

THE FLAVOUR OF ARMENIAN FOOD

True Armenian cooking is relatively simple fare, often of a kind necessary in a cold climate. It is subtly herbed and spiced with overtones of the colourful era of Byzantium. The combination of rice, currants, onions and pine nuts is a legacy from that era, a legacy which, in fact, belongs to those of the Orthodox faith, be it Armenian, Greek or Eastern. Fasting is a very important requirement of the religion and the ingenuity of the Armenians in preparing dishes without any animal products is evident in recipes. Many such recipes in other chapters are also used in Armenian cooking.

To illustrate their staunch upholding of tradition, the founder of Armenia is immortalized in the recipes Haigagan Parak Hatz and Haigagan Keteh. The former is a bread similar to the flat breads of Persia and Lebanon, only cooked a little longer so that it dries out. Try the Khoubiz recipe (see Index), but cook immediately it is shaped, sprinkling breads with sesame seeds. Bake for 6-7 minutes, long enough to dry it. This keeps well and is served as a dry bread or moistened with water. Haigagan Keteh is the same as Glor Keteh, recipe for which is in this chapter, only with the circle folded in on itself then pressed flat rather than rolled into a rope and coiled.

Another recipe worthy of mention is Topig, one dating back to the days of Byzantium. His Grace, the Armenian Bishop of the Diocese of Sydney, is not only renowned amongst Sydney's Armenian community as a cook of great standing, he is also remembered for his culinary achievements in Los Angeles and Washington. His Topig and his Oologantch Litzk are the envy of every Armenian cook in these three cities. The Topig recipe I have given does not quite follow his Grace's in that I refuse to soak chick peas for the length of time he recommends (my comments on this matter are documented in the section on Pulses at the beginning of this book). Investigation and testing found that I did not need to cook the Topig for the length of time he recommends. My taste testers, members of his congregation, assured me that it was a very good Topig, not quite as good as His Grace's, but near enough, and just like their mothers used to make. Perhaps I should give you details of the famous Topig so that you might judge for yourself.

Apparently the secret is to soak the chick peas for 3 days, changing water daily and letting them ferment, as he claims this is necessary for the success of the dish. By then the peas are much easier to skin. His method is to wrap the peas in a cloth and rub vigorously. The skins come off easily. Put into a bowl of water and skim off the floating skins. Put drained peas through a food grinder. The onions should be boiled in a generous amount of water and drained, reserving the water. Regarding the filling, we both agree on that point, so mix the onions with the remaining ingredients listed. Now, to prevent the water penetrating the cloth used for boiling, it should be soaked in the reserved onion water, and wrung out well. Spread out a quarter of the ground pea mixture (mixed with mashed potato) on the cloth in a very thin square as thin as you can make it. Fill as described, then fold corners over, sealing joins. Knot the cloth and prepare the remaining Topigs in the same way. Boil them in salted water for 1 hour. Drain and leave in the cloth until completely cold before removing. Now you know.

The Oologantch Litzk recipe given is also His Grace's, minus 3 onions. Trust a woman never to leave well enough alone!

AN ARMENIAN MEAL

Rather than discuss Armenian meals as served in the Armenian SSR, it is preferable to give the usual way an Armenian, wherever he may live, may take a meal following tradition. It is served in the Western manner, that is with Western table appointments. All the prepared dishes for the meal are placed on the table at the one time so that the diners may take what they wish. In cooler weather the meal could begin with a bowl of soup, probably spiced with mint and thickened with yoghurt. A meat, chicken or fish dish and vegetable, rice or pasta accompaniment, salad, bread and pickles. Tan (yoghurt drink) accompanies every meal served in the Armenian tradition. When fasting, the meal could feature fish or one of their delicious dishes made from dried beans, peas or bulgar (burghul). The full range of foods, from meats to desserts, could be Armenian, but they are just as likely to be from any of the Arabic countries (Egypt, Lebanon, Syria), Greece or Iran, in fact from countries where they or their parents had sought a new home.

COOKING METHODS

Armenians, particularly in the United States, are renowned for their success in the food industry. They operate speciality food stores, delicatessens, restaurants and bakeries, and while Armenian foods feature in their commercial endeavours, their affinity with food extends to preparing dishes from any nation. Perhaps it is an inherited gift; to be able to adapt to a situation is either born in us or thrust upon us. It has been thrust upon the Armenians for generations and it has held them in good stead. In other words, it is difficult to say that the Armenian uses this pot or that method of cooking, for it could be anything you might be using yourself.

An Armenian kitchen would be well stocked and well equipped with all the items necessary for producing good, wholesome food. You would not find cupboards filled with cans or freezers filled with TV dinners, but you would be likely to find pantry shelves lined with jars of pickles and preserves, with perhaps a basderma (pastourma) hanging. I tested the latter recipe

but as a principal part of my work is involved with the meat industry, I am afraid that I cannot bring it upon myself to advise you to prepare this pungent, spiced meat at home as it requires days of hanging in the open air to dry it. I would prefer you to patronize your local Armenian or Greek food store and buy it ready prepared, as its commercial preparation is carried out under controlled conditions. Basderma is similar to the Romanian pastrami, except that a large quantity of chaiman (fenugreek) is included in the garlic and spice coating.

INGREDIENTS FOR ARMENIAN COOKING

There is hardly an ingredient in Armenian cooking with which the Western cook would not be familiar. Had I written this book ten years previously it would have been a different matter, but with the ever-increasing trend to use pulses and grains, what might once have been strange is no longer so. One recipe included in this chapter, called Harissa, is made in Armenia with a special wheat unavailable outside the Near and Middle East. Pearl barley is a more than reasonable substitute; consequently in this recipe barley has been given as the ingredient.

Chick peas (garbanzo beans) are usually preferred without the skin. These are available at Armenian food shops but are very difficult to find elsewhere. It may be necessary for you to follow instructions on page 12 for removing the skins.

One flavouring ingredient which should be explained is sumak. It is a coarse powder with a sour flavour, prepared from the dry red berries of a species of the sumach tree. It is also used in Iran and other countries of the region.

NIVIK
CHICK PEAS WITH SPINACH

Serves: 6
Cooking time: 3 hours

1½ cups chick peas (garbanzo beans)
water
1 large onion, chopped
¼ cup olive oil
¼ cup tomato paste
salt
freshly ground black pepper
1 teaspoon sugar
750 g (1½ lb) spinach

1. Wash chick peas well, place in a bowl and cover with 4½ cups cold water. Leave to soak overnight — in a cool place if weather is hot.
2. Next day put chick peas and soaking water into a deep pan and bring to the boil. Cover and simmer gently for 2 hours or until tender.
3. In a separate pan gently fry onion in oil until transparent. Add tomato paste, about 2 teaspoons salt, a generous grinding of black pepper and the sugar. Add to the cooked chick peas.
4. Wash spinach well, remove roots and discoloured leaves. Chop leaves and stems roughly and add to chick pea mixture.
5. Cover and simmer for further 20-30 minutes, adding more water only if necessary. Nivik should be moist, not too liquid. Serve with bread, salad and pickles as a light meal. Also good served cold.

DEREVE PATTOUG
STUFFED GRAPE VINE LEAVES

Makes 6 dozen
Cooking time: 1¼ hours

Rice Filling:
2 large onions, finely chopped
½ cup olive oil
1 cup short grain rice
¼ cup pine nuts
¼ cup currants
1 teaspoon ground allspice
2 tablespoons finely chopped fresh dill
salt
freshly ground black pepper

To finish:
80 fresh or preserved grape vine leaves
water
1 lemon, thinly sliced
¼ cup olive oil
lemon wedges and madzoon (yoghurt) for
   serving

1. In a pan fry onion gently in olive oil until transparent. Add rice and stir over heat for 5 minutes. Add pine nuts, currants, allspice, dill, and salt and pepper to taste. Cover and cook on gentle heat for 5 minutes. Remove and leave aside.
2. Blanch fresh or preserved vine leaves in boiling water for 3 minutes, adding them in 3 lots. As each lot is blanched, remove to a bowl of cold water, then drain well.
3. Spread a vine leaf on work surface, shiny side down, and place a heaped teaspoon of the rice filling towards stem end. Roll once, fold in sides and roll into a neat package. Repeat with remaining ingredients.
4. Line base of a heavy pan with 4 vine leaves and pack rolls, folded side down, in closely packed rows. As each row is completed place 3 thin slices of lemon on top before beginning next row.
5. When all rolls are in pan, top with 3 lemon slices and cover with remaining vine leaves. Pour 2 cups water and olive oil over rolls and invert a heavy plate on top to keep rolls in shape during cooking.
6. Bring to a slow simmer, reduce heat, cover pan and simmer gently for 50 minutes. Remove pan from heat and leave until cool.
7. Carefully remove rolls to serving dish, discarding lemon slices. Serve at room temperature, or cover dish and chill before serving. Garnish platter with lemon wedges and serve with a bowl of yoghurt.

NIVIK (Chick Peas with Spinach) recipe above

TOPIG
LENTEN CHICK PEA KOFTA

Serves: 8-12
Cooking time: 35 minutes

2 cups chick peas (for skinning, see page 12)
6 cups cold water
2 small potatoes, boiled in jackets
1½ teaspoons salt
freshly ground white pepper

Filling:
3 large onions, halved and sliced
2 tablespoons water
¼ teaspoon ground allspice
½ teaspoon ground cumin
⅓ cup pine nuts
⅓ cup currants
¾ cup tahina
salt
freshly ground black pepper

To finish and serve:
boiling, salted water
olive oil
ground cinnamon or paprika
lemon wedges
parsley sprigs

1. Soak chick peas in the cold water for 24 hours, in a cool place if weather is warm. Remove skins by either of the methods described under Skinning Pulses. Drain well.
2. Pass skinned chick peas through food grinder twice, using fine screen. Alternatively place in food processor container in 2 lots and process to a paste.
3. Peel skin from boiled potatoes and mash finely with a fork. Combine with ground chick peas, add salt and a good grinding of white pepper. Blend thoroughly and keep aside.
4. Put sliced onions in a pan with the water, cover and steam over medium heat for 10 minutes, then remove cover and leave until moisture evaporates. Turn into a bowl and cool.
5. Add allspice, cumin, pine nuts and currants to the onion. Blend well, then mix in tahina, and salt and pepper to taste.
6. Take 4 pieces of unbleached calico or similar cloth, each about 50 cm (20 inches) square and scald in boiling water. Cool a little, then wring out well.
7. Open out a square of cloth on work surface and put a quarter of the chick pea paste in the centre. Spread evenly with a spatula to a 20 cm (8 inch) square and place a quarter of the filling in the centre, spreading it a little.
8. Bring each corner of the paste over the filling by lifting up corners of cloth. Paste should enclose filling in envelope fashion. Smooth joins to seal well.
9. Make a single tie with each pair of diagonally opposite corners of cloth, then tie a second time.
10. Complete another 3 topigs in the same way.
11. Half fill a large pot with water, bring to the boil and add about 1 tablespoon salt.
12. When briskly boiling, lower prepared topigs into pot and return to the boil. Cover and boil steadily for 12-15 minutes or until topigs float and feel firm to the touch.
13. Lift out immediately and place on a tray, draining off water in tray.
14. Untie and invert topigs onto platter. Leave until cool.
15. When ready to serve, pour a little olive oil over each topig and dust lightly with cinnamon or paprika. Garnish platter with lemon wedges and parsley. To serve, cut each topig in half, then slice in thick pieces. Olive oil and lemon juice are added to individual taste.

Note: Ready skinned chick peas are available at some Armenian and Greek food stores. These look like split peas, but are larger and nut coloured.

YEREPOUNI
BRAIN FRITTERS

These delicately flavoured brain fritters are from Yerevan, the capital of Soviet Armenia, as the recipe name suggests.

Serves: 4 as an appetizer
Cooking time: 25 minutes

6 sets lamb brains
2 tablespoons vinegar
salt
water
2 egg yolks
1 tablespoon finely chopped fresh dill
¼ cup finely grated kasseri cheese
olive or corn oil for frying
lemon wedges for serving

1. Soak lamb brains in water to cover, adding vinegar and 2 teaspoons salt. Leave for 15-20 minutes, then drain. Remove skin and any veins. If lamb brains have been frozen, it is very difficult to remove the skin — this does not matter so much, but cut out any veins present as the blood discolours the brains.
2. Place brains in a pan with fresh water to cover, add 1 teaspoon salt and bring almost to the boil. Cover and simmer gently over low heat for 15 minutes or until tender.
3. Drain the brains well and turn into a bowl. Mash finely with a fork and leave until cool.
4. Add egg yolks, dill and finely grated cheese. Mix to a soft paste and add salt if necessary.
5. Put oil in a frying pan to a depth of 5 mm (¼ inch). Place 6 egg poaching rings in the oil, turning them to oil surfaces.
6. Heat oil over medium high heat. Spoon a generous tablespoon of brain mixture into each ring and fry until golden brown on each side. Once mixture is set, rings may be removed.
7. Drain on paper towels and add remaining mixture to rings in pan. Serve hot or warm as an appetizer, garnished with lemon wedges.

HARISSA
MEAT AND BARLEY PUREE

There are versions of harissa in various other countries of the region covered. The Armenians use a special wheat for harissa which is unavailable outside the Middle East, so barley is used instead in this version. Harissa is traditionally served on the first day after New Year.

Serves: 6-8
Cooking time: 4½-5 hours

1½ cups pearl barley
water
1 kg (2 lb) chuck steak
salt
freshly ground black pepper
⅓ cup butter
1 teaspoon ground cinnamon
1 teaspoon ground cumin

1. Wash barley well in cold running water. Place in a bowl and add cold water to cover. Leave to soak overnight.
2. Put barley and soaking water in a heavy pan. Set on medium heat and bring to the boil. Reduce heat, cover pan, and simmer gently for 1½ hours until barley is just tender.
3. Cut the steak into 3 cm (1¼ inch) cubes and put in a separate pan with water to cover. Bring slowly to the boil, skimming as required.
4. Put barley and chuck steak together with the liquids into a large casserole dish, add salt and pepper to taste and cook in moderately slow oven 170°C (325°F) for 3 hours. Stir occasionally during cooking, adding water if mixture looks like scorching.
5. In a small frying pan heat butter until browned, stir in cinnamon and cumin. Remove from heat.
6. When meat is very tender and falling apart, remove casserole from oven and beat mixture with a wooden spoon until puréed. The meat should break up into stringy pieces and blend with the barley.
7. Spread on a heated serving platter, smoothing surface. Make indentations over surface with the back of a spoon and fill with the melted butter mixture. Serve with bread and salads.

CHROD BOUREK
WATER-DIPPED PASTRY WITH CHEESE FILLING

Occasionally during the compilation of this book I almost resorted to coin-tossing to decide in which chapter I should place a certain recipe. When I tried this particular gem, I thought I just might have to do so as both the Turks and the Armenians lay claim to it.

As the Armenian Mante uses a noodle-type dough with its origin probably dating from the influence of the Mongols (which did not reach as far south as Turkey), it is possible that this water-dipped pastry could have been developed at the same time.

Serves: 12 as a first course, 6 as a main course
Oven temperature: 180°C (350°F)
Cooking time: 1-1¼ hours

Cheese Filling:
2 cups crumbled feta cheese
1 cup cottage or ricotta cheese
1 cup grated kasseri cheese
4 eggs, lightly beaten
¼ cup finely chopped parsley
2 tablespoons chopped fresh dill
freshly ground black pepper

Water-dipped Pastry: **(for rolling, see page 16)**
3 cups plain flour
1 teaspoon salt
3 eggs, beaten
½ cup tepid water
additional flour for kneading and rolling
water for boiling
½ cup melted butter for assembling

1. Mash feta cheese finely with a fork and blend with remaining cheese filling ingredients. Refrigerate until required.
2. Sift flour and salt into a mixing bowl and make a well in the centre. Beat eggs well and add to flour with ½ cup water. Gradually stir flour into liquid to form a soft dough.
3. Knead dough well in bowl. If still sticky, gradually add a little more sifted flour until dough is smooth and comes cleanly from sides of bowl. Amount of flour depends on size of eggs and the flour's absorption qualities. Shape dough into a ball and stretch a piece of plastic film over bowl. Rest dough for 30 minutes.
4. Divide dough into 10 even-sized balls. Using a light dusting of flour on work surface, shape one ball of dough into a square, dust with flour and roll out thinly, following directions given in section on 'Rolling Pastry Thinly'. Final pastry sheet should be about 28 x 33 cm (11 x 13 inches) in size. Stack and cover as directed as each sheet is rolled. All but 2 sheets of pastry are to be boiled.
5. Three-parts fill a large boiler with water and bring to the boil. Have a large basin of cold water next to the boiler, and spread a large, folded cloth next to this.
6. Lift up one pastry sheet and lower it gradually into the boiling water. Boil for 1 minute and scoop out carefully with a large sieve, guiding pastry into sieve with a wooden spoon. Plunge pastry into cold water, leave for 2 minutes, lift out and drain over bowl. Turn it onto cloth and open pastry out carefully to drain and dry a little. Boil another three sheets, laying them on cloth separately to drain. Any sheets which tear may still be used.
7. Brush a 25 x 30 cm (10 x 12 inch) baking dish with melted butter and spread 1 uncooked sheet of pastry in dish. Brush with butter and place the 4 boiled sheets of pastry on top, brushing each with butter as they are positioned. Spread cheese filling evenly in dish.
8. Boil another 4 sheets of pastry as in Step 6, using a dry cloth for draining. Place on top of filling, buttering each as it is spread in dish. Top with last uncooked sheet and trim edges with a sharp knife level with top of dish. Brush top of pie with remaining butter.
9. Bake in a moderate oven for 1 hour until top is golden brown and crisp. Centre sheets will be soft and tender. Rest pie for 10 minutes before cutting into serving portions. Serve hot as an appetizer, or as a main course for a light meal.

Note: Spinach, meat or chicken fillings may be used with this pastry. See Index for Savoury Pie fillings.

DZAGHAGAGHAMPI TTVASH (Cauliflower Pickles) and KHARENI TTVASH (Mixed Pickles) *recipes page 164*

KHARENI TTVASH
MIXED PICKLES

½ small cauliflower
1 sweet green pepper
1 sweet red pepper
2-3 stalks celery
2 medium-sized carrots
2 medium-sized green tomatoes
cooking salt

Brine Mix:
4 cups water
¼ cup pickling salt
1 cup white vinegar
3 teaspoons sugar

To finish:
1-2 hot fresh or dried chilis
1-2 sprigs dill, optional
1-2 cloves garlic

1. Wash vegetables well. Break cauliflower into florets. Core and seed peppers and cut into wide strips. Cut celery into 5 cm (2 inch) pieces. Peel carrots and slice into 5 mm (¼ inch) slices. Cut tomatoes into thick wedges.
2. Place prepared vegetables in layers in a bowl, sprinkling about 2 tablespoons cooking salt on each layer. Leave for 5-6 hours, then rinse well and drain.
3. Heat water and pickling salt in a stainless steel or enamelled pan, stirring until salt is dissolved. Add vinegar and sugar and bring to the boil. Leave until cool.
4. Pack vegetables into 1 or 2 sterilized jars, arranging them attractively. To each jar add a cut clove of garlic, 1 whole chili and a sprig of dill amongst the vegetables.
5. Pour cooled brine over prepared vegetables. Seal with glass or plastic lids and leave at room temperature for 1 week before opening. Once opened, store pickle in refrigerator. Pickles should keep for 2 months in a cool dark place, longer once stored in refrigerator.

LOUPIA TTVASH
GREEN BEAN PICKLES

1.5 kg (3 lb) green string beans
cooking salt
2 hot fresh or dried chilis
2 cloves garlic
1 quantity Brine Mix, see Khareni Ttvash
   (above)

1. Wash beans well. Top and tail, remove strings if necessary (some varieties today are stringless). Cut diagonally into 8 cm (3 inch) lengths, or leave whole if desired.
2. Place beans in layers in a bowl, sprinkling about 2 tablespoons salt over each layer. Leave for 6 hours, rinse well and drain.
3. Make brine as directed and leave until cool.
4. Pack beans in 2 sterilized jars, placing a chili and a cut clove of garlic in each jar. Pour on cooled brine, seal with glass or plastic lids and leave for 1 week before opening. Once opened, store pickle in refrigerator. Should keep for 2-3 months in a cool dark place.

DZAGHAGAGHAMPI TTVASH
CAULIFLOWER PICKLES

1 quantity Brine Mix, see Khareni Ttvash
   (above)
1 medium-sized cauliflower
salted water
1-2 hot chilis
1-2 cloves garlic

1. Make brine mix as directed and leave until cool.
2. Break cauliflower into florets, removing thick stems. Place cauliflower in a bowl and cover with cold, salted water. Leave for 15-20 minutes to remove any insects trapped in the vegetable. Drain and rinse well under cold water. Drain in a colander.
3. Bring a large pan of water to the boil and blanch cauliflower in 2 lots, for 3 minutes each lot. Time blanching from when water returns to the boil after adding the cauliflower.
4. Drain cauliflower well and pack into 1 large or 2 smaller sterilized jars, adding a chili and a cut clove of garlic to each jar.
5. Pour cooled brine over cauliflower, seal and store in a cool, dark place for 1 week before using. Cauliflower will keep 2-3 months. Once opened, store in refrigerator.

GLOR KETEH
BUTTER-FLAKE BREADS

Makes 6 breads
Oven temperature: 190°C (375°F)
Cooking time: 12-15 minutes

Yeast Dough:
1 sachet active dry yeast
¼ cup warm water
4 cups plain flour
1 cup warm evaporated milk
1 egg, beaten
1 teaspoon salt
1 tablespoon caster sugar
¼ cup melted, unsalted butter

To finish:
½ cup melted, unsalted butter
1 small egg, beaten
sesame seeds or black cumin seeds

1. Soak yeast in the water and stir to dissolve.
2. Sift flour into a mixing bowl, remove about 1 cup flour and keep this aside.
3. Blend evaporated milk with beaten egg, add salt and sugar and stir until dissolved.
4. Pour yeast liquid and evaporated milk into centre of flour. Stir in a little flour to thicken liquid, cover and leave in a warm place for 10 minutes or until frothy.
5. Blend in remaining flour in bowl, beat by hand for 2 minutes, then gradually beat in warm, melted butter with a little of the reserved flour. Beat dough for further 5 minutes by hand or in electric mixer with dough hook.
6. Knead in reserved flour, adding as much as dough will take. Knead for 10 minutes until dough is smooth and satiny. Form into a ball.
7. Grease bowl with a little butter, add dough and turn to coat with butter. Stretch plastic film over bowl and leave to rise in a warm place for 1 hour or until doubled in bulk.
8. Punch down dough and turn onto a lightly floured board. Knead until smooth, divide into 6 even sized portions and roll each into a ball. Cover with a cloth.
9. Dust board and 1 ball of dough with flour and roll dough into a large, thin circle about 40 cm (16 inches) in diameter.
10. Brush circle of dough evenly with some of the ½ cup melted butter. Roll up into a long rope. Take each end and swing it up and down, letting dough hit the work surface. This stretches the rope to twice the original length.
11. Coil into a round with ends of dough on top. Press ends onto coil and flatten a little. Shape remaining dough.
12. When all are shaped, press firmly with hands and flatten each into an 18 cm (7 inch) round — use rolling pin if you prefer. Place on greased baking sheets. Cover and leave for 45 minutes or until doubled in size.
13. When risen, glaze breads with beaten egg and sprinkle with sesame or black cumin seeds. Bake in a moderately hot oven for 12-15 minutes until golden brown and cooked. Serve warm with fruit preserves or cheese.

SHEHREHI YEGHINTZ
RICE WITH VERMICELLI

Serves: 6
Cooking time: 25 minutes

¼ cup butter
1 cup fine vermicelli noodles
1½ cups long grain rice
3½ cups chicken or other light stock
1½ teaspoons salt

1. Lightly crush bundles of vermicelli before measuring.
2. Melt butter in a heavy-based pan and add noodles. Stir over medium heat for 5 minutes until noodles are golden brown.
3. Add rice and stir over heat for 5 minutes, then add stock and salt. Bring to the boil and reduce heat to low.
4. Cover pan and cook gently for 15 minutes. Switch off heat and leave pan covered for 5 minutes before serving.

HARSANIK YEGHINTZ
SPICED LAMB PILAF

Serves: 6
Cooking time: 1 hour

250 g (8 oz) lean boneless lamb
1 medium-sized onion
¼ cup butter
¼ cup blanched slivered almonds
½ teaspoon ground allspice
4 cups light stock (chicken or lamb)
salt
freshly ground black pepper
2 cups long grain rice
½ teaspoon saffron threads
2 tablespoons hot water

1. Cut lamb into thin strips 4 cm (1½ inch) long. Halve onion lengthwise and cut into slender wedges.
2. Heat butter in a heavy pan and brown lamb strips and onion over high heat, stirring constantly. Add almonds and fry 2 minutes longer. Reduce heat and stir in allspice.
3. Add 1 cup stock, about 1 teaspoon salt and a good grinding of black pepper. Cover and simmer gently for 20 minutes. Increase heat, and add remaining stock and bring to the boil.
4. Wash rice well and drain. Add to boiling stock, stir and add a little more salt. When boiling, reduce heat to low, cover pan and simmer for 25 minutes.
5. Meanwhile pound saffron threads and steep in the hot water. After rice has been cooking for 20 minutes pour saffron liquid over rice, cover pan and cook for further 5 minutes. Turn off heat and leave covered for 5 minutes before serving.

MANTIABOUR
LAMB PASTA AND YOGHURT SOUP

Shades of Italy again? No — more likely a descendant from the man-ton *of the nomadic Mongolians, and a relative of the* manty *of Russia. Here mante is used in a satisfying soup. You will find mante as a lamb pie later in this chapter.*

Serves: 6
Cooking time: 40 minutes

Dough:
2 cups plain flour
½ teaspoon salt
1 egg
cold water

Filling:
200 g (1 lb) finely ground lamb
1 medium-sized onion, grated
¼ cup finely chopped parsley
salt
freshly ground black pepper

To finish:
water
salt
5 cups chicken stock
1 cup drained yoghurt (see page 21)
1 clove garlic, crushed, optional
2 teaspoons dried mint

1. Sift flour and salt into a mixing bowl. Beat egg with fork in a cup measure and make up to ½ cup with cold water. Pour into flour and mix to a firm dough. Add a little more water if necessary. Knead until smooth, cover and rest for 20-30 minutes.
2. Combine filling ingredients thoroughly (lamb should not be too lean), adding salt and pepper to taste.
3. Roll out half of dough as thinly as possible on a floured board. Cut into 4 cm (1½ inch) squares, stack and cover while remainder of dough is rolled and cut.
4. Place a teaspoon of meat filling in the centre of a square of dough, fold over into a triangle and press edges well to seal. Bring the two narrow angles of the triangle together and press well, making a shape somewhat resembling the Italian tortellini. Place on a cloth-lined tray and cover while preparing remainder.
5. Bring 8 cups water to the boil in a large pot and add 1 tablespoon salt. Add about 20 mante, return to the boil and boil for 10 minutes. Remove with slotted spoon to a colander and boil remaining mante. These may be kept in a sealed container in the refrigerator if not required immediately.
6. When ready to serve, bring chicken stock to the boil, add mante and boil gently for 10 minutes. Add yoghurt and crushed garlic if used and stir gently over heat for 2-3 minutes without allowing soup to boil. Rub mint to a powder and stir into soup. Serve immediately.

SEMPOOGI YEV MISOVGHOROVATZ (Baked Eggplant with Lamb) *recipe page 172*

HAVGOTOV SHIOMIN
EGGS WITH SPINACH

Serves: 6
Oven temperature: 180°C (350°F)
Cooking time: 40-45 minutes

750 g (1½ lb) spinach
4 small onions
⅓ cup olive oil
salt
freshly ground black pepper
6 eggs
additional olive oil
madzoon (yoghurt) for serving

1. Trim off roots and discoloured leaves from spinach. Wash spinach in several changes of water, drain well and chop leaves and stalks coarsely.
2. Place in a large pan (not aluminium), cover and cook for 15 minutes, stirring spinach occasionally. There is no need to add water to pan as the moisture on the leaves is sufficient for cooking. When cooked, strain spinach in a colander, pressing with back of a spoon to extract moisture.
3. Halve onions lengthwise and slice into semicircles. Heat oil in a pan and fry onions until transparent and lightly browned. Add spinach and stir over heat for a few minutes. Season to taste with salt and pepper.
4. Turn spinach mixture into a large, shallow oven dish and make 6 depressions with the back of a spoon. Break an egg in each depression. Drizzle a little oil on top of each egg.
5. Bake in a moderate oven for 10 minutes or until eggs are set. Serve hot as a light meal with madzoon.

DZEDZADZ TANABOUR
YOGHURT AND BARLEY SOUP

Serves: 6
Cooking time: 3½ hours

Stock:
1.5 kg (3 lb) lamb soup meat with bone (neck, breast, shank)
water
2 carrots, quartered
1 onion, quartered
leafy top of 1 celery stalk
freshly ground black pepper
salt

To finish:
½ cup barley, washed
3 cups yoghurt
1 egg
1 tablespoon dried mint
2 tablespoons butter, optional

1. Rinse lamb soup meat and place in a large pot with water to cover. Add remaining stock ingredients except salt and bring to the boil. Skim when necessary before liquid boils.
2. When well skimmed and boiling gently, add salt to taste, cover and simmer on low heat for 1½ hours.
3. Strain stock into another pan and discard or otherwise use stock ingredients.
4. Add barley to stock and stir occasionally until boiling. Cover and simmer on low heat for 1½ hours or until barley is very soft and soup is thick.
5. Beat yoghurt with egg and blend in half of dried mint crushed to a coarse powder.
6. Stir yoghurt mixture into simmering soup, and return to a slow simmer, stirring occasionally. Do not boil.
7. Serve hot in soup bowls with a little of the remaining mint sprinkled on top of each bowl. If desired, butter may be heated in a pan and the remaining mint blended in. Drizzle mint butter on each serve.

VOSBOV ABOUR
LENTIL SOUP

Serves: 6
Cooking time: 3 hours

1 quantity lamb stock (see Dzedzadz
   Tanabour, page 168)
water
1 cup red lentils, washed
3 medium-sized onions
¼ cup butter
salt
freshly ground black pepper
paprika for serving

1. Make stock as directed and strain into a measuring jug. Add water if necessary to make up to 6 cups.
2. Put stock in a deep pan and bring to the boil. Add lentils and return to the boil, skimming when necessary. Boil gently with lid partly on pan while onions are prepared.
3. Chop 2 onions finely. Heat half the butter in a frying pan and fry onions until lightly browned. Add to lentils, cover pan tightly and simmer for 1 hour until lentils are tender. Add salt and pepper to taste.
4. Cut remaining onion in half lengthwise and slice into semicircles. Put remaining butter in frying pan and fry onions until golden brown.
5. Serve hot soup in bowls garnished with a sprinkling of paprika and some fried onions.

ARAPGIRI TOPIG
BURGHUL AND POTATO BALLS

Serves: 6
Cooking time: 1 hour

6 medium-sized potatoes, about 750 g (1½ lb)
¾ cup fine bulgar (burghul)
water
¾ cup plain flour
salt
freshly ground black pepper

Filling:
2 medium-sized onions
2 tablespoons water
¼ teaspoon ground allspice
¼ cup pine nuts
¼ cup currants
⅓ cup tahina
salt
freshly ground black pepper

To finish:
oil for deep frying

1. Scrub potatoes and boil in their jackets until tender. Drain, remove skins and mash.
2. Place burghul in a bowl, cover with cold water and leave for 5 minutes. Drain through a fine sieve, pressing well with the back of a spoon to extract moisture.
3. Put potato in a bowl with burghul, flour and salt and pepper to taste. Blend thoroughly to a paste.
4. Put onion in a pan with 2 tablespoons water, cover and steam on medium heat for 10 minutes. Remove lid and let moisture evaporate. Turn into a bowl, add remaining filling ingredients, seasoning to taste with salt and pepper. Blend thoroughly.
5. Shape burghul and potato paste, a scant tablespoon at a time, into balls. Moisten hands with water during shaping. Flatten a ball in your hand, put a generous teaspoon of filling in the centre and close paste over filling, moulding into a smooth oval shape. Repeat with remaining ingredients.
6. Heat oil and deep fry 6 at a time for 6-8 minutes, turning to brown evenly. When golden brown, remove with a slotted spoon and drain on paper towels. Serve hot or warm.

ZADIG AGHTZAN
SPINACH SALAD

Serves: 6
Cooking time: 10 minutes

750 g (1½ lb) spinach (about 1 bunch)
3 cups drained yoghurt (see page 21)
1 clove garlic
salt
½ cup finely chopped parsley
pinch of sugar

1. Remove roots and coarse stems from spinach. Wash leaves well, shake off as much moisture as possible and shred fairly finely. Place in a large pan over medium heat, cover and cook for 10 minutes. Stir occasionally. When just cooked, drain in a colander, pressing out moisture with back of a spoon. Leave until cool.
2. Place drained yoghurt in a mixing bowl. Crush garlic with ½ teaspoon salt and stir into yoghurt with cooled spinach, parsley and sugar. Check seasoning and add more salt and sugar to taste. Cover and chill well before serving.

OOLOGANTCH LITZK
STUFFED MUSSELS

It is claimed by the Armenians that Stuffed Mussels is a creation of Armenian cooks at the time of Constantinople and the Byzantium era. It is a valid claim, as the basic combination of rice, onions, pine nuts and currants is used by Orthodox Armenians and Greeks as a filling for foods during fasts when meat must not be taken.

Many cooks have trouble closing mussels after filling with the rice mixture. Near the pointed end of the mussel, close inspection reveals a fine white ligament. Sever this and the mussel can be closed easily after filling, but take care as you can completely unhinge it.

For further information on preparing mussels, see Midye Dolmasi recipe, page 136.

Serves: 8-10
Cooking time: 1 hour

Filling:
3 large onions, finely chopped
½ cup olive oil
1 cup short grain rice, washed
⅓ cup pine nuts
⅓ cup currants
½ teaspoon ground allspice
1 tablespoon chopped fresh dill
salt
freshly ground black pepper

To finish:
5 dozen large mussels
2 cups water
lemon wedges for serving

1. Gently fry onions in oil until transparent. Stir in remaining filling ingredients and keep aside.
2. Prepare mussels as directed in Midye Dolmasi recipe, severing the fine white ligament near the hinge.
3. Place 2 generous teaspoons of filling in each mussel, close up and arrange in layers in a deep pan. Invert a heavy plate on top of mussels and keep them intact during cooking. Add water and set pan over medium heat. Bring to the boil, cover, and simmer gently on low heat for 35-40 minutes.
4. Remove pan from heat and leave mussels to cool in pan.
5. Remove mussels, wipe with paper towels and rub shells with a cloth dipped in oil for a better appearance. Arrange on serving dish and garnish with lemon wedges. Serve at room temperature. If desired, mussels may be chilled before serving.

KHORSHAAF (Dried Fruit Compote) *recipe page 176*;
DARTCHINOV TEY (Cinnamon Tea) *recipe page 177.*

SEMPOOGI YEV MISOVGHOROVATZ
BAKED EGGPLANT WITH LAMB

Serves: 4 as a main course, 8 as a first course
Oven temperature: 180°C (350°F)
Cooking time: 45 minutes

8 long eggplants, each about 250 g (8 oz)
salt
500 g (1 lb) finely ground lamb
1 medium-sized onion, finely chopped
2 tablespoons finely chopped parsley
1 sweet green pepper
freshly ground black pepper
¼ teaspoon ground allspice
¼ cup tomato paste
¾ cup water
2 tablespoons butter

1. Remove stems from eggplants. Cut almost through eggplants crosswise at 2 cm (¾ inch) intervals. Take care not to cut right through.
2. Sprinkle salt liberally into cut surfaces and leave for 30 minutes. Rinse in cold water and squeeze dry by pushing ends of each eggplant together.
3. Put ground lamb into a mixing bowl with onion and parsley. Core and seed the pepper, keep a quarter of it aside and chop remainder finely. Add to lamb with a generous grind of pepper, allspice and about 1 teaspoon salt. Blend ingredients thoroughly.
4. Stuff some meat mixture in each slit in the eggplants, filling slits generously. Put finished eggplants in a baking dish.
5. Blend tomato paste in ¾ cup water and add salt and pepper to taste. Pour over eggplants and place reserved piece of pepper in the liquid. Dot tops with butter and bake, uncovered, in a moderate oven for 45 minutes. Baste during cooking with the juices. Serve hot with salad and bread.

MANTE
LAMB PIE

Serves: 4-5
Oven temperature: 180°C (350°F)
Cooking time: 1 hour

Pastry:
2 cups plain flour
½ teaspoon salt
¼ cup oil
½ cup cold water

Filling:
500 g (1 lb) finely ground lamb
1 small onion, finely chopped
1 tablespoon oil
2 tablespoons finely chopped parsley
salt
freshly ground black pepper

To finish:
melted butter
1 cup hot chicken stock

1. Sift flour and salt into a mixing bowl, add oil and rub into flour with fingertips. Add water, mix to a soft dough and knead lightly until smooth. Cover and rest for 30 minutes.
2. Place ground lamb in a mixing bowl — it should not be too lean. Gently fry onion in oil and add to lamb with parsley and salt and pepper to taste.
3. Roll out a third of the pastry to fit a 25 x 30 cm (10 x 12 inch) baking dish. Put aside and cover with a cloth.
4. Roll out remaining pastry thinly and cut into 4 cm (1½ inch) squares. Place a teaspoon of meat filling in centre of each, fold up sides and press to seal. Finished pastries will look like miniature canoes with the meat filling showing (see photograph page 171).
5. Place pastries side by side in rows in buttered baking dish. Top with reserved pastry, tucking edges in neatly. Brush with butter.
6. Bake in a moderate oven for 45 minutes. Pour hot chicken stock over pastry and return to oven for further 10-15 minutes until most of stock is absorbed.
7. Cut into squares and serve with yoghurt.

Note: Sometimes this is prepared without the top covering of pastry. It is a more attractive way to present the dish. Brush the meat filling with butter before baking.

AGHT'ZIVADZ KEDNAHUNZOUR
LAMB SAUSAGES WITH POTATOES

As with many Armenian recipes, this cumin-flavoured lamb dish also features in Turkish and Greek cookery (Turkish – İzmir Köftesi, Greek – Souzoukakia). While the sausage-shaped meatballs are browned first, then simmered in tomato sauce in these latter versions, the Armenians arrange them in a baking dish alternately with pieces of potato, pour on the sauce and bake them in the oven for a one-dish main course.

Izmir is a province of Turkey and at one time was home to many Armenians and Greeks.

Serves: 6
*Oven temperature: 180°C (350°F), reducing to
    160°C (300°F)*
Cooking time: 1½ hours

750 g (1½ lb) finely ground lamb
3 slices stale white bread, crusts removed
2 cloves garlic, crushed
1 tablespoon chopped parsley
1 teaspoon ground cumin
salt
freshly ground black pepper

Tomato Sauce:
¼ cup tomato paste
½ small sweet green pepper
1 cup water
½ teaspoon sugar
salt
freshly ground black pepper

To finish:
¼ cup melted butter
750 g (1½ lb) medium-sized potatoes

1.   Put lamb into a bowl. Soak bread in cold water, squeeze dry and crumble into lamb. Add garlic, parsley, cumin and season to taste with salt and pepper.
2.   If you have a meat grinder, pass mixture through it once, using fine screen, then knead to a paste. If not, knead well until thoroughly blended and paste-like in consistency.
3.   Moisten hands and shape generous tablespoons of lamb mixture into oval sausage-like rolls. Keep aside.
4.   Combine tomato paste with chopped pepper, water, sugar and salt and pepper to taste.
5.   Peel potatoes and cut in half so that pieces are about the same size and shape as the meatballs.
6.   Brush a baking dish with some of the butter. Arrange meatballs in rows in dish, placing pieces of potato, cut side down, between meatballs. Brush with melted butter.
7.   Pour tomato sauce mixture evenly over the top and bake uncovered in a moderate oven for 10 minutes, basting occasionally with sauce in dish. Reduce heat to slow, cover dish with foil and cook for further hour. Add a little more water to dish if necessary. Serve hot with a green vegetable or salad accompaniment and pickles.

KHARENI LITZK BULGHOUROV
STUFFED VEGETABLES

Serves: 6 as a main course, more for a buffet
Cooking time: 1½ hours

6 medium-sized sweet green peppers
6 medium-sized tomatoes
6 long eggplants (aubergines) or 3
    medium-sized oval eggplants

Stuffing:
750 g (1½ lb) finely ground lamb
1 small onion, finely chopped
1 cup chopped, peeled tomatoes
¼ cup tomato paste
¼ cup finely chopped sweet green pepper
¼ cup short grain rice
½ cup coarse bulgar (burghul), rinsed
pinch of hot chili pepper
1½ teaspoons salt

To finish:
2 cups water
¼ cup sumak
1 tablespoon tomato paste
pulp from tomatoes
1½ teaspoons salt
1 teaspoon sugar

1. Wash vegetables. Cut tops from peppers and reserve. Remove core, seeds and white membrane, rinse and drain. Cut off tops of tomatoes (stem end) and set aside. Scoop out tomato pulp with a spoon and keep pulp separate. Drain tomatoes. Remove stalks from eggplants. Cut off 2 cm (¾ inch) from this end and keep aside. Scoop out eggplant flesh, leaving 5 mm (¼ inch) of flesh. Place eggplants in salted water and soak for 20 minutes. Rinse and drain.
2. For the stuffing, be sure that lamb has some fat with it. Combine with remaining stuffing ingredients and blend thoroughly.
3. Place stuffing in vegetables — do not fill completely as there must be space for expansion. Replace reserved tops. For the eggplants, pare down reserved ends to form a cork.
4. Combine water and sumak, bring to the boil, then drain through a fine sieve. Discard sumak. Make liquid up to 2 cups with water if necessary.
5. Place pulp from tomatoes in the base of a deep, heavy pan and arrange stuffed peppers upright in pan. Put eggplants on top of peppers, placing them on their sides. Place tomatoes upright on top of eggplants.
6. Blend sumak liquid with tomato paste, salt and sugar and pour over vegetables. Cover pan tightly and bring to the boil. Reduce heat to low and simmer gently for 1¼ hours.
7. Arrange vegetables in serving dish and keep warm. Boil liquid in pan to reduce a little, pour over vegetables. Serve hot or warm.

ANOUSHABOUR
CHRISTMAS PUDDING

Serves: 8-10
Cooking time: 2½ hours

1 cup pearl barley
cold water
small piece cinnamon bark
1 cup granulated sugar

For serving:
ground cinnamon
blanched almonds and hazelnuts
chopped walnuts
sultanas (white raisins)
rose water, optional

1. Wash barley well, place in a bowl and cover with 4 cups cold water. Soak overnight.
2. Next day put barley, soaking water and cinnamon bark into a heavy pan and bring to the boil. Boil gently, uncovered, until barley is very soft and porridge-like in consistency — about 2 hours. Remove cinnamon bark.
3. Stir in sugar and cook for further 10 minutes. Turn into individual bowls and sprinkle with ground cinnamon. Decorate with nuts and sultanas.
4. Serve warm or chilled with additional nuts and sultanas, and rose water for adding to individual taste if desired.

ANOUSHABOUR (Christmas Pudding) *recipe above.*

TAHINOV HATZ
TAHINI COOKIES

Makes about 5 dozen
Oven temperature: 180°C (350°F)
Cooking time: 15 minutes

½ cup butter
1 cup tahina
1 cup caster sugar
½ cup firmly packed brown sugar
1 egg
2½ cups plain flour
1½ teaspoons baking powder
pinch salt
1 cup finely chopped walnuts

1. Cream butter, tahina and sugars until light. Add egg and beat well.
2. Sift flour, baking powder and salt twice, then fold into tahina mixture with the walnuts.
3. Take portions of dough and roll into balls the size of a small walnut. Place on greased baking sheets and press to flatten slightly — with tines of fork if desired to give a good finish.
4. Bake in a moderate oven for 15 minutes or until lightly coloured. Cool on baking sheets for 5 minutes, then lift onto racks to cool completely. Store in an airtight container.

KHORSHAAF
DRIED FRUIT COMPOTE

Serves: 6
Cooking time: 45 minutes

1 cup pitted prunes
1 cup dried apricot halves
1 cup sultanas (white raisins)
water
½ cup granulated sugar
thin strip of lemon rind
2 cloves
¼ teaspoon ground allspice, optional
chopped walnuts for serving

1. Wash dried fruits well and place in a pan with cold water to cover. Bring to the boil, then simmer, covered, on low heat for 15 minutes.
2. Add sugar, lemon rind, and spices. Stir to dissolve and add a little more water if necessary. Simmer gently, uncovered, until fruit is soft but not mushy, and syrup is thick. Remove lemon rind and whole spices.
3. Turn into a bowl and chill well. Serve in sweet glasses sprinkled with chopped nuts.

TAN
YOGHURT DRINK

Many countries in the region covered use a yoghurt beverage with meals. It is most refreshing, particularly in summer. In Turkey and Iran it is made similarly and called Ayran and Abdug respectively; in Lebanon, Syria and Jordan it is 'Ayraan when salt is used, Laban bi Sikkar when sweetened with sugar.

Makes about 3 cups

2 cups yoghurt (page 20)
1 cup water
pinch of salt

1. Put yoghurt in blender jar or bowl and beat until smooth.
2. Add water gradually, beating constantly. If too thick add a little more water, as yoghurts vary in consistency. Beat in salt and chill well before serving. Tan accompanies every Armenian meal.

DARTCHINOV TEY
CINNAMON TEA

To make 2 tea cups:

1½ cups water

4 x 8 cm (3 inch) pieces cinnamon bark·

sugar for serving

1. Put water in a long-handled coffee pot with cinnamon bark left intact.

2. Bring to the boil and boil gently for 15 minutes. Remove cinnamon bark and pour into tea cups. Serve sugar separately.

SYRIA, LEBANON, JORDAN

In writing this book I was faced with many a dilemma. This chapter was one of them. Should I treat each country separately or place them together? So many dishes, though different in name, are basically the same, and are claimed by each nation. In the interests of avoiding repetition it seemed best to put them together. You will find a mixture of Arabic dialects in the names because recipes were given to me by Lebanese, Syrians, Jordanians and Palestinians.

The area which is Lebanon, Syria and Jordan has played a significant part in history for thousands of years, a trading link with East and West and a melting pot of Arabic cultures and creeds. Their dishes have been developed through the wide variety of foods available and the diverse nature of the people in the cities, towns and the remotest desert areas. Collectively this has produced a cuisine which epitomizes the Arabic people, adopted by other nations in the region and in turn adopting dishes from neighbouring regions.

THE FLAVOUR OF ARABIC FOODS

In my time I have tried many a Kibbeh, some excellent, others good, and an occasional disappointing one. The excellence of an Arabic cook is measured by her Kibbeh, and in trying to find how a cook goes about making an excellent Kibbeh or a Kibbeh bil Sanieh, I was left thoroughly bewildered, since no two cooks seemed to agree. Keep the mixture cold, I was told; it doesn't matter, said someone else. Use only hogget, not lamb, for cooked kibbeh; lamb is fine if it is not too young. Bake it for a long time; bake it for a short time. What confusion! Try my Kibbeh bil Sanieh and you can start on the merry-go-round of kibbeh making! I am dizzy!

One modernization which will probably have traditional Kibbeh makers throw their hands up in horror is the use of the food processor. But try it before you condemn. Though I enjoy using a pestle and mortar, I lack the stamina to use it for Kibbeh making. Furthermore I doubt if many do use it away from their native home as even the hand-operated food grinder makes light of the task in comparison.

Following Kibbeh in popularity is Tabouleh, the delicious parsley and burghul salad of the region. Again there will be those who disagree with my recipe — more about that in the introduction to the recipe.

Parsley, mint, the understated spiciness of cinnamon and allspice, the somewhat acid flavour of yoghurt, the refreshing tartness of

LABNEH MAKBUS (Yoghurt Cheese Balls) *recipe page 184.*

lemon, the fruitiness of olive oil, the earthiness of burghul, tahini, eggplant, dried beans, rice — these are the flavours of the cuisine of this region. Never overpowering, subtly blended, a delight to the palate.

Arab hospitality is frequently expressed with the offering of *mezze,* a variety of appetizers only limited by the availability of ingredients and the capacity of the cook to prepare them. Hummous bi Tahini, Baba Ghannouj and Bakdounis bi Tahini are three bread dips almost always on hand for *mezze* as they keep very well under refrigeration. With the food processor they can be prepared very quickly and efficiently.

More time consuming in their preparation, but nevertheless prepared frequently, are Mihshi Warak Enib, stuffed grape vine leaves; recipes for these most popular morsels are to be found in the sections on Armenia and Cyprus, as both versions are similar to the Arab versions.

A diligent cook prepares pastries and stores them in her freezer, to be reheated at a moment's notice. Fatayer, Sfiha and Lahm bi'Ajeen, flat or shaped lamb pies and rolls and delicious spinach pies, are piled on platters and served with yoghurt or lemon wedges. Khoubiz bread dough, a kind of short crust pastry, or the fine fillo pastry can form the basis of the pies and rolls. You can take short cuts by using frozen bread dough for some of them, and the advantages of fillo pastry are already well known.

Other *mezzes* could be: Labneh Makbus, yoghurt cheese balls; Tabouleh, a good salad to have on hand for any situation; Falafel, dried bean croquettes, and fried or baked kibbi balls. All these can be prepared ahead; store Labneh and Tabouleh as directed in recipes; Falafel and kibbi balls freeze very well and may be defrosted and heated in a moderate oven. With modern refrigeration, freezers and food preparation appliances, the Arab cook has a much easier task when entertaining than her predecessors, even in her native land.

All *mezze* are served with Khoubiz, the Arabic flat bread now so widely available to the Westerner. Even if your local store does not keep it in stock, you will find the recipe given quite easy to follow, particularly if you bake bread. The Khoubiz Sorj of Lebanon and the Shirak of the Palestinians and Jordanians are one and the same. The same dough is rolled and stretched as thinly as possible without breaking the dough, and baked on a large metal dome called a *sorj*. The *sorj* is heated over a fire until very hot, and the bread draped over it. Cooking time is short — about 3 minutes — and after cooking the bread is wrapped in a cloth to keep it soft. The *sorj* is available in varying sizes, but I have found that a good iron Chinese wok inverted over a charcoal fire works very well, even if the breads are not as large as they should be. Bread sheets, as they are commonly called, are used cut in squares and rolled up with grilled meats and salad ingredients for an Arabic-style hamburger. Khoubiz has a convenient pocket for the same kind of filling, or anything you would conceivably put between two slices of bread.

Tahini is a most important ingredient in the Arabic cooking of the region. It is a paste made from toasted sesame seeds and sometimes a little experimentation is required to find the blend to your liking as they do vary in quality. I have found considerable variation between tahinis, though they all separate to some degree. Store the unopened cans upside-down for some time before use; this way the blending usually required is considerably minimized.

The making of yoghurt is an art handed down from mother to daughter and is almost a daily occurrence in traditional homes. Instructions have been given in the introductory chapter of the book with two methods detailed. It is through the cooking of this region that I learned how to stabilize yoghurt and for those who might be watching saturated fat intake, cooked skim milk yoghurt, Laban Mutboukh, is an excellent substitute for sour cream. The people of the region never, ever, serve yoghurt with fish, for what reason I really do not know, though the reasons given have varied considerably.

The pastries of the region are renowned worldwide: every Western city now has Lebanese or Syrian pastry shops. I have always made it a practice to patronize such shops as I have found their pastries are superb. My favourite version of baklava is the Lebanese Baklawa Be'aj. In my quest to find and develop this recipe for the home I had a problem in finding a name for it. Though to me the shape resembles the petals of a flower, it seems that the Lebanese or Syrian is reminded of a cloth wrapped bundle which is called a *be'aj,* and this is the name they give this pastry, though it is generally referred to as baklawa. The other version of baklawa I have given, Kul'wa'shkur, has a delightful translation which describes the pastry admirably — eat and praise.

EATING IN THE STYLE OF THE REGION

With such a diverse group of peoples it is difficult to give a general method of serving a meal, as the meal could be taken in a city home, a village dwelling or a desert tent. As I have described the traditional Arabic feast as served in a tent in the chapter on the Gulf States, I shall concentrate on the city or village meal service.

Once again foreign influences have been felt widely in the area and Beirut is considered a very Western city, though still with an essentially Arabic character. The meal is likely to be set on a conventional table spread with a cloth or it could be set up on a large, low, brass table, depending on the atmosphere that the hostess wishes to create. The one single feature of any meal is abundance, with a large variety of foods served at the meal. There could be Kibbeh prepared in one of the many ways, Tabouleh, perhaps a fish dish, rice, a vegetable stew, crisp cos (romaine) lettuce, and other salad ingredients, khoubiz, pickles, olives and fresh fruit. Individual serving plates, cutlery and glassware are part of the table appointments. The setting could be as refined as any Western dining room or colourfully Arabic in flavour. After the meal coffee is taken in a separate room, perhaps with sweets though these are more likely to be eaten at a later time. With coffee comes conversation and sharing the *narghile,* the water pipe of the area.

COOKING METHODS

The *madaqqa* and *jorn,* pestle and mortar of the region, is a necessary part of cooking equipment. The mortar is usually very large and made of stone for Kibbeh making, with smaller versions in stone or brass for Hummus and other purées and for pounding spices. A *sanieh,* a large, round baking tray is an ideal cooking utensil for the oven and readily available at Middle Eastern food stores. For shaping Ma'amoul a *tabi* can also be obtained from such stores, though I have given a means of shaping using equipment you will have on hand. Coring zucchini is an art which requires an implement more slender than an apple corer, and zucchini corers are also available. For general cooking, standard pots and pans may be adapted, though I recommend heavy pans, particularly for dishes containing yoghurt and thick soups.

INGREDIENTS FOR ARABIC COOKING

Stock up on fine and coarse burghul, tahini, dried beans, chick peas, dried mint and a spice mix called za'tar used as a topping with oil on khoubiz before baking. Flat leaf parsley is used in abundance, and it is worthwhile having a sizable patch in your herb garden. The favoured fats are olive oil and samneh, though substitutes can be used in many recipes. Where a recipe's flavour is dependent on the right oil or fat, no substitute is given.

Rose water and orange flower water for flavouring syrups and pastries; walnuts, almonds, pine nuts with the occasional use of unsalted pistachio nuts. Salted nuts, toasted and salted chick peas and pumpkin seeds are favoured for nibbling with arak, the potent aniseed-flavoured spirit of the region, and no Arabic household of this region would be without them. Dibs, carob syrup, is also very much a part of the cuisine. It is mixed with tahini and spread on khoubiz.

SAMNEH

While ghee is popularly used in place of samneh, the flavour is not quite the same as the clarified or drawn butter prepared by the Arabic cook.

Melt salted or unsalted butter in a pan on low heat. When the froth rises, skim it off — it contains some of the milk solids and the salt if salted butter is used. Pour the clear oil into a container through a folded piece of butter muslin set in a sieve, leaving the milk solids in the pan. These can be combined with the froth for adding to meat and chicken stews or tossed through vegetables not prepared in the Middle Eastern tradition.

TARATOUR BI TAHINI
TAHINI SAUCE

Makes 1¼-1½ cups

2 cloves garlic
salt
½ cup tahini
¼-½ cup cold water
½ cup lemon juice

1. Crush garlic cloves with ½ teaspoon salt in a mixing bowl. Gradually add tahini and beat well with a wooden spoon.
2. Beat in a little water and lemon juice alternately. The water thickens the mixture, lemon juice thins it.
3. Add all the lemon juice and enough water to give a thin or thick consistency, depending on use. Add more salt to taste and use as directed in recipes. Flavour should be tart.

Food processor or blender method: Place tahini and garlic in blender or processor container and process for a few seconds to crush the garlic. Add lemon juice and water alternately, a little at a time, until desired consistency is reached. Blend in salt to taste.

BAKDOUNIS BI TAHINI
PARSLEY AND TAHINI SAUCE

Follow directions for Taratour bi Tahini, adding 1 cup finely chopped parsley after a ¼ cup water and all the lemon juice has been blended into the tahini. Beat well and add more water only if it is necessary. In food processor or blender add coarsely chopped parsley at end and process just long enough to chop it finely. Parsley must still be visible. Serve as a dip as part of *meze,* or as an accompaniment to simple fish dishes.

Note: In Cyprus this sauce is known as Tahinosalata.

LABAN MUTBOUKH
COOKED YOGHURT

Yoghurt is used in Lebanese and other Middle Eastern dishes in much the same way as sour cream is used in Western cuisine. If goat's milk yoghurt is available, it may be added as it is to any dish which requires yoghurt to be cooked for a time. However the yoghurt generally available (or home-made) is made with cow's milk. This curdles when heated for a long period, so it has to be stabilized beforehand. Cow's milk yoghurt can be added to a cooked dish just before serving without being previously stabilized, providing the sauce is not allowed to boil.

2 cups yoghurt
1 egg white
2 teaspoons cornflour
1 teaspoon salt

1. Place yoghurt in a heavy-based pan.
2. Beat egg white with a fork until frothy and blend into yoghurt with cornflour and salt. Stir in the same direction until thoroughly combined.
3. Place pan over medium heat and stir constantly with a wooden spoon. Heat until it begins to boil, stirring continuously in the same direction. This is important.
4. Lower heat and leave to simmer gently, uncovered, for 3-5 minutes until thick. Use as required in recipes.

BABA GHANNOUJ (Eggplant and Sesame Purée) *recipe page 185*;
BAKDOUNIS BI TAHINI (Parsley and Tahini Sauce) *recipe above*
HUMMUS BI TAHINI (Chick Pea and Sesame Purée) *recipe page 185.*

KAREESHEE
COTTAGE CHEESE

This is the Syrian version of the Greek Mizithra, and as there is little difference, follow the directions for making Mizithra, page 27.

However, if you wish to make the following recipe, be sure to collect all the whey, as it is required for Kareeshee bi Limoon, a whey cheese similar to the Italian ricotta cheese.

KAREESHEE BI LIMOON
WHEY CHEESE

whey from Kareeshee
4 cups whole milk
juice of 1 lemon, strained

1. Put whey in a large pan and heat until lukewarm. Pour in milk and continue to heat until milk rises to the surface. Keep heat low.
2. Add lemon juice and leave until cheese thickens, still keeping pan on low heat. Takes about 15 minutes.
3. Line a colander or large sieve with a doubled piece of butter muslin and ladle cheese into this. Leave until well drained, scraping down sides of cloth occasionally. Gather ends of cloth, tie and suspend from a fixed object until completely drained. Remove from cloth and store in a sealed container in refrigerator until required. Keeps for 1 week. Use as for ricotta cheese in recipes.

LABNEH
YOGHURT CHEESE

Makes about 2 cups cheese

6 cups laban (yoghurt, page 20)
2 teaspoons salt

1. Yoghurt made from full cream milk must be used for labneh. Measure into a bowl and stir in salt.
2. Place yoghurt into centre of a doubled piece of butter muslin or a soft piece of cotton cloth, gather up corners and tie securely. Suspend from a fixed object over a bowl and leave to drain for at least 10 hours. It is best to do this at night as it is cooler then.
3. When well drained and the consistency of ricotta cheese, remove from cloth to a bowl. Cover and store in refrigerator. Use as directed in recipes or as a spread on Khoubiz (flat bread). Labneh is a popular breakfast food; it is spread on bread with a drizzle of olive oil and eaten with olives.

LABNEH MAKBUS
YOGHURT CHEESE BALLS

1 quantity Labneh (above)
olive oil

1. Make labneh according to directions. When well drained, take a tablespoonful at a time and roll into smooth balls. Place side by side on a tray.
2. Chill cheese balls in refrigerator for several hours until firm. When firm and a little dried, pack into a sterilized jar and cover with olive oil. Seal and store at room temperature.
3. When serving as an appetizer or for spreading on flat bread, serve in a bowl with a little of the oil, so that the oil may be used to soften the cheese.

HUMMUS BI TAHINI
CHICK PEA AND SESAME PUREE

Makes 3 cups
Cooking time: 3 hours

1 cup chick peas
3 cups water
⅓ cup tahini
½ cup lemon juice
2 cloves garlic, crushed
salt

For serving:
chopped parsley
1 tablespoon olive oil
paprika or cayenne pepper

1. Wash chick peas well, cover with the water and soak for 12 hours or overnight.
2. Put on to boil in the water in which they were soaked. Boil gently for 2 hours, add 1 teaspoon salt and cook until very tender — about 3 hours in all. Drain and reserve some of the cooking liquid and 1 tablespoon of the peas.
3. Press peas through a sieve or food mill, adding about 2 tablespoons of the cooking liquid to separate the last of the peas from the skins.
4. Slowly blend the tahini and most of the lemon juice into the purée.
5. Crush garlic with ½ teaspoon salt in a mortar and add to purée. Adjust flavour and consistency with lemon juice or cooking liquid and add salt if necessary. Hummus should be thick and smooth.
6. Spread in a shallow serving dish, swirling it with back of a spoon. Pour olive oil in centre and garnish with reserved chick peas, chopped parsley and a sprinkling of paprika or cayenne pepper.

Blender or food processor method: Purée peas to separate skins, add to container or processor bowl with remaining ingredients, holding back some lemon juice and salt to adjust flavour. Blend or process until thick and smooth.

Note: Even if using a modern appliance the chick peas must be separated from their skins for a successful hummus. Preparation time can be shortened by removing the skins either after the initial soaking, or after boiling. See page 12 for more detail.

BABA GHANNOUJ
EGGPLANT AND SESAME PUREE

Serves: 4-6

1 medium-sized eggplant, about 375 g (12 oz)
¼ cup lemon juice
¼ cup tahini
2 cloves garlic
2 teaspoons salt or to taste
1 tablespoon olive oil
¼ cup finely chopped parsley

1. Grill eggplant over a charcoal fire for 30-40 minutes, turning frequently. Alternatively place on centre shelf in a hot oven and cook until soft, again turning often.
2. Peel off skin while hot and remove stem and end of eggplant if firm.
3. Chop flesh and pound in a mortar with pestle to a purée or place in a blender or food processor and purée.
4. Blend in most of the lemon juice and gradually add the tahini.
5. Crush garlic to a paste with 1 teaspoon salt and add to eggplant. Beat well and adjust flavour with more lemon juice and salt.
6. Beat in olive oil and parsley. If using an appliance put about 4 parsley sprigs into container and process until parsley is chopped but still visible.
7. Place in a shallow dish, garnish with parsley and serve with Khoubiz as an appetizer.

Note: If making ahead, store in sealed container in refrigerator. Bring to room temperature before serving.

TABOULEH
BURGHUL AND PARSLEY SALAD

I once prepared this salad on my television cookery show and received much criticism from members of the Lebanese community in Sydney. It was said that I used far too much burghul and should have had tomato mixed through it, not just as garnish. I concede the latter point, with one reservation. If you wish to have the salad on hand for a few days in the refrigerator for convenience, then leave the tomato out and add to the portion being served.

As to the former criticism, I still believe that Tabouleh should have a large proportion of burghul to parsley. While in the Middle East I spoke with many excellent exponents of Lebanese cookery, and found they agreed with me. If you beg to differ, then decrease burghul to ¼ cup and increase chopped parsley to 3 cups or more.

Serves: 6-8

¾ cup fine burghul
2 cups cold water
2 cups chopped parsley
½ cup finely chopped spring onions
¼ cup finely chopped mint
¼ cup olive oil
2 tablespoons lemon juice
1½ teaspoons salt
½ teaspoon freshly ground black pepper
2 firm ripe tomatoes
crisp lettuce leaves
¼ cup lemon juice mixed with ½ teaspoon
   salt

1. Place burghul in a bowl and cover with the cold water. Leave to soak for 30 minutes. Drain through a fine sieve, pressing with back of a spoon to extract moisture. Spread onto a cloth and leave to dry further.
2. Meanwhile prepare parsley. Wash well, shake off excess moisture and remove thick stalks. Wrap in a tea towel and place in refrigerator to crisp and dry.
3. Put burghul into a mixing bowl and add spring onions. Squeeze mixture with hand so that burghul absorbs onion flavour.
4. Chop parsley fairly coarsely, measure and add to burghul with mint.
5. Beat olive oil with lemon juice and stir in salt and pepper. Add to salad and toss well.
6. Peel and seed tomatoes and cut into dice. Gently stir into salad. Cover and chill for at least 1 hour before serving.
7. Serve in salad bowl lined with crisp lettuce leaves. Lemon juice and salt mixture is served in a jug so that it may be added according to individual taste.

LSANAT MTABBLI
LAMB TONGUE SALAD

Serves: 6-8
Cooking time: 1½-2 hours

10 lamb tongues
water
salt
1 clove garlic
1 quantity Dressing (see Fattoush, page 198)
or
1 quantity Bakdounis bi Tahini (page 182)
2 tablespoons finely chopped parsley for
   garnish

1. Wash lamb tongues well, scrubbing if necessary. Put in a pan and cover with cold water. Bring to the boil, then add about 3 teaspoons salt and halved garlic clove. Cover pan and simmer on low heat for 1½-2 hours. Test with a skewer to determine when tender.
2. Remove tongues, cool a little and take off skin, gristle and bone from root end. Cut into 2 cm (¾ inch) cubes and place in a bowl.
3. Pour the olive oil and lemon dressing or half the Bakdounis bi Tahini over the tongue and toss well. Serve at room temperature or chilled with parsley sprinkled on top. May be served as an appetizer or part of main meal.

TABOULEH (Burghul and Parsley Salad) *recipe above.*

FATAYER SBANIKH
TRIANGLE SPINACH PIES

Makes about 30
Oven temperature: 200°C (400°F)
Cooking time: 40 minutes

½ quantity Khoubiz dough (page 190)

Spinach Filling:
750 g (1½ lb) spinach
⅓ cup olive oil
1 large onion, finely chopped
½ cup snoober (pine nuts) or chopped
    walnuts
¼ teaspoon nutmeg
salt
freshly ground black pepper
¼ cup lemon juice

1. Make khoubiz dough according to directions, using full amount of yeast specified if making half quantity. Cover and leave to rise.
2. Remove roots and damaged leaves from spinach. Wash spinach well in several changes of water, shake off excess moisture and chop leaves and stalks fairly finely.
3. Place spinach into a deep pan (not aluminium) and cook over medium heat, uncovered, for 5-8 minutes until wilted and juices run out. Toss with a fork while cooking.
4. Turn into a colander and press with back of spoon to remove as much moisture as possible.
5. Heat oil in a pan and gently fry onion until transparent. Add spinach and fry for 5 minutes, stirring frequently.
6. Add pine nuts or walnuts, salt and pepper to taste, nutmeg and lemon juice. Cook for further 5 minutes or until moisture has evaporated. Leave until cool.
7. Punch down dough and roll out on a lightly floured board until 5 mm (¼ inch) thick. Cut into 10 cm (4 inch) rounds; place rounds on a cloth and cover with another cloth.
8. Place a tablespoon of spinach filling in centre of each round and bring up sides at three points to form a triangular shape. Press edges very firmly with fingertips to seal pies completely. Care must be taken that the oily juices of the spinach filling do not get onto the edge of the dough. If this happens, dip finger in flour and dab onto dough before sealing.
9. Place pies close together on lightly oiled baking sheets and bake in a moderately hot oven for 15 minutes or until lightly coloured and cooked. For a golden brown top place briefly under a hot grill. Serve hot or warm.

ARDISHAWKI MIHSHI
STUFFED ARTICHOKES

Serves: 4
Cooking time: 1¼ hours

8 large globe artichokes (see page 9 for
    preparation)
water
juice of 1 lemon
1 medium-sized onion, finely chopped
1 tablespoon olive oil
¼ cup snoober (pine nuts)
500 g (1 lb) finely ground lamb
salt
freshly ground black pepper
1 tablespoon finely chopped parsley
2 cups water
2 tablespoons butter
2 tablespoons flour

1. Wash and prepare artichokes as directed for whole artichokes. Open carefully with fingers to expose choke and remove this with a teaspoon. Drop prepared artichokes into a bowl of cold water with half the lemon juice added.
2. Gently fry onion in oil until transparent, add pine nuts and stir over heat until lightly browned.
3. Combine meat with onion and pine nut mixture, 1 teaspoon salt, pepper to taste and parsley.
4. Drain artichokes and fill centres with meat mixture, forcing in as much as they will take, and mounding meat at top.
5. Arrange artichokes upright in a large pan, in a single layer if possible. Add water and 1 teaspoon salt and sprinkle remaining lemon juice over artichokes.
6. Cover and bring to a simmer. Simmer gently for 45-60 minutes until artichokes are tender.
7. Drain off liquid into a measuring jug and make up to 1½ cups with water if necessary. Keep artichokes hot.
8. Melt butter in a small saucepan and stir in flour. Cook 1 minute, then add cooking liquid, stirring constantly. Bring to the boil, still stirring, then boil gently for 2 minutes.
9. Arrange artichokes on platter and pour sauce over them. Serve hot.

ZAYTUN MSABBAH
SPICED OLIVES

fresh green olives
3 small, dried hot chilis for each kg (pound)
    olives
water
rock salt

1. Either leave olives as they are, or cut 3 or 4 slits in each with a fine-bladed, stainless steel knife or razor blade. Discard any damaged olives.
2. Pack into sterilized glass jar or jars, and cover with cold water. Soak for 3 days, changing water each day. Measure last amount of water.
3. Measure same amount of fresh water into a pan and add rock salt in the proportion of ⅓ cup to each 4 cups water. Heat and stir until salt dissolves. Cool.
4. Pack chilis into jar or jars, placing them amongst the olives. Pour cool brine on top, filling jars. Remove any air bubbles and seal with plastic lid. Store in a cool, dark place for 5 months before using.
5. To serve, remove required amount of olives and rinse under cold water. Drain and place in a bowl. Squeeze on the juice of a lemon and pour on ¼ cup olive oil. Stir to blend and leave for an hour or two before serving.

KABES EL KARNABEET
PICKLED CAULIFLOWER

1 medium-sized cauliflower
salted water
2 cups water
⅓ cup pickling salt
3 cups white vinegar
1 beetroot (beet), optional
2 cloves garlic
hot chilies

1. Break cauliflower into florets and place in a bowl of salted water to remove insects. Leave for 10 minutes, then drain and rinse well. Drain in colander.
2. Heat 2 cups water with salt until boiling and salt is dissolved. Cool and add vinegar.
3. Peel beetroot if used and slice, halving slices.
4. Pack cauliflower into 2 sterilized jars, placing slices of beetroot between layers and adding a garlic clove and 1 hot chili to each jar.
5. Fill jars with pickling solution and seal with glass or plastic lids. Store in a cool place for 1 week before using. Once opened, store in refrigerator. Unopened pickles can be kept in a cool, dark place.

KHOUBIZ
LEBANESE FLAT BREAD

Of all the Middle Eastern breads this is the most widely known. In recent years its popularity has increased enormously as Western tastes become more adventurous. Though widely available commercially in the cities, khoubiz is easily made in the domestic oven or electric frypan. Though the home product is not as evenly browned, it has a better flavour and finer texture. Traditionally khoubiz contains no shortening, but I find a little oil in the dough improves the flavour and texture. Many Lebanese cooks include oil also.

You will find more details re baking, storing and serving in All About Bread (page 13).

Makes 8 loaves
Oven temperature: 260°C (500°F)
Cooking time: 4-5 minutes

6 cups plain flour
1 sachet active dry yeast
2 cups warm water
1½ teaspoons salt
1 teaspoon sugar
2 tablespoons oil

1. Sift flour into a large mixing bowl and warm in a low oven.
2. Dissolve yeast in ¼ cup warm water, add remaining water and stir in salt and sugar.
3. Remove about 2 cups flour from bowl and set aside. Pour yeast liquid into centre and stir in some flour to make a thick liquid. Cover with cloth and leave in a warm place until frothy.
4. Stir in rest of flour, adding oil gradually, then beat until smooth, either by hand for 10 minutes, or on electric mixer using dough hook for 5 minutes.
5. Sprinkle some of the reserved flour onto a board, turn out dough and knead for 10 minutes, using more flour as required. Dough is ready when it is smooth and satiny with a slightly wrinkled texture. Shape dough into a ball.
6. Oil bowl, put in dough smooth side down then turn over so that top is coated with oil. Stretch plastic wrap over bowl and leave in a warm place to rise until almost doubled in bulk — about 1-1½ hours. Preheat oven.
7. Punch down dough and turn out onto lightly floured board. Knead for a minute or so, then divide into 8 equal pieces, rolling each into a ball.
8. Roll each piece into a 25 cm (10 inch) round and place on a lightly floured cloth. Cover with another cloth and leave for 20 minutes.
9. Heat a large baking sheet or flat griddle on the lowest shelf in an electric oven; in a gas oven select the section of the oven with the most even heat, probably near the top.
10. Place a round of dough on a lightly floured baking sheet with one flat edge or on a piece of plywood, spreading it evenly. Shake to ensure that it will slide off easily.
11. Rub heated baking sheet or griddle with wad of paper towel dipped in oil then slide dough onto it. Bake in hot oven for 4-5 minutes until it puffs up like a balloon. If you would like it browned on top, turn quickly and leave for a minute. Remove bread and wrap in a cloth to keep it warm and soft. Bake remaining loaves.

To bake in electric frypan (a good alternative if your gas oven does not heat evenly): Preheat frypan on highest setting with metal lid on, vent closed. When heated, oil base quickly and slide dough onto base. Cover and cook for 3 minutes, remove lid, turn bread over, re-cover and cook further 2 minutes.

MNA'ISH BI ZA'TAR
SEASONED FLAT BREAD

Make Khoubiz as directed to Step 8, but do not rest dough. Flute edge of each round with fingertips and brush generously with olive oil. Sprinkle 2 tablespoons za'tar (spice mix, see Glossary) evenly on top and bake as for Khoubiz, Steps 9 to 11. Do not turn over — brown top under hot grill if desired.

ADAS BIS SILQ (Lentil and Silverbeet Soup) *recipe page 192.*

RIZ MUFALFAL
PLAIN RICE

Serves: 5-6
Cooking time: 35 minutes

2 cups good quality long grain rice
2 tablespoons samneh (clarified butter)
   or ghee
3 cups hot water
2 teaspoons salt or to taste

1. Place rice in a bowl and cover with cold water. Stir with fingers to loosen starch, then pour through a sieve to drain. Rinse under running water. Drain thoroughly.
2. Heat samneh in a heavy pan, add rice and stir over medium heat for 2 minutes until grains are well coated with fat.
3. Pour in hot water and add salt. Stir occasionally until boiling, reduce heat, cover pan tightly and leave over low heat for 25 minutes. Turn off heat and leave for 10 minutes before serving — may be left for longer if desired. Fluff up with fork before serving.

FALAFEL
DRIED BEAN CROQUETTES

Makes about 35
Cooking time: 5-6 minutes each lot

1 cup fava beans (dried broad beans, see
   (page 12)
1 cup chick peas (page 12)
water
1 medium-sized onion
2 cloves garlic
½ cup finely chopped parsley
pinch hot chili pepper
1 teaspoon ground coriander
½ teaspoon ground cumin
½ teaspoon bicarbonate of soda
salt
freshly ground black pepper

To finish:
oil for deep frying

1. Put broad beans in a bowl and cover with 3 cups cold water. Leave to soak for 48 hours, changing water once each day, twice in hot weather.
2. Put chick peas in 3 cups cold water and soak for 12-15 hours.
3. Drain beans and peas and remove skins as directed in section on Skinning Pulses. Skin may be left on the chick peas.
4. Combine uncooked beans and peas with roughly chopped onion and garlic and grind twice in food grinder using fine screen, or process in food processor in 2 lots.
5. Combine with parsley, chili pepper, coriander, cumin and soda and add salt and pepper to taste. Knead well and leave to rest for 30 minutes.
6. Shape a tablespoon of the mixture at a time into balls, then flatten into thick patties 4 cm (1½ inches) in diameter. Place on a tray and leave for 30 minutes at room temperature.
7. Deep fry in hot oil, 6-8 at a time, and cook for 5-6 minutes, turning to brown evenly. When well browned, remove and drain on paper towels.
8. Serve hot as an appetizer with Taratour bi Tahini or in split khoubiz with the same sauce and salad vegetables.

ADAS BIS SILQ
LENTIL AND SILVERBEET SOUP

Serves: 5-6
Cooking time: 1½ hours

1½ cups brown lentils
6 cups cold water
8-10 leaves silverbeet (Swiss chard)
¼ cup olive oil
1 large onion, finely chopped
3 cloves garlic, finely chopped
¼ cup chopped coriander leaves
salt
freshly ground black pepper
¼ cup lemon juice
lemon wedges for serving

1. Wash lentils well and place in a heavy pan with the cold water. Bring to the boil, skimming if necessary, then cover and simmer gently for 1 hour or until lentils are soft.
2. Wash silverbeet well and cut off stems. (Stems may be used as a separate vegetable for later meals.) Slit leaves down the middle, then shred coarsely.
3. Heat oil in a separate pan, add onion and fry gently until transparent. Stir in garlic and cook for a few seconds longer.
4. Add shredded silverbeet to pan and fry, stirring often, until leaves wilt.
5. Pour onion and silverbeet mixture into lentils, add coriander, salt and pepper to taste and the lemon juice. Cover and simmer gently for further 15-20 minutes. Serve soup in deep plates with lemon wedges for squeezing into soup according to individual taste. Khoubiz or other bread is a necessary accompaniment.

SHURABAT MOZAAT
MEAT SOUP

Serves: 6
Cooking time: 2 hours

1 kg (2 lb) lamb soup bones
500 g (1 lb) lamb stew meat, diced
water
salt
freshly ground black pepper
small piece cinnamon bark
3 small carrots, quartered
½ cup chopped celery
½ cup chopped, peeled tomatoes
½ cup short grain rice, or 1 cup fine noodles
¼ cup finely chopped parsley for serving

1. Rinse bones and place in a soup pot. Add meat, cover with 8 cups water and bring to the boil, skimming when necessary.
2. When well skimmed add salt and pepper to taste and cinnamon bark. Cover and simmer for 45 minutes.
3. Add vegetables, cover and cook for further 30 minutes. Remove soup bones and discard.
4. Stir in washed rice or crumbled noodles, adjust seasoning and simmer, covered, for further 20-25 minutes. Remove cinnamon bark.
5. Serve in soup bowls, sprinkled with chopped parsley.

SHURABAT AL KISHK
SOUP WITH KISHK

The preparation of kishk is a once-a-year effort when the wheat crop is harvested. Villagers, particularly in isolated areas, depend on kishk for nutritious winter breakfasts, and add it to soups for substance.

Basically kishk is burghul fermented with milk and yoghurt, a long process which takes 2 weeks altogether. After the fermentation process, the mixture is salted, spread on cloth and allowed to dry thoroughly, then rubbed to a fine powder.

Middle East food stores sell kishk – though it is expensive, a little goes a long way. It is also used in Iran.

Serves: 6
Cooking time: 20-25 minutes

250 g (8 oz) lean, ground lamb
1 tablespoon samneh (clarified butter) or oil
1 large onion, finely chopped
3 cloves garlic, finely chopped
1 cup kishk
4 cups cold water
salt
freshly ground black pepper

1. Put lamb, samneh or oil and onion in a heavy pan and stir over high heat until meat loses pink colour and is crumbly. Add garlic and cook until juices evaporate.
2. Stir in kishk and cook on medium heat for 3 minutes, stirring constantly. Remove pan from heat and add water gradually, stirring constantly. Taste and add salt if required, and pepper to taste.
3. Return to medium heat and stir constantly until thickened and bubbling. Consistency should be that of a thick cream soup; add a little more water if necessary.
4. Remove from heat and serve immediately in bowls.

Note: This soup can be served at any time. For breakfast in Lebanon and Syria, it is often prepared without the meat and garlic.

SHURABAT AL KIBBEH
KIBBI SOUP

Serves: 6
Cooking time: 1 hour

½ quantity Kibbeh mixture (page 205)
⅓ cup pine nuts
¼ cup samneh (clarified butter)
1 large onion, finely chopped
6-7 cups water
small piece cinnamon bark
salt
freshly ground black pepper
½ cup short grain rice, washed
¼ cup chopped parsley for serving

1. Make kibbeh as directed and shape into balls the size of a walnut. Make a hole in each ball, insert ½ teaspoon pine nuts and re-form into balls.
2. Heat samneh in a large frying pan and brown kibbeh balls, shaking pan so that they keep the round shape and brown evenly. Remove to a plate, leaving samneh in frying pan.
3. Add onion to pan and fry gently, stirring often, until soft. Add 1 cup water and bring to the boil, stirring to lift browned juices.
4. Tip pan contents into a deep pot and add remaining water, cinnamon, salt and pepper to taste and rice. Bring to the boil, stirring occasionally, then simmer, covered, for 10 minutes.
5. Add kibbi balls, cover and simmer for further 20 minutes. Ladle into bowls, sprinkle with chopped parsley, and serve with warm khoubiz (flat bread).

LABAN BIL BAYD
EGGS IN YOGHURT GARLIC SAUCE

Serves: 6
Oven temperature: 200°C (400°F)
Cooking time: 20-25 minutes

1 quantity Laban Mutboukh (page 182)
2 cloves garlic
salt
2 teaspoons dried mint
¼ cup samneh (clarified butter)
freshly ground white pepper
6 eggs

1. Make laban mutboukh as directed and leave to simmer gently, uncovered.
2. Crush garlic with ½ teaspoon salt and blend in mint crumbled to a coarse powder.
3. Heat samneh in a small frying pan and add garlic mixture. Fry for 5 minutes, stirring often.
4. Pour hot laban mutboukh in a shallow ovenproof dish. Break the eggs on top, spacing them evenly. Pour garlic-samneh mixture over the eggs and bake in a hot oven for 15-20 minutes until eggs are set hard. Serve hot.

Note: For an interesting first course, put yoghurt mixture in 6 individual dishes, break an egg into each dish and top with garlic samneh mixture. Bake as above.

'IGGIT AN NUKHAAT
BRAIN OMELET

Serves: 4-5

4 sets lamb brains
water
salt
1 clove garlic
juice of 1 lemon
¼ cup samneh (clarified butter)
1 medium-sized onion, finely chopped
6 eggs
⅓ cup chopped parsley
freshly ground black pepper

1. Cover brains with cold, salted water and leave to soak for 20 minutes. Drain and remove skin if possible (not possible if brains were frozen) and remove any dark veins.
2. Place in a pan with water to cover, salt to taste, whole garlic clove and lemon juice. Bring to a slow simmer, uncovered, and simmer for 15 minutes until tender.
3. Drain the brains and cut into tiny pieces.
4. Heat samneh in a frying pan and fry onion until transparent. Remove onion to a bowl, and drain samneh back into pan. Cool onion.
5. Break eggs into bowl with onion and beat lightly with a fork. Add parsley, brains and salt and pepper to taste. Stir to blend.
6. Reheat frying pan on medium heat and pour in egg mixture. Cover pan with lid and cook on low heat for 10-15 minutes until set and puffed. Serve hot, cut in wedges.

KIBBIT BATATA BI SANIEH (Potato Kibbi) recipe page 197;
LUBYI BI ZAYT (Green Beans in Oil) recipe page 197.

KOUSA MIHSHI BI LABAN
STUFFED ZUCCHINI WITH YOGHURT

Serves: 6-8 as an appetizer, 4-5 as a main course
Cooking time: 1¼ hours

1 kg (2 lb) even-sized zucchini (courgettes)
cold salted water

Meat Stuffing:
1 medium-sized onion, finely chopped
1 tablespoon samneh (clarified butter) or oil
1 tablespoon snoober (pine nuts), optional
250 g (8 oz) ground lamb or beef
¼ cup short grain rice
1 tablespoon chopped parsley
½ teaspoon ground allspice
salt
freshly ground black pepper

To finish:
1¼ cups cold water
1 quantity Laban Mutboukh (page 182)
2 cloves garlic, crushed
1 teaspoon dried mint

1. Choose either medium-sized or small zucchini, as long as they are all about the same size. Wash well and cut off stem end. Using an apple corer, hollow out zucchini, leaving rounded end intact. Try not to puncture skin. Soak in salt water for 10 minutes, then drain.
2. Gently fry onion in samneh until transparent. If using pine nuts add to pan after 10 minutes, and cook with onions for at least another 5 minutes, stirring occasionally.
3. Add pan contents to ground meat with rice, parsley, spice, about a teaspoon of salt, a good grinding of pepper and ¼ cup water. Combine ingredients thoroughly.
4. Fill zucchini with stuffing. Though rice expands during cooking, the meat shrinks, so there is no need to allow room for expansion.
5. Arrange zucchini in layers in a heavy-based pan, sprinkling layers lightly with salt. Add water, invert a plate on top of the zucchini and bring to a slow simmer. Cover and simmer gently for 1 hour or until tender.
6. Meanwhile prepare Laban Mutboukh (cooked yoghurt) as directed. When it begins to boil, add garlic, boil 2 minutes, then remove from heat.
7. When zucchinis are cooked remove plate and pour Laban Mutboukh over them and leave over medium heat for 10 minutes to boil gently. Cook uncovered until sauce is thick.
8. Crush the dried mint to a coarse powder and sprinkle on top. Cover pan and leave off the heat for 10 minutes before serving. For a main course, serve with mashed potatoes or steamed rice.

Note: Middle Eastern food suppliers usually stock a special corer for preparing vegetables for stuffing. It is not as wide as an apple corer, and much longer.

KOUSA MIHSHI BI BANDOURA
STUFFED ZUCCHINI WITH TOMATO SAUCE

Prepare stuffed zucchini as for Kousa Mihshi bi Laban to Step 4. Keep aside.

In a frying pan gently fry one large chopped onion in ¼ cup samneh (clarified butter) or oil. When transparent, add 2 finely chopped garlic cloves, cook for a few seconds and add 1 cup chopped peeled tomatoes, ¼ cup tomato paste, 1 cup water, ⅛ teaspoon cinnamon, and salt and pepper to taste.

Bring to the boil. Pour ¼ of the sauce into a heavy pan and arrange filled zucchini in layers in pan, spooning sauce over each layer. Cover and simmer gently for 1¼ hours. Serve hot or warm with the sauce.

KARNABIT BI TAHINI
CAULIFLOWER WITH TAHINI SAUCE

Serves: 6
Cooking time: 10-12 minutes

1 medium sized head cauliflower
water
salt
1 cup Tahini bi Taratour (page 182)

1. Break cauliflower into florets and place in a bowl with cold water and salt. Leave for 15 minutes so that any insects trapped in can be removed. Drain.
2. Cook cauliflower rapidly in boiling, salted water, uncovered, for 10-12 minutes until just tender and still a little crisp. Drain in a colander.
3. Put cauliflower in a bowl and spoon half the tahina sauce evenly over it. Serve hot or cold with remaining sauce in a bowl for adding to individual taste.

LUBYI BI ZAYT
GREEN BEANS IN OIL

Serves: 6
Cooking time: 45 minutes

500g (1 lb) green beans
¼ cup olive oil
1 medium-sized onion, chopped
2 cloves garlic, chopped
1 cup chopped, peeled tomatoes
1 tablespoon tomato paste
½ cup water
salt
freshly ground black pepper
½ teaspoon sugar
2 tablespoons chopped parsley

1. Wash beans well. Top and tail and remove strings if present. Cut into 5 cm (2 inch) lengths, or slit them lengthwise (French cut).
2. Heat olive oil in a pan and add onion. Fry gently until transparent, add garlic and cook a few seconds longer.
3. Add tomatoes, tomato paste, water, sugar and salt and pepper to taste. Cover and simmer for 15 minutes.
4. Add prepared beans and parsley, cover and simmer for further 15-20 minutes until beans are tender. Serve hot or lukewarm in the traditional way. Very good served chilled.

KIBBIT BATATA BI SANIEH
POTATO KIBBI

Serves: 6-8
Cooking time: 1¼ hours

6 medium-sized potatoes, about 750 g (1½ lb)
water
1½ cups fine burghul
1 medium-sized onion, grated
½ cup finely chopped parsley
1 teaspoon dried mint
½ teaspoon ground cinnamon
2-3 teaspoons salt
freshly ground black pepper
½ cup plain flour, optional

To finish:
1 large onion, halved then sliced
¾ cup olive oil

1. Scrub and cook potatoes in boiling, salted water until tender. Peel and mash.
2. Place burghul in a fine sieve and rinse with cold water. Press with back of spoon to extract moisture, then turn into a large bowl and leave for 15 minutes.
3. Add potatoes, grated onion, parsley, mint, cinnamon, 2 teaspoons salt and plenty of pepper. Mix, taste and add more salt if necessary.
4. Knead well with hand, moistening it occasionally with water. If mixture is too soft add enough flour to make a firm paste, kneading well.
5. Put sliced onion and half the oil in a 25 x 30 cm (10 x 12 inch) baking dish or 30 cm (12 inch) round dish. Dot potato paste over onions, then spread evenly with a spatula. Cut into diamond shapes using an oiled knife.
6. Pour remaining oil evenly on top and bake in a hot oven for 40 minutes or until golden brown. Cool in dish, then serve at room temperature with salad. Good served hot, in which case cool for 10 minutes before serving.

BAMYI BI ZAYT
OKRA IN OIL

Substitute 500 g (1 lb) okra for beans in Lubyi bi Zayt recipe (page 197) and prepare as directed on page 9.

Heat oil in pan and fry okra quickly, stirring carefully so as not to break them. Remove to a plate with a slotted spoon and keep aside.

Make tomato and onion sauce as directed (Steps 2 and 3) and simmer for 15 minutes. Add okra and ¼ cup chopped fresh coriander leaves instead of the parsley. Cover and simmer for 20 minutes or until tender. Pour ¼ cup lemon juice over okra, cover and cook for further 5 minutes. Serve hot or lukewarm.

Note: Canned or frozen okra may be used instead of fresh okra. Do not fry in oil.

FATTOUSH
TOASTED BREAD SALAD

Serves: 6

1 Khoubiz (flat bread, page 190)
6 leaves cos (romaine) lettuce or 4 leaves other
   lettuce, crisped
1 slender green cucumber
2 medium-sized tomatoes
½ cup chopped spring onion
½ cup chopped parsley
¼ cup chopped fresh mint
1 cup chopped sweet green pepper
1 cup ba'le (chickweed or purslane), optional

Salad Dressing:
1 clove garlic
1 teaspoon salt
½ cup lemon juice
½ cup olive oil
freshly ground black pepper

1. Toast khoubiz under a hot grill until golden brown. Break into small pieces, or cut into small squares using kitchen scissors. Keep aside.
2. Shred lettuce or break into small pieces. Peel cucumber, quarter lengthwise and cut into chunks. Cut tomatoes into small cubes. Prepare other salad vegetable ingredients. When picking the ba'le, select leaves near the top of the stalks and the young leafy ends.
3. Crush garlic in a bowl with the salt and mix to a paste, stir in remaining dressing ingredients, then beat thoroughly with a fork.
4. Combine bread and prepared vegetable ingredients and herbs in a salad bowl, pour on dressing, toss well and serve.

BATATA MTABBLI
POTATO SALAD

Serves: 6

8 medium-sized potatoes
salted water
1 medium-sized onion, finely chopped
½ cup finely chopped parsley
½ teaspoon dried mint
salt
freshly ground black pepper
1 quantity Salad Dressing (see Fattoush,
   above)

1. Scrub potatoes and boil in their jackets in salted water. Peel, and when cool cut into 2 cm (¾ inch) cubes.
2. Place potatoes in a bowl with onion, parsley, mint rubbed to a powder and salt and pepper to taste.
3. Make salad dressing as directed in Step 3 of Fattoush recipe and pour over potatoes. Toss and serve at room temperature.

MIHSHI MALFUF BI ZAYT
MEATLESS CABBAGE ROLLS

Serves: 6
Cooking time: 1 hour

Rice and Chick Pea Stuffing:
1½ cups chopped spring onions
¼ cup olive oil
1 cup long grain rice
1 cup drained, canned chick peas
½ cup finely chopped parsley
1 cup chopped, peeled tomatoes
½ teaspoon ground allspice
salt
freshly ground black pepper

To finish:
24 cabbage leaves
water
3 cloves garlic
1 teaspoon salt
1 teaspoon dried mint
¼ cup lemon juice
½ cup olive oil

1. Gently fry spring onion in ¼ cup olive oil for 2-3 minutes. Turn into a bowl and add remaining stuffing ingredients, adding salt and pepper to taste.
2. Remove leaves from cabbage carefully so as not to tear them, counting larger leaves as 2. Par-boil cabbage leaves in boiling water until limp enough to handle, cooking leaves in 2 or 3 lots. Drain in a colander.
3. Cut out larger part of centre rib in each leaf and cut larger leaves in half down centre. Line the base of a deep pan with ribs and any torn leaves.
4. Place a generous tablespoon stuffing on base of each leaf, roll up once and tuck in sides to contain filling. Roll to end of leaf. Repeat with remaining ingredients.
5. Crush garlic with salt and blend in crumbled, crushed mint and lemon juice.
6. Pack rolls flap side down in lined pan, sprinkling some of the garlic-lemon mixture and olive oil between the layers of rolls. Invert a plate on top of the rolls to keep them intact during cooking. Add enough cold water to just cover rolls and put lid on firmly.
7. Bring to the boil on medium heat, reduce to low and simmer gently for 45 minutes. Remove from heat and leave aside for 30 minutes. Serve lukewarm or cold.

WARAK MIHSHI BI SILQ
STUFFED SILVERBEET LEAVES

Follow Mihshi Malfuf bi Zayt recipe and make rice and chick pea stuffing, substituting 1½ cups cooked brown lentils for the chick peas.

Instead of the cabbage leaves, use silverbeet (Swiss chard) leaves halved lengthwise and cut into 10 cm (4 inch) squares. You will require about 50 squares.

Dip briefly in boiling water, or just run hot tap water over leaves to soften enough for handling. Drain and place squares shiny side down on work surface. Put 1 scant tablespoon stuffing on each square and roll up into a small, neat roll. Finish as for Mihshi Malfuf bi Zayt, omitting mint and adding ½ cup lemon juice instead of ¼ cup.

SAMKE BI TARATOUR
FISH WITH TAHINI SAUCE

Serves: 6-8
Oven temperature: 180°C (350°F)
Cooking time: 30 minutes

1 snapper or other baking fish,
    about 2 kg (4 1b)
juice of ½ lemon
salt
¼ cup olive oil
double quantity Taratour bi Tahini (page 182)

To garnish:
pomegranate seeds, pine nuts fried in oil till golden, thinly peeled cucumber skin, lemon wedges or slices, olives, parsley sprigs, ¼ cup finely chopped parsley

1. Clean and scale fish if necessary. Leave head on but remove eyes. Rinse and wipe dry with paper towels. Slash skin on body of fish in 3 places on each side.
2. Rub fish inside and out with lemon juice and salt, cover and refrigerate for 1 hour.
3. Oil a large baking dish. Put fish in it and pour remaining oil over top. Bake in a moderate oven for 30 minutes or until fish is cooked when tested at thickest part. Baste occasionally with pan juices during baking and do not overcook.
4. Carefully lift fish onto platter, cover with food wrap and chill. Alternatively cool a little, cut off head and tail neatly and put aside. Remove side fins and lift flesh from body in 2 sections from each side. Take off skin and remove any bones. Discard backbone and fins. Rearrange fish in original shape on clean platter, cover and chill.
5. Make Taratour bi Tahini as directed, using enough water to give a thick sauce. Spread half the sauce over the fish, leaving head and tail uncovered. Smooth with a small spatula and decorate as desired with whatever garnish ingredients listed are available or appeal. Cucumber skin can be used to simulate fins by making fringe-like cuts along the length of the strips. Use an olive or parsley sprig for eye. Cover and chill until serving time.
6. Garnish platter with lemon slices or wedges and parsley sprigs. Stir most of chopped parsley into remaining sauce, place in a bowl and sprinkle with chopped parsley. Serve Samke bi Taratour as part of a buffet spread or as a first course.

KIBBEH SAMAK
FISH KIBBI

Serves: 6
Oven temperature: 200°C (400°F)
Cooking time: 45-50 minutes

Fish Kibbeh:
3 cups fine burghul
1 kg (2 lb) white fish fillets
1 large onion
¼ cup finely chopped coriander leaves
¼ cup finely chopped parsley
grated rind of 1 orange
3 teaspoons salt
freshly ground black pepper

Filling:
¼ cup olive or other oil
⅓ cup pine nuts
2 large onions, halved and sliced

To finish:
½ cup olive or other oil

1. Put burghul in a fine sieve and rinse under running water. Press out moisture with back of a spoon. Put aside.
2. Remove skin from fish and any bones present. Chop roughly.
3. Put fish and onion through food grinder using fine screen, or process in food processor.
4. Combine fish and onion with burghul, coriander, parsley, orange rind, salt and pepper to taste. Knead to a firm paste consistency. Mixture may be processed in food processor in 4 lots.
5. In a frying pan heat the ¼ cup oil and brown pine nuts. Remove with a slotted spoon and add onion to pan. Fry gently until transparent. Return pine nuts to pan and remove from heat.
6. Grease a 25 x 30 cm (10 x 12 inch) baking dish with oil and add half the fish kibbi. Spread evenly and top with onion and pine nut mixture.
7. Dot remaining kibbi over filling, then spread evenly with a spatula. This keeps filling in place.
8. Cut through in diamond shapes with a sharp knife. Pour remaining oil over kibbi and bake in a hot oven for 30-35 minutes until golden brown. Serve hot or cold.

SAMKE HARRAH AL-SAHARA
BAKED FISH WITH HOT CHILI SAUCE

Many versions of this famous Lebanese fish dish exist. Even pronunciations and the resultant transliteration vary considerably. The regional Arabic for fish is samke *(singular) and* samek *(plural), the 'a' pronounced as the 'u' in up, and the 'e' as in end. Thus spellings vary from samke, sumke, sumki to samek, samak and sumak.*

This delicious version was graciously provided by Mrs Landy Jammal and Mr Jimmy Antoon of the popular Al-Sahara Lebanese restaurant in Chatswood, a Sydney suburb, so I have just as graciously used their translation.

Serves: 4
Oven temperature: 180°C (350°F)
Cooking time: 40-45 minutes

1 snapper or other baking fish,
    about 2 kg (4 lb)
salt
½ cup olive oil for frying
4-6 cloves garlic
salt
¼ cup finely chopped coriander leaves
1 cup tahini
½ cup cold water
½ cup lemon juice
¼-½ teaspoon hot chili pepper
1 tablespoon snoober (pine nuts)
lemon wedges and coriander sprigs to
    garnish

1. Clean and scale fish, wipe dry with paper towels. Leave heads on but remove eyes. Slash body in 2 places on each side. Sprinkle inside and out with salt, cover and refrigerate for 1-2 hours. Pat dry before cooking.
2. Heat all but 1 tablespoon oil in a large frying pan and fry fish on high heat for a few minutes each side. Do not cook through. Lift out of pan with a fish slice and place in baking dish.
3. Pound garlic cloves with 1 teaspoon salt, and mix in coriander. Tip most of oil out of frying pan, leaving about 2 tablespoons, heat and add garlic mixture. Fry quickly until mixture is crisp without being burnt. Cool.
4. Place tahini in a bowl, beat well, then gradually add water, beating constantly. Mixture will thicken. Then beat in lemon juice gradually and stir in garlic mixture and chili pepper to taste. Add more salt if necessary.
5. Pour sauce over fish in baking dish, covering it completely. Bake in a moderate oven for 30-35 minutes or until fish is cooked through and sauce is bubbling.
6. While fish cooks, heat reserved tablespoon of oil in a clean pan and fry pine nuts until golden brown.
7. Lift cooked fish onto platter and spoon sauce on top. Sprinkle with pine nuts and garnish platter with lemon wedges and coriander sprigs. Serve hot.

MOUSAKHAN
CHICKEN ROASTED WITH BREAD

Mousakhan is a Palestinian speciality which calls for a very thin flat bread called Shirak. This bread requires considerable expertise in making the dough paper thin, and also should be baked on a large metal dome (sorj) over a charcoal fire, so I have given a substitute bread as Mousakhan is well worth trying.

Serves: 8
Oven temperature: 180°C (350°F)
Cooking time: 1¾-2 hours

2 chickens, each about 1 kg (2 1b)
salt
freshly ground black pepper
⅓ cup olive oil
3 medium-sized onions, sliced
3 teaspoons sumak
2 Khoubiz (page 190)

1. Wipe chickens dry with paper towels. Rub inside and out with salt and pepper. Tie the legs together and tuck wings under body.
2. Heat half the oil in a large pan and fry the chickens over medium heat until lightly browned, turning them often. Remove to a plate and keep aside.
3. Add remaining oil to pan with sliced onion and fry gently, stirring often, until transparent. Sprinkle in sumak and cook for further 2 minutes. Remove from heat.
4. Split each khoubiz into two, to give four flat pieces of bread. Place two pieces slightly overlapping in the base of a baking dish.
5. Place a mound of onion in the centre of each, using about ¼ of the onion mixture. Put a chicken on top of each mound, and spread remaining onion mixture over the top of each chicken. Pour oil from pan over chicken and bread.
6. Cover chickens with remaining rounds of bread, with white surface of bread downwards. Sprinkle bread lightly with water.
7. Bake in a moderate oven for 1½ hours or until chickens are tender and cooked thoroughly. If bread begins to burn, cover top with a piece of aluminium foil. The bread covering keeps the chickens moist, while the bread in the base of the dish absorbs the flavoursome juices.
8. Serve cut into portions with a piece of the bread for each serving.

MIHSHI MALFUF
CABBAGE ROLLS

Serves: 6
Cooking time: 1¼ hours

1 large head cabbage
boiling salted water

Stuffing:
1 medium-sized onion, finely chopped
2 tablespoons samneh (clarified butter) or oil
750 g (1½lb) finely chopped or coarsely
   ground lamb shoulder
1 cup short grain rice, washed and drained
½ teaspoon ground allspice
salt
freshly ground black pepper
¼ cup water

To finish:
4 cloves garlic, chopped
salt
¼ cup lemon juice or 3 teaspoons debis roman
   (pomegranate molasses)
1 teaspoon dried mint
water

1. Core cabbage and remove leaves carefully. Heart may be reserved for making salad. Boil leaves in salted water, a few at a time, until limp. Drain in a colander.
2. Cut larger leaves in half, removing rib. Cut thicker part of rib from smaller leaves. Line a deep pan with ribs and any torn leaves.
3. Gently fry onion in samneh or oil until soft and add to the finely chopped or ground lamb with remaining stuffing ingredients. Combine thoroughly.
4. Place a tablespoon of filling on bottom edge of leaf and roll, tucking in sides to contain filling. Press with hand into a neat sausage shape.
5. Pack finished rolls flap side down in lined pan. Place close together in layers, sprinkling each layer with a little garlic, salt and lemon juice. If using debis roman in place of lemon juice, blend into ¼ cup water and sprinkle onto rolls.
6. Crush remaining garlic and mix with coarsely powdered mint. Sprinkle over final layer of rolls and add enough water to pan to just cover rolls.
7. Invert a heavy plate on top of rolls, cover pan and bring to a simmer. Simmer on low heat for 1 hour. Serve hot or warm.

Note: Lean lamb bones may be used to line the base of the pan instead of the cabbage trimmings. Another alternative is to use lamb stock instead of water.

MIHSHI MALFUF (Cabbage Rolls) *recipe above;*
BATATA MTABBLI (Potato Salad) *recipe page 198.*

KIBBEH

The preparation of kibbeh, virtually the national dish of both Lebanon and Syria, is an exercise in patience and stamina. Or rather this *was* the case, and still is for the purists of Middle Eastern cookery. Modern appliances can replace the traditional *madaqqa* and *jorn* (pestle and mortar) for the tedious preparation — the kibbeh will be just as good and the cook far less exhausted.

The basic essentials of kibbeh making are to have the right meat and to keep the mixture cool. Ideally hogget (yearling mutton) should be used; if you cannot obtain this in your area, lamb may be used provided it is not too young. Look for lamb with a deep pinky red colour and a good fat cover. Very young lamb is a definite pink in colour, very lean and velvety in texture, and may be used for the making of Kibbeh Nayye only. Beef topside (US bottom round) may be used as a last resort, providing it is prime quality. Whatever the meat, it must be trimmed of all fat and gristle before preparation, so allow for this trimming when making your purchase.

In cities with large Lebanese and Syrian communities it is sometimes possible to find a butcher who specializes in providing ready ground kibbeh meat. A Lebanese or Syrian acquaintance might know of one.

Use the fine burghul for kibbeh. With modern processing this usually does not require rinsing, but a little soaking helps to soften it and retain some moisture for a lighter, more tender finished dish.

KIBBEH BIL SANIEH
BAKED STUFFED KIBBI IN A TRAY

Serves: 6-10
Oven temperature: 180°C (350°F)
Cooking time: 45 minutes

2 medium-sized onions, finely chopped
¼ cup samneh (clarified butter)
¼ cup snoober (pine nuts)
250 g (8 oz) coarsely ground lamb or veal
salt
freshly ground black pepper
¼ teaspoon ground cinnamon
1 quantity Kibbeh (page 205)
additional pine nuts to garnish, optional
¾ cup melted samneh (ghee) or olive oil
cold water

1. Gently fry onion in samneh until transparent. Add pine nuts and fry until nuts are lightly browned.
2. Increase heat and add meat. Stir and cook until juices evaporate and meat begins to brown. Remove from heat, add salt and pepper to taste and cinnamon.
3. Make kibbeh mixture according to directions — no need to chill unless making ahead of time required.
4. Brush a 28 x 33 cm (11 x 13 inch) baking dish or a 35 cm (14 inch) round dish with samneh or oil. Press a little less than half the kibbeh mixture onto the base, smoothing it with wet hand.
5. Top with ground meat and nut mixture, spreading it evenly. Dot the top with mounds of remaining kibbeh mixture, then carefully press it out evenly so that the filling stays in place. Smooth top.
6. Run a knife blade around edge of dish, then score deeply into diamond shapes. Press a pine nut into centre of each diamond if desired. Pour melted samneh or oil mixed with 2 tablespoons cold water over top, making sure some runs down between sides of dish and kibbeh.
7. Bake in a preheated moderate oven for 30 minutes. To brown top, sprinkle lightly with water 3 or 4 times during cooking. Cut through scored sections and serve hot or cold with yoghurt, salads and Khoubiz.

Note: Use the oil if planning to serve cold. Kibbeh bil Sanieh may also be cooked without the filling. Spread evenly in dish, score as required and pour on melted samneh or oil. Bake as above.

KIBBEH
GROUND LAMB AND BURGHUL

3 cups burghul
1 kg (2 1b) lean lamb or hogget (yearling
   mutton) from leg
1 large onion
3 teaspoons salt
1 teaspoon freshly ground black pepper
1 teaspoon ground allspice
iced water or ice chips (about ½ cup)

Food grinder method:
1. Place burghul in a bowl, cover with cold water and leave to soak for 10 minutes. Drain in a sieve and press with back of spoon to remove as much moisture as possible. Tip into a flat dish, spread out and chill in refrigerator for 1-2 hours. This also dries it further.
2. Trim all fat and fine skin from meat and cut into cubes. Chill for 1 hour if not very cold.
3. Pass meat through grinder twice, using fine screen. Grind onion twice and combine with meat, burghul, salt, pepper and allspice.
4. Pass through grinder twice, adding a little iced water or ice chips if mixture feels warm.
5. Knead to a smooth, light paste with hands, adding iced water or ice chips when necessary. Cover and chill until required.

Food processor method:
Prepare burghul and meat as above, Steps 1 and 2. Using steel cutting blade, process a quarter of the meat cubes at a time until paste-like in consistency. Transfer to a large bowl. Process onion to a thick liquid and add to meat. Combine meat with onion, seasoning, spices and burghul. Process again in 6 lots, adding a tablespoon of iced water or ice chips to each lot. Combine again in a bowl and give a final knead by hand. Cover and chill until required.

KIBBEH MISHWEY OR KIBBEYET
STUFFED KIBBI BALLS

Use the same ingredients as for Kibbeh bil Sanieh, replacing ¾ cup samneh or olive oil with sufficient oil for deep frying.

1. Take lumps of kibbeh the size of a small egg and shape into balls.
2. Dip hands in cold water, roll ball of kibbeh in palms until smooth, then make a hole in the ball with your forefinger. Work finger round in hole until you have a shell of even thickness. Fill hole with filling mixture and close opening. Moisten with cold water to seal well. If any breaks appear in shell, close with wet fingers.
3. Complete the shape to resemble either a torpedo, pointed at each end, or a spinning top, rounded at one end, pointed at the other. Place finished kibbi shells on a tray.
4. Heat oil and deep fry a few at a time until a deep brown without being burnt. Turn to brown evenly. Lift out with slotted spoon and drain on paper towels. Keep warm in low oven until remainder are cooked. Alternatively place shaped kibbi side by side in a large greased baking dish, brush well with melted samneh or oil and bake in a moderate oven, 180°C (350°F) for 20-25 minutes.
5. Serve hot or cold with salads, yoghurt and Khoubiz.

Note: Torpedo shaped Kibbeyet are usually fried in oil. The spinning top shaped ones can be cooked over glowing charcoal or oven baked.

LAHM BI'AJEEN
LAMB FILLED PASTRY ROLLS

These delicate pastries often appear on restaurant menus as Ladies' Fingers. Sometimes they are called Sambusik bi Lahm, but any combination of lamb and pastry or dough is usually called Lahm bi' Ajeen or similar, literally meaning 'meat with dough'. As there is another recipe by this name in this chapter, I am depending on the translation to indicate the difference.

Makes about 60
Oven temperature: 200°C (400°F)
Cooking time: 40 minutes

Lamb Filling:
½ cup snoober (pine nuts)
2 tablespoons samneh (clarified butter)
500 g (1 lb) finely ground lean lamb
1 large onion, finely chopped
¼ teaspoon ground cinnamon
salt
freshly ground black pepper
¼ cup finely chopped parsley
1 tablespoon finely chopped fresh mint

To finish:
15 sheets fillo pastry
½-¾ cup melted samneh

1. In a frying pan heat ghee and fry pine nuts until golden. Remove to a plate with a slotted spoon.
2. Add lamb to pan and stir over medium high heat until colour changes and lamb is crumbly. Add onion and continue to fry until onion is transparent.
3. Reduce heat and add cinnamon and salt and pepper to taste. Cover and simmer for 15 minutes until juices evaporate. Stir occasionally. When cooked, stir in parsley and mint and remove from heat. Leave covered until cool. Add pine nuts.
4. Take a sheet of fillo pastry and brush lightly with samneh. Fold in half to give almost a square shape. Brush again with samneh and place about 2 tablespoons of filling towards edge of longer end of pastry. Fold pastry over filling, fold in sides to contain filling and roll up firmly so that finished pastry looks like a long cigar about the thickness of a finger. Repeat with remaining ingredients, keeping finished pastries covered.
5. Lightly grease baking sheets with samneh and place rolls on sheets. Brush rolls lightly with samneh.
6. With a sharp knife make shallow slits on top of each roll about 8-10 cm (3-4 inches) apart so that rolls are evenly marked. This helps when cutting the finished rolls into finger lengths as fillo pastry shatters easily when cooked.
7. Bake rolls in a moderately hot oven for 12-15 minutes until golden brown. Cut into finger lengths and serve hot, piled on platters.

Note: Alternatively small rolls may be made. Shape as directed on page 17, using pastry strips 12 cm (5 inches) wide.

FATAYER
TRIANGLE LAMB PIES

Makes about 30
Oven temperature: 200°C (400°F)
Cooking time: 40 minutes

½ quantity Khoubiz dough (page 190)
Lamb Filling (see Sfiha, page 210)
oil for brushing

For serving:
lemon wedges or laban (yoghurt)

1. Make khoubiz dough as directed, cover and leave to rise. (If making only half quantity, use full amount of yeast given in recipe.)
2. Prepare lamb filling according to directions, making filling a little drier than for Sfiha.
3. Punch down dough and turn onto a lightly floured board. Roll out until 5 mm (¼ inch) thick and cut into 10 cm (4 inch) rounds. Alternatively roll dough into balls the size of an egg and flatten out with hand or rolling pin.
4. Place a tablespoon of lamb filling in centre, moisten edge of dough with a little water and bring up sides at three points to form a triangular shape. Press edges firmly to seal, leaving the top of the pie open a little to show filling.
5. Place pies on oiled baking sheets and brush with oil. Bake in a moderately hot oven for 15 minutes until golden and cooked. For a golden brown top, place under a hot grill for a few seconds.
6. Serve hot or warm with lemon wedges so that juice may be squeezed into centre of pie. Alternatively serve with a bowl of yoghurt on the side.

FATAYER (Triangle Lamb Pies) *recipe above;*
SFIHA, LAHM BI'AJEEN (Flat Lamb Pies) *recipe page 210.*

KIBBEH NAYYE
RAW KIBBI

Serves: 10-12 as an appetizer or first course

1 quantity Kibbeh (page 205)
¼ cup olive oil
1 cup sliced spring onions, including green
   tops
2 cos (romaine) lettuce
lemon wedges
4-6 khoubiz cut into quarters

1. Make kibbeh according to directions using 2 cups burghul instead of 3.
2. After final kneading, place on a large oval platter and spread it out flat. Round the edges and smooth the top, using hand dipped in iced water. Make a depression in the centre with thumb and with the side of forefinger make 2 grooves along and across kibbeh to the edges. Alternatively shape on individual dishes.
3. Place kibbeh uncovered in refrigerator and chill for about an hour, or until colour of kibbeh changes to a pleasant red. The cold plus the oxygen brings up the colour. If not serving immediately, cover with plastic food wrap. Do not stack if individual plates are used, otherwise colour will change.
4. To serve, drizzle olive oil in centre depression and along grooves. Garnish with a ring of sliced spring onions around edge. Place washed and crisped lettuce leaves in a bowl, lemon wedges in another bowl, and khoubiz (flat bread) in a basket. The kibbeh is scooped up with either lettuce leaves or bread, and lemon juice squeezed on if desired.

Note: Kibbeh Nayye should be eaten the day it is made. Any left over should be used for a cooked kibbeh dish.

SHEIKH AL MIHSHI
STUFFED EGGPLANT

Serves: 6
Oven temperature: 190°C (375°F)
Cooking time: 1 hour

12 small long eggplants or 6 medium-sized
   oval eggplants
¼ cup samneh (clarified butter) or oil

Meat Filling:
500 g (1 lb) finely ground lamb or beef
2 tablespoons oil
1 large onion, finely chopped
1 clove garlic, finely chopped
¼ cup pine nuts
¼ teaspoon ground cinnamon
¼ teaspoon ground allspice
¼ cup finely chopped parsley
salt
freshly ground black pepper

To finish:
1 cup tomato purée
salt and pepper
water, optional

1. Remove stalk from eggplants and remove peel in 1 cm (½ inch) intervals to give a striped effect.
2. Heat oil in a pan and fry eggplants, browning lightly on all sides. Remove to a plate.
3. Add ground meat, oil, onion and garlic to pan and fry, stirring often, until juices evaporate. Add pine nuts, spices, parsley, and salt and pepper to taste. Remove from heat.
4. Cut a deep slit along one side of each eggplant and fill with meat mixture.
5. Arrange in baking dish and pour tomato purée on top. Season with salt and pepper and bake in a moderately hot oven for 30 minutes, adding water to dish during cooking if necessary, and basting eggplants occasionally.

MANSAAF
SPICED LAMB IN YOGHURT

Apparently it is a popular misconception to regard Mansaaf as a Jordanian feast. I have been assured by Jordanian friends that Mansaaf is actually a dish served at feasts. The Palestinians also prepare this, calling it Mansi.

As a favour to my friends, I shall now set the record straight, and give you the recipe. Of course in Jordan they would probably use a whole lamb, though it is scaled down for normal meals.

Serves: 6
Cooking time: 2 hours

1.5 kg (3 1b) lamb shoulder on the bone
water
salt
freshly ground black pepper
¼ cup samneh (clarified butter) or ghee
¼ cup snoober (pine nuts)
1 large onion, chopped
1½ teaspoons turmeric
½ teaspoon ground allspice
1 small piece cinnamon bark
1 quantity Laban Mutboukh (page 182)

1. Have meat retailer cut shoulder into 6 even-sized pieces. Alternatively ask for thickly cut lamb shoulder chops.
2. Place lamb in a pan and just cover with cold water. Bring slowly to the boil, skimming as required. When well skimmed and boiling, add salt and pepper to taste, cover and simmer gently for 30 minutes.
3. Heat samneh in a frying pan and add pine nuts. Fry until golden and remove pine nuts to a plate, draining samneh back into the pan.
4. Add onion to pan and fry gently until transparent. Stir in turmeric, allspice and cinnamon bark and cook for further 2 minutes. Add this mixture to the simmering lamb.
5. Meanwhile make Laban Mutboukh according to directions and keep aside.
6. After lamb has been cooking for 1 hour, remove lid and let liquid reduce until it half covers lamb.
7. When reduced, add Laban Mutboukh, shaking pan to blend it evenly with liquid. Let Mansaaf simmer gently on low heat until lamb is tender and sauce is thick. If sauce must be stirred, do so in the one direction. Adjust seasoning with salt and pepper and remove cinnamon.
8. Pile Mansaaf in serving platter and sprinkle with the browned pine nuts. Serve hot with Riz Mufalfal. To serve in the traditional manner, line serving platter with split khoubiz as a substitute for the paper-thin shirak bread of Jordan, pile on the rice and cover with the lamb and yoghurt mixture. Sprinkle with pine nuts.

KIBBEH BI LABAN
KIBBI BALLS IN YOGHURT

Serves: 6
Cooking time: 30-35 minutes

½ quantity Kibbeh Mishwey (page 205)
double quantity Laban Mutboukh (page 182)
½ cup water
1 clove garlic
salt
2 teaspoons dried mint
¼ cup samneh (clarified butter)
Riz Mufalfal for serving (page 192)

1. Make kibbi balls as directed, filling with the stuffing and shaping into torpedo shapes. Do not cook finished balls. Set aside.
2. Prepare laban mutboukh as directed, using 1 egg white only and adding water after it has simmered 3-5 minutes. Bring to the boil and simmer for further 5 minutes, uncovered.
3. Add prepared kibbeh balls and simmer on low heat, uncovered, while preparing garlic mint mixture.
4. Crush garlic with ½ teaspoon salt and blend in crushed mint. Heat samneh in a small pan, add garlic mixture and fry for 2-3 minutes.
5. Add to yoghurt and kibbi balls, stir gently in one direction and add more salt to taste. Leave to simmer gently, uncovered, for 15 minutes. Do not stir again.
6. At end of cooking yoghurt sauce should be thick; if not, leave to simmer for further 5 minutes. Serve hot with Riz Mufalfal.

SFIHA, LAHM BI'AJEEN
FLAT LAMB PIES

Sfiha is the Syrian equivalent of Lahm bi'Ajeen, a flat lamb pie popular throughout this region known as the Fertile Crescent (which also includes Iraq).

Khoubiz dough is used in Syria for Sfiha – the Lebanese cook often uses a pie crust pastry base for a more tender, crisp crust and a lot less fuss.

Makes about 30
Oven temperature: 200°C (400°F)
Cooking time: 40 minutes

½ quantity Khoubiz dough (page 190)

OR

Pastry:
4 cups plain flour
1 teaspoon salt
1 cup melted samneh (clarified butter) or
    other shortening
⅔ cup warm water

Lamb Filling:
1 tablespoon oil
500 g (1 lb) ground lamb
1 large onion, finely chopped
⅓ cup snoober (pine nuts)
¼ teaspoon ground cinnamon
¼ teaspoon ground allspice
salt
¼ teaspoon freshly ground black pepper
¼ teaspoon freshly ground white pepper
½ cup chopped, peeled tomatoes
3 teaspoons debis roman (pomegranate
    molasses) or lemon juice

To finish:
oil for brushing
pomegranate seeds, lemon wedges or yoghurt
    for serving

1. Make khoubiz dough, using full amount of yeast even if making ½ quantity and leave to rise. Alternatively make pastry — sift flour and salt into a bowl, add cool melted samneh and rub thoroughly and lightly into flour with fingertips. Sprinkle in most of water and mix to a pliable dough, adding more water if necessary. Knead lightly until smooth, wrap and leave to rest for 30 minutes.

2. Heat oil in a frying pan, add ground lamb and stir over medium high heat until colour changes and meat is crumbly. Add onion and cook for 10 minutes, stirring often, until onion is soft.

3. Add pine nuts, spices, salt to taste and pepper, fry 1 minute longer, then add tomatoes. Cover and cook on low heat until tomato softens — about 10 minutes.

4. Stir in debis roman or lemon juice. Remove from heat and cool. Mixture should be moist, but not liquid.

5. Punch down dough if used. Roll out dough or pastry on a lightly floured board until 5 mm (¼ inch) thick and cut into 10 cm (4 inch) rounds; roll out and shape trimmings also. Place rounds on a cloth, covering with another cloth. Alternatively take balls of dough the size of an egg and press each into a round with hand.

6. Take a round of dough and flute edge with finger tips. Spread a tablespoon of filling onto dough and place pies close together on oiled baking sheets. Brush meat and crust lightly with oil.

7. Bake pies in a moderately hot oven for 12-15 minutes. Serve hot or warm, sprinkling with a few fresh pomegranate seeds if available. Lemon wedges for squeezing onto pies, or yoghurt, may be served with them.

KIBBEH MISHWEY OR KIBBEYET (Stuffed Kibbi Balls) *recipe page 205.*

SHISHBARAK
LAMB PASTIES IN YOGHURT SAUCE

Serves: 6
Oven Temperature: 180°C (350°F)
Cooking time: 45 minutes

Pastry:
2 cups plain flour
½ teaspoon salt
¾ cup cold water
¼ cup melted samneh (clarified butter) for
   baking

Filling:
2 tablespoons samneh
¼ cup pine nuts
500 g (1 lb) finely ground lean lamb
1 large onion, finely chopped
¼ teaspoon ground allspice
pinch of ground cinnamon
salt
freshly ground black pepper

Yoghurt Sauce:
5 cups yoghurt
1½ cups water
1 tablespoon cornflour
1 egg white, lightly beaten
2 teaspoons salt

To finish:
2 cloves garlic
½ teaspoon salt
¼ cup samneh
1 tablespoon dried crushed mint
Riz Mufalfal for serving (page 192)

1. Sift flour and salt into a mixing bowl, add water and mix to a soft dough, adding a little more flour if necessary. Knead lightly until smooth, cover and rest dough for 30 minutes.
2. Meanwhile make filling. Heat half the samneh in a pan and fry pine nuts until golden brown. Lift out with a slotted spoon and keep aside.
3. Heat remaining samneh in pan and add meat. Stir over high heat to break up meat and fry until meat changes colour. Add onion and fry for further 10 minutes until onion is transparent. Stir in spices and salt and pepper to taste. Add pine nuts and leave to cool.
4. Roll out pastry on lightly floured board and cut into 5 cm (2 inch) rounds. Place a teaspoon of meat filling in centre and fold pastry over into a crescent. Press edges to seal and crimp with fingers or press with tines of fork. Wrap crescent around finger and press the two points together to give a hat shape. Place on baking sheets greased with some of the melted samneh. When pasties are filled and shaped brush with remaining samneh.
5. Bake pastries in a moderate oven for 10-15 minutes until lightly browned. Pastries do not have to be completely cooked.
6. Place yoghurt in a large heavy pan and stir until smooth. Blend cornflour into water and add to yoghurt with egg white and salt. Stir, then place pan over medium heat and stir constantly in one direction until thickened and bubbling.
7. Add pastries to bubbling yoghurt, stir gently, then cook uncovered over medium low heat for 10 minutes. Stir twice more during cooking.
8. Crush garlic with salt. Heat samneh in a small pan, add garlic and fry gently for a few seconds. Stir in mint and remove pan from heat.
9. Pour garlic mixture into Shishbarak, stir and cook for 2 to 3 minutes longer. Serve hot in deep plates with riz.

KASBI MISHWI BI TOUM
GRILLED LIVER WITH GARLIC

Serves: 4-6
Cooking time: 3-4 minutes

500 g (1 lb) lamb liver
cold salted water
3-4 cloves garlic
½ teaspoon dried mint
¼ cup olive oil
salt
freshly ground black pepper
lemon wedges for serving

1. Soak liver in cold, salted water for 20 minutes. Drain, remove skin from liver and cut into 1 cm (½ inch) slices. Cut slices into roughly 2 cm (¾ inch) squares. Dab liver with paper towels to dry.
2. Crush garlic and combine with finely crumbled mint. Spread each side of liver pieces with garlic paste and place in a dish. Sprinkle with olive oil and salt and pepper to taste. Cover and leave for 30 minutes.
3. Thread pieces of liver onto skewers, passing them through the sides of the squares so that liver is flat on the skewers.
4. Cook over glowing charcoal for 1-2 minutes each side, taking care not to overcook. Brush with oil from the dish during cooking.
5. Serve hot with lemon wedges so that juice may be squeezed on to individual taste. Serve as a *mezze* or main meal.

USHTA
CLOTTED CREAM

Where buffalo's milk is available in the Middle East you will find Ushta. The rich milk is boiled and left to stand until the cream forms solidly on top. It is so thick that it can be cut with a knife. The cream is enjoyed with certain pastries, used as a filling for 'Ataif as it does not melt on heating, or enjoyed on its own with sweet preserves or honey.

As the flavour of the genuine ushta is rather strong, it is an acquired taste. The version given uses dried cow's milk so the flavour, though different, would be more widely acceptable.

If you have access to rich milk fresh from the cow, it is possible to make clotted cream — in other words Devonshire cream is a good substitute where this is available.

Ushta (sometimes transliterated as kishta with a deep guttural sound for the 'k') is the Arabic name in the region covered in this chapter. In Turkey it is known as kaymak, and in Iraq, gaimer.

Makes about 1 cup

2 cups full cream powdered milk
2½ cups water

1. Thoroughly blend powdered milk with water, beating if necessary to break up lumps.
2. Pour into a 23 cm (9 inch) frying pan, preferably one with a thick base. A non-stick coating on the pan is an advantage as the milk does not scorch in such a utensil.
3. Place on medium low heat and bring slowly to a gentle simmer — do not boil.
4. When a skin forms on the top, pull this to one side of the pan with a large spoon. Lift out, pouring any liquid in spoon back into the pan. Place cream in a bowl.
5. Each 10 minutes or so for the next 2-2½ hours, remove the skin as it forms. At the end only a thin layer of thick milk remains in the pan. This may be discarded or used in cooking.
6. Place collected cream in blender or food processor and process until smooth. Pour back into bowl and chill thoroughly. Cream sets solidly and, if kept covered, will keep in the refrigerator for 1 week or more. Use as directed in recipes or with stewed fruits and desserts.

'ATAIF MIHSHI
STUFFED PANCAKES

Makes 16-18
Cooking time: 6 minutes

1 quantity 'Ataif batter (page 214)
1 cup cold 'Atar (pages 214, 216)
corn or peanut oil for deep frying

Nut Filling:
1½ cups finely chopped walnuts
¼ cup granulated sugar
1½ teaspoons ground cinnamon

OR

Cheese Filling:
1 cup Kareeshee (page 184), or Italian ricotta
   cheese

1. Make pancakes, cooking them on one side only. Cook until top loses all trace of whiteness — about 3 minutes. Stack on a plate.
2. Prepare selected filling. Combine nuts, sugar and cinnamon, or mash cheese with a fork to soften it.
3. Place 2 generous teaspoons filling in the centre of each pancake (on uncooked side). Fold over and pinch edges well together to seal.
4. Heat oil to 200°C (400°F) or when a cube of bread turns golden in 30 seconds. Fry stuffed pancakes 3 or 4 at a time, turning to brown evenly (about 2 to 3 minutes).
5. Lift out with slotted spoon and drain on paper towels. Dip while hot into 'atar (syrup) and pile onto a plate. Serve warm or cold.

Note: Ushta, a thick clotted cream (above) may be used as a filling. Do not use any other cream as a substitute as it will melt.

213

'ATAIF
PANCAKES

Makes: 16-18
Cooking time: 4-5 minutes each pancake

1 sachet active dry yeast
1 teaspoon sugar
1½ cups warm water
1½ cups plain flour
pinch of salt

For serving:
'Atar (pages 214, 216)
Ushta (page 213) or thick whipped cream

1. Blend yeast with sugar and ¼ cup of the water. If active dry yeast is used, water may be a little warmer than lukewarm. Stir to dissolve.
2. Sift flour and salt into a warm mixing bowl and make a well in the centre.
3. Pour 1 cup water and yeast mixture into centre, then gradually stir in flour with a wooden spoon. Stir until smoothly blended. If lumpy, stir with a balloon whisk until smooth.
4. Cover bowl with a cloth and leave in a warm place for 1 hour or until batter has risen and surface is bubbly.
5. Heat a heavy-based frying pan and grease with a wad of paper towelling dipped in ghee or oil. Medium heat should be sufficient for cooking the pancakes.
6. Pour in about 1½ tablespoons of the batter and tilt pan immediately so that batter spreads a little into a round approximately 10 cm (4 inches) in diameter. Use a ladle so that batter goes into pan in one lot. If batter is too thick, stir in remaining water. Pancake should be thick, but should spread a little.
7. Cook until golden brown on underside, flip over and cook other side. Lift out and stack on a plate.
8. Dip into cold 'atar syrup and serve with ushta or thick whipped cream.

Note: Flours vary in their absorbing quality, so it is necessary to hold back some of the liquid and adjust the consistency before cooking.

'ATAR I
SCENTED SYRUP

Makes about 2½ cups

3 cups granulated sugar
2½ cups cold water
1 teaspoon lemon juice
1-2 tablespoons rose or orange flower water

1. Dissolve sugar in water in a heavy pan over medium heat, stirring occasionally.
2. Bring to the boil, add lemon juice and boil over medium heat for 12 minutes or until thick when tested on a cold saucer. When cool, consistency should be similar to thin honey.
3. Add rose or orange flower water to taste, boil 1 minute longer.
4. Strain, cool and store in a sealed container in refrigerator until required.

Note: Once syrup has begun to boil it is important that it is not stirred again, as this makes the syrup cloudy.

'ATAIF (Pancakes) recipe page 214.

'ATAR II
SYRUP

Makes 2½ cups

3 cups granulated sugar
2 ½ cups cold water
1 tablespoon lemon juice
1 piece cinnamon bark

1. Dissolve sugar in water in a heavy-based pan over medium heat.
2. Add lemon juice and cinnamon bark and bring to the boil.
3. Boil over medium heat for 12 minutes until thick. Test a little on a cold saucer. When cooled it should be the consistency of thin honey.
4. Strain, cool and store in a sealed container in refrigerator until required.

KUL'WA'SHKUR
ALMOND PASTRY OR EAT AND PRAISE

Makes 40 pieces
Oven temperature: 170-180°C (325-350°F)
Cooking time: 1 hour

500 g (1 lb) fillo pastry
¾ cup melted samneh or unsalted butter
½ cup chopped pistachio nuts, optional

Almond Filling:
3 cups coarsely ground almonds
1 cup caster sugar
1 egg white
1½ teaspoons orange flower water
2 drops almond essence

'Atar Syrup:
2 cups granulated sugar
1½ cups water
2 teaspoons lemon juice
2 teaspoons rose water

1. Brush a 25 x 33 cm (10 x 13 inch) baking dish with clarified butter and place a sheet of fillo pastry in dish. Brush fillo with butter and top with another sheet. Repeat until half the fillo sheets are used.
2. Combine almonds with sugar. Beat egg white until stiff and fold in nuts, orange flower water and almond essence.
3. Spread nut filling over fillo in dish.
4. Place a sheet of fillo on top, butter and repeat until all are used.
5. Brush top with butter and with a sharp knife cut through layers in diamond shapes (see diagram page 17 for details). Sprinkle top lightly with cold water.
6. Bake on middle shelf in a moderate oven for 30 minutes, raise to one shelf above centre and cook for further 30 minutes.
7. Meanwhile blend sugar and water in a pan, stir over heat until dissolved and add lemon juice. Bring to the boil and boil for 15 minutes over medium heat. Stir in rose water and leave till cool. Syrup should be consistency of thin honey when cool.
8. Pour cooled syrup over hot pastry and leave until cold. Sprinkle with pistachio nuts if desired.
9. Cut through pastry again and lift out pieces with a spatula. Store in a sealed container at room temperature.

MUHALLABIA
ALMOND CREAM PUDDING

Serves: 6
Cooking time: 15 minutes

¼ cup ground rice
3 cups milk
pinch of salt
¼ cup sugar
¾ cup ground almonds
1 tablespoon rose water
pistachios or almonds for serving
pomegranate seeds, optional

1. Blend ground rice in ¼ cup of the milk. Bring remainder of milk to the boil in a heavy-based pan and blend in ground rice mixture, salt and sugar.
2. Stir constantly with a wooden spoon over medium heat until mixture bubbles gently, then simmer gently for 5 minutes, stirring often. Reduce heat if necessary so that mixture cooks slowly.
3. Stir in the ground almonds until blended smoothly, then add the rose water.
4. Remove from heat and stir occasionally till mixture cools a little, then pour into serving bowl or six individual dishes.
5. Chill and serve garnished with nuts and pomegranate seeds if available.

SAMBUSIK
DATE CRESCENTS

Makes 30
Oven temperature: 180°C (350°F)
Cooking time: 20-25 minutes

2½ cups plain flour
½ teaspoon ground mahlab, optional
¼ cup melted butter
⅓ cup milk
¼ cup granulated sugar
¼ cup olive or nut oil

Date Filling:
250 g (8 oz) dates
¼ cup butter
1 teaspoon rose water

1. Sift flour into mixing bowl with mahlab if used, and rub in butter until evenly distributed.
2. Heat milk and sugar, stir until dissolved and cool to luke-warm.
3. Pour milk into flour with oil and mix to a soft dough. Knead until smooth.
4. Chop dates and put in a pan with ¼ cup butter. Stir over medium heat until mixture is combined and paste-like in consistency. Remove from heat and add rose water.
5. Roll out dough on a lightly floured board until 5 mm (¼ inch) thick. Cut into 5 cm (2 inch) rounds.
6. Place a teaspoon of date filling in centre of each round, and turn pastry over filling to form a crescent. Crimp edge with fingers or press with tines of a fork to seal.
7. Place sambusik on ungreased baking sheets and bake in a moderate oven for 20-25 minutes until lightly coloured. Cool 5 minutes on sheets, then lift onto a rack to complete cooling. Store when cold.

Note: A walnut filling may be used instead of dates. Use filling as for Ma'amoul B'jowz (page 220).

BAKLAWA 'BE'AJ'
NUT PASTRIES

Makes about 40
Oven temperature: 180°C (350°F) reducing to 150°C
   (300°F)
Cooking time: 45 minutes

500 g (1 lb) fillo pastry
¾ cup melted samneh or unsalted butter
½ cup chopped pistachio nuts, optional

Nut Filling:
2 egg whites
½ cup caster sugar
2 cups coarsely ground walnuts
2 cups coarsely ground almonds
1 teaspoon rose water

'Atar Syrup:
2 cups granulated sugar
1½ cups water
1 teaspoon lemon juice
1 teaspoon orange flower water
1 teaspoon rose water

1. Stack 10 sheets fillo pastry on a flat surface, keeping remainder covered with a dry, then a damp tea towel.
2. Brush top sheet of stack with butter, lift sheet and replace on stack buttered side down. Brush top with butter, lift top two sheets and turn over on stack. Repeat until all 10 sheets are buttered, lifting an extra sheet each time. Top and bottom of finished stack should remain unbuttered.
3. With kitchen scissors cut buttered stack of fillo into approximately 10 cm (4 inch) squares. Stack and cover. Prepare remainder of fillo. Depending on size of fillo sheets, you may have fewer than 10 left at the end. Halve sheets if necessary to give 10 layers.
4. Beat egg whites until stiff and beat sugar in gradually. Fold in nuts and rose water.
5. Butter top of fillo square and place a tablespoonful of nut mixture in the centre. Gently squeeze into a lily shape, with four corners of square as petals and filling in centre.
6. Place in a buttered 25 x 33 cm (10 x 13 inch) baking dish. Repeat with remaining ingredients, placing finished pastries close together in dish.
7. Bake in a moderate oven for 30 minutes, reduce to slow and cook for further 15 minutes.
8. Meanwhile dissolve sugar in water over heat, add lemon juice and orange flower water and bring to the boil. Boil for 15 minutes, stir in rose water and cool.
9. Spoon cool thick syrup over hot pastries. Leave until cool and sprinkle pistachio nuts in centres of pastries if desired.

Note: If you are not used to working with fillo pastry, then it is advisable to fill and shape the first lot of buttered squares before going onto the next lot. The butter firms fairly quickly and it could be difficult to shape the pastries if the buttered sheets are left for a time.

K'NAFI JIBNI
SHREDDED PASTRY WITH CHEESE

Oven temperature: 180°C (350°F)
Cooking time: 45 minutes

500 g (1 lb) konafa (kataifi) pastry
1 cup samneh (clarified butter), melted

Filling:
500 g (1 lb) ricotta or mizithra cheese
1 tablespoon granulated sugar
grated rind of 1 lemon
1 quantity cold 'Atar (pages 214,216)

1. Loosen konafa pastry by pulling gently with fingers. Place in a large bowl and pour on melted samneh. Toss pastry shreds so that they are evenly coated with samneh, using a fork or fingers.
2. Place half the strands in the base of a 25 x 30 cm (10 x 12 inch) oven dish, or in a 25 cm (10 inch) round baking dish (sanieh). Press down to make it more compact.
3. Combine cheese with sugar and lemon rind and beat until softened.
4. Spread cheese evenly over pastry in dish and top with remaining pastry.
5. Bake in a moderate oven for 45 minutes until golden brown.
6. When K'nafi is cooked, remove from oven and pour on cooled 'atar (syrup). Leave until cold and serve cut in squares or diamond shapes. Store any remaining K'nafi in a covered container in refrigerator.

MUHALLABIA (Almond Cream Pudding) *recipe page 217.*

MA'AMOUL B'JOWZ
EASTER WALNUT CAKES

Makes 45
Oven temperature: Preheat at 230°C (450°F), reduce
*   to 180°C (350°F)*
Cooking time: 20-25 minutes

4½ cups fine semolina
½ cup caster sugar
250 g (8 oz) butter
1 cup milk
½ teaspoon bicarbonate of soda
icing (confectioner's sugar)

Walnut Filling:
1½ cups coarsely ground walnuts
¼ cup caster sugar
1 teaspoon ground cinnamon

1. Combine semolina and sugar in a mixing bowl.
2. Melt butter in a pan and heat until bubbling. Pour into semolina and sugar and mix with wooden spoon until butter is evenly distributed.
3. Heat milk in pan until bubbles begin to rise, remove from heat and stir in soda. Pour into semolina mixture.
4. Mix with wooden spoon to a soft dough. When it cools a little, knead lightly by hand. Cover bowl with a sheet of plastic cling film to make an airtight seal. Leave for at least 5 hours or overnight.
5. Mix nut filling ingredients together.
6. Knead dough again to make it pliable. Take a tablespoonful of dough at a time and roll into balls the size of a large walnut.
7. Flatten a ball of dough in your palm and push up sides to make a pot shape. Fill hollow with a generous teaspoonful of nut filling and mould dough over filling. Press edges to seal well and roll into a ball again.
8. Press into a decorated mould (a *tabi*) and tap out on board. Place on ungreased baking tray. Alternatively place ball of dough on tray, flatten slightly and press tines of fork obliquely around sides to give cakes a slightly conical shape. Press top with fork.
9. Have oven preheated to very hot, place Ma'amoul in oven and reduce heat to moderate. Bake at moderate for 20-25 minutes until lightly coloured. Remove and cool on trays for 10 minutes.
10. Sift some icing sugar onto a sheet of waxed paper. Place Ma'amoul on sugar and sift more sugar on top to coat thickly. When cool, store in an airtight container.

Note: Traditionally Ma'amoul are shaped using the same technique as when making Stuffed Kibbi Balls (page 205).

SHARAB EL WARD
ROSE WATER SYRUP

2 cups sugar
1 cup water
strained juice of ½ lemon
few drops pink food colouring
⅓ cup rose water

1. Put sugar and water into a pan and stir over medium heat until dissolved. Bring to the boil and add lemon juice.
2. Boil, without stirring, for 10 minutes, skimming when necessary.
3. Add colouring to syrup to achieve a deep pink — it will be lighter when diluted later.
4. Add rose water and boil 3 minutes longer. Remove from heat, cool, bottle and seal.
5. To serve, put 2-3 tablespoons syrup in a glass and fill with iced water.

QAHWI
COFFEE

Coffee making in this part of the world is taken as seriously as it is in Turkey and the Gulf States. Every household has its *rakwi* (long-handled coffee pot) and *tahrini* (brass coffee grinder).

To impress your Arabic host or your guests, know the right coffee talk — *murrah* for sugarless coffee, *mazboutah* for medium sweet and *hilweh* for very sweet.

Coffee is always served in tiny, bowl-shaped, handle-less cups, sometimes placed in decorative brass holders. The rakwi is frequently made of brass and attractively worked; very old pieces are complete with lid to keep the coffee hot. It is often taken to the coffee drinkers with the cups. Speed in transferring from the stove to the serving area is necessary as the grounds must not be given time to settle in the pot. When drinking coffee, however, you must allow a little time before drinking it to allow the grounds to settle.

To each Arabic coffee cup measure of water add a level teaspoon sugar for medium sweet, a heaped teaspoon for very sweet. Stir sugar in water over heat until dissolved and boiling. Add 1 heaped teaspoon pulverized coffee (usually a dark roasted coffee) for each cup water, stir well and cook until foam rises to the top of the pot. The pot is removed from the heat and the base rapped on a flat surface to reduce foaming. Heat twice more, with raps in between. Pour immediately into the cups.

To flavour the coffee, either cardamom pods are ground with the beans (3 or 4 with each 250 g or 8 oz beans) or one pod added to pot for each 4 cups coffee being brewed, though this is the particular flavouring of the Arab Gulf countries. Traditionally a little silver urn of rose water or orange blossom water would accompany the coffee so that a few drops may be added to individual taste.

GHERFER or AINAR
SPICED TEA WITH NUTS

Serves: 4

2 cups water
4 large pieces cinnamon bark
sugar to taste
⅔ cup finely chopped walnuts

1. Put water in a long-handled coffee pot (*rakwi*) and add cinnamon bark. Bring to the boil and boil gently for 5 minutes. Remove cinnamon bark.
2. Put 2 tablespoons nuts in each of 4 tea glasses. Pour tea into glasses and add sugar to taste. Serve with a spoon.

IRAQ

In northern Iraq lies Kurdistan, an area stretching across to eastern Turkey and western Iran. It is here that man first began farming, planting grain crops and raising livestock to be able to control food production.

Before 5000 B.C. saw the birth of the Sumerian civilization founded in the fertile valley between the Tigris and Euphrates Rivers, and called Mesopotamia by the Ancient Greeks. This area is regarded as the birthplace of civilization. Towards the southern part of the valley Babylon and Ur grew, flourished and died around 500 B.C., leaving a legacy for civilizations to come.

After the unification of the Arab people under the banner of Islam some 1,300 years later, the region came under Arab rule, with Baghdad succeeding Damascus as the capital of the Islamic world. Baghdad became the centre of Arabic culture and trade, with caravans bringing foods and spices from China, India and Persia.

In the courts of the Caliphs of Baghdad the art of cooking thrived with strong Persian influence, a legacy of the Persia civilization. Arabic cooking and food tastes flourished and expanded, with the vast variety of foods brought from Asia. As they swept westward, spreading Islam, they took with them the foods to which they had become accustomed — saffron from Asia minor, citrus fruits, almonds, rice and sugar cane from Asia, many to be planted in their conquered lands, thus introducing new foods to Europe.

The Mongols, then the Ottoman Turks, swept into Baghdad and her glory diminished, but her culinary glories spread far and wide, influencing the cuisine of the Arab world in general; that influence is still evident today.

THE FLAVOUR OF IRAQI FOOD

One usually enters a country with preconceived ideas about their foods. Though I expected an extension of Arabic cuisine, all I could associate with Iraq was the Lion of Babylon dates I had been buying for years, and I wondered in what other ways the date was used on its home ground.

When dates are being dried for export and for use throughout the remainder of the year, a thick dark amber syrup is exuded from the fruit. It is used in Hemooth Heloo, a lamb and dried fruit dish reminiscent of Persian meat and fruit combinations, but with a flavour more sweet than sweet-sour. Marees is a combination of date syrup and butter, heated and blended with squares of Khoubiz and eaten with gaimer, the thick buffalo cream of the area, similar to the Ushta and Kaymak of neighbouring countries. The Kurds in the north of Iraq use a raisin syrup for Marees.

For a simple date sweetmeat, try Holwah Tamar, or the more intricate Murabba Tamar, and Klaicha for a mouth-melting pastry filled with dates and perfumed with rose or orange flower water.

Ingredients for BAHARAT (Mixed Spice) *recipe page 245*

Iraqi date varieties dried for export are Kahastawari, Khadrowi and Zhehdik, the first two being the varieties exported to the West. Baban and Berhi are delicate dates best eaten fresh, though they freeze very well. Baban is a black date with a fairly firm skin — when squeezed gently the flesh pops out and literally melts in the mouth. Berhi, a light golden date with a tender skin, is not skinned before eating. It is stringy sweet and delicious, with a slightly peppery undertone, and the texture of fresh sugar cane. If left too long Berhi dates become overripe and squashy, rather the way bananas do.

The rice dishes of Iraq, though not extensive in range, are somewhat similar to those of Persia: Timman, steamed rice very similar to Chelou, and Timman Z'affaran, a rice dish reminiscent of Persian Polous with the spiciness of Gulf Arabic cooking, but essentially Iraqi in concept and presentation.

Dolma are as popular here as elsewhere and I was fascinated with Mumbar, basically a Dolma meat filling in sausage casing; a long length of casing is filled and coiled into a pot. After long, slow simmering the Mumbar is sliced into portions and served as an appetizer.

Though potatoes are relative newcomers to Middle East cooking and in Iraq not readily available all year round, the Iraqis make the most of the potato when it is in season, using it for delightful potato cakes called Batata Charp, filled with a spicy meat or a tomato and parsley stuffing.

In discussing foods with our Iraqi contact, I would frequently ask how a particular dish was served. His reply always was 'as part of a feast', giving me the impression that Iraqis are always feasting. After visiting his home unexpectedly, I found that every meal *is* a feast, with huge quantities served. It was at this meal that another side of Arabic hospitality was revealed. Our host did not eat while we were his guests, as it is the custom for the host to look after their needs exclusively; his were not considered until after their departure. I was impressed and amazed at his self-control in not even venturing to take a nibble during the many hours we enjoyed his hospitality. However he did take care of his thirst with a few glasses of beer, Australian beer at that.

One typically Iraqi dish, and a speciality of Baghdad outdoor restaurants bordering the Tigris, is Masgoof. It is a dish which is seldom prepared in the home though it is possible to do so. The Tigris River teems with a vast variety of freshwater fish — very large, firm-fleshed and flavourful. The fish is gutted and slit, opened out and impaled on two green sticks secured in the earth and set alongside a fire of fragrant woods. As the fish is rather oily it needs little attention from the cook, except perhaps light seasoning with salt, pepper and paprika before cooking. The fish is barbecued slowly with the inner flesh exposed to the heat. After almost an hour's cooking in this way the fish is removed from the sticks and thrown skin side down on top of the now-glowing embers to complete the cooking. It is served on a platter with sliced onion and tomato, and plenty of bread. The right way to eat Masgoof is with your fingers so that you may feel the bones — it makes a lot of sense. Though the variety of fish is large, the most popular fish for Masgoof is the Shabboot, though Booni and Theka are also available and equally good. The diner is given a choice of which fish to have prepared as they are all kept in a tiled pond on the premises for your selection. There is certainly no doubt about the freshness.

Beautiful parks and gardens stretch along the banks of the Tigris, with bronzed statues set in groups, the tableaus depicting tales from the Arabian Nights, a reminder of the glorious days of the Caliphs of Baghdad and their contribution to the art and culture of the Arabic world.

Zlabiya, a kind of sweet, syrupy pastry rosette and a favourite of the Iraqis, is immortalized in the stories of the *Arabian Nights:* 'Of sweet Zlabiya chain I hung a necklace around her neck. From its delicious loops I made a ring on her ears.' The same confection is prepared in neighbouring countries to the west and as far east as India, but its home is Iraq.

One particular dish served at feasts, that is real feasts, is Khouzi. A version which I found fascinating, Khouzi Khasibi, needs very special facilities for its preparation. A rice is prepared similar to Timman Z'affaran but with little cooking of the grain. The lamb is steamed beforehand in a conventional oven until half done. It is then skewered with two green ribs from palm branches passing through the leg and shoulder on each side. The rice is placed on a deep tray on top of a bed of glowing coals set in the base of a *tannour* oven. The lamb is lowered head down into the tannour with the fat tail of the lamb at the top of the carcase so that the meat is basted as the fat melts. The opening of the oven is criss-crossed with green palm leaves and wet clay is packed on top to seal the opening completely. The lamb cooks slowly, the juices dripping onto the rice below, and when the clay seal begins to crack the lamb is cooked. The use of the green palm ribs is all part of the flavour of the whole dish as they begin to smoulder towards the end of cooking, imparting a special fragrance to the meat. The Khouzi of the city dweller is prepared similarly to the Khouzi of Saudi Arabia and you might find that recipe easier to duplicate for an Arabic feast.

Khoubiz, the flat bread of Iraq, is similar to the Mafrooda Burd of the Gulf States and the Nane Lavash or Taftoon of Iran. Samoon is a diamond-shaped thick loaf similar to the Barbari of Iran but only a quarter of its size. Khoubiz is served with every meal; Samoon is a popular bread for breakfast.

EATING IRAQI STYLE

A meal in a town house is served on a dining table spread with a cloth, with china and cutlery. All the dishes for the meal are placed on the table at the one time. Soup is seldom, if ever, served. Rice is always part of the meal and served with Murag, a meat stew with bamia (okra), eggplant, green peas or beans. A roast chicken could also be served with a platter of Batata Charp, a large bowl of salad containing cos (romaine) lettuce, crisp cucumbers, tomatoes, onion rings and a cress-like herb called barbeen. Another herb which could be included is rashad, resembling coarse dill and with the peppery flavour of cress. Date vinegar is used as the dressing on salads with a little salt and pepper. The beverage is more than likely to be beer, and when one recalls the area's earliest history it is understandable as beer was made by the Sumerians as far back as 3000 B.C. At the conclusion of the meal, coffee, prepared in the Turkish manner, and sweet pastries are served in another room. If you are a guest, on your departure your hostess sprinkles the top of your head with rose water dispensed from a long silver decanter fitted with a perforated top. The significance is to carry the pleasure of the visit away with you, the lingering fragrance serving as a reminder.

INGREDIENTS FOR IRAQI COOKING

Favourite meats are lamb, beef and chicken. The rice preferred is the basmati rice of Pakistan. You will need baharat, the spice mix popular in the Gulf States, although the Iraqi cook is quite likely to substitute ground allspice, adding a little pepper and paprika for added heat and colour. Flat leaf parsley is essential, watercress for salads in place of the rashed and barbeen which would be difficult to obtain outside the region. Dried dates and, if you can get them, fresh dates for preserves and sweets; rose water, orange flower water, saffron, almonds, walnuts and dried fruits. The dried lime of the Gulf States and Iran is also used in Iraq where it is called noomi Basra. Basra is a seaport on the Arabian Gulf, and as the dried limes would arrive from there the locals added the name of the seaport to the name for the lime. I have referred to the lime as noomi in the recipes and the directions for making your own can be found on page 245.

PRONUNCIATION OF ARABIC NAMES

Pronounce 'a' as in *past*; 'e' as in *egg*; 'eh' as in *egg*, slightly aspirated; 'ou' as in *soup*; 'i' as in *pit*; 'u' as in *put*; ' (inverted comma) before a vowel is a barely perceptible 'k' (Lebanon, Syria and Jordan only).

This guide serves for all Arabic-speaking countries: Iraq, Lebanon, Syria, Jordan, the Gulf States, Yemen and Egypt, and for Iran and Afghanistan.

BATATA CHARP I
POTATO CAKES WITH MEAT FILLING

Makes 40
Cooking time: 30 minutes plus frying time

1 kg (2 lb) potatoes
1 large egg, beaten
¼ cup plain flour
salt
freshly ground black pepper

Meat Filling:
1 medium-sized onion, finely chopped
1 tablespoon oil
1 clove garlic, finely chopped
250 g (8 oz) finely ground lamb or beef
1 teaspoon Baharat (page 245)
salt
½ cup chopped, peeled tomatoes
¼ cup chopped parsley

To finish:
flour for coating
oil for shallow frying

1. Scrub potatoes and boil in their jackets until tender. Drain, peel and mash to a smooth purée. Leave to cool, then blend in egg, flour and salt and pepper to taste.
2. Gently fry onion in oil until transparent, add garlic and ground meat and stir over high heat until mixture is crumbly and meat begins to brown. Stir in spices, salt to taste, tomatoes and parsley. Reduce heat, cover and simmer for 15 minutes. Mixture should be fairly dry when cooked.
3. Take about a tablespoon of potato mixture and flatten in palm of hand. Put a teaspoon of meat filling in centre and close potato around filling. Roll into a ball and place on a tray. During shaping moisten hands with water to prevent potato sticking.
4. Roll balls in flour and flatten to make thick cakes. Arrange on a tray.
5. Place oil in a frying pan to a depth of 5 mm (¼ inch). Heat well and fry potato cakes until golden brown on each side — about 3 minutes in all. Drain on paper towels and serve hot, piled on a plate. Garnish as desired.

BATATA CHARP II
POTATO CAKES WITH VEGETABLE FILLING

Vegetable Filling:
1 large onion, finely chopped
2 tablespoons oil
1 teaspoon turmeric
2 large ripe tomatoes
½ cup finely chopped parsley
salt
freshly ground black pepper

1. Prepare potato mixture as for Batata Charp I.
2. Gently fry onion in oil until transparent, add turmeric and fry for further minute. Remove from heat.
3. Peel tomatoes, halve crosswise and remove seeds and juice. Chop finely and place in a bowl. Add onion mixture, parsley and salt and pepper to taste.
4. Make potato cakes as instructed in Batata Charp I from Step 3, using vegetable filling in place of the meat filling.

HAMUTH HELOO (Lamb with Dried Fruits) *recipe page 232.*

TIMMAN
STEAMED WHITE RICE

Iraqi steamed rice is rather like the neighbouring Iranian Chelou, but there is sufficient difference in the preparation to warrant its inclusion. As with Chelou, it can be just steamed to a light fluffy grain, or cooked in such a way as to achieve a crisp golden rice crust on the base of the pot.

Serves: 5-6
Cooking time: 50 minutes

2 cups basmati or other good quality long
    grain rice
⅓ cup melted ghee or oil
8 cups warm water
2 tablespoons salt

1. Pick over rice and wash well in cold water. Drain well in a sieve.
2. Heat 1 tablespoon ghee in a heavy pot and add rice. Stir over high heat for 2 minutes, then add warm water and salt and bring to the boil, stirring occasionally. Boil for 5 minutes, then pour through a sieve to drain rice.
3. Heat another tablespoon ghee in the same pot, add drained rice and spread evenly. Pour remaining ghee on top of rice.
4. Cover tightly with lid and place pot over medium heat for 10 minutes, then reduce to low and cook for further 30 minutes. For rice without a crust, cook on constant low heat for 40 minutes.
5. To remove crust easily, place pot in cold water for 5 minutes to loosen rice from base of pot, otherwise fluff up rice with fork and pile into serving dish. If crust is present break into pieces and place around rice on dish.

TIMMAN Z'AFFARAN
SAFFRON RICE

Serves: 5-6
Cooking time: 1 hour

2 cups basmati or other good quality long
    grain rice
water
½ teaspoon saffron threads
2 tablespoons rose water
⅓ cup ghee or oil
¼ cup blanched, split almonds
1 medium-sized onion, finely chopped
250 g (8 oz) ground lamb or beef
½ teaspoon Baharat (page 245)
salt
¼ cup sultanas (white raisins)
3 cups chicken stock

1. Pick over rice, place in a bowl and wash well until water runs clear. Cover with cold water and leave to soak for 30 minutes.
2. Pound saffron threads, place in a small bowl, add rose water and leave to steep until required.
3. Heat half the ghee or oil in a frying pan, add almonds and fry until golden. Remove to a plate with a slotted spoon and reserve.
4. Add onion to pan and fry gently until transparent. Increase heat, add ground meat and cook, stirring often to make meat crumbly. Fry until juices evaporate, add baharat, ½ teaspoon salt and sultanas and fry for 1 minute longer. Remove pan from heat, cover and leave aside.
5. Heat remaining ghee or oil in a deep, heavy pan and add 2 teaspoons of the saffron-rose water mixture and the chicken stock. Bring to the boil.
6. Drain rice and add to boiling stock with salt to taste. Stir occasionally until rice returns to the boil, reduce heat to low and cover pan tightly. Simmer gently for 30 minutes.
7. Fold meat mixture gently through rice, cover rim of pan with a cloth or 2 paper towels and set lid on tightly. Leave on low heat for 5 minutes, remove from heat and leave for another 5 minutes or longer if necessary. Rice should not spoil, though this depends on its quality.
8. Pile rice in serving dish or platter and sprinkle with browned almonds and remainder of saffron-rose water mixture. Excellent served with roast chicken and lamb, or serve as part of a buffet.

TASHREEB DIJAJ
POT ROASTED CHICKEN

Serves: 6
Cooking time: 2 hours

1 chicken, about 1.7 kg (3½ lb)
1 lemon
salt
freshly ground black pepper
2 tablespoons ghee or oil
1 head garlic, left whole and unpeeled
1 cup water

1. Clean chicken and wipe dry with paper towels. Cut half the lemon into quarters and rub chicken inside and out with lemon quarters. Season cavity and outside of chicken with salt and pepper and leave for 30 minutes to absorb flavours.
2. Heat ghee or oil in a heavy pan and brown chicken on all sides.
3. Remove outer layers of skin on head of garlic, exposing the cloves. Leave unpeeled and attached to the root. Wash well and add to chicken. Reduce heat, cover and cook on low heat for 10 minutes.
4. Juice remaining lemon half and add to pot with water. Cover pan tightly and simmer gently over low heat for 2 hours, turning chicken twice during cooking.
5. When tender, remove chicken to a platter and keep hot. Skim fat from juices in pan, and remove garlic and discard. Reduce juices over high heat until half original quantity remains. Adjust seasoning with salt and pepper.
6. Cut chicken into serving portions and pour juices over chicken. Serve with Timman or Timman Z'affaran.

DIJAJ ALA TIMMAN
ROAST STUFFED CHICKEN

Serves: 6
Oven temperature: 180°C (350°)
Cooking time: 3 hours

Rice Stuffing:
½ cup basmati or other good quality long grain rice
¼ cup ghee
1 small onion, finely chopped
¼ cup pine nuts or blanched, slivered almonds
¼ cup chopped walnuts
¼ cup sultanas (white raisins)
½ teaspoon Baharat (page 245) or allspice
1 cup water
salt
freshly ground black pepper

To finish:
1 chicken, about 1.7 kg (3½ lb)
salt
freshly ground black pepper
¼ cup melted butter or ghee
½ cup water or light stock

1. Pick over rice and wash until water runs clear. Drain well.
2. Heat ghee in a pan, add onion and fry gently until transparent. Stir in pine nuts or almonds, walnuts and rice and fry for 5 minutes, stirring often.
3. Add sultanas, baharat, water, and salt and pepper to taste. Stir well, cover and cook on low heat for 10 minutes until water is absorbed. Remove from heat and cool.
4. Clean chicken and wipe dry with paper towels. Fill cavity with rice stuffing and truss. Rub chicken with salt and pepper.
5. Melt butter or ghee in a baking dish. Put chicken in dish and baste well with the butter or ghee. Add water or stock to dish and roast chicken in a moderate oven for 2½ hours, basting often with juices in dish.
6. Serve chicken cut in portions with stuffing piled in centre of the platter. Though not usual, juices in dish may be skimmed, diluted with a little stock, brought to the boil and served separately in a jug.

HABEET I
STEWED LAMB

Serves: 6
Cooking time 3-3 ½ hours

1.5 kg (3 lb) lamb shoulder cut in 6 pieces on the bone
water
1 noomi (dried lime) or thinly peeled rind of ½ lemon
salt
freshly ground black pepper
6 cloves garlic, chopped
½ cup cider or malt vinegar

1. Place lamb pieces in a large pan and cover with cold water. Pierce lime on each side with a skewer if used and add to pot. Alternatively add lemon rind.
2. Bring slowly to the boil, skimming frequently as froth rises. When well-skimmed and simmering add about 2 teaspoons salt, a good grinding of pepper, garlic and vinegar.
3. Cover and simmer gently for 2½-3 hours until liquid is reduced to a thick sauce and meat falls off bones.
4. Remove bones and dried lime or lemon rind and serve habeet on a platter with bread as part of an Iraqi meal.

HABEET II
SPICED STEWED LAMB

Reduce garlic in above recipe to 3 cloves and omit pepper and vinegar. When well skimmed, add salt, chopped garlic, 1 teaspoon turmeric and 1 tablespoon Baharat (page 245). Continue from Step 3 and serve with Timman (page 228).

KHOUZI ALA TIMMAN
LAMB SHANKS AND RICE

A restaurant speciality in Baghdad, this dish is a scaled-down version of the festive Arabic Khouzi — whole lamb stuffed with rice — the cooking method and the stuffing varying according to the region. (See page 260 for Khouzi as prepared in the Gulf States.) Though the lamb is not stuffed in this recipe, the final dish has the basic components of Khouzi.

Serves: 6
Cooking time: 2 ½ hours

6 lamb shanks, cracked
cold water
1 noomi (dried lime) or strip of lemon rind
1 large onion, finely chopped
¼ cup oil
1 teaspoon Baharat (page 245)
½ teaspoon turmeric
2 cups chopped, peeled tomatoes
salt
freshly ground black pepper

For Serving:
Timman or Timman Z'affaran (page 228)

1. Rinse lamb shanks in cold water and place in a large pot with cold water to just cover meat. Add noomi or lemon rind and bring slowly to the boil, skimming as required.
2. In a separate pan gently fry onion in oil until transparent. Add baharat and turmeric and fry for further 1 minute. Add tomatoes, about 2 teaspoons salt and pepper to taste.
3. When lamb shank liquid is well skimmed and simmering, add tomato mixture, cover and simmer gently for 1½-2 hours until meat is very tender. Towards end of cooking, place lid on an angle on the pot so that the liquid can reduce to a thick sauce.
4. Arrange lamb shanks on a bed of Timman or Timman Z'affaran, pour sauce over and serve with salad and Khoubiz.

KHOUZI ALA TIMMAN (Lamb Shanks and Rice) *recipe above*

HAMUTH HELOO
LAMB WITH DRIED FRUITS

When dates are being dried they exude a thick molasses-like syrup. The Iraqi cook adds some of this when making Hamuth Heloo; dried dates soaked and puréed and the addition of brown sugar give a somewhat similar flavour.

Serves: 5-6
Cooking time: 2 hours

1 kg (2 lb) boneless lamb stew meat
¼ cup ghee or oil
1 medium-sized onion, chopped
2 cups water
salt to taste
small piece cinnamon bark
1 noomi (dried lime) or thinly peeled rind of
    ½ lemon
½ cup chopped dates
¾ cup dried apricots
¾ cup dried prunes, pitted
¼ cup sultanas (white raisins)
2 tablespoons brown sugar
Timman for serving (page 228)

1. Cut meat into 2 cm (¾ inch) cubes and brown in half the ghee in a heavy pan.
2. Push meat to one side, add onion and cook for 5 minutes. Reduce heat and add 1 cup water, salt to taste, cinnamon bark and noomi (pierced twice with a skewer) or lemon rind. Cover and simmer for 45 minutes.
3. Place chopped dates in a small pan with remaining cup of water and heat until dates soften. Press through a sieve to purée.
4. Add date purée to meat with apricots, prunes, sultanas and brown sugar. Stir, then cover tightly and simmer for further hour or until lamb is tender. Check during cooking to ensure fruit does not catch, adding a little more water if necessary.
5. Remove cinnamon bark and noomi or lemon rind and serve hot with Timman.

MUMBAR
LAMB AND RICE SAUSAGE

Mumbar is another Iraqi innovation, popular during winter when the variety of available vegetables is limited.

Serves: 6-8
Cooking time: 2½ hours

Lamb Filling:
1 kg (2 lb) finely ground lamb with a little fat
3 cloves garlic, finely chopped
1 small onion, finely chopped
¼ cup finely chopped parsley
¼ cup tomato paste
½ cup long grain rice, washed
1 teaspoon Baharat (page 245)
salt
freshly ground black pepper

To finish:
750 g (1½ lb) lamb breast (riblets)
water
1 noomi (dried lime), optional
salt
freshly ground black pepper
thick lamb or beef sausage casings

1. Combine lamb filling ingredients, adding salt and pepper to taste. Mix thoroughly and refrigerate until required.
2. If lamb breast is in one piece, cut into strips between the bones. Place in a large pot and cover with cold water. Bring slowly to the boil, skimming as required.
3. When well-skimmed and simmering, add dried lime pierced twice with a skewer (if used), and salt and pepper to taste. Cover and simmer for 30 minutes.
4. Rinse sausage casing and leave in one piece. You will require a piece about 60 cm (24 inches) in length. Open casing under running water and slip onto the end of a large funnel. Push length of casing onto funnel.
5. Place filling in funnel and push it through with the end of a wooden spoon. As filling comes through, pull end of casing over it and knot. Fill casing as evenly as possible.
6. When filled, run hands along casing to distribute filling evenly, then knot other end.
7. Remove pot with lamb from heat. Coil mumbar into pot on top of lamb, keeping coil flat. Invert a heavy plate on top to keep mumbar in place and return to low heat. Cover pot and simmer for further 1½ hours. Check liquid after 30 minutes and add water if necessary to just cover mumbar.
8. When cooked, leave pot at side of stove for 15 minutes, then remove mumbar to a plate. Slice in 4 cm (1½ inch) pieces and serve with Murag and Timman.

DOLMAS
STUFFED VEGETABLES

Dolmas are as popular in Iraq as in other countries of the region. The filling given for Mumbar is used in the Iraqi version, with the usual vegetables — eggplants (aubergines), tomatoes, sweet peppers, zucchini (courgettes), cabbage, grape vine and silver-beet (Swiss chard) leaves. The Iraqis, still the innovators in Arabic cuisine as they were centuries ago, fill egg shells with any meat mixture left after preparing the vegetables. These are placed on top of the vegetables for cooking.

Use lamb filling as for Mumbar. Prepare vegetables as for Khareni Litzk Bulghourov, page 174, then fill. Place in an oiled dish, brush with oil, cover with foil and bake in a moderate oven for 30 minutes. Remove foil and bake for further 20-30 minutes.

LAHAM AJEEN
FLAT LAMB PIES

Many Middle East countries have their favourite version of Laham Ajeen. In Iraq they are made in great quantities and sold for between-meal snacks. As I rather enjoyed these in Baghdad, this is the version of Laham Ajeen I have chosen to include.

They freeze well, so it is worthwhile having a quantity on hand for the lunch-box or picnic hamper as they are equally good served cold. Another way to present them is to make smaller versions and serve hot as a finger food with pre-dinner drinks.

Makes 24
Oven temperature: 220°C (425°F)
Cooking time: 45 minutes

Yeast Dough:
5-6 cups plain flour
1 sachet active dry yeast
2 cups warm water
2 teaspoons sugar
2 teaspoons salt
2 tablespoons oil

Lamb Topping:
1 large onion, finely chopped
2 tablespoons oil
2 cloves garlic, finely chopped
500 g (1 lb) finely ground lamb
1½ cups chopped, peeled tomatoes
1½ cups grated zucchini
2 tablespoons chopped parsley
½ teaspoon dried thyme
1 small chili, seeded and finely chopped
salt
freshly ground black pepper

1. Sift flour into a large mixing bowl and warm in a low oven.
2. Dissolve yeast in ¼ cup warm water, stir in remaining water with sugar and salt.
3. Remove about 2 cups flour from bowl and keep aside. Pour yeast mixture into centre and blend in a little of the flour to thicken liquid. Cover with cloth and leave until frothy.
4. Stir in rest of flour in bowl to make a soft dough, adding oil gradually. Beat by hand for 10 minutes, or on electric mixer with dough hook for 5 minutes.
5. Turn onto board dusted with some of the reserved flour and knead until smooth and elastic, using just enough flour to stop dough sticking. Shape into a ball.
6. Oil bowl, put dough in and turn over to oil top. Cover top of bowl with plastic wrap and leave in a warm place until doubled in bulk — about 1 hour.
7. Meanwhile make topping. Gently fry onion in oil until transparent, add garlic and increase heat. Add lamb and stir over high heat until juices evaporate and meat begins to brown. Add remaining topping ingredients, cover and simmer over gentle heat for 30 minutes, removing lid towards end of cooking so that excess moisture can evaporate. Mixture should be thick. Cool.
8. Punch down dough and turn onto floured board. Knead for 2 minutes, then divide into 24 equal portions, shaping each into a ball.
9. Roll out each ball to a 12 cm (5 inch) round and place on greased baking sheets. Spread a generous tablespoon of topping on each and bake in a hot oven for 12-15 minutes until cooked. Serve hot or cold.

TASHREEB
STEWED LAMB SHANKS AND TRIPE

For a genuine Tashreeb, lambs' feet are required. As these are difficult to obtain, often being prohibited from sale by health regulations, I have used lamb shanks instead. This is just one version of Tashreeb as prepared in Iraq.

Serves: 6
Cooking time: 2½-3 hours

500 g (1 lb) tripe
4 lamb foreshanks, cracked
½ cup chick peas, soaked overnight
water
2 noomi (dried limes) or thinly peeled rind of
   ½ lemon
1 head garlic, left whole and unpeeled
1 large onion, finely chopped
¼ cup ghee or oil
2 cups chopped, peeled tomatoes
2 teaspoons Baharat (page 245)
salt
freshly ground black pepper
2 Khoubiz (page 190) or 4 slices dry toast

1. Wash tripe well and cut into 3 cm (1¼ inch) squares. Place in a large pot with lamb shanks and drained chick peas, cover with cold water and bring to the boil. Drain off water.
2. Add fresh water to pot to just cover contents. Add dried limes, each pierced twice with a skewer, or lemon rind. Wash head of garlic well and strip off the outer layers of skin, leaving the unpeeled garlic cloves exposed. Leave the garlic intact and add to the pot. Bring to a slow simmer, skimming as required.
3. Meanwhile gently fry onion in ghee or oil until transparent, add tomatoes and baharat.
4. When lamb and tripe mixture is well-skimmed and simmering, add tomato mixture with salt and pepper to taste. Cover and simmer gently for 2-2½ hours until lamb and tripe are tender.
5. Remove dried limes and head of garlic and discard. Lift out lamb shanks and strip meat from bones. Cut meat into pieces and return to pot. Bring to the boil to reheat meat.
6. Cut khoubiz into squares, or halve toast slices if used. Place in the base of a deep serving dish or casserole. Pour liquid from tashreeb over bread, then top with meat and tripe mixture. Serve in deep plates.

MURAG
MEAT STEW

Though the literal translation of murag *is sauce or gravy, it is the Iraqi version of the popular Middle Eastern meat stew. A vegetable is usually added — green beans, peas, eggplant or okra being the most popular. When murag is served with rice, as it almost always is, the dish is then called Timman Murag.*

Serves: 5-6
Cooking time: 2-2¼ hours

1.5 kg (3 lb) boneless stewing beef or lamb
¼ cup oil
2 large onions, finely chopped
2 cups chopped, peeled tomatoes or ¼ cup
   tomato paste
1 cup water
1 teaspoon sugar
1 teaspoon Baharat, optional (page 245)
salt
freshly ground black pepper

1. Trim meat and cut into 4 cm (1½ inch) squares. Heat half the oil in a heavy pan and brown meat over high heat, removing to a plate when browned.
2. Reduce heat and add remaining oil with onion. Fry gently until transparent.
3. Add tomatoes or tomato paste, water (1½ cups if using paste), sugar, baharat if used, about 2 teaspoons salt and pepper to taste. Bring to the boil, reduce heat and return meat to pan. Cover and simmer for 45 minutes for lamb, 1¼ hours for beef.
4. Add prepared vegetable, cover and simmer for further hour or until meat is tender. Serve with Timman or Timman Z'affaran, Khoubiz and pickles.

Add one of the following:
500 g (1 lb) green beans, topped and tailed and cut in half
500 g (1 lb) okra (see page 9 for preparation)
2 cups shelled green peas
500 g (1 lb) eggplant, cubed, salted 30 minutes and rinsed

Note: When using okra as the vegetable, add 2 chopped cloves of garlic to the onion.

MURAG (Meat Stew) *recipe above.*

HOLWAH TAMAR
DATE SWEETMEAT

500 g (1 lb) dried, pitted dates
¼ cup ghee
2 cups walnut pieces
2 tablespoons toasted sesame seeds

1. Chop dates roughly and place in a heavy pan with the ghee.
2. Cook over medium heat, stirring often, until dates soften and are combined with the ghee.
3. Spread half the date mixture in a 23 cm (9 inch) square cake pan. Sprinkle walnut pieces over the dates, pressing them in lightly. Place remaining date mixture on top, spreading it evenly.
4. Sprinkle evenly with toasted sesame seeds, pressing them on lightly. Leave until cold and cut into small squares or diamond shapes. Store in a sealed container and serve as a sweetmeat.

MURABBA TRINGE
CITRON PEEL IN SYRUP

2 citrons
water
3 cups sugar
1 tablespoon lemon juice

1. Lightly grate entire surface of each citron. Score peel deeply from stem end to base into 6 or 8 segments, depending on size of citrons. Remove peel carefully.
2. Cut each segment into 3 pieces, then, as the piece from the centre will be square, cut it in half diagonally so that all pieces are triangular in shape.
3. Place peel in a pan and cover with cold water. Bring to the boil and pour off water. Cover with fresh cold water, boil again and drain. Do this 5 times in all, then cover with cold water and leave to stand for 6-8 hours.
4. Drain and cover with fresh cold water. Bring to the boil and boil gently until tender — about 45 minutes. Drain again and spread out on paper towels to dry.
5. In a clean pan dissolve sugar in 3 cups cold water over medium heat, stirring occasionally. When dissolved, bring to the boil and add lemon juice. Boil without stirring for 5 minutes.
6. Add citron peel to syrup and return to the boil. Boil on medium heat for 10 minutes, skimming when necessary. Remove pan from heat, cover and leave overnight.
7. Next day return pan contents to the boil and boil gently for 15-20 minutes or until syrup is thick when tested on a cold saucer.
8. Cool a little, then ladle peel and syrup into warm, sterilized jars. Seal when cold and store in a cool, dark place. Serve as a confection in small dishes with a spoon.

KLAICHA
DATE-FILLED PASTRIES

Makes 30
Oven temperature: 170°C (325°F)

3 cups plain flour
½ cup caster sugar
250 g (8 oz) unsalted butter (1 cup)
3 teaspoons orange flower or rose water
¼ cup water

Date Filling:
250 g (8 oz) pitted dates
2 tablespoons butter

1. Sift flour and sugar into a large mixing bowl. Cut butter into pieces and rub into flour with fingertips until distributed evenly.
2. Blend orange flower or rose water with water and sprinkle onto flour mixture. Mix to a firm dough and knead lightly until smooth. Rest the dough for 30 minutes.
3. Meanwhile chop dates. Place in a pan with the butter and heat gently till dates soften, stirring often. Remove from heat and keep aside.
4. Roll dough into balls the size of a large walnut (about a tablespoonful).
5. Flatten a ball of dough in the palm of your hand and place a teaspoonful of date filling in the centre. Mould dough around filling and reshape into a ball.
6. Press ball into a carved mould similar to a *tabi* and place on an ungreased baking tray. Alternatively place on tray, flatten slightly and press tines of a fork obliquely around sides and across top, giving pastries a slightly conical shape.
7. Bake in a preheated moderately slow oven for 30-35 minutes, until lightly browned.
8. Cool on tray — pastries will become firm and crisp on cooling. Store in a sealed container when cool.

Alternative shaping: Divide pastry into 3 equal portions and roll each portion into a rectangle 1 cm (½ inch) thick and 10 cm (4 inches) wide. Put one-third of the date mixture, shaped in a long roll, along one edge of pastry and roll up to enclose filling. Press edges and ends to seal and place rolls, join side down, on ungreased baking sheet. Decorate top with pastry crimper or any other means to make a design. Bake as for klaicha above, cool and slice at an angle to serve. Store in a sealed container.

MANALSAMA
WALNUT-FILLED PASTRIES

Makes 30
Oven temperature: 170°C (325°F)
Cooking time: 30-35 minutes

1 quantity pastry, see Klaicha (above)

Walnut Filling:
2 cups coarsely ground walnuts
¼ cup caster sugar

To finish:
icing (confectioner's) sugar

1. Make pastry as directed in Klaicha recipe, Steps 1 and 2.
2. Combine filling ingredients, kneading with hand to form a coarse paste.
3. Roll dough, a tablespoon at a time, into balls the size of a large walnut. Flatten out in the palm of the hand and put a generous teaspoon of nut filling in the centre. Close dough around filling, sealing well.
4. Reshape into a ball and press into a decorated mould (a *tabi*), then tap out onto ungreased baking sheet. Alternatively place balls on baking sheet, press to flatten slightly and decorate sides and top with tines of a fork, giving pastries a slightly conical shape.
5. Bake in a moderately slow oven for 30-35 minutes until very lightly browned.
6. Cool on baking sheet for 10 minutes.
7. Sift a layer of icing sugar onto a sheet of waxed paper and place manalsama on sugar. Sift more icing sugar on top to coat thickly. Leave until thoroughly cooled and store in a sealed container.

MURABBA TAMAR I
DATES IN SYRUP

Cooking dates are required for this confection. The fresh dates available in non-date growing countries are table varieties, usually imported frozen. These are too soft to be prepared in the traditional way. If these are the only dates available then follow the directions for Murabba Tamar II.

750 g (1½ lb) fresh cooking dates
water
walnut halves
3 cups granulated sugar
thin strip lemon rind
strained juice of ½ lemon
4 cloves
small piece cinnamon bark

1. Wash dates and remove stems. Peel off the skin with a sharp knife. Place in a pan and cover dates with cold water. Bring to the boil and boil gently for 15 minutes or until tender. Drain dates, reserving cooking liquid.
2. When dates are cool enough to handle, push date seeds out with a knitting needle.
3. Cut walnut halves in half to give quarters about the size of the date seed. Insert a piece of walnut in each date.
4. Place prepared dates in a bowl in layers, sprinkling sugar generously between each layer and on top. Leave for 12 hours or overnight.
5. Measure reserved date cooking liquid and make up to 2 cups with water if necessary. Pour over dates and leave for 2 hours to dissolve sugar, shaking bowl contents occasionally.
6. Drain sugar liquid into a heavy pan and bring to the boil. Add lemon rind and juice, cloves and cinnamon bark. Boil uncovered on medium heat for 10 minutes without stirring. Skim as required.
7. Add dates and return to the boil. Boil for 10 minutes or until syrup is thick when tested on a cold saucer.
8. Remove lemon rind and cinnamon bark. Pack dates into sterilized jars and pour syrup over them. Seal when cold and store at room temperature. Serve in small dishes with a spoon, or as a sweetmeat.

MURABBA TAMAR II
TABLE DATES IN SYRUP

1. Use same ingredients as for Murabba Tamar I, substituting table dates for the cooking dates. Leave dates unpeeled, wash well and remove seeds. Insert walnut pieces in each date. If you prefer, slit side of date to remove seed and insert walnut.
2. Combine 2 cups water with the sugar and dissolve over medium heat, stirring occasionally. Add lemon rind, juice and spices and boil, uncovered, for 10 minutes without stirring. Add prepared dates and return to the boil. Remove from heat. Leave aside for 12 hours.
3. Remove dates from syrup and place in a heat-proof bowl.
4. Bring syrup to the boil and boil without stirring for 10 minutes. Skim when necessary. Strain syrup over dates and leave until cool. Pack into sterilized jars, seal and store in refrigerator.

MURABBA TAMAR (Dates in Syrup) *recipes above;*
KLAICHA (Date-Filled Pastries) *recipe page 237*

ZLABIYA
FRIED SWEET ROSETTES

Makes about 30
1 sachet active dry yeast
1½ cups warm water
2½ cups plain flour
½ teaspoon salt
2 teaspoons sugar
corn or peanut oil for frying

Syrup:
2 cups sugar
1½ cups water
2 teaspoons lemon juice
2 teaspoons rose water or orange flower water

1. Dissolve yeast in ¼ cup warm water.
2. Sift flour into a bowl and make a well in the centre.
3. Add remaining warm water, salt and sugar to the yeast mixture and pour into centre of flour. Gradually stir in flour to form a thick liquid batter, then beat vigorously for 10 minutes. This can be done with an electric mixer using ordinary beaters. Cover and leave to rest in a warm place for 30 minutes.
4. Meanwhile make syrup. Dissolve sugar in water over medium heat. Bring to the boil, add lemon juice and boil briskly for 15 minutes. Add rose water or orange flower water, boil mixture 1 minute longer, then leave aside to cool.
5. Beat batter again for 5 minutes, then let it rest for further 30 minutes.
6. Heat sufficient oil for deep frying in a wide pan — a depth of 4 cm (1½ inches) is sufficient. Heat to a temperature of 190°C (375°F), as pastries must fry without colouring too much.
7. Beat batter again briefly and place some in a pastry bag fitted with a 5 mm (¼ inch) plain nozzle. Hold finger over nozzle while filling bag.
8. Squeeze batter into oil in a 10 cm (4 inch) circle and fill in circle with a lacy pattern of squiggles or zig-zags, ensuring that batter touches outer circle in places. Finished pastry must look like a rough lacy rosette.
9. Fry for about 3 minutes, turning once to cook evenly. When golden, lift out with slotted spoon, drain briefly, then place into cool syrup. Using a second spoon or a fork, turn pastry in syrup and lift out onto a plate. Repeat until batter is used. (A second pair of hands will make the process much less complicated for the cook.)
10. Serve Zlabiyas piled on a plate. These remain crisp for some time if syrup is very thick.

THE GULF STATES

UNITED ARAB EMIRATES
SAUDI ARABIA
BAHRAIN

KUWAIT
QATAR
OMAN

While each is a separate country rather than a state, the collective grouping in one chapter is necessary as their cooking varies little. One can trace the origin of certain recipes to one particular place but you would also find the same dish prepared in the other countries.

The aspect of Arabic life that impresses one most is their hospitality, and the single food (if it could be called such) with which this is expressed is coffee. The coffee pot is ever present, though nowadays coffee is likely to be prepared early in the day and kept hot in a vacuum flask ready for any person who comes by.

There are certain rules which should be observed if ever you are offered coffee in this region. First, do not refuse a cup: to do so is an insult to the host. Your cup will be replenished a second time and a third, and more if you do not indicate to the host that you are satisfied. A simple little jiggle of your empty cup from side to side indicates that you have had sufficient. Only a small portion of coffee is served — a third of a cup is poured each time and the handle-less cups are very small. It is always served unsweetened and

flavoured with cardamom. Taking three cups of coffee is expected of you, rather than just one.

First impressions of Gulf food, particularly in the *suk* (market) quash any notion originally held that the staple diet was boiled meat (lamb, mutton or camel) served on a huge mound of spiced rice. While this might be true of the nomadic Bedouin, camped far from places which could provide anything else, it is not so of the food of townspeople. The variety of fresh vegetables, fruits, spices, meat, fish and poultry from which to choose would delight any serious cook and amaze at the same time, as an aerial view of the region with its vast, arid landscape does not indicate abundance, not of the edible kind anyway.

THE FLAVOUR OF ARABIC COOKING

The Gulf Arabs are very fond of skewered meats, either succulent cubes of lamb similar to the kebabs of other Middle Eastern countries, or

Kabab Mashwi, a meat paste moulded on flat skewers and grilled over coals. These are often served folded into khoubiz together with salad ingredients.

Their rice dishes are of the kind one would expect, knowing the colourful history of the Arabs, as it was they who opened the spice routes to India and the East, and to the West, trading their own cardamom, coriander and cumin for cinnamon, nutmeg, cassia, ginger, pepper, turmeric and cloves. The most popular spicing is a mixture of most of these, called baharat, and it is used in rice, soups, fish, poultry and meat dishes, usually with the addition of whole spices to emphasize certain flavours and turmeric or saffron for colour. Often the saffron is steeped in rose water and poured over the dish towards the end of cooking or on serving for a final dash of colour and fragrance.

Shades of near-Indian cooking are to be expected with the historical links going probably even further back than those already documented. The Indus Valley civilization mysteries have yet to be unravelled, but recent archaeological finds in Bahrain and elsewhere in the Gulf region revealed seals similar to those found in the Indus Valley.

Machbous is a particularly interesting dish of meat, fish, prawns or chicken cooked in spices with rice. The rice itself must be basmati as the Arab refuses any other substitute. It is an aromatic rice from Pakistan, hard of grain, which holds up to the long cooking involved. However times have been shortened in the recipes, in anticipation of possible substitutes.

One ingredient which intrigued me is the loomi (dried lime). In the Gulf region it is used extensively, either whole or pound into a powder, and it imparts an interesting and unusual flavour to foods. It is difficult to give a substitute, but in some recipes the thinly peeled rind of a lemon may be used instead. The lime itself is dried naturally on the tree; it is grown in Oman and also imported from Thailand. Loomi is also to be found in Iran and Iraq, where it is called respectively limu omani and noomi, but in these countries it is only used whole. I have given details in this chapter on how to prepare your own dried limes.

The cucumbers of the Gulf are much loved by the people and after tasting them I could understand why. The long green cucumber which we know is picked before it reaches maturity and this is when cucumbers are at their best. One other variety, a long slender cucumber with a dark green and deeply grooved skin, is available in Western countries under a variety of names. In the Gulf it is called trooh and the locals claim that when the moon is full one can hear the cucumber groaning as it twists itself into the circles and other squiggly shapes in which it comes.

The waters of the Gulf teem with prawns and an infinite variety of fish. The most popular fish for the table are gugurfan and shehen (similar to bream), wahar (called flathead in the waters of Australia), beyah (mullet), chanad (mackerel) and a popular Kuwaiti fish called zubaidi (pomfret). Generally fish is cooked over glowing coals, oven-baked, fried or stewed.

The khoubiz (flat bread) of the area is made in a similar way to the Persian Nane Lavash and Taftoon. Though the general term is khoubiz, the breads are known as Mafrooda and Mafrooda Burd, depending on the flour used. Quite often Iranian bakers run the bakeries and the same ovens and equipment are used as in Iran. Samouli, a white bread similar to long French bread sticks, is baked in a conventional oven.

EATING ARABIC STYLE

Today the region, while still keeping its traditions, is likely to cater also to Western tastes. A town house is likely to have a living room with one part furnished with floor and wall cushions for Arabic visitors, and a table and seating for Western visitors, emphasizing the innate hospitality of the Arab.

Whether served on a cloth spread over a carpet on the floor or on a dining table, the food is presented in the same way. All the components of the meal are placed in dishes and platters, with plates, spoons, forks and glassware. Only in a Bedouin tent is one likely to have the experience of eating from a communal platter, using the fingers of the right hand.

SAMAK QUWARMAH (Fish Curry) *recipe page 253.*

The main dish could be meat, fish or chicken, either cooked in a rich sauce, or roasted, baked or grilled. Muhammar (a sweet rice), Mashkoul (rice and onions) or Muaddas (a combination of rice and lentils) is served separately unless rice is incorporated with the meat dish. A dish of fresh salad is always served, consisting of cos (romaine) lettuce, crisp firm cucumbers, tomatoes, sweet peppers, radishes and a cress-like green herb. The salad is simply dressed with vinegar. Bowls of yoghurt and pickles accompany the meal and bread is always served.

If you want to serve a meal with all the exotic elements of a feast in a desert sheikh's tent, then the dish to prepare is Khouzi. While Khouzi is prepared throughout the Gulf States and other Arabic countries, the Saudi Arabian Khouzi reigns supreme. First you require a whole lamb including the head. A rice stuffing, redolent with nuts, onions, sultanas and spices, is prepared. Some of this is packed into a chicken with shelled hard-boiled eggs; then the chicken is placed in the cavity of the lamb with the bulk of the rice mixture. The cavity is sewn up and the lamb trussed. Though frequently roasted on the spit, it is traditionally placed in a large tray with the ribs of palm leaves serving as a rack. Water is added to the tray and a lid is sealed over the tray with a flour-and-water paste. It is then oven-baked to succulent perfection. The lamb is cooked until it is so tender that the meat comes away from the bones easily. The stuffing is removed and spread on a serving platter with the lamb resting on top.

This is served with great ceremony. Servants present pitchers and bowls for guests to wash their hands before the meal. All the components of the meal are spread on a cloth over a colourful and usually expensive carpet, with cushions scattered around. The guests sit in their places with the most important guest seated next to the host, and the host delights in selecting the most succulent pieces of lamb to offer to the principal guest. The most highly regarded parts of the lamb are the eyes and though that may repel, the Arabs consider them great delicacies. I should imagine it would be somewhat like tackling your first oyster. To serve such a feast in the traditional manner would of course mean that only men would be present, but you can overcome this problem by proclaiming any woman guest to be an honorary male. (There are most reputable precedents for this: the Queen of England was accorded this honour during a visit to Saudi Arabia in 1979.) At feasts of this type eating is regarded as a serious business and there is little, if any, conversation. When the meal is finished hands are washed again and the guests adjourn to another area for coffee, conversation and the water pipe.

INGREDIENTS FOR GULF COOKING

Basmati rice is a necessary ingredient for authentic Gulf cooking. The meat is usually lamb, but now that more food is imported, beef is gaining in popularity. Coarsely ground coffee, preferably moccha, cardamom, saffron, turmeric, flat-leaf parsley, coriander, rose water, loomi (dried lime) and dates are frequently used. Tamarind is still used in certain dishes though tomato has replaced tamarind to a great extent. A large quantity of onions should be on hand, as they are much used in Gulf cooking. The recipes, glossary and introductory chapters give more detail on Gulf foods.

BAHARAT
MIXED SPICES

Makes about 2 cups

½ cup black peppercorns
¼ cup coriander seeds
¼ cup cassia bark
¼ cup cloves
⅓ cup cumin seeds
2 teaspoons cardamom seeds
4 whole nutmegs
½ cup ground paprika

1. Place peppercorns, coriander seeds, cassia, cloves, cumin and cardamom seeds in jar of blender and grind to a powder. It may be necessary to combine whole ingredients and grind ½ cup of mixture at a time.
2. Grate nutmeg and blend into spices with ground paprika. Store in an airtight jar and use as specified.

BAHARAT *using ground spices*
Use the above quantities of ready ground spices. Four nutmegs yield approximately ¼ cup ground nutmeg. Total amount of baharat will be greater than above quantity.

DUKKOUS AL-TAMAT
TOMATO SAUCE

Cooking time: 35 minutes

1 tablespoon oil
4-6 cloves garlic, crushed
750 g (1½ lb) ripe tomatoes, peeled and chopped
salt
1½ teaspoons Baharat (above)

1. Heat oil in a pan and add crushed garlic, cook only for a few seconds.
2. Add tomatoes and salt to taste. Cover and leave to simmer on low heat for 30 minutes.
3. Add baharat, cook with lid off for 2-3 minutes, then remove from heat. Serve with rice or as specified. Sauce may be stored in a sealed jar in the refrigerator and heated as required.

LOOMI
DRIED LIMES

Dried limes are a necessary flavour additive to Gulf cooking, and are also used in Iran and Iraq. While the Gulf cooks use loomi either whole or powdered, they are only used whole in Iran and Iraq. When using them intact, they must be pierced with a skewer or fork on each side so the cooking liquid can travel through the lime to take the flavour. In the dry heat of the Middle East the limes are very brittle and holes can be made by simply pressing with two fingers. I live in a humid climate and find that the humidity toughens the lime, so more forceful means of piercing and powdering need to be adopted.

As loomi are not readily available outside the Middle East, instructions are given for preparing them. The species of lime used alters the flavour a little, but it is still a most interesting spice.

By the way, a sprinkling of powdered loomi does wonders for steaks — rub in before grilling or pan frying.

small fresh limes, preferably Tahitian limes
salted water

1. Leave limes whole, but if they are very large they can be halved to speed the drying process.
2. Put limes in a pan of boiling water with about 1 tablespoon salt. Return to the boil, and boil rapidly for 3-5 minutes, depending on size. Drain.
3. Place on a mesh metal cake rack and place in the sun to dry. This takes up to a week, depending on strength of sun. Turn daily. If there is insufficient heat in the sun, and this could be the case as limes are a late autumn and winter fruit, it might be necessary to resort to other means.
4. Alternatively then, place rack with limes in a very low oven, set on lowest possible heat. Put in coolest part of oven and leave for 3-4 days. A warming drawer would be even better, or if you can get one, use an electric food dryer.
5. Limes are ready when they are dark and the flesh completely dehydrated. Take care not to make them too dark. Store in an airtight container.

To powder loomi: Pound in a mortar with pestle or process in blender.

DUKKOUS AL-BADINJAN
EGGPLANT SAUCE

Oven temperature: 180°C (350°F)
Cooking time: 30 minutes

2 medium-sized oval eggplants, each about
     250 g (8 oz)
4 cloves garlic
salt
2 tablespoons oil
¼-½ teaspoon hot chili pepper
1 teaspoon paprika

1. Place eggplants on a baking sheet in a moderate oven and bake for 30 minutes or until soft.
2. Crush garlic cloves with 1 teaspoon salt in a mortar or bowl.
3. When eggplants are cooked, peel off skin while hot and place flesh in a bowl. Chop up flesh, then mash with a fork.
4. Stir in crushed garlic, oil, chili pepper to taste, paprika and more salt if necessary. Serve warm with Muaddas (page 250) or other rice dishes.

ACHAR LEFET
PICKLED TURNIPS

2 cups water
¼ cup pickling salt
1 kg (2 lb) small white turnips (about 8)
1 small beetroot (beet)
1 clove garlic
1 cup white vinegar

1. Combine water and salt in a pan and bring to the boil, stirring until salt is dissolved. Cool.
2. Peel turnips and cut into quarters or sixths. Peel beetroot and cut into thick strips. Peel and halve garlic clove.
3. Pack turnips in a sterilized jar, placing beetroot strips and garlic between layers.
4. Combine cooled brine with vinegar and pour over turnips. Remove air bubbles by pressing a fine skewer down sides of jar.
5. Seal with lid — if a metal lid is used, place a piece of plastic wrap over top of jar, then secure lid in position.
6. Leave in a cool place for at least 3 weeks before opening. Once opened, store in refrigerator. Unopened pickles will keep in a cool, dark place for up to 3 months.

ACHAR TAMAT
PICKLED TOMATOES

1 kg (2 lb) firm, ripe tomatoes
¼ cup coarse pickling salt
3 teaspoons freshly ground black pepper
3 teaspoons paprika
2 teaspoons ground coriander
6 cloves garlic, halved
3 cups white vinegar

1. Choose small or medium-sized tomatoes with no sign of decay. Wash well.
2. Slit tomatoes almost half way through at stem end and fill slits with salt. Place upright in a bowl and leave for 3 days. Drain off liquid as it accumulates.
3. Invert tomatoes in a colander and leave until the excess liquid drains off.
4. Combine pepper, paprika and coriander and sprinkle about a half teaspoon of the mixture into each tomato.
5. Pack tomatoes into sterilized jars, adding pieces of garlic between layers. Fill jars with vinegar and seal with glass or plastic lids. Leave for 1 week before opening. Use pickles within 6 weeks.

DUKKOUS AL-BADINJAN (Eggplant Sauce) *recipe above;*
DUKKOUS AL-TAMAT (Tomato Sauce) *recipe page 245.*

ACHAR FILFIL
PICKLED PEPPERS

500 g (1 lb) sweet peppers
2 cups water
¼ cup coarse pickling salt
2 cups white vinegar
2 cloves garlic
1 hot chili

1. Wash peppers well, dry, trim stems but do not remove. Cut a long slit in each pepper.
2. Combine water and salt in a pan and heat, stirring until salt is dissolved. Bring to the boil, then add vinegar and return to the boil.
3. Pack peppers into a warm sterilized glass jar, adding halved garlic cloves and the washed and trimmed hot chili.
4. Pour boiling hot brine and vinegar mixture over peppers, filling jar to overflowing. Let peppers absorb brine, top up when they settle and remove air bubbles.
5. Seal jar with glass or plastic lid; if metal lid is used, place a doubled layer of plastic film over top of jar before securing lid. Leave in a cool place for 3 weeks before opening. Once opened, store pickles in refrigerator. Pickles will keep in a cool, dark place for 3-4 months.

KHOUBIZ
FLAT BREAD

Though khoubiz is a general term for bread in the Arabian Gulf region, there are more precise names for the various breads. As there are so many similar bread recipes already given, it will suffice to give the names and tell you which bread recipe to follow to make them Gulf style breads.

MAFROODA
WHITE FLAT BREAD

A white flat bread without a pocket. Follow Khoubiz recipe, page 190. Do not rest bread after shaping, and prick with a fork or pinwheel. Bake on hot griddle or baking sheet for 4 minutes, pressing bread with a cloth if it looks as though a pocket is forming. Turn to brown other side after 2 minutes or brown under hot grill after baking.

MAFROODA BURD
WHOLEMEAL FLAT BREAD

Follow same directions as for Mafrooda, substituting wholemeal flour for two-thirds of the white flour in the Khoubiz recipe (4 cups wholemeal flour, 2 cups white flour).

SAMOULI
WHITE BREAD

This is similar to French bread sticks, and comes in sizes ranging from short sticks to the very long 'husband beaters' (that is not a Gulf term — it would never happen!) The top is glazed with water or egg glaze and sprinkled with coarse salt, sesame seeds or caraway seeds.

Follow Kouloura recipe, page 90, and roll dough into a 40 cm (16 inch) circle. Cut circle into quarters. Beginning at curved side, roll up to the point of the section. Put loaves on baking sheets, cover with a cloth and leave in a warm place until doubled in bulk. Glaze with beaten egg or water, sprinkle with coarse salt, sesame or caraway seeds, then sprinkle lightly with cold water. Bake in a moderately hot oven for 15 minutes or until loaves sound hollow when tapped.

MUHAMMAR
SWEET RICE

Known as the Bahraini pearl divers' rice, Muhammar is one of those recipes which falls into the 'necessity is the mother of invention' category.

Though early pearl divers were doubtlessly not aware of the physiological implications of diving, at some stage they must have found they could dive more frequently and with less ill-effect if they had sweet foods (maintained blood sugar levels) and sustaining foods (carbohydrates and fats). The combination of date juice, rice and fat fulfilled these requirements.

Diving enthusiasts might be interested in the skills of these intrepid men. Using a rope to guide them, they would rapidly descend to a depth of up to 40 metres (130 feet) with a weight tied to their toes. They would stay down 10 to 15 minutes, scoop up any oysters in sight, then ascend. Diving at such a depth even with modern scuba gear has its hasards, let alone with no breathing apparatus at all. Needless to say the mortality rate was high, with sharks, sea snakes and jellyfish adding to the dangers involved.

Serves: 5-6 (1 if you are diving)
Cooking time: 30-35 minutes

¼ teaspoon saffron threads
3 cardamom pods, cracked
2 tablespoons rose water
2 cups basmati rice
6 cups water
1 tablespoon salt
⅓-½ cup granulated sugar or honey
¼ cup ghee or butter

1. Place saffron and cardamom in the rose water and leave aside to steep.
2. Pick over rice and wash until water runs clear.
3. Bring 6 cups water to the boil in a heavy pan, add salt and rice and stir occasionally until water returns to the boil. Leave uncovered and boil for 8 minutes. Drain in a colander.
4. Pour sugar or honey onto hot rice and mix through with a fork.
5. Heat ghee or butter in pan in which rice was cooked and add sugared rice. Sprinkle rose water mixture on top. Make 3 holes in rice with end of a wooden spoon.
6. Cover rim of pan with a paper towel and place lid on tightly. Cook rice over low heat for 20-25 minutes until tender. Serve with grilled fish and roast lamb.

MASHKOUL
RICE WITH ONION

Serves: 5-6
Cooking time: 1 hour

2 cups basmati or other good quality long
  grain rice
cold water
1 tablespoon salt
1 large onion, finely chopped
¼ cup ghee or oil

1. Pick over rice and wash with cold water until water runs clear, then drain.
2. Bring 6 cups water to the boil in a large pot, add rice and salt and return to the boil, stirring occasionally to keep grains separate. Boil for 8 minutes, then strain into a large sieve.
3. Heat ghee in a heavy pan and add onion. Fry gently until transparent, increase heat and fry until crisp and lightly coloured. Remove half of the onion and ghee and put aside.
4. Add strained rice to pan and toss with fork to mix onion through rice. Put reserved onion and ghee on top of rice. Cover pan tightly with lid and cook on low heat for 35-40 minutes or until rice is tender. Fluff up with fork and serve piled on a platter. This is a standard accompaniment to most Gulf meals.

MUADDAS
RICE WITH LENTILS

Serves: 6
Cooking time: 1 hour

2 cups basmati or other good quality long
  grain rice
½ cup brown or green lentils
1 large onion, finely chopped
¼ cup oil or ghee
4 cups boiling water
salt

1. Pick over rice and wash in several changes of cold water until water runs clear. Drain well in a sieve.
2. Pick over lentils to remove small stones and discoloured seeds. Put in a bowl of water and remove any that float. Wash lentils well and drain thoroughly.
3. In a heavy, deep pan heat oil or ghee and add onion. Fry until transparent and lightly flecked with brown. Add rice and lentils and stir over medium heat for 3 minutes.
4. Add boiling water and about 2 teaspoons salt or to taste. Return to the boil, stirring occasionally. Reduce heat to low, cover pan and simmer gently for 45 minutes.
5. Remove pan from heat. Take off lid and place two paper towels over rim of pan. Replace lid and leave aside for 10-15 minutes before serving. Serve as a rice accompaniment to meat and fish dishes or as directed in recipes.

SHAURABAT ADAS
LENTIL SOUP

Serves: 6
Cooking time: 1¼-1½ hours

1½ cups small red lentils
water
1 large onion, finely chopped
¼ cup samneh (ghee) or oil
4-5 cloves garlic, crushed
2 teaspoons Baharat (page 245)
2 cups chopped, peeled tomatoes
2 loomi (dried limes)
salt
1 cup crushed fine noodles, optional

1. Pick over lentils, place in a sieve and rinse under cold running water. Put into a large pot and add 6 cups water. Bring to the boil, skimming if necessary.
2. In a frying pan heat ghee or oil and add onion. Fry gently until transparent, do not brown. Stir in garlic and spices, cook a few seconds, then add tomatoes.
3. After lentils come to the boil, add onion mixture to pot with dried limes, each pierced twice with a skewer or fork.
4. Return to the boil and boil gently, uncovered, for 40 minutes. Add noodles, salt to taste, and a little more water if soup looks too thick. Simmer gently for further 25-30 minutes, uncovered, until lentils and noodles are tender. Stir occasionally.
5. Serve hot in deep bowls with khoubiz (flat bread), salad and pickles.

CHEBEH RUBYAN (Prawns Balls) *recipe page 252,*
served with MUHAMMAR (Sweet Rice) *recipe page 249*

MAZZA BISHURBA
LAMB KNUCKLE SOUP

Serves: 6
Cooking time: 2½-3 hours

4 lamb knuckles (shanks)
8 cups cold water
1 loomi (dried lime, page 245)
1 large onion, finely chopped
2 tablespoons ghee
1 tablespoon Baharat (page 245)
2 small pieces cinnamon bark
1½ cups chopped peeled tomatoes
salt
freshly ground black pepper
½ cup long grain rice, preferably basmati

1. Wash lamb shanks if necessary, place in a soup pot and add the water. Pierce dried lime on each side with a skewer and add to pot.
2. Bring to a slow simmer over medium heat, skimming frequently as scum rises.
3. When well-skimmed and almost boiling, cover and simmer over low heat for 30 minutes.
4. In a frying pan gently fry onion in ghee until transparent, add spices and fry for further 3 minutes.
5. Add to soup with tomatoes and salt and pepper to taste. Cover and simmer for 1½ hours.
6. Remove lime and cinnamon bark and discard. Lift out lamb knuckles and trim off meat. Cut meat into small pieces and return to soup.
7. Pick over rice, wash well and add to soup. Cover and simmer gently for further 30 minutes or until rice is very tender. Serve hot with Khoubiz (flat bread).

CHEBEH RUBYAN
PRAWN BALLS

Serves: 4-6
Cooking time: 1¼ hours

1 kg (2 lb) uncooked prawns (shrimp)
¼ cup coriander leaves
½ teaspoon turmeric
½ teaspoon ground loomi (dried lime),
    optional
¾ cup ground rice
1 teaspoon salt

Filling:
1 large onion, finely chopped
2 tablespoons ghee
1 teaspoon Baharat (page 245)
½ teaspoon ground loomi (dried lime) or
    grated rind of ½ lemon

Tamarind Sauce:
piece of tamarind the size of a small egg
2 cups warm water
1 small onion, finely chopped
1 tablespoon ghee
1 large tomato, peeled and chopped
1 teaspoon Baharat (page 245)
¼-½ teaspoon hot chili pepper
salt
2 teaspoons sugar

For serving:
Muhammar (page 249)
cooked prawns and coriander sprigs to
    garnish

1. Shell and devein prawns, rinse and dry well. Mix prawns with coriander leaves and pass through food grinder using fine screen, or process to a paste in food processor.
2. Combine prawn mixture with turmeric, ground loomi if available and ground rice. Add salt and mix well with hand until thoroughly blended. Cover and refrigerate until required.
3. In a pan gently fry onion in ghee until transparent, stir in baharat and loomi or lemon rind and remove from heat. Keep aside.
4. Soak tamarind in 1 cup warm water for 10 minutes and rub with fingers. Pass through a sieve, pressing pulp through with back of a spoon. Reserve tamarind liquid.
5. In a large, wide-based pot gently fry small chopped onion in ghee until transparent. Add tamarind liquid, remaining water, tomato, spices, salt to taste and sugar. Cover and simmer gently for 15-20 minutes.
6. While sauce is simmering, make chebeh. Take about a tablespoon of prawn paste and flatten in moistened palm. Place a teaspoon of onion filling in centre and close up, shaping into a ball. Keep hands moist during shaping. Repeat until ingredients are used.
7. Drop completed chebeh into simmering sauce. Cover and simmer gently for 35-40 minutes. Chebeh will swell during cooking. Serve hot with Muhammar and garnish with a few cooked prawns and coriander sprigs if desired.

252

SAMAK QUWARMAH
FISH CURRY

Serves: 6
Cooking time: 1 hour

750 g (1½ lb) fish steaks or fillets
salt
2 tablespoons ghee or oil
2 medium-sized onions, chopped
1 teaspoon grated fresh ginger
2 cloves garlic, crushed
½ teaspoon hot chili pepper
1 teaspoon Baharat (page 245)
1 teaspoon turmeric
1 small piece cinnamon bark
1 cup chopped, peeled tomatoes
2 loomi (dried limes) or thinly peeled rind of
    ½ lemon
½ cup water

For serving:
Muhammar (page 249)
OR
Mashkoul (page 250)

1. Wipe fish dry with paper towels, cut into serving pieces and sprinkle lightly with salt. Cover and leave aside in a cool place.
2. Heat ghee or oil in a heavy pan, add onion and fry gently until transparent. Add ginger, garlic, chili, baharat, turmeric and cinnamon bark and stir over heat for 2 minutes.
3. Add tomatoes, loomi (pierced twice with a skewer) or lemon rind, and water. Add salt to taste and bring to a slow simmer. Cover and simmer gently for 15 minutes.
4. Place fish pieces in sauce, cover and simmer gently for 15-20 minutes until fish is cooked through. Lift fish onto prepared Muhammar or Maskhoul. Remove loomi or lemon rind and cinnamon bark from sauce and spoon sauce over fish.

MACHBOUS
SPICED PRAWNS AND RICE

Serves: 4-5
Cooking time: 50 minutes

1 kg (2 lb) uncooked prawns (shrimp)
2–3 tablespoons ghee
2 cloves garlic, chopped
1 large onion, chopped
2 teaspoons Baharat (page 245)
1 teaspoon turmeric
1½ cups chopped peeled tomatoes
2 teaspoons salt
freshly ground black pepper
1 tablespoon chopped parsley
1 teaspoon chopped coriander leaves
2½ cups water
2 cups basmati or other good quality long
    grain rice

1. Shell prawns and devein if necessary.
2. In a large pot heat 1 tablespoon ghee with garlic and add prawns. Stir over moderately high heat until prawns stiffen and turn pink — no need to cook them through. Lift out of pan and keep aside.
3. Add remaining butter to pot, add onion and fry gently until transparent and lightly browned.
4. Stir in baharat and turmeric and fry for 1 minute.
5. Add tomatoes, salt, pepper and chopped herbs, bring to the boil and add water. Cover pot and boil over moderate heat for 5 minutes.
6. Wash rice until water runs clear. Stir into sauce, bring to the boil, and boil, covered, for 10 minutes. Reduce heat to low.
7. Stir pot contents, then put prawns on top of rice, stirring them in lightly.
8. Cover pot and simmer gently over low heat for 20 minutes, stirring halfway through cooking.
9. Stir, then leave covered, off the heat, for 5 minutes. Serve with Khoubiz, pickles and salad.

SAMAK MAHSHI
FRIED STUFFED FISH

Serves: 4-6
Cooking time: 20 minutes

1 kg (2 lb) small, whole fish
salt
1 large onion, finely chopped
2 cloves garlic, finely chopped
2 tablespoons ghee
1½ teaspoons Baharat (page 245)
½ teaspoon ground loomi (dried lime)
½ teaspoon turmeric
flour for coating
oil or ghee for frying

1. Scale fish. Remove gills and clean out insides through small opening. Rub cavity with a wad of paper towelling dipped in salt to clean thoroughly. Rinse fish and dry well.
2. Fry onion and garlic in ghee until lightly browned. Stir in 1 teaspoon baharat, the dried lime and salt to taste. Remove from heat.
3. Stuff fish with onion mixture, placing a small wad of greaseproof paper or foil in opening to keep stuffing in.
4. Combine remaining baharat with turmeric and 1 teaspoon salt and rub over fish. Leave fish aside for 15 minutes to absorb flavours.
5. Heat oil or ghee. Coat fish lightly in flour and shallow fry until cooked through. Drain on paper towels and serve hot, garnished with lemon and parsley.

Note: Often curry powder is used instead of baharat in Bahrain.

SAMAK MASHWI
BARBECUED FISH WITH DATES

The traditional Gulf way to grill fish is in a special cut-away dome-shaped clay barbecue with glowing coals in the base. The fish is impaled on a firm stick, with the stick passing through the mouth and into the body. The end of the stick protruding from the mouth is stuck into the earth under the bed of coals, at a 45° angle. Perhaps you could try a similar method, using a fire on a low grid, with galvanized iron set around 3 sides to deflect the heat.

Serves: 6
Cooking time: 8-12 minutes

1 cup dried, pitted dates
water
6 whole firm-fleshed fish, each about
    375 g (12 oz)
salt
2 large onions, finely chopped
2 cloves garlic, crushed, optional
1½ teaspoons Baharat (page 245)
1 teaspoon turmeric

1. Put dates in cold water to cover and leave to soak for 30 minutes or until soft.
2. Purchase fish suitable for barbecuing, preferably a round-bodied variety such as red mullet. Do not have them scaled.
3. Gut fish and clean cavities well. Rinse and dry with paper towels. Sprinkle with salt and leave for 15 minutes or longer.
4. Mix together onions, garlic if used and spices and add a little water.
5. Fill cavities with mixture and close cavities with poultry skewers or wooden cocktail picks previously soaked in cold water for 30 minutes.
6. Rub dates through a sieve to purée, adding some of the soaking water, or purée in blender or food processor, adding enough date liquid to make a soft paste.
7. Spread date purée on each side of fish and leave on a rack for 10 minutes.
8. Cook fish over glowing charcoals for 4-5 minutes each side, depending on thickness of body.
9. Serve fish hot. The scales keep the flesh intact and the skin with scales attached is removed before eating. The dates give the fish a very pleasant flavour.

MACHBOUS ALA DAJAJ
SPICED CHICKEN AND RICE

Serves: 4-5
Cooking time: 1¾-2 hours

2 large onions, chopped
2 tablespoons ghee
1 tablespoon Baharat (page 245)
1 teaspoon turmeric
1 chicken, about 1.5 kg (3 lb), jointed
1½ cups chopped, peeled tomatoes
3 cloves
½ teaspoon powdered loomi (dried lime),
   or 1 strip lemon rind
2 pieces cinnamon bark
6 cardamom pods
3 teaspoons salt
2½ cups water
2 cups basmati or other good quality long
   grain rice
2 tablespoons chopped coriander leaves
2 tablespoons chopped parsley

1. In a deep, heavy pan, gently fry onion in ghee until transparent and beginning to brown. Stir in baharat and turmeric and cook two minutes longer.
2. Add chicken pieces and turn in onion mixture over medium heat to brown lightly. Add tomatoes, cloves, loomi, cinnamon, cardamom pods and salt, stirring well to combine.
3. Add water, cover and simmer over gentle heat for 45 minutes.
4. Pick over rice to remove discoloured grains. Place in a bowl and wash with cold water until water runs clear. Drain.
5. Stir rice gently into pot contents, add herbs and bring back to a slow simmer. Cover with lid and simmer on low heat for 35-40 minutes until chicken is tender, stirring gently once or twice during cooking. Remove from heat and leave aside for 10 minutes.
6. Pile onto large platter with chicken pieces in centre and serve hot with pickles, salad and khoubiz (flat bread).

QUWARMAH ALA DAJAJ
CURRIED CHICKEN

Serves: 5-6
Cooking time: 2-2½ hours

1 chicken, about 1.5 kg (3 lb), jointed
salt
1½ teaspoons Baharat (page 245)
1 teaspoon turmeric
¼ cup ghee
2 large onions, finely chopped
2 cloves garlic, crushed
1 teaspoon grated fresh ginger
¼-½ teaspoon hot chili pepper
small piece cinnamon bark
1 cup chopped, peeled tomatoes
2 loomi (dried limes) or thinly peeled rind
   of ½ lemon
¾ cup water

For serving:
Muhammar (page 249) or
Mashkoul (page 250)

1. Cut chicken joints into smaller pieces if desired. Wipe dry and sprinkle with salt. Combine baharat and turmeric and rub half of the mixture onto the chicken. Leave for 15 minutes.
2. Heat ghee in a heavy pan and brown chicken pieces on each side. Remove to a plate.
3. Add onion to pan and fry gently until transparent. Add garlic, ginger, remaining spice mixture, chili pepper to taste and cinnamon bark. Fry for 5 minutes, stirring often.
4. Add tomatoes, dried limes pierced twice with a skewer, or lemon rind, and water. Add salt to taste and bring to the boil.
5. Add chicken pieces, reduce heat to low and cover pan tightly. Simmer very gently for 1½-2 hours until chicken is tender and sauce is thick.
6. Serve hot with Muhammar or Mashkoul.

KABAB MASHWI
GROUND MEAT KEBAB

It is quite a sight to see these flavoursome kababs being prepared in the Gulf States, with many shops and food stalls specializing in them.

Lightning-quick hands shape the herbed and spiced meat paste onto long, flat skewers. Iron troughs running the length of the shop glow hotly with their charcoal fires ready to cook the kababs quickly to juicy tenderness. The skewers sit across the top of the troughs in neat formation, with the cooks working their way up and down the passageway between, turning the skewers or removing them when cooked.

The finished kabab is deftly slid off the skewer onto soft, flat khoubiz; shredded lettuce, sliced tomato, chopped onion and cucumber are added and it is handed to the waiting customer. Hamburger Gulf style!

Serves: 8
Cooking time: 2-3 minutes

1 kg (2 lb) ground lamb or beef
1 cup coarsely chopped parsley
2 large onions, chopped
2 teaspoons salt
2 teaspoons Baharat (page 245)
oil for cooking

To serve:
Khoubiz (page 190)
cos (romaine) lettuce, in leaves or shredded
sliced tomatoes
sliced cucumber
finely chopped onion or spring onion

1. Combine meat with parsley, onion, salt and baharat. Pass through a meat grinder twice, using fine screen. Alternatively process in 4 lots in food processor.
2. Knead to a smooth paste by hand if meat grinder is used; if processed, knead to blend flavours evenly.
3. Moisten hands with water, take generous tablespoons of the paste and mould it around flat, sword-like skewers in finger shapes about 10 cm (4 inches) long. Place 2 such shapes on long skewers, one if skewers are short. Keep hands moistened during shaping.
4. As skewers are prepared, set them across a baking dish with ends of skewers resting on each side.
5. Have charcoal fire at the glowing stage and remove grid if possible. A rectangular shaped barbecue such as the Japanese hibachi is an advantage as medium-length skewers fit across it without the need for a grid.
6. Brush kababs lightly with oil and grill for 2-3 minutes, turning frequently. If it is impossible to cook them without a grid, then try to place skewers so that meat lies between the grid bars.
7. Remove cooked kababs from skewers and serve immediately in warmed Khoubiz with salad ingredients. Also may be served on a plate with vegetable or salad accompaniment.

THARYD
BRAISED MEAT AND POTATOES

Serves: 5-6
Cooking time: 3 hours

1 kg (2 lb) boneless stewing lamb or beef
2 large onions, chopped
2 tablespoons ghee or oil
2 teaspoons Baharat (page 245)
1 clove garlic, crushed
2 cups chopped, peeled tomatoes
¼ cup tomato paste
2 teaspoons salt
½ teaspoon freshly ground black pepper
¼ cup chopped parsley
750 g (1½ lb) potatoes
1 khoubiz (flat bread)
chopped parsley to garnish

1. Trim meat and cut into cubes.
2. In a heavy based pan gently fry onions in ghee or oil until transparent.
3. Increase heat and add meat cubes. Stir until meat loses red colour, add spices and garlic and cook 1 minute.
4. Add tomatoes, tomato paste, salt, pepper and parsley. Cover and simmer very gently for 1½ hours.
5. Peel potatoes and halve if large. Add to pan, cover and simmer for further 1½ hours.
6. Cut khoubiz into small pieces and place in serving dish. Ladle meat, potatoes and sauce on top and sprinkle with chopped parsley. Serve with salad and pickles.

BASAL MAHSHI
STUFFED ONIONS

Serves: 6-8 as a meal, 12 as an appetizer
Cooking time: 1¾ hours

tamarind pulp the size of a walnut
1 cup warm water
5 large onions
water
750 g (1½ lb) ground beef or lamb
½ cup long grain rice, rinsed
1½ teaspoons Baharat (page 245)
½ teaspoon turmeric
salt
freshly ground black pepper
½ cup chopped tomatoes
2 tablespoons tomato paste
2 tablespoons chopped parsley
1 tablespoon oil
1 tablespoon melted ghee or oil
2 teaspoons sugar

1. Soak tamarind in ½ cup of warm water for 30 minutes. Strain into a bowl, pressing with back of spoon to separate pulp. Reserve liquid and discard seeds and fibres.
2. Peel onions and carefully cut out root with a pointed knife. Slit onion on one side through to the centre, cutting from top to root end.
3. Drop onions into boiling water and boil gently for 8-10 minutes until softened. Drain and cool.
4. In a mixing bowl thoroughly combine ground meat with rice, baharat, turmeric, seasoning to taste, tomatoes, tomato paste, parsley and oil.
5. Separate onion layers carefully. Outer layers may be cut in half, leave inner layers intact.
6. Place about a tablespoonful of meat mixture on a layer of onion and roll up firmly.
7. Grease a heavy pan with ghee or oil and pack rolls in pan with seam down. Sprinkle layers lightly with salt.
8. Combine tamarind liquid with remaining ½ cup water and the sugar and pour over rolls.
9. Invert a heavy plate on top to keep rolls intact during cooking and cover pan with lid.
10. Bring to a simmer over medium heat, reduce to low and simmer gently for 1½ hours. Serve hot with salads, pickles and flat bread. May also be served lukewarm as an appetizer.

KUBA AL-AISH
STUFFED MEAT ROLLS

Serves: 4
Cooking time: 10 minutes

Filling:
¼ cup yellow split peas
1 cup water
2 medium onions, finely chopped
1 tablespoon ghee
¼ cup sultanas
¼ teaspoon ground cardamom
½ teaspoon Baharat (page 245)
salt

Meat Mixture:
500 g (1 lb) lean lamb or mutton
1½ cups boiled, strained short grain rice
2 cloves garlic, chopped
1½ teaspoons Baharat (page 245)
1½ teaspoons salt
1 egg for shaping
oil for frying

1. Wash split peas and boil gently in the water for about 45 minutes until tender. Drain.
2. Gently fry onions in ghee until transparent and beginning to brown. Stir in sultanas, spices and add split peas. Add salt to taste and leave aside.
3. Chop meat in small pieces and mix with rice, garlic, spices and salt. Grind twice using fine screen, or process in 2 lots in food processor. If grinder is used, beat meat mixture to a paste-like consistency.
4. Beat egg in a bowl. Take a lump of the meat mixture about the size of a small egg. Coat palms with egg and shape meat smoothly, then using thumb make a hollow in the ball, moulding meat to a fairly thin shell. Fill with split pea mixture and press opening firmly to close. Reshape into either an oval or an oblong shape with rounded edges. Place finished kubas on a tray.
5. Heat about 1 cm (½ inch) oil in a frying pan and fry kubas for about 5 minutes each side. Drain on paper towels and serve hot with salad and flat bread.

MARAQ AL-BAMIYA
MEAT WITH OKRA

Serves: 5-6
Cooking time: 2-2½ hours

piece of tamarind the size of a walnut
½ cup warm water
1 kg (2 lb) stewing beef or lamb
¼ cup oil
2 large onions, chopped
3 cloves garlic, crushed
1½ cups chopped peeled tomatoes
½ cup water
salt
2 teaspoons Baharat (page 245)
2 teaspoons sugar
500 g (1 lb) bamiya (okra, see page 9 for
    preparation)
Mashkoul for serving (page 250)

1. Place tamarind in warm water and leave aside to soak.
2. Cut meat into 2 cm (¾ inch) cubes and brown in half the oil in a heavy pan. Remove to a plate.
3. Add remaining oil to pan, add onion and fry gently until transparent. Add garlic, cook a few seconds then stir in tomatoes, water, salt, baharat and sugar. Return meat to pan, cover and simmer for 1-1½ hours until meat is almost tender. Time depends on type of meat used.
4. Prepare bamiya as directed. Rub tamarind to separate pulp from seeds and fibres, then pass through a sieve, reserving liquid.
5. Place bamiya on top of meat in pan and pour tamarind liquid over bamiya. Cover and simmer for further 30 minutes or until meat and vegetables are tender. Do not stir once bamiya is added —just shake pan gently to distribute flavours. Serve with Mashkoul or other simple rice dish.

MACHBOUS
SPICED LAMB AND RICE

Serves: 4-5
Cooking time: 3 hours

2 large onions, chopped
2 tablespoons ghee
1 tablespoon Baharat (page 245)
1 teaspoon turmeric
1.5 kg (2 1b) lamb shoulder cut in 4-5 pieces
    on the bone
1½ cups chopped, peeled tomatoes
3 cloves
½ teaspoon powdered loomi (dried lime)
2 pieces cinnamon bark
3 cardamom pods
3 teaspoons salt
2½ cups water
¼ cup chopped parsley or coriander
2 cups basmati or other good quality long
    grain rice

1. In a large pot gently fry onion in ghee until transparent and beginning to brown. Stir in baharat and turmeric and cook 2 minutes longer.
2. Add lamb pieces and turn in onion mixture over medium heat, lightly browning meat. Add tomatoes, spices and salt, stirring well to combine. Cover and simmer 10 minutes.
3. Add water and chopped herb, cover and simmer over gentle heat for 2-2½ hours until meat is fork tender.
4. Pick over rice if necessary, place in a bowl or sieve and wash until water runs clear. Drain and stir gently into pot contents. Return to the boil, reduce heat and cover tightly.
5. Simmer for 20 minutes, stirring once or twice during cooking. When cooked, stir carefully once more, cover and leave off the heat for 5 minutes.
6. Pile onto a large platter, with meat pieces in centre. Serve hot with pickles, salad and Khoubiz (flat bread).

TAMAR AL GIBNA (Dates with White Cheese) *recipe page 263.*

KHOUZI
BAKED WHOLE LAMB

Serves: 20
Oven temperature: 180°C (350°F)
Cooking time: 4-5 hours

1 small lamb, about 10-12 kg (20-25 lb)
salt
¼ cup Baharat (page 245)
2 teaspoons turmeric
1 small chicken, about 1 kg (2 lb), optional
3 hard-boiled eggs, optional
½ cup rose water
2 teaspoons saffron threads, pounded
5 cups basmati or other good quality long
   grain rice
1 cup ghee
3 large onions, finely chopped
5 cups water
1 cup blanched almonds or cashew nuts
½ cup pine nuts
½ cup pistachio nuts
½ cup sultanas

1. Wipe lamb inside and out with a damp cloth. Rub cavity and outer surface with salt, half the baharat, and 1 teaspoon turmeric. Put aside.

2. If chicken is used, wipe dry with paper towels and rub cavity and skin with a little baharat, turmeric and salt. Insert shelled hard-boiled eggs in chicken cavity. Leave chicken aside until rice stuffing is ready.

3. Put rose water in a bowl and add pounded saffron threads; leave to soak for 10 minutes.

4. Pick over rice, put in a strainer and wash well under cold running water. Drain.

5. In a large pan melt half the ghee and add chopped onions, fry gently until transparent, stir in remaining baharat and turmeric and add rice. Stir for 5 minutes on medium heat, then add 5 cups water and bring to the boil, stirring occasionally. Add salt to taste, reduce heat, cover and simmer on low heat for 10 minutes.

6. Add nuts and sultanas and fold into the rice. Sprinkle half rose water mixture into the rice mixture. Cover pan and leave off the heat for 10 minutes until liquid is absorbed.

7. Put some of this rice mixture in the chicken, filling it loosely. Secure opening with poultry pins.

8. Sew up the cavity of the lamb half way and leave thread hanging. Fill cavity with some of the rice mixture, put chicken in if used and complete filling with the remaining rice mixture. Finish sewing up cavity.

9. Place a large rack in a very large catering-size baking dish and sit the lamb on the rack. Brush lamb with remaining ghee. Cover dish with large sheets of foil, sealing joins with double folds. Press foil under edge to seal completely.

10. Bake in a moderate oven for 2 hours. Baste lamb with juice in dish and pour remaining rose water mixture over lamb. Cover dish again, return to oven and bake for a further 2-3 hours until very tender, basting twice more with dish juices. Remove foil 30 minutes before end of cooking.

11. Lift lamb onto a large platter, remove string and spoon stuffing out on the platter, setting chicken (if used) on top of stuffing.

12. Lamb can be carved, but it is much more fun to break off very soft tender chunks of meat. Enjoy your feast and feel like a sheik!

Note: Kid may be used instead of lamb.

KEBAT AL BATATIS WAL BURKUL
BURGHUL AND POTATO CAKES WITH LAMB AND APRICOT FILLING

Serves: 6
Cooking time: 1 hour

4 medium-sized potatoes, about 500 g (1 lb)
¾ cup fine burkul (burghul)
¼ cup plain flour
1 egg
salt
freshly ground black pepper

Lamb and Apricot Filling:
2 tablespoons oil or ghee
1 large onion, finely chopped
500 g (1 lb) finely ground lamb
¼ cup chopped almonds
½ cup chopped, dried apricots
½ teaspoon Baharat (page 245), optional
salt
freshly ground black pepper
¼ cup water

To finish:
oil for deep frying

1. Scrub potatoes and boil in their jackets until tender. Drain, remove skins and mash.
2. Place burghul in a bowl and cover with 2 cups cold water. Soak for 15 minutes and drain through a fine sieve, pressing with the back of a spoon to extract moisture.
3. Put potatoes and burghul in a bowl and add flour, egg and salt and pepper to taste. Blend thoroughly to a paste and shape tablespoons of the mixture into balls with moistened hands.
4. To make filling, heat oil or ghee in a frying pan, add onion and fry gently until transparent. Increase heat, add ground lamb and cook over high heat, stirring often, until lamb is crumbly and begins to brown. Reduce heat to low, stir in remaining filling ingredients, seasoning to taste with salt and pepper and adding water last. Cover and simmer for 10 minutes on low heat. Remove from heat and cool a little.
5. Flatten a ball of burghul and potato paste in the palm of the hand and place a generous teaspoon of filling in centre. Close up paste and reshape into a ball, then flatten to a thick cake. Repeat with remaining ingredients.
6. Deep fry 6 at a time in hot oil for 7-8 minutes, turning to brown evenly. Drain on paper towels and serve hot.

LAHM BIL BAYD
GROUND MEAT WITH HARD-BOILED EGGS

Serves: 3-6
Cooking time: 5-7 minutes

500 g (1 lb) ground lamb
1 small onion, chopped
¼ cup finely chopped parsley
½ cup soft breadcrumbs
salt
freshly ground black pepper
6 hard-boiled eggs
1 egg white, beaten

To finish:
1 egg, beaten
1 cup dry breadcrumbs
oil for deep frying

For serving:
Dukkous al-Tamat (page 245)

1. Combine lamb with onion and pass through meat grinder twice using fine screen. Alternatively process in food processor to a paste.
2. Turn into a bowl and add parsley, soft crumbs, and salt and pepper to taste. Knead to a fairly soft paste. Divide into 6 equal portions.
3. Shell eggs and coat with beaten egg white. Shape a portion of the meat paste around each egg, moulding it smoothly.
4. Brush coated eggs with beaten egg, roll in dry breadcrumbs to coat, then deep fry in hot oil, cooking for 5-7 minutes in all. Turn to brown evenly. Do not have oil too hot, as outside will brown before inside is cooked. Serve hot, cut in half, with Dukkous al-Tamat, or cold with salad.

AL-SALOOQ
FRIED CARDAMOM SWEETMEATS

Makes 24
Cooking time: 5 minutes each batch

½ cup milk
2 cups plain flour
1 teaspoon baking powder
½ teaspoon ground cardamom
½ cup melted butter
oil for deep frying
icing (confectioner's) sugar

1. Bring milk to the boil, then cool.
2. Sift flour, baking powder and cardamom into mixing bowl, add melted butter and blend with a wooden spoon until combined and crumbly.
3. Pour in cooled milk and mix to a soft dough. Knead lightly for 1 minute until smooth.
4. Roll into balls the size of a walnut, then roll into thick fingers and press around forefinger to make a crescent shape.
5. Heat oil to 190°C (375°F) or when a cube of bread turns golden in 45 seconds. Add 6 salooq at a time and fry for 5 minutes, turning to brown evenly.
6. Lift out with slotted spoon and drain on paper towels.
7. After 2 batches are cooked, place in a bag of sifted icing sugar and shake to coat. Lift out. Cook and coat remaining salooq. Serve warm or cold.

SABB AL-GAFSHA
SWEET PUFFS

Makes about 40

1 sachet active dry yeast
2 tablespoons warm water
1 cup tdaheen hummus (chick pea flour)
½ cup plain flour
3 teaspoons ground rice
5 large eggs (at room temperature)
½ teaspoon ground cardamom
¼ teaspoon saffron threads, pounded
¼ cup ghee, melted and cooled
oil for deep frying

Syrup:
2 cups sugar
2 cups water
2 tablespoons strained lemon juice
½ teaspoon ground cardamom
¼ teaspoon saffron threads, pounded

1. Add yeast to warm water, leave to soak, then stir to dissolve.
2. Sift chick pea flour, plain flour and ground rice into a bowl and make a well in the centre.
3. Beat eggs well and stir in cardamom, saffron and yeast mixture.
4. Add egg-yeast mixture to dry ingredients, pour in cooled ghee and gradually blend to a thick batter, beating until smooth.
5. Stretch a piece of plastic wrap over bowl and leave in a warm draught-free place for at least 4 hours — it may be left for longer.
6. To make syrup, dissolve sugar in water in a heavy pan over medium heat, stirring occasionally. When dissolved, bring to the boil, add lemon juice, cardamom and saffron and boil for 15 minutes. Remove from heat and leave until cool.
7. Heat oil in medium-sized deep pan to 190°C (375°F). Stir dough, then drop teaspoonfuls of dough into hot oil, pushing it off the end of the spoon with a round-bladed knife. Drop 10-12 balls in at a time and fry for 3-4 minutes, turning balls over to brown evenly.
8. When golden brown and cooked through, lift out with a slotted spoon and place in cool syrup.
9. When all are cooked, stir sabb in syrup to coat evenly, then lift out with slotted spoon and pile onto plate. Serve warm.

TAMAR
DATES

Not so long ago the date palm was the fountain of life to the people of the Gulf region – their fruit for trade and sustenance, the palm itself for building materials, household and personal articles and fuel. Today it is still revered by many, particularly the Bedouin and the impoverished.

In Oman the date is enjoyed in simple ways — indeed it is all this nectar-sweet fruit requires. Fresh dates are dipped in samneh (ghee or clarified butter), or eaten with camel milk curds. The date molasses gathered after drying the fruit features in their cooking — for making a sweet bread or adding to Muhammar (page 249).

To be able to enjoy the date all year round, various sweetmeats are made. The simplest is dates formed into a ball and rolled in ash as a protection against insects. Other date recipes follow.

TAMAR AL GIBNA
DATES WITH WHITE CHEESE

Serves: 6

750 g (1 lb) fresh dates
500 g (1 lb) keereesh, mizithra or anari
 (see Index) or ricotta cheese, or
2 cups yoghurt

1. Pit dates and place in individual dishes. Serve with cheese or yoghurt.

AL BATHEETH
DATE SWEETMEAT

Makes 20
Cooking time: 12 minutes

1 cup wholemeal flour
¼ cup ghee or clarified butter
1 cardamom pod, bruised
1 cup chopped dates
½ teaspoon ground ginger
icing (confectioner's) sugar for serving

1. Place flour in a heavy-based pan and stir over medium heat until lightly browned — about 10 minutes.
2. While flour is browning heat ghee in a small pan with the cardamom pod. Heat for 5 minutes and leave aside.
3. Add dates to flour, and heat for 2 minutes until dates feel soft. Stir constantly.
4. Remove cardamom pod from ghee and add ghee to date mixture with ginger. Stir until ghee is evenly distributed and remove from heat. Mixture will be crumbly. Leave until cool enough to handle.
5. Take about a tablespoonful of mixture at a time and knead in hands, tossing from one hand to the other. When mixture holds together squeeze into an oval shape, moulding it smoothly. Place on a plate and leave until cool.
6. Pack in airtight container. Serve sprinkled with icing sugar.

RANGINA
FRESH DATE SWEET

Serves: 6
Cooking time: 5-8 minutes

500 g (1 lb) fresh dates
½ cup butter
¾ cup plain flour
1 teaspoon ground cardamom

1. Pit dates and arrange in individual dessert dishes.
2. Melt butter in a heavy pan and stir in flour. Cook over medium heat, stirring constantly, until flour becomes a golden brown — take care not to burn it.
3. Remove from heat and stir in cardamom. Leave to cool down a little, stirring occasionally as it cools. Pour while warm over the dates. Let rangina cool to room temperature before serving.

Note: Some chopped walnuts stirred into the browned flour give an interesting taste and texture to the sweet.

GHIRAYBAH
SHORTBREAD COOKIES

Makes 35-40
Oven temperature: 170°C (325°F)
Cooking time: 20-25 minutes

1 cup samneh (clarified butter)
1 cup icing (confectioner's) sugar, sifted
2½ cups plain flour

1. Chill samneh in refrigerator if too soft. Put firm samneh in mixing bowl and beat until light. Gradually add sifted icing sugar, beating until very creamy and light.
2. Sift flour and fold into butter mixture. Knead lightly until smooth. If kitchen is hot, chill dough in refrigerator for 1-2 hours.
3. Roll pieces of dough into balls the size of a walnut and place on ungreased baking sheets. Press thumb into centre of each ball to make a dimple and to flatten dough slightly. Flour thumb lightly if necessary.
4. Bake in a moderately slow oven for 20-25 minutes until very lightly coloured. Cool on baking sheets, then remove and store in a sealed container. These are very delicate biscuits and must be handled carefully.

Note: Ghiraybah are prepared in most countries of the Middle East. Sometimes they are topped with a blanched almond or pine nut instead of being dimpled; cooks in other areas prefer not to let the cookies colour at all; still others finish Ghiraybah with a dusting of icing sugar. Caster sugar is often used in the mixture rather than the icing sugar used in the Gulf States.

NASHAB
FRIED NUT ROLLS

Makes about 40
Cooking time: 2-3 minutes each lot

Nut Filling:
1 cup finely ground cashew nuts
1 cup finely ground walnuts
½ cup caster sugar
1-1½ teaspoons ground cardamom

To finish:
10 sheets fillo pastry
water for sealing
ghee or oil for deep frying

1. Combine nut filling ingredients, adding cardamom to taste.
2. Cut pastry sheets into quarters. Pieces should be about 15 cm (6 inches) wide and 20 cm (8 inches) long. Stack and cover with a cloth.
3. Take a strip of pastry and place on work surface with narrow edge towards you. Sprinkle 2 teaspoons nut filling thinly across base of strip, keeping 1 cm (½ inch) of pastry clear of filling at sides and base.
4. Moisten sides of strip with water and fold sides over filling, pressing folds along length of sides. Roll up firmly to within 5 cm (2 inches) of end of strip. Moisten this section lightly and evenly with water and complete the roll. Repeat using remaining ingredients, placing completed rolls on a cloth.
5. Heat oil or ghee in a deep pan to a temperature of 190°C (375°F) and deep fry 5 at a time for 2-3 minutes, turning rolls to brown evenly. When deep golden brown, remove with slotted spoon and drain on paper towels. Cool before serving. Store nashab in a sealed container at room temperature.

SAMBOOSA HOLWAH
FRIED NUT TRIANGLES

Samboosa Holwah should be very tiny and literally bulging with sugar and nuts. You might find it difficult to contain the nut filling in the narrow confines of the pastry strip as it is folded. Push filling in during first 2 or 3 folds — if you go off-course with the shaping do not be concerned, as the final shape will be near enough to a triangle. Try one or two strips before cutting all the pastry. If it proves too difficult, cut remaining strips 5 cm (2 inches) wide, using same amount of filling.

Makes about 60
Cooking time: 2-3 minutes each lot

Nut Filling:
1 cup coarsely ground raw cashew nuts
½ cup coarsely ground walnuts
½ cup caster sugar
½-1 teaspoon ground cardamom
2 teaspoons cold water

To finish:
10 sheets fillo pastry
water for sealing
ghee or oil for deep frying

1. Combine cashew nuts and walnuts in a bowl with sugar and ground cardamom to taste. Add water and knead well with hand until mixture clings together in a coarse paste.
2. Cut sheets of fillo pastry in 4 cm (1½ inch) strips across the width of the sheet. If fillo sheet measures 30 x 40 cm (12 x 16 inches), strips may be a little longer or shorter, according to size of sheet. Cover strips with a cloth.
3. Take a strip of pastry and place a teaspoon of filling on one end of strip. Fold pastry diagonally over filling forming a triangle, then a straight fold up, followed by another diagonal fold in the opposite direction to the first fold. Continue folding to the end of the strip. Moisten end of pastry with water and press to seal. Repeat using remaining ingredients, placing finished pastries on a cloth.
4. Heat ghee or oil in a deep pan to a temperature of 190°C (375°F), or when a cube of bread turns golden in 45 seconds. Deep fry triangles 10 at a time for about 2-3 minutes, turning to brown evenly. Pastries must not cook too quickly as the inner layers must cook before the outside becomes too brown.
5. When pastries are a deep golden brown, remove with slotted spoon and drain on paper towels. Leave until cold before serving. Samboosa Holwah will keep crisp for a number of days stored in a sealed container at room temperature.

QAHWAT
ARABIC COFFEE

Serves: 8

6 cardamom pods
1 cup cold water
¼ cup coarsely pulverized dark roast coffee

1. Bruise cardamom pods by hitting with a mallet or pound briefly in a mortar.
2. Put water in a long-handled coffee pot and add cardamom pods and coffee. Bring to the boil, then reduce heat to low. Leave to simmer on low heat for 20 minutes so grounds settle.
3. Pour into Arabic coffee cups, only half filling cups. It is traditionally served without sugar.

QAHWAT AL-HILO
SWEET ARABIC COFFEE

This is actually a spice infusion, and though called a coffee, there is no coffee in it.

Serves: 6
1½ cups water
3 whole cardamoms, bruised (see Qahwat)
3 teaspoons saffron threads, pounded
sugar to taste

1. Combine ingredients in a small pan or large long-handled coffee pot. Stir to dissolve, then leave on low heat for 30 minutes until reduced and thick.
2. Serve in Arabic coffee cups, filling them. An exotic brew.

YEMEN

Once known as North and South Yemen, and later as the Arab Republic of Yemen and the Democratic People's Republic of Yemen, the two countries put aside their ideological differences and merged in 1990, becoming the Republic of Yemen. Yemeni hospitality is typically Arabic; indeed many years ago in a remote part of the Hadramaut to the South, one Yemeni host would be so incensed if a traveller passed by without calling that he would shoot over their heads. Perhaps that was going a little too far!

THE FLAVOUR OF YEMENI FOOD

Hot, spicy foods are particularly loved by the Yemenis, so be warned when tackling a recipe calling for chilis.

Zhug, a hot relish fired with chilis and pepper and flavoured with cardamom, caraway, fresh coriander and garlic, is used as a bread dip. Breads and cereals are the staples of the Yemeni diet and zhug, together with a fenugreek-based mixture called hilbeh, add flavour and interest to these foods. Hilbeh is used in southern Yemen while another version called hulba is used in the north. Though the basic ingredients are the same, there is a slight difference in the pronounciation between the two areas, and the preparation is also slightly different.

The basic sauce is combined with bone stock and placed on a small fire close to where the meal is taken. At the end of the meal any remaining food, such as rice, vegetables, lentils and meat pieces, are added to the pot. The whole is heated and mixed and the resultant hash is scooped up with fresh-baked flat bread, usually khobz or malvj. I have given a version in the recipes following as it is a good way to use up leftovers, having included foods and flavouring ingredients likely to be present on the Yemeni table. It is rather like a Middle Eastern meal of hash or bubble and squeak.

The Yemeni cook makes quite a variety of breads, some leavened with yeast, others somewhat similar to the Indian chapati. One bread much loved by the Yemenis is malvj, a barley bread, and though recipes vary considerably you will find my version an easy bread to make and quite delicious.

Bint-al-Sahn is a fine-textured yeast bread formed into very thin leaves and smothered with samneh. The leaves are placed one on top of the other forming dough cakes, then baked. They are served hot from the oven with more samneh and honey, and served at the beginning of a meal on festive occasions. While on the subject of honey, in the early days honey was frequently poured over meat and rice, however the men allowed this luxury only to themselves as honey was considered an aphrodisiac and it was thought improper for the womenfolk to partake.

While yoghurt is used in large towns and cities, the Yemenis in remote rural areas use sour milk instead. Flavourwise there is little difference and no doubt the Yemenis have their particular utensils set aside for making the sour milk. It is impossible for the Westerner to make an equivalent as milk is usually pasteurized, which kills the bacteria essential for the souring process. Yoghurt is used in these recipes, even though the Yemeni version would often specify sour milk.

Meat and chicken are popular foods, but so little is available that the Yemenis, particularly the poorer ones, would have meat perhaps once a week or even less. However they do tend to use a lot of bones for basic stock.

Though Moccha is renowned for its coffee, very few Yemenis can afford it and to satisfy their taste for coffee they grind the husks and make a brew with ground ginger. It is called Qishr and I have given you a recipe as it is a very pleasant brew.

EATING YEMENI STYLE

Of all the countries covered, Yemen has been the least touched by Western customs. Generally the men eat first and the women and children have their meal afterwards or in another room. A cloth is spread on a carpet and cushions placed on the floor and around the walls for seating and back support. All the food is placed in pots, platters or bowls with no separate bowls or plates for individual diners. Hands are washed before the meal and the meal is eaten using the fingers of the right hand. The food is likely to include boiled rice, a cereal dish made of ground sorghum or flour, a soup, cooked and raw vegetables, a hot relish such as zhug, and plenty of bread. Bint-al-Sahn precedes the meal on festive occasions and on Fridays, the Moslem holiday. If fruits are available then these are included. Though parts of the country are fertile and capable of producing a large variety of fruits including grapes, mangoes and bananas, the land is not fully productive.

After the meal any food left is put into the hulba dish and heated on the small wood burner, called a *mauqad,* and it is scooped out with fresh bread. Soup is passed around in a ladle so that each diner may sip from it to cleanse the palate.

The meal is taken with little or no conversation and as soon as a person has had enough to eat, he leaves the table, washes his hands and retires into the *mafraj,* a sitting room furnished with carpets and cushions. Here coffee is taken, the *mada'* (water pipe) shared, and conversation flows.

COOKING METHODS

Cooking facilities are rather primitive with much of the cooking carried out on fires out of doors. Bread is baked on the sides of a beehive-shaped oven or cooked on a flat iron over the fire. While traditional cooking vessels were made of iron or carved out of stone similar to basalt, aluminium pots and pottery vessels are more likely to be used today. The traditional shape is rather shallow with a ridge half-way up the side of the vessel, forming two handles, rather like a shallow Dutch oven or casserole. You will require a heavy-based frying pan or griddle for cooking breads, otherwise any cooking utensil can be used according to the dish being prepared.

INGREDIENTS FOR YEMENI COOKING

Wholemeal, barley and white flour for breads, dried beans and lentils, beef or lamb, any vegetable used in Middle East cooking including eggplant and okra, plus fresh coriander leaves, hot chilis, fenugreek, cardamom, black cumin, caraway seeds, turmeric and saffron — with these foods you will be able to duplicate Yemeni cooking. As you probably will not be able to obtain coffee husks, use finely ground moccha coffee for Qishr.

HULBA
FENUGREEK PASTE

Serves: 6
Cooking time: 15-20 minutes

¼ cup ground hulba (fenugreek)
1 cup cold water
2-4 bisbas (hot chilis), depending on taste
salt
1 tomato, peeled and chopped
¼ cup chopped onion or spring onion
2 cloves garlic, crushed
¼ teaspoon Hawayij (below)
1 cup finely chopped boiled lamb or chicken
1 cup boiled lentils
1 cup boiled rice
1 tablespoon chopped kizbara (coriander
   leaves)
2 tablespoons samneh (clarified butter) or oil
bone or chicken stock

1. Place fenugreek in a bowl and add cold water. Leave to soak for 5 hours. Pour off water and beat until frothy with a fork.
2. Remove stalks and seeds from chilis and chop finely (take care in handling them). Blend into fenugreek paste with salt to taste and place in a pot. This is the actual Hulba.
3. Add remaining ingredients listed except the stock, or substitute some of the ingredients with whatever is on hand, e.g. diced boiled potatoes for rice, cooked dried beans for lentils. (For 1 cup cooked lentils, simmer ½ cup red lentils in 1½ cups water for 15-20 minutes until thick.)
4. Blend ingredients in pot and add enough stock to moisten. Place over medium heat and cook, stirring occasionally, until bubbling and thick. Add a little more stock during heating if necessary.
5. Adjust seasoning with salt and serve in a deep bowl with khobz, malvj, or the readily available Lebanese flat bread for scooping up the mixture. Serve in individual bowls if preferred.

HILBEH
FENUGREEK AND CORIANDER PASTE

2 teaspoons fenugreek seeds
cold water
2 cloves garlic
¾ cup chopped coriander leaves
½ teaspoon salt
2 teaspoons lemon juice
1 small hot chili, seeds removed, optional

1. Soak fenugreek seeds in ½ cup cold water for 12-18 hours until a jelly-like coating is evident on seeds. Drain off water.
2. Place fenugreek in blender jar with garlic and coriander and blend to a coarse purée, adding salt, lemon juice, chili if used and enough cold water to draw ingredients over blades.
3. Turn into a jar, seal and store in refrigerator. Use as a bread dip or as specified in recipes.

ZHUG
HOT RELISH

3 cardamom pods
1 teaspoon black peppercorns
1 teaspoon caraway seeds
4-6 hot chilis
1½ cups coriander sprigs, washed and
   drained
6 cloves garlic
½ teaspoon salt
¼ cup cold water

1. Place cardamom pods, peppercorns and caraway seeds in jar of blender and blend to a coarse powder.
2. Cut stems from chilis, leaving rest of chili intact. Add to blender jar with remaining ingredients and blend to a coarse purée.
3. Turn into a small saucepan and bring to the boil. Simmer uncovered for 10 minutes, then place in a jar, seal and store in refrigerator. Use as a bread dip or as specified in recipes.

HAWAYIJ
SPICE MIX

6 teaspoons black peppercorns
3 teaspoons caraway seeds
1 teaspoon saffron threads
1 teaspoon cardamom seeds
2 teaspoons turmeric

1. Pound peppercorns, caraway seeds, saffron and cardamom seeds in a mortar, or grind in a blender.
2. Stir in turmeric and store spice mix in a sealed jar. Use according to recipes.

SALUF BI HILBEH
FLAT BREAD WITH FENUGREEK AND CORIANDER PASTE

Makes 12 loaves
Oven temperature: 260°C (500°F)
Cooking time: 4 minutes each lot

1 sachet active dry yeast
1½ cups warm water
2 cups plain flour
2 cups wholemeal flour
½ teaspoon salt
oil or samneh (ghee)
1 quantity Hilbeh (page 268)

1. Soak yeast in ¼ cup water and stir to dissolve.
2. Sift flours into a mixing bowl, remove 1 cup flour and keep aside.
3. Blend remaining water and salt into yeast liquid and pour into flour. Mix in a little of the flour to thicken liquid, cover and leave in a warm place for 10-15 minutes until frothy.
4. Blend in remaining flour in bowl, then beat by hand for 10 minutes, or on electric mixer using dough hook for 5 minutes.
5. Turn onto a floured board and knead in enough of the reserved flour to make dough smooth and satiny. Return to bowl, sprinkle top of dough lightly with flour and stretch a sheet of plastic film over top of bowl. Leave in a warm place until doubled in bulk — about 30 minutes. Preheat oven.
6. Punch down dough and turn out on board. Knead a little, then divide into 12 equal portions.
7. Place a heavy flat griddle or baking sheet on centre shelf in oven and heat for 10 minutes. Grease with a wad of paper towelling dipped in oil.
8. Roll out each portion to a 15 cm (6 inch) round and prick with a fork. Brush top lightly with oil and spread on 1 teaspoon hilbeh. Lift 2 loaves onto a lightly floured, flat-edged baking sheet or plywood board and slide onto heated griddle or baking sheet.
9. Bake in hot oven for 4 minutes. Top may be lightly browned under a hot grill.
10. As breads are removed, wrap in a cloth to keep them warm and soft. Serve warm.

Note: If breads begin to puff up during cooking, press top with a folded cloth. Breads should be bubbly, but should not form a pocket.

LAHUH
SOUR DOUGH FLAT BREAD

This sour dough bread is cooked in a pan as you would cook pancakes. It is favoured during Ramadan and other Moslem feasts when enormous quantities of food are prepared and consumed. No doubt its popularity lies in the simplicity of ingredients and preparation.

Makes about 10 rounds
Cooking time: 5-6 minutes each bread

2 cups wholemeal flour
1 teaspoon salt
1½ cups water
oil for cooking

1. Sift flour into a mixing bowl, add water and stir to make a thin batter.
2. Stretch a piece of plastic food wrap over bowl and leave at room temperature for 2-3 days until fermented. Length of time depends on temperature. It is fermented when bubbles pepper the surface and batter has a sour smell.
3. Place just enough oil in a heavy frying pan to finely coat the base. Put over medium heat. Stir batter.
4. When oil is heated, pour about ⅓ cup batter into the pan, shaping it into a round with the back of a spoon.
5. Cook for 2-3 minutes until browned and surface looks dry, then turn and cook for further 2-3 minutes. Lift out and place on a plate.
6. Repeat with remaining batter, stacking lahuh on the plate as they are cooked. Add more oil to pan as required.
7. Serve warm as an accompaniment to Yemeni meals, or eat lahuh warm, drizzled with melted butter and honey.

KHOBZ
WHOLEMEAL FLAT BREAD

Makes 12 rounds
Cooking time: 2-3 minutes each round

3 cups wholemeal flour
1 teaspoon salt
1 cup tepid water
oil for cooking

1. Combine flour and salt in a bowl, pour in water and mix to a soft dough.
2. Knead in bowl for 10 minutes. Dough will feel slightly sticky at first but will become smooth as it is kneaded.
3. Form into a ball, stretch plastic film over bowl and leave dough to rest for 2 hours or even longer.
4. Divide dough into 12 even-sized balls the size of a large egg. Roll out to rounds 15 cm (6 inches) in diameter. Dough can be shaped without flour — if it sticks, dust work surface and dough very lightly with white flour.
5. Place rounds side by side on a cloth, cover and leave to rest for 20 minutes.
6. Heat a heavy frying pan or flat griddle. Cooking surface is hot enough when a little water sprinkled on bounces off the surface. Rub with cloth dipped in oil.
7. Put in a round of dough and cook for about 1 minute, pressing top lightly with a folded cloth to encourage even bubbling of dough. When browned on base, turn over and cook for further minute or until bread looks cooked. As breads are cooked, wrap in a cloth to keep them soft and warm. Rub cooking surface occasionally with oiled cloth.

MALVJ
BARLEY BREAD

Makes 8 breads
Cooking time: 2-3 minutes each bread

½ sachet (1 teaspoon) active dry yeast
¼ cup warm water
½ cup skim milk yoghurt at room
   temperature
½ teaspoon bicarbonate of soda
1 cup barley flour
1 cup wholemeal flour
½ teaspoon salt

1. Dissolve yeast in warm water.
2. Stir yoghurt until smooth and mix in soda. Yoghurt will froth.
3. Combine flours in a mixing bowl with salt. Add yeast liquid and yoghurt. Stir to a soft dough, then knead by hand for 10 minutes.
4. Cover bowl with plastic film and leave in a warm place for 1-1½ hours or until almost doubled in bulk.
5. Turn dough onto board and knead a little. Divide into 8 equal portions and roll into balls.
6. Press or roll each ball into a flat 15 cm (6 inch) round. Place on a cloth, cover and leave for 20 minutes.
7. Heat a griddle or electric frypan on medium high heat. Rub pan with a wad of paper towel dipped in oil. Put in 1 round of dough and after a few seconds press dough with a folded cloth to encourage small bubbles. If dough is not pressed, the bread forms a pocket. Cook for 1½ minutes, turn and cook for further 1 minute or until done. Bread will have a slightly moist appearance around edges. Remove and wrap in a cloth to keep warm while other breads are cooked. Serve warm.

SHOURBA BILSEN (Thick Lentil Soup) *recipe page 272;*
SHOURBA FUL (Dried Bean Soup) *recipe page 272.*

SHOURBA BILSEN
THICK LENTIL SOUP

Serves: 6
Cooking time: 2½ hours

250 g (8 oz) soup bones (beef or lamb)
7 cups water
2 cups bilsen (brown lentils)
1 large onion, finely chopped
¼ cup oil
3 cloves garlic, chopped
2 cups chopped, peeled tomatoes
¼ cup kizbara (coriander leaves)
salt
freshly ground black pepper

1. Rinse soup bones and place in a pot with the water. Bring to a slow simmer, skimming when necessary.
2. When well skimmed and boiling, add washed lentils. Return to the boil, reduce heat to low, cover and simmer gently for 1 hour. Do not stir.
3. Meanwhile in a separate pan fry onion in oil until soft and lightly browned, add garlic and cook for 1 minute more. Stir in tomatoes, coriander and salt and pepper to taste.
4. Remove bones from pot and discard. Add onion mixture to lentils, cover and simmer gently for further hour or until thick. Take care that soup does not catch to base of pot.
5. Serve hot in small bowls with flat bread and salad.

SHOURBA FUL
DRIED BEAN SOUP

Make as for Shourba Bilsen, substituting 2 cups dried haricot (navy) beans for lentils. Wash beans well, place in a pot with the 7 cups cold water and bring to the boil. Boil for 2 minutes, remove from heat and leave until beans are plump. Add washed bones and return to the boil, skimming as required. When well skimmed, cover and simmer for 1 hour. Proceed from Step 3.

FATUT
FRIED BREAD WITH EGGS

Serves: 4
Cooking time: 5-6 minutes

2 Khobz (page 270)
¼ cup samneh (clarified butter) or ghee
4 eggs, lightly beaten
salt

1. Break up khobz into small pieces. (If desired Lebanese flat bread may be used instead of khobz.)
2. Heat samneh or ghee in a large frying pan and add bread pieces. Stir over medium heat until beginning to become crisp and lightly browned.
3. Pour in eggs and salt to taste, and stir over heat for 2 minutes, as you would scrambled egg. When egg is just set, pile onto plates and serve hot. A good breakfast dish — scrambled eggs and toast from one pan!

FATUT BIL HULBA
FRIED BREAD WITH EGGS AND FENUGREEK

This is a combination of Fatut (previous recipe) and Hulba. Make the basic fenugreek paste with chilis and salt to taste as directed in Hulba recipe, Steps 1 and 2, page 268.

Blend in 2 cups chicken stock and pour into pan with cooked Fatut. Bring to the boil and serve in bowls with lemon juice added to taste.

BANADURA SALATA BIL KIZBARA
TOMATO AND CORIANDER SALAD

Serves: 6

6 medium-sized firm tomatoes
½ cup chopped kizbara (coriander leaves)
1 small bisbas (hot chili) or freshly ground
    black pepper
juice of ½ lemon
salt
¼ cup olive oil

1. Peel tomatoes by placing in a bowl and pouring boiling water over them. Pour off water after 10 seconds and peel off skins.
2. Slice tomatoes into a bowl and sprinkle with chopped coriander.
3. If using chili, cut off stalk, slit open and remove seeds. Take care that you do not put fingers near eyes or mouth. Chop chili finely. Otherwise use plenty of black pepper.
4. Combine chopped chili or pepper with lemon juice and about 1 teaspoon salt. Beat in ¼ cup olive oil. Pour over tomatoes and leave for 15 minutes before serving.

SHAWAYUH
SPICED CHARCOAL GRILLED MEAT

Though very little meat is available for the Yemeni diet, when it is possible to obtain meat suitable for grilling, these cuts are spiced with hawayij and cooked over glowing charcoal. If the meat is tough, then it is simmered after the grilling in a little water flavoured with onion or spring onion. We are more fortunate in that we can choose suitable cuts of meat.

Serves: 6
Cooking time: 12-15 minutes

6 thickly cut grilling steaks or lamb chops
2-3 teaspoons Hawayij (page 268)
oil for basting
salt

1. Slit fat selvedge on steaks or chops to prevent meat curling while cooking. Sprinkle meat on each side with hawayij and leave for 30 minutes at room temperature.
2. When coals are red hot, dab meat with oil and place over fire. Cook until seared on each side and raise grid or move meat to a cooler part of the fire. Continue to cook until done to taste, though the Yemeni taste is for well-done meat. Brush occasionally with oil during cooking.
3. When cooked, season with salt and serve immediately.

HOR'EE
STEWED BEEF SHANK

Serves: 5-6
Cooking time: 4½-5 hours

1.5 kg (3 lb) beef fore shank on the bone
water
2 large onions, quartered
6 cloves garlic
2 cups chopped, peeled tomatoes
2 teaspoons Hawayij (page 268)
salt
freshly ground black pepper
1-2 bisbas (hot chilis), optional

1. Have meat retailer cross cut the fore shanks on the bone into thick slices.
2. Place meat in a large pot and just cover with cold water. Bring slowly to the boil, skimming when necessary.
3. When well-skimmed and boiling, add onion, whole peeled garlic cloves, tomatoes, hawayij and salt to taste. Add plenty of pepper or 1-2 whole chilis, depending on how hot a dish you can take.
4. Cover and simmer gently on low heat for 4 hours or until meat is very tender and liquid reduced to a thick sauce. Serve hot.

AKUW'A
OXTAIL STEW

Serves: 5-6
Cooking time: 3½- 4 hours

2 oxtails, jointed
water
2 cups chopped, peeled tomatoes
3 small onions
4-5 cloves garlic
2 teaspoons Hawayij (page 268)
salt

1. Wash oxtail and place pieces in a large pot. Cover with cold water and bring to a slow simmer, skimming when necessary.
2. When boiling gently and well skimmed, add tomatoes, whole peeled onions, whole peeled garlic cloves, hawayij and salt. Cover and simmer gently for 3-3½ hours or until meat is tender and liquid considerably reduced.
3. Serve hot with rice or boiled potatoes, Khoubiz (flat bread) and salad.

KIRSHUH
STEWED LIVER AND KIDNEY

Though Kirshuh is usually made with a selection of variety meats (offal), depending on what is available to the Yemeni cook, it is just as good using liver and kidney (or liver and lung if you don't mind the sound of lung frying).

Serves: 5-6
Cooking time: 1½-2 hours

500 g (1 lb) lamb liver
salted water
2 lamb kidneys
¼ cup oil
1 large onion, finely chopped
3 cloves garlic, finely chopped
1 teaspoon turmeric
1 cup chopped, peeled tomatoes
1 teaspoon ground coriander seeds
½ teaspoon ground cumin
2 cardamom pods
½ cup water
salt
freshly ground black pepper
1 tablespoon finely chopped kizbara
   (coriander leaves) or parsley

1. Place liver in salted water for 30 minutes. Drain, dry and pull off fine skin. Cut into 2 cm (¾ inch) cubes, removing any large tubes.
2. Skin and core kidneys. Dice, rinse briefly under cold running water, drain and dry with paper towels.
3. Heat oil in a deep pan, add onion and fry gently until transparent. Add garlic and turmeric, cook for 2 minutes longer, then add prepared liver and kidney. Increase heat and fry quickly until colour changes, stirring often.
4. Reduce heat, add tomatoes, ground coriander seeds, cumin, and cardamom pods, water and salt and pepper to taste. Cover and simmer gently on low heat for 1-1½ hours or until liver and kidneys are tender. As mixture should be thick, add more water only if stew looks like scorching.
5. Stir in chopped coriander leaves or parsley and serve hot.

AKUW'A (Oxtail Stew) *recipe above*

BINT-AL-SAHN
DOUGH CAKE WITH HONEY

Serves: 8
Oven temperature: 190°C (375°F)
Cooking time: 25-30 minutes

1 sachet active dry yeast
¼ cup warm water
3 cups plain flour
1 teaspoon salt
4 eggs
¾ cup melted samneh (clarified butter) or
   ghee
To serve:
melted butter or samneh
warm honey

1. Soak yeast in warm water and stir to dissolve.
2. Sift flour and salt into a mixing bowl and make a well in the centre.
3. Beat eggs well and pour into flour with yeast liquid. Stir to blend, then knead well. Gradually add ¼ cup of the melted samneh (this should be just warm), kneading well into the dough. Keep kneading until dough is smooth and fairly elastic. If dough looks too dry add water, but this depends on size of eggs used.
4. With floured hands divide dough into 16 balls, each the size of a large egg. Place on a tray as they are formed.
5. Take a ball of dough, place on lightly floured board and form into a very thin round shape by working the heel of your hand in a rotary motion on the dough. (I am right handed, and I found that I could best do this with my left hand, using the right hand to move the dough round in order to flatten it evenly.) If you have any trouble flattening it, resort to a rolling pin.
6. Brush a baking sheet well with some of the samneh and place completed round on one side of this. Brush top of dough generously with samneh. Shape another 7 balls of dough and place on top of first round. As each round is placed on the previous round, press the edges with fingertips, then brush generously with melted samneh.
7. Shape remaining 8 balls of dough the same way and stack on baking sheet in another pile, pressing edges together and brushing with samneh as before. Top layers should also be coated with samneh. Leave in a warm place for 45 minutes.
8. Bake bint-al-sahn in a moderately hot oven for 25-30 minutes until lightly golden and cooked. Tap base of tray — it should sound hollow when cakes are cooked.
9. Serve hot on a platter with melted butter or samneh and warm honey poured on top — amount should be generous, but it depends on your taste. Traditionally this is broken off in flakes with the fingers, dipping pieces in the butter-honey mixture in the platter. You may serve it cut in wedges if preferred with butter and honey from platter spooned on top.

QISHR
COFFEE WITH GINGER

Though coffee is a major export from Moccha in the Republic of Yemen, the locals can rarely afford it. They generally use the ground coffee husks and flavour it with ground ginger. As you are unlikely to have access to ground coffee husks, the recipe given uses coffee and ground ginger for a delightfully different brew.

Serves: 4-6

1 cup cold water
6 teaspoons powdered coffee
6 teaspoons sugar
2 teaspoons ground ginger

1. Put water in a long-handled coffee pot.
2. Add coffee, sugar and ginger and stir well to combine. Set on medium heat and bring to the boil. Remove from heat until bubbling subsides, then return to the boil. Do this 3 times in all.
3. Put into tiny Arabic coffee cups or demitasse cups and serve. Amount makes 6 cups of the former, 4 cups if served in demitasse cups.

EGYPT

With a history so ancient and so awesome in its magnificence, perhaps too much is expected of Egypt's foods. Events earlier this century saw a cosmopolitan Egypt, with foods influenced by French, Italians, Turks and Greeks more than Arabs. However the new Egypt has loosened her links with the West and regained her own national identity. Consequently food preferences have reverted to those linked with the past, retaining tradition.

Taking a broad look at Egyptian food, bread stands out as being the most important component of the Egyptian diet. Vendors, flat wicker baskets piled high with aish and perched precariously on their heads, wind their way through the crowded streets of Cairo to their favourite selling spot. Aish is the flat bread of Egypt, usually made with a combination of plain and wholemeal flour with sufficient leavening to form a pocket and a soft crust, its basic character unchanged by the passage of millennia, and a constant reminder of the role Ancient Egypt played in developing the staff of life.

Barley, millet and wheat were the principal grains of earliest civilizations. According to anthropologists studying evidence, bread baked during these times was hard and chewy. Barley and millet do not contain adequate amounts of the gluten-forming proteins essential to make a light-textured bread. Wheat on the other hand does contain these proteins, but their nature can be altered if heat is applied at the wrong stage of preparation. The early wheat strains had to be heated before threshing so that the husk could be removed, so destroying these essential properties in the grain and giving wheat bread characteristics similar to those made of barley and millet.

The Ancient Egyptians developed a strain of wheat which could be threshed without the preliminary heating, taking a giant step towards the improvement of bread. Whether by accident or by design, they also found a means to leaven bread made from this wheat. Because of the shortage of the new grain, some centuries passed before other civilizations were introduced to leavened bread.

THE FLAVOUR OF EGYPTIAN FOOD

Even an ex-patriate Egyptian living in a land where vast varieties of food are constantly available will still yearn for the bean dishes of his homeland. Ful Medamis, the brown bean purée made with ful (tiny broad beans, also known as fava beans) would probably be preferred, if offered, to the most exquisite French culinary creation, as it evokes nostalgia. He is likely to remember the ful vendors of his native homeland with huge *idras* of ful simmering day and night, ready to provide a satisfying breakfast in the morning, a midday meal, or just a snack at any time. Ful Medamis is served as a *mazza* or as a

substantial meal with hard-boiled eggs mashed into it and crowned with golden olive oil, tart with lemon, pungent with garlic, subtly flavoured with cumin and topped with a generous sprinkling of parsley. While basically a simple peasant dish, it is the kind of dish which the Westerner now endeavours to duplicate after his forays in what are commonly called health food stores. Flat or crusty bread is a must and a variety of salad vegetables may be served with it, plus Salata Tahina. Similar foods which will equally stir the Egyptian far from home are Tameya, broad bean patties, Ful Nabed and Besara, a soup and a purée respectively, both made with skinned broad beans. A prized vegetable is bamia (okra), mostly favoured in meat and vegetable stews.

Many of Egypt's favoured recipes appear in other chapters which they themselves acknowledge as belonging to other countries, so if you are looking for a particular dish tried during a stay in Egypt, then you are likely to find it elsewhere. For example the Yiouvetsi of Cyprus and Greece is as popular in Egypt where it is called Lissan al Assfour. While pigeons are highly regarded and bred for the table, in the interests of conservation I have preferred not to give a recipe. However if you can buy specially raised pigeons and wish to try an Egyptian recipe using them, then prepare the Farroog Mahshi recipe using four pigeons instead of the two chickens specified. The stuffing for this particular recipe is usually made with a green wheat called fireek, rarely obtainable outside the Middle East. Coarse burghul or barley are substitutes, with the burghul the best for this recipe.

Whatever the meal or the occasion, aish is served with all meals. As you have no doubt gathered, there is much repetition in the foods of the various countries in the region covered, with many foods of one country being similar to those nearby. Aish, the Egyptian flat bread, is similar to the Saluf of Yemen. Follow the Saluf recipe, omitting the potent Hilbeh topping. Allow the shaped bread to rise for 15 minutes before baking and do not prick with a fork; this ensures that a pocket forms when cooked. Even if you include the Hilbeh topping, you will not be far from the flavour of Egyptian food, as Hilbeh is known in Alexandria where it is used as a bread dip.

EATING EGYPTIAN STYLE

Western influence is still in evidence in the dining table of Egypt. The table is spread with a cloth and all the components of the meal are placed in their respective dishes and set on the table at the beginning of the meal. Individual plates or bowls are set out, with knives, forks and spoons. The meal could comprise a soup, chicken, fish or meat stew such as Bamia, rice, pickles, olives, salad and bread.

If a bean purée or soup is served, then lemon wedges, chopped onions, salad vegetables and Salata Tahina accompany it. Quite often such a meal is served without other foods, excepting plenty of bread of course.

COOKING METHODS

Most homes are not well equipped as far as cooking facilities are concerned. A single burner often is the only means by which to cook. For the making of Ful Medamis, the Egyptians have a small electric hotplate which plugs into the standard power point. This keeps a constant low heat and is just large enough to take the small *idra*, a special pot which tapers at the top, in which the beans are cooked slowly for several hours. A casserole dish with a wide base tapering to a narrow opening will substitute for the idra.

For any other Egyptian cooking, modern pots, pans and casserole dishes can be used successfully.

INGREDIENTS FOR EGYPTIAN COOKING

The dried beans, ful and ful nabed, are available at Greek and Middle Eastern food stores and specialist food stores. Though I have not come across them, I am informed that broad beans are available already skinned. These look white (the unskinned ones are green to almost purple) and should be used for Besara, Ful Nabed and Tameya, saving considerable time. A shorter soaking time is necessary, and though your yield will be greater, use the quantities given in the recipes, adjusting flavourings slightly.

Ground cumin, dried mint, fresh dill, flat leaf parsley and garlic are the principal flavour givers, with butter and olive oil the favoured fats.

BAMIA (Lamb and Okra Casserole) *recipe page 290*

TA'LEYA I
GARLIC SAUCE

This is more of a condiment to be added to cooked dishes than a sauce in the accepted sense. I have given a somewhat modified version — usually 6 or 7 cloves of garlic are used in Egypt for adding to a dish serving 6 or so. As garlic increases in pungency when cooked as directed, be warned and decrease amount even further if you wish. Of course it depends on the size of the garlic cloves used and the pungency of the variety.

3-4 cloves garlic
¼ teaspoon salt
2 tablespoons samneh or clarified butter
1 teaspoon ground coriander
pinch of hot chili pepper

1. Crush garlic with salt in a mortar. Alternatively crush in a garlic press and mix with salt.
2. Heat samneh or butter in a small pan and add garlic. Cook, stirring constantly, until golden brown, remove pan from heat and stir in coriander and pepper. Use while sizzling hot as directed in recipes.

TA'LEYA II
ONION SAUCE

2 large onions
¼ cup olive oil
1-2 cloves garlic, finely chopped

1. Halve peeled onions lengthwise then slice thinly to give semicircles.
2. Heat olive oil in a pan, add onions and fry over medium heat until golden brown. Add garlic and cook a minute longer. Use as directed in recipes.

TAMEYA
BROAD BEAN PATTIES

Makes 30
Cooking time: 5 minutes each lot

2 cups ful nabed (dried broad beans)
water
1 cup chopped spring onions
¼ cup chopped parsley
2 tablespoons chopped coriander leaves
3 cloves garlic
1½ teaspoons salt
freshly ground black pepper
¼ teaspoon hot chili pepper
¼ teaspoon bicarbonate of soda
sesame seeds, optional
oil for deep frying

1. Place beans in a bowl and cover well with cold water. Leave to soak for 2 days, changing water 2 or 3 times.
2. Drain beans and remove skins by pressing each firmly with fingers. Bean should pop out, otherwise tear skin with fingernail then squeeze. Do not cook beans.
3. Pass cleaned beans through food grinder using fine screen. Combine with spring onion, parsley, coriander, garlic, salt, peppers and soda. Pass through grinder twice more, then knead to a paste. Let mixture rest for 30 minutes.
4. With wet hands shape about a tablespoon of mixture at a time into thick patties about 4 cm (1½ inches) in diameter. Dip each side in sesame seeds if desired. Place on a tray and leave at room temperature for 20 minutes.
5. Heat oil to 180°C (350°F) or until a cube of bread turns golden in 1 minute. Fry tameya a few at a time until deep golden brown, turning to brown evenly. Each lot should take 5 minutes to cook. Drain on paper towels. Serve hot with flat bread such as Khoubiz (page 190), Salata Tahina (page 281) and assorted salad vegetables such as tomato, cucumber, sweet peppers and lettuce.

Food processor method: Combine prepared ingredients and process in 2 lots using steel blade. Mix well to evenly distribute flavours, rest mixture 30 minutes and continue from Step 5.

BESARA
BROAD BEAN PUREE

Large dried broad beans (ful nabed) are used for Besara. Those sold skinless are white and though not readily available, are well worth using if you can find them. Soak skinned beans for 24 hours in a cold place and use the soaking water in the cooking. The beans with skin intact require longer soaking so that the tough seed covering can be removed (see page 12).

The melokhia in the recipe is optional; its use imparts a green colour to the purée without affecting the flavour. An aluminium cooking utensil is likely to cause discoloration of the purée; use stainless steel, tin-lined copper or an enamelled utensil if possible.

Serves: 5-6
Cooking time: 1 ¾ hours

3 cups ful nabed (dried broad beans)
cold water
salt
freshly ground black pepper
3 teaspoons dried mint
1 teaspoon dried melokhia, optional

For serving:
Ta'leya II (page 280)
olive oil
chopped onions
lemon wedges

1. Cover beans well with cold water and soak for 48 hours, changing water 2 or 3 times. Remove skins.
2. Place beans in a pot with 5 cups water and bring to a slow simmer. Cover and simmer gently for 1½ hours until very soft.
3. Pass through sieve or purée in a blender and return to pot. Add salt and pepper to taste, rubbed mint and well-rubbed melokhia if used. Cook gently, uncovered, until bubbling.
4. Serve hot in small bowls, garnishing each with ta'leya. Have on hand a cruet of olive oil, chopped onions and lemon wedges in bowls so that these may be added to individual taste. Serve with flat bread or crusty bread.

SALATA TAHINA
TAHINI SALAD

Makes about 1 ¾ cups

2 cloves garlic
salt
¾ cup tahini
1 tablespoon white vinegar
juice of 1 lemon
½ cup water
½ teaspoon ground cumin
½ cup chopped parsley

1. Crush garlic cloves with ½ teaspoon salt.
2. Place tahini in mixing bowl and beat well. This preliminary beating reduces the strong flavour of the tahini.
3. Beat in garlic and vinegar. Gradually add lemon juice alternately with water. To make a cream salad of good consistency add enough lemon juice to make the tahini very thick before adding water. This way you have more scope in adjusting the flavour and consistency of the sauce.
4. Add salt to taste, and more lemon juice if a sharper sauce is required. Blend in cumin and parsley and chill until required. Serve as a mazza or as directed in recipes.

SEMIT
SESAME BREAD RINGS

Makes about 18
Oven temperature: 220°C (425°F)
Cooking time: 15 minutes

1 sachet active dry yeast
¾ cup warm water
½ cup milk, boiled and cooled to lukewarm
4 cups plain flour
1 teaspoon salt
2 teaspoons sugar
2 teaspoons oil
1 small egg, beaten
sesame seeds
water

1. Soak yeast in ¼ cup warm water and stir to dissolve.
2. Sift flour into a mixing bowl, remove about 1 cup flour and set aside.
3. Add remaining warm water and warm milk to yeast with salt and sugar and stir to dissolve sugar.
4. Pour liquid into centre of flour and stir in a little of the flour to thicken liquid. Cover and leave in a warm place for 10 minutes until frothy.
5. Blend in remaining flour in bowl and beat until smooth, then beat by hand for 10 minutes or on electric mixer with dough hook for 5 minutes. Gradually beat in oil, adding a little of the reserved flour.
6. Turn onto a floured board and knead in as much of the reserved flour as the dough will take. Knead for 10 minutes or until smooth and satiny. Shape into a ball.
7. Oil bowl lightly, add dough and turn it in bowl to oil top. Stretch plastic film over bowl and leave dough in a warm place for 30 minutes or until doubled in bulk.
8. Punch down dough and turn onto a lightly floured board. Knead a little, then break off pieces the size of a small egg.
9. Roll a piece of dough into a rope 1 cm (½ inch) thick and 20 cm (8 inches) long. Form into a ring, overlapping ends and pressing to seal.
10. Make about 5 rings, then glaze with beaten egg and dip tops in a dish of sesame seeds. Place on a lightly oiled baking sheet.
11. Shape remainder of dough into rings, 5 at a time, finishing each lot with egg glaze and sesame seeds.
12. Cover finished semit with a cloth and leave in a draught-free place until doubled — about 30 minutes.
13. Place a baking dish of hot water on the bottom shelf of a hot oven. Bake semit on centre shelf of oven for 15 minutes until semit sounds hollow when tapped. When cooked, brush semit while hot with water and leave on baking sheets to cool. This crisps the crust.

Note: Normally each semit is shaped, glazed and coated separately, but preparing them in small batches speeds up the job. If you shape all of them before glazing, the first begin to rise and they are more difficult to handle.

TAMEYA (Broad Bean Patties) *recipe page 280.*

COUSCOUS
COUSCOUS

Though couscous is the national dish of Morocco, Tunisia and Algeria, it is also popular in Egypt. The other North African nations serve steaming mounds of couscous with their flavoursome stews; in Egypt it is generally prepared as a dessert, and occasionally makes its appearance with stews.

Couscous is available from Middle Eastern and Greek food stores; for the curious, adventurous and patient, I have given directions for making your own. Allow plenty of time and give yourself lots of space. Once you have mastered the art, increase ingredients proportionately to make a larger quantity and store in an airtight container.

Makes about 2 cups

1 cup fine semolina
¼-⅓ cup cold water
¼-⅓ cup plain flour
¼ teaspoon salt

1. Place semolina in a large round baking dish or a basin with a flat base. Form into a circle leaving centre clear.
2. Pour 2 tablespoons water in centre, flick semolina into the water with fingers, then work with palm of hand in a circular motion to moisten the semolina evenly.
3. Mix flour with salt and sprinkle half of this over the semolina. Work into semolina, again using palm of hand and circular movements. Add a little more of the water and flour so that small, round grains about the size of sesame seeds begin to form. The aim is to coat semolina grains with flour.
4. Turn into a wide, medium-meshed wire sieve (a wooden framed sieve is ideal) set over a large cloth. Sieve and return the grains from the cloth to the dish or basin with any large lumps left on top of the grains in the sieve. The smaller grains in the sieve are the couscous — tip these into a bowl.
5. Work a little more flour and water into the dish or basin contents, sieve, sort and work again until ingredients are formed into pellets of couscous, adding more flour and water as required. No more than ⅓ cup flour and ⅓ cup water should be used to 1 cup semolina.
6. Line the top section of a couscousier or a colander with a piece of butter muslin and put the couscous in it, spreading it evenly.
7. Bring about 3 cups water to the boil in the bottom section of the couscousier or a deep pan and place container with couscous on top. If using a colander, drape a tea towel around edge if colander does not fit snugly, so that steam does not escape. Cover couscous with lid and steam for 10 minutes. Container with the couscous must not touch the water.
8. Turn couscous onto a cloth and break up any lumps with fingers. Spread out and leave for several hours in an airy place to dry thoroughly. Store in an airtight container and use as directed in recipes.

ROZ
BOILED RICE

Serves: 6
Cooking time: 20 minutes

2 cups rice, long or short grain
water
salt
2 tablespoons samneh (ghee) or butter

1. Place rice in a sieve and wash under running water. Put into a bowl with 1 teaspoon salt and cover with cold water. Soak for 10 minutes, then drain in sieve. Do this well ahead of time required for cooking so that grains can dry. Spread it out in a dish if you like.
2. Heat samneh or butter in a heavy pan and add rice. Stir over medium heat for 2 minutes or until grains are well coated with fat.
3. Add 3½ cups water and 1 teaspoon salt and bring to the boil, stirring occasionally. Reduce heat.
4. Cover pan tightly and leave to cook on low heat for 15-20 minutes. Turn off heat and leave for 5-10 minutes. Fluff up with a fork and serve.

Alternative cooking method: Drain rice after soaking — no need to let grains dry. Put 3½ cups water, samneh or butter and salt into pan, bring to the boil and add rice. Return to the boil, stirring once or twice, reduce heat, cover and finish as above.

KOUSHARI
LENTILS, MACARONI AND RICE IN OIL

This is classed as an 'oil' dish by Coptic Egyptians and is prepared during periods of fasting when animal products cannot be taken. You may cook the lentils, macaroni and rice simultaneously in 3 pots, or if, like me, you like to keep pots to a minimum, use the method given. This is the way they prepare it in Egypt anyway.

Serves: 6
Cooking time: 1½-1¾ hours

1 cup ads iswid (brown lentils)
water
salt
1 cup small macaroni noodles
1 cup short grain rice
2 tablespoons olive oil
Ta'leya II (page 280)
1 cup tomato purée

1. Place lentils in a sieve and wash well under running water. Place in a large pot and add 3 cups water and 1 teaspoon salt. Bring to the boil, then simmer for 1 hour until tender but still intact. Drain and keep aside.
2. Clean same pot and add 4 cups water. Bring to the boil, add 2 teaspoons salt and the macaroni. Stir constantly until water returns to the boil and cook, uncovered, for 15 minutes until tender. Stir occasionally. Drain and keep aside. Clean pot again and dry.
3. Wash rice well in sieve under running water and drain. Heat oil in pot and fry rice over medium heat for 2-3 minutes. Add 2 cups water and 1 teaspoon salt and bring to the boil, stirring occasionally. Cover and simmer over low heat for 15 minutes or until tender. Leave covered off the heat for 5 minutes for grains to separate.
4. Prepare ta'leya II according to directions, add tomato purée and bring to the boil.
5. Add lentils and macaroni to cooked rice and toss together lightly with a fork. Pour hot ta'leya and tomato mixture on top, toss again and cover pot. Leave over low heat for 10 minutes. Serve hot with salads, grilled fish or prawns.

FUL MEDAMIS
SIMMERED FUL BEANS

*Though Ful Medamis is proclaimed as the national
dish of Egypt, it is also enjoyed in other countries
of the region.*
*In Egypt the ful beans (small broad beans) are
cooked very slowly in an idra, a special pot which
tapers to a narrow neck. The shape is deliberate so
that the small amount of water used in the cooking
is not lost. As steam condenses on the upper sloping
sides, it drops back into the pot. There are casserole
dishes with a somewhat similar design, and these
may be used successfully for the preparation of ful.
Otherwise use a heavy pan with a tight fitting lid.*

Serves: 6
Cooking time: 5-6 hours

2 cups dried ful (small broad beans)
4 cups cold water
¼ cup ads asfar (red lentils), optional
salt
3 cloves garlic
pinch of ground cumin

For serving:
6 hard-boiled eggs, optional
finely chopped parsley
lemon wedges
olive oil
freshly ground black pepper

1. Wash beans well, then cover with the cold water. Leave to
soak overnight, in a cool place if weather is warm.
2. Place beans and their soaking water in a heavy pan, add
lentils if used, cover tightly and simmer very gently for 5-6
hours. Alternatively place beans and water with lentils in a
casserole dish with tapering sides, cover tightly and place in a
very slow oven, 120°C (250°F) and cook for 6 hours.
3. Check beans occasionally, and add a little water if they look
dry. Do not stir while cooking, as doing so will cause them to
stick to utensil.
4. Crush garlic with a little salt and add to beans with additional salt to taste and a pinch of ground cumin. If desired,
beans may be passed through a sieve to purée, otherwise serve
them as they are.
5. Serve in soup bowls, adding a quartered hard-boiled egg if
used, and a sprinkling of chopped parsley to each. Each diner
squeezes on lemon juice and adds olive oil and pepper to
individual taste. The beans and egg are usually crushed with a
fork and bowl contents blended. Serve with flat or crusty bread,
crisp salads and Salata Tahina (page 281).

To serve as an appetizer: Purée the beans, add garlic, salt,
pepper, cumin and blend in lemon juice and olive oil to taste.
Serve spread on a dish with a good sprinkling of parsley. Flat
bread cut into quarters should accompany the Ful Medamis.

SHOURBA ADS
LENTIL SOUP

Serves: 6
Cooking time: 1-1 ¼ hours

1½ cups ads asfar (red lentils)
6 cups meat or chicken stock, or water
1 medium-sized onion, grated
1 teaspoon ground cumin
salt
freshly ground black pepper
1 tablespoon lemon juice

For serving:
Ta'leya II (page 280)
lemon wedges
olive oil

1. Place lentils in a sieve and wash under running water.
2. Bring stock or water to the boil in a large soup pot and add
lentils and onion. Return to a slow boil, cover and simmer over
low heat for 45-60 minutes until lentils are tender. Do not stir
during cooking.
3. After this cooking, lentils should be a purée; for a finer
texture pass through a sieve or purée in a blender.
4. Add cumin and salt and pepper to taste. If a thinner soup is
required, add water to achieve desired consistency. Stir in lemon
juice and heat gently until bubbling.
5. Serve hot in deep bowls, topping each serving with ta'leya.
More lemon juice is added according to individual taste. Have
olive oil on hand as the amount in the ta'leya may not be
sufficient for some tastes.

MELOKHIA
GREEN HERB SOUP

*Though in Egypt a stock made from any available
vegetables is often used, it is preferable to have a meat
stock base. This can be from lamb, beef or chicken. If
chicken is used, the bird is roasted with butter after the
initial boiling and served separately as part of the meal.
Egyptians living abroad find our mass-produced
chickens lack flavour, and many add a stock cube so
that the end result is just like 'back home'. For more
information on melokhia, see Glossary.*

Serves: 6
Cooking time: 15-20 minutes

6 cups chicken or meat stock flavoured with
   onion
1 chicken stock cube
salt
freshly ground black pepper
1½ cups dried melokhia leaves
2 leaves silq (silverbeet or Swiss chard)
1 quantity Ta'leya I (page 280)

For serving:
chopped onion
vinegar or lemon juice

1. Bring strained stock to the boil and add crumbled stock cube if chicken stock is used. Adjust seasoning with salt and pepper.
2. Measure melokhia leaves, then crumble finely. Remove white stalks from silq and chop leaves finely.
3. Add melokhia and silq to boiling stock, return almost to the boil and simmer, uncovered, for 10 minutes. The melokhia swells and stays suspended in the stock.
4. Make ta'leya and add to the soup, cover pot and simmer for 2 minutes. Serve piping hot with a bowl of chopped onions bathed in vinegar or lemon juice to be added to individual taste.

Note: If a whole chicken has been simmered for the stock, oven-roast with butter and serve at the same meal. Plain boiled rice (Roz, page 285) completes the meal.

FUL NABED
BROAD BEAN SOUP

Serves: 6
Cooking time: 1 ¾ hours

3 cups ful nabed (dried broad beans, for
   preparation see page 12)
cold water
1 teaspoon ground cumin
salt
freshly ground black pepper
¼ cup olive oil
1 tablespoon lemon juice

For serving:
finely chopped parsley
lemon wedges

1. Cover beans well with cold water and soak for 48 hours, changing water 2 or 3 times. Remove skins as directed in preparation instructions.
2. Put into pot with 6 cups water, bring to a slow simmer, cover and simmer gently for 1½ hours until very soft.
3. Press through a sieve or purée in a blender. Return to pot and add cumin, salt and pepper to taste, olive oil and lemon juice. Stir over gentle heat until bubbling.
4. Serve hot in deep bowls garnished with chopped parsley. Lemon juice is squeezed on according to individual taste. Flat bread or other bread should accompany this soup.

FATA
LAMB AND BREAD SOUP

Serves: 6
Cooking time: 2 hours

750 g (1½ lb) lean, boneless lamb
6 cups water
1 large onion, finely chopped
salt
freshly ground black pepper
1 clove or pinch of ground mastic, optional
¾ cup water
½ cup rice
2 tablespoons samneh (ghee) or butter

To finish:
¼ cup samneh (ghee) or butter
2-3 cloves garlic, crushed
¼ cup vinegar
2 rounds Khoubiz (page 190), toasted

1. Cut lamb into small cubes and place in a large pot with cold water. Bring slowly to the boil, skimming when necessary.
2. Add onion and salt and pepper to taste. If you find the aroma of boiling lamb unpleasant, add clove or mastic to overcome this. (I find it unnecessary.)
3. Cover and simmer gently for 1½ hours or until lamb is tender without falling apart.
4. While soup is cooking, wash rice and drain. Boil 1 cup water in a separate pan, add 1 tablespoon samneh, ½ teaspoon salt and the rice and return to the boil, stirring occasionally. Cover and simmer over low heat for 15-20 minutes until tender.
5. Lift cooked meat from soup with a slotted spoon, drain and fry in another tablespoon samneh in a frying pan. Remove and keep hot.
6. Add the ¼ cup samneh to the frying pan and heat. Add garlic and fry until lightly coloured. Pour in vinegar off the heat, return pan and boil for a few seconds. Keep aside.
7. Place a round of toasted bread in a large tureen or casserole; cut it in quarters if you like. Spoon a little of the garlic mixture over the bread and top with half the cooked rice. Pour on some of the soup and add another layer of bread and remainder of rice. Put fried meat cubes on top and spoon on remaining garlic mixture. Add remaining soup and garnish with chopped parsley before serving.

Note: To cut down on the rather complex preparation of this dish, the rice may be boiled in the soup after the meat cubes have been removed.

SAYYADIAH
FISH WITH RICE

Serves: 4
Cooking time: 1 hour

4 whole fish, each about 375 g (12 oz)
juice of 1 lemon
salt
freshly ground black pepper
3 cloves garlic, finely chopped or crushed
1 teaspoon ground cumin
2 medium-sized onions, finely chopped
2 tablespoons oil
2 cups long grain rice
3½ cups hot water
flour
oil for frying
lemon wedges and parsley sprigs to garnish

1. Scale and gut fish and leave heads on. Rinse and wipe dry. Rub surfaces and cavities with lemon juice and season with salt and pepper. Cover and leave aside for 30-45 minutes. Prepare garlic and mix with the cumin.
2. Gently fry onions in oil in a deep pan for 15-20 minutes until very soft and golden. Wash rice, drain and add to onions. Stir over medium heat for 2-3 minutes, then add the hot water. Bring to the boil, reduce heat to low, cover pan and cook gently for 20 minutes.
3. Make 3-4 deep slits on each side of the fish and fill slits with garlic-cumin mixture. Coat fish with flour and shallow fry in hot oil until golden brown and cooked.
4. Remove fish to a dish and keep hot.
5. Add about 2 tablespoons of the oil in which the fish was cooked to the cooked rice. Stir through with a fork, cover pan and leave rice for 5 minutes.
6. Pile rice on a platter, arrange fish on top and garnish with lemon wedges and parsley sprigs.

FARROOG MAHSHI
ROAST STUFFED CHICKEN

Serves: 6
Oven temperature: 180°C (350°F)
Cooking time: 2 hours

2 chickens, each about 1 kg (2 lb)
salt
freshly ground black pepper
¼ cup melted butter

Stuffing:
1 cup coarse burghul
water
livers and hearts from chickens
1 large onion, finely chopped
2 tablespoons butter
2 tablespoons finely chopped parsley
1 teaspoon dried mint
salt
freshly ground black pepper
1 cup chicken stock made from remaining
  giblets

1. Wipe chickens with paper towels and season inside and out with salt and pepper. Cover and refrigerate until required.
2. Place burghul in a bowl and soak for 5 minutes in water to cover. Strain in a sieve, pressing with the back of a spoon to extract all moisture.
3. Clean and finely chop livers and hearts. If chickens are without giblets, use 125 g (4 oz) chicken livers.
4. Heat butter in a frying pan and gently fry onion until transparent. Add chopped liver and heart and fry just long enough for colour of meats to change. Remove pan from heat.
5. Stir in soaked and drained burghul, parsley, mint rubbed to a powder, and salt and pepper to taste. Add chicken stock, cover pan and cook on low heat for 5 minutes. Cool stuffing.
6. Fill chickens with stuffing, then truss.
7. Put melted butter in a baking dish, add chickens breast side up and baste with the melted butter. Bake in a moderate oven for 1½ hours, turning chickens on their sides during cooking, then breast side up during last 10 minutes to complete browning.
8. Remove chickens to a plate and spoon stuffing onto serving platter. Joint chickens and place on top of stuffing. Keep hot.
9. Dissolve browned juices in dish with a little hot water, bring to the boil and strain over the chicken.

KOLKAS
MEAT WITH TARO

I had been led to believe that of Middle Eastern countries only Cyprus used kolokassi (taro). That in itself is strange as the root is indigenous to the Pacific Islands. Surprisingly, the Egyptians use it also. They call the root kolkas and call the dish they use it in by the same name. More detail in the Glossary; just remember not to wet the root once peeled and cut up as it can go slimy. The Egyptians do not chip off the pieces as they do in Cyprus.

Serves: 6
Cooking time: 2¼ hours

1 kg (2 lb) stewing beef or lamb
¼ cup butter
1½ cups water
salt
freshly ground black pepper
1 kg (2 lb) kolkas (taro)
juice of ½ lemon
15 silq (silverbeet or Swiss chard) leaves
1 tablespoon finely chopped coriander leaves
2 cloves garlic, crushed

1. Trim meat and cut into cubes. If using lamb, amount specified is for boneless lamb.
2. Melt 1 tablespoon of the butter in a deep pan and fry meat lightly — just enough for it to lose red colour. Do not brown. Add water, about 2 teaspoons salt and pepper to taste, cover and simmer gently for 1 hour or until half-cooked.
3. Wash kolkas root and dry well. Peel and cut into squarish pieces about 2 cm (¾ inch) thick.
4. Add lemon juice to meat with the kolkas. Make sure kolkas is totally immersed in the liquid otherwise it could discolour. Cover and simmer for further hour or until meat is tender. Do not stir once kolkas is added.
5. Wash silq well and strip leaves from white stalks (stalks can be used as a vegetable for later meals). Drain leaves.
6. Heat remaining butter in a large frying pan and add leaves. Stir over medium heat until well wilted and darkened in colour. Chop finely while in pan, add coriander and garlic and stir over heat for 1 minute.
7. Add silq mixture to cooked meat, cover pan and leave off the heat for 5 minutes before serving. Serve with bread.

KORUMB MAHSHI
CABBAGE ROLLS

Serves: 6
Cooking time: 1¼ hours

24 cabbage leaves
boiling salted water

Stuffing:
1 medium-sized onion, finely chopped
2 tablespoons butter
750 g (1½ lb) finely ground beef
½ cup short grain rice
1 tablespoon chopped dill
½ teaspoon ground cumin
¼ cup tomato purée
salt
freshly ground black pepper

To finish:
1 cup tomato purée
½ cup meat stock
juice of ½ lemon
2 cloves garlic, chopped
½ teaspoon sugar
salt and pepper
2 tablespoons butter

1. If cabbage leaves are large, halve and count as two leaves. Blanch a few leaves at a time in boiling salted water for 3-5 minutes or until softened enough to roll.
2. Drain leaves in a colander and remove hard centre rib. Line pan with cabbage ribs and additional leaves if necessary.
3. To prepare stuffing, gently fry onion in butter until soft. Add to ground meat with remaining stuffing ingredients, adding salt and pepper to taste. Combine thoroughly.
4. Place a generous tablespoon of filling on one edge of cabbage leaf and roll into a neat package, folding in sides. As leaves are filled, place fold side down in lined pan.
5. Combine tomato purée with stock, lemon juice, garlic, sugar and salt and pepper to taste. Pour over rolls and add butter to pan. Invert a heavy plate on top of rolls, cover pan and bring to a slow simmer over medium heat. Reduce heat to low and simmer for 1 hour. Serve hot.

BAMIA
LAMB AND OKRA CASSEROLE

Serves: 5-6
Oven temperature: 150-160°C (300-325°F)
Cooking time: 2-2½ hours

1 kg (2 lb) boneless stewing lamb or beef
2 tablespoons ghee or butter
1 large onion, finely chopped
½ teaspoon ground cumin
1 cup chopped peeled tomatoes
2 tablespoons tomato paste
½ cup stock or water
salt
freshly ground black pepper
½ teaspoon sugar
500 g (1 lb) fresh okra (see page 9)
1 tablespoon ghee
Ta'leya I (page 280)
Roz (page 285) for serving

1. Trim meat and cut into 3 cm (1¼ inch) cubes. Heat ghee or butter in a heavy-based pan and brown meat on all sides, adding a single layer of meat to pan at a time. Transfer to casserole dish.
2. Reduce heat, add onion to pan and fry gently until transparent. Add cumin, tomatoes, tomato paste and stock and stir well to lift browned sediment.
3. Pour over lamb in casserole, add salt and pepper to taste and the sugar. Cover tightly and cook in a moderately slow oven for 1½ hours.
4. Prepare okra as directed, rinse, drain and dry. Heat ghee in a pan, add okra and fry over medium heat for 3 minutes, tossing gently.
5. Arrange okra on top of meat in casserole, cover and cook for further 40 minutes or until meat is tender.
6. Prepare ta'leya and pour while hot over bamia. Serve at the table from the casserole dish with Roz in another dish.

COUSCOUS BI SUKKAR (Sweet Couscous with Nuts)
and BASBOUSA (Semolina Cake) *recipes page 292*

COUSCOUS BI SUKKAR
SWEET COUSCOUS WITH NUTS

Serves: 6-8
Cooking time:45 minutes
2 cups Couscous (page 284)
water
½ cup melted, unsalted butter

For serving:
icing (confectioner's) sugar
toasted peanuts or almond slivers

1. Put couscous in a bowl and cover with cold water. Stir with fingers then drain off water. Leave couscous to stand for 15 minutes. Grains will swell.
2. Place couscous in top section of couscousier and set over 4 cups boiling water. Alternatively place couscous in a fine sieve or muslin-lined colander which fits snugly over a deep pan of boiling water, ensuring that bottom of sieve or colander does not touch the water.
3. Drape a tea towel over the top of the couscous container and fit lid on, bringing ends of cloth over the top of the lid. Steam for 15 minutes, then turn couscous into a bowl.
4. Break up any lumps with fingers or a fork and sprinkle with 2 tablespoons cold water. Fluff up with fork and return to steaming container, adding more boiling water if necessary.
5. Cover as before and steam for 30 minutes, regulating heat so that water boils gently. When cooking is completed, couscous should be tender without being mushy.
6. Turn into a bowl and fluff up with fork, breaking up any lumps. Add melted butter and toss through to coat grains evenly.
7. Serve warm, piled in individual sweet dishes and sprinkle with icing sugar and peanuts or almonds.

BASBOUSA
SEMOLINA CAKE

Oven temperature: 180°C (350°F)
Cooking time: 30 minutes

½ cup butter, preferably unsalted
¾ cup caster sugar
1 teaspoon vanilla essence
2 eggs
2 cups fine semolina
1 teaspoon baking powder
½ teaspoon bicarbonate of soda
¾ cup yoghurt
blanched split almonds

Syrup:
2 cups sugar
1½ cups water
1 tablespoon lemon juice

1. Cream butter, sugar and vanilla essence until light and fluffy. Add eggs one at a time and beat well.
2. Sift semolina, baking powder and soda twice. Fold into butter mixture alternately with yoghurt.
3. Spread batter into a greased 20 x 30 cm (8 x 12 inch) slab cake pan and place almonds on top in rows (4 across and 7 down). Arrange evenly so that when cake is cut, an almond will be centred on each piece.
4. Bake in a moderate oven for 30-35 minutes until cake is cooked when tested.
5. While cake cooks, make syrup. Dissolve sugar in water over medium heat, add lemon juice and bring to the boil. Boil rapidly for 10 minutes, then cool by standing pan in cold water.
6. When cake is cooked, spoon cooled syrup over the hot cake. Cool thoroughly and cut into diamond shapes or squares to serve. Ushta or thick whipped cream may be served with basbousa.

IRAN

While Iran is its official name, I cannot help referring to the country as Persia, as this seems to me to be an expression of the essence of the country and its people. Do not be confused with my Irans and Iranians, Persias and Persians: they are all one and the same. Most countries of the Middle East were influenced in one way or another by Persia, particularly as regards food. The dolmeh of Persia became the dolma with sundry variations of Iraq, Turkey, Greece, Cyprus, Armenia, Lebanon, Syria and the Gulf States, even though many of these countries use a term meaning stuffed or filled rather than a derivation of dolmeh.

THE FLAVOUR OF PERSIAN FOOD

One of the most popular dishes in Tehran is Chelou Kebab, and restaurants specialize in its preparation alone. It is a simple dish, depending on the perfection of the basic elements which are melded into a culinary delight with a simple stir of the diner's fork.

My first taste of Chelou Kebab won me over to Persian cooking, for in it I could see the true art and dedication of the Persian cook. To behold, it is a simple dish of rice and grilled lamb. But once tasted it is much, much more. Only the best portion of the lamb will do — the tender, lean eye of the rib, trimmed so that not a trace of fat or gristle mars its purity, sliced thinly and marinated in lemon and onion juice to melt-in-the-mouth tenderness. Charcoal grilled only seconds before, it is served nestling into a pile of steaming hot chelou, with a tomato or two for colour. Pats of butter, a generous dusting of sumak and raw egg yolk accompany it, to be stirred into the rice for an amalgamation of subtle flavours complementing the lamb. The rice is the most important element of the dish and Persian rice is aromatic, hard-grained and almost without equal. Pakistan's basmati rice is the nearest and certainly the best substitute. Once you make chelou and taste it, you will never cook plain rice any other way again.

Polous are an extension of chelou and the recipes are well worth trying. The imaginative use of fruits is another high point in Persian cooking, with sweet-sour flavours the Western palate has learned to appreciate. Fruits are frequently combined with meats in Iran's polous. The Persian cook, like her Western counterpart, does take short cuts and if you find chelou and polous are too time-consuming in their preparation, then try kateh in place of chelou, and dami instead of polous. The most important factor is using the right rice. Experiment by trying basmati rice first, then you have a yardstick against which to measure the success of future efforts using another more readily available long grain rice. The quantities of rice have been trimmed to suit Western tastes and appetites but the essence of the dishes has not suffered.

The Persian khoresh, though loosely translated as a sauce, is a combination of meat or poultry with vegetables, fruits, herbs and spices to make a substantial sauce for serving with rice dishes. Abgusht on the other hand is a meat stew and can become, with the addition of more liquid, a substantial meat-based soup, while aash is always regarded as a soup.

The fruits of Persia are highly regarded and are served during the day, preceding meals. The cucumber is regarded as a fruit and if you have ever tasted a Persian cucumber you will understand why.

Herbs are an important part of Persian cooking. Sabzi Khordan is a platter of mixed herbs served with Nane Lavash, panir (goats' milk cheese), and Mast va Khiar (yoghurt and cucumber salad) as a refreshing start to a meal. More detail is given in the recipe.

Spinach is native to Persia and how it came to be known as English spinach I cannot say. It features in boranis (salad), khoresh, abgusht and kuku (egg casseroles or omelets).

Sweet-sour flavours are essentially Persian in character, with dishes featuring fruit such as pomegranates, peaches, sour cherries, apples and quinces with lime or lemon juice added for good measure. Verjuice, the juice of green (unripened) grapes, is widely used in Iran for a really sour flavour.

The samovar is an essential item in every Persian household as tea ranks with abdug (yoghurt drink) as Persia's principal beverages. Tea is taken in small, slender glasses and served with lumps of sugar. To drink it in the Persian way one must hold the lump of sugar between the teeth and sip the tea through it. The sugar can be conventional cube sugar or small 'cushions' of clear white toffee.

NOW ROOZ

Though Iran is predominantly a Muslim country, their most joyous feast has its origins long before Islam, in the time of the prophet Zoroaster and the great kings of Ancient Persia. It is a celebration of Now Rooz, the Persian new year, actually beginning on the first day of spring, 21 March. The new year means new life to the Persian and this celebration places constant emphasis on the newness of life. About two weeks before Now Rooz, wheat or other grain is sown in a sandy bed. By Now Rooz Eve the green shoots are well in evidence and the clump is usually divided according to the number of family members, each tied with a colourful ribbon and set on the *haft seen* (seven S's) table, symbolic of the roots of life. Altogether seven food items beginning with an 's' must be placed on the table, the number seven probably relating to the seven days of the week or the seven planets of the solar system. Apples (sib), garlic (sir), sumak (a kind of spice), herbs (sabzi), vinegar (sarkh), coin (sekeh), and a sweet pudding made with a special wheat and called samanoo, are the usual items. The table would also have a bowl of water with a green leaf floating in it, fresh fruit, eggs, meat, fish, fowl, sweetmeats, pastries, grains and nuts — in other words a harvest festival in miniature. These are raw foods all used for meals throughout the holiday period.

We arrived in Iran on the thirteenth day of Now Rooz. On that day every person who is able to leaves his home and travels as far away as possible so that their bad luck can be left behind. Persians love picnics and this is one massive picnic day. Food is packed along with the samovar to supply the copious amounts of tea consumed. A clump of green shoots is placed jauntily on the bonnet, roof or trunk of the family car, and during the picnic it is thrown into a running stream. In Tehran the deep gutters which carry the spring water from the mountains behind the city were dotted with these clumps, as those who cannot get to the country picnic at one of the city's beautiful parks or gardens. Now Rooz celebrations last for about 2 weeks.

PERSIAN BREADS

Bread is the staff of life: in Iran as in most other Middle East countries, you are constantly aware of the importance of this most ancient of foods. As Persia has influenced the bread making of so many of the countries surrounding it, a description of the process should be part of this chapter.

Bread is still baked traditionally, though the oven is likely to be heated by oil-fed burners rather than wood.

One bakery we visited in Shiraz was baking Nane Lavash. In one room was the dough maker, tending the modern bread mixer in the centre. Along the full length of three walls ran a waist-high bench structure made of a stone compound, with straight-sided holes 50 cm (20 inches) in diameter formed into the structure. There were at least thirty of these proving vats, each with softly rounded cushions of dough gently billowing above the level of the bench. We were looking at just one of the three 'bakes' of the day.

Next door was a room filled with cream-coloured flour, shovel at the ready. Then came the bakehouse. The heat exuding from this area was sufficient to keep the proving room warm enough for the dough to rise, though with these flat breads the rising of the dough is not necessary.

The procedure in the bakehouse goes something like this: one lad breaks off lumps of dough from the huge mass on his table, shaping them into balls. These are rolled out to an oval shape by another lad. A more experienced baker takes the rolled out dough, expertly throws it back and forth across the backs of his hands, enlarging it even further, runs a *jella* (a spiked wheel on a handle) across the dough three times, then throws it onto the *manjak* — a slightly domed oval cushion about 60 cm (2 feet) long and 30 cm (1 foot) across. After all the rolling, throwing and tossing the sheet of now-thin dough covers this completely. The baker then slips his hand into a pocket in the back of the *manjak,* takes it up and presses the dough deftly onto the scorching hot wall of the *tannour,* the beehive clay oven of the Middle East and India. In thirty to forty seconds the bread bubbles and cooks to golden brown crispness. Another baker armed with a *mengash* (a long rod finished with a metal hook) pulls off the cooked bread and flicks it through a waist-high opening into the actual shop where it is sold immediately.

The whole procedure is carried out with rhythmic precision and at a pace so rapid that the onlooker almost becomes mesmerized. The aroma of the baking bread alone is enough to keep one in a state of euphoria.

Other breads baked in Iran are:

Taftoon: similar to Nane Lavash in preparation and baking, only it is round and somewhat smaller. Usually made with flour resembling wholemeal with the bran removed.

Sangyak: about 75 cm (30 inches) long and 30 cm (12 inches) wide. Top oiled and well-indented with fingertips. Baked in a traditional oven on a bed of hot pebbles, it is a bubbly, crisp flat bread, usually made with wholemeal flour. At its best when warm.

Barbari: shaped in long loaves about 60 cm (24 inches) long, 25 cm (10 inches) wide and 4 cm (1½ inches) thick when cooked. The top is oiled and four grooves running the length of the bread are made with the fingers. Baked on trays in a traditional oven, it is the most popular breakfast bread. Excellent when warm, not as pleasant when cold as the texture is rather coarse. White flour is used for Barbari.

EATING PERSIAN STYLE

The midday and evening meals are almost identical, with the same variety of foods served.

The Persians use their carpets well and their meals are served on one. The carpet is spread with a leather cover called a *sofreh,* which serves as protection and makes a firm base for the dishes. This is covered with a white cloth *sofreh* and the carpet surrounded with cushions for seating. China dinner plates are set out with spoons and forks which have now replaced the traditional method of eating from the fingers of the right hand. A rice dish, either chelou, polou, dami or kateh, is always served with a khoresh. Abgusht, either as a soup or as a stew, could also be served or perhaps a baked chicken or fish. A borani (salad), if made with a yoghurt base, often replaces the khoresh, particularly in summer. A mixed green salad with cos (romaine) lettuce, cucumber, tomatoes, radishes and herbs, and dressed with olive oil and vinegar, is frequently included. Yoghurt, pickles, flat bread and fresh fruit complete the meal. Abdug (yoghurt drink) is usually served as the beverage.

Tea, sharbat (fruit sherbet), or sekanjabin (a sweet-sour mint-flavoured beverage) are usually taken as refreshments between meals. Kuku is often included at the table, particularly for festive occasions, or served as the main dish for a light meal. Kababs and kuku are favourite foods for serving on picnics.

INGREDIENTS FOR PERSIAN COOKING

Basmati rice or a suitable substitute is a must for Persian cooking. Meats generally preferred are lean lamb, veal, venison if available, lean beef and poultry. Though recipes state a particular meat and may give two choices, often any other of these meats may be used. Turmeric, cinnamon, saffron, sumak and dried mint are the popular spices and seasonings. For cooking, ghee (clarified butter) is preferred, though oil, butter or margarine may be substituted. Limu omani (dried lime) is used whole in Persian cooking, generally when the cook wishes to remove strong flavours from meats. Directions for making your own dried limes are given in the chapter on the Gulf States; see Loomi, page 245. The introductory chapters, recipes and glossary cover any other queries you might have regarding Persian foods.

NANO DOK
SPICING MIX

Persian cooks frequently spice their soups and boranis (yoghurt salads) just before serving. Nano Dok is a favourite, and one I found to my liking. Sometimes this basic mix is combined with crisp fried onion, and where this is the case I have included the spicing within the recipe as the onion is often used both in and on top of the prepared dish.

Another popular seasoning for soup is a combination of dried mint, cinnamon and pepper (no ghee), but as these ingredients are often used in the soup, the Nano Dok given is the one I recommend for a final dash of colour and fragrance to soups and boranis.

1-3 tablespoons ghee
1 teaspoon turmeric
1½ teaspoons dried mint

1. Heat ghee in a small pan, stir in turmeric and cook for a few seconds until turmeric colours a golden brown.
2. Crush mint, add to pan, stir and remove from heat immediately. The heat in the pan will be sufficient to bring out the flavour of the mint.

Note: Use amount of ghee according to recipe — the smaller amount if a lot of ghee has been used in the soup, and for boranis; use the larger amount if only a little ghee has been used in the soup.

SABZI KHORDAN
MIXED HERB PLATTER

Herbs feature prominently in Iranian foods. Sabzi Khordan is a popular appetizer, often served at the beginning of a meal. Many restaurants in Iranian cities place this on the table as soon as you are seated, whether previously ordered or not. I found it delightfully refreshing and appetite stimulating, and certainly most welcome. The plates are left during most of the meal for between-course nibbles.

Herbs:
flat-leaf parsley
mint sprigs
tender radish leaves
spring onion tops
chives or tareh (garlic chives)
tarragon
coriander leaves
watercress or shahat
fenugreek

Serve with:
panir (feta) cheese
Mast va Khiar, optional (page 300)
Nane Lavash or other flat bread

1. Select a variety of herbs from those listed. Wash well and remove coarse and discoloured leaves. Cut bladed herbs in finger lengths; break other herbs into small sprigs; separate radish leaves. Drain and wrap in a tea towel. Place in a plastic bag and chill for 3-4 hours to crisp them.
2. Arrange attractively on a platter or in a flat basket.
3. Cube cheese and place in a bowl. Prepare Mast va Khiar as directed, place in a bowl and chill.
4. Cut flat bread into 8 cm (3 inch) squares and place in a napkin-lined basket.
5. Arrange ingredients on table before guests are seated. Alternatively serve with pre-dinner drinks.

Note: To eat Sabzi Khordan, wrap a selection of herbs and a piece of cheese in bread; if desired add Mast va Khiar. Panir is the goat's milk cheese of Iran, similar to feta.

BORANIS

These simply prepared, cooling Persian salads are most versatile. While they may replace the traditional salad at a meal, they also serve as appealing appetizers. In this role the only accompaniment necessary is flat bread such as Nane Lavash or Nane Sangyak, or the readily obtainable Khoubiz, the Arabic flat bread. Cut the bread in manageable squares for scooping up the borani.

Their other role, popular in summer, is as a substitute for a khoresh when serving a full Persian meal, and they make an interesting 'sauce' for polous and kababs served with chelou.

Always use a thick, drained yoghurt for boranis — see page 21 for draining yoghurt.

BORANI BADEMJAN
EGGPLANT SALAD

Serves: 6-8
Cooking time: 20 minutes

2 large, oval eggplants (aubergines),
    each about 375 g (12 oz)
salt
½ cup oil
2 cups drained yoghurt (page 21)
2 cloves garlic, crushed
salt
freshly ground black pepper
chopped walnuts to garnish, optional

1. Cut eggplants in half lengthwise, then slice 5 mm (¼ inch) thick. Sprinkle slices liberally with salt (stack if necessary) and leave for 30 minutes. Rinse and dry with paper towels.
2. Heat half the oil in a large frying pan and fry eggplant until golden brown on each side. Drain on paper towels. Add more oil to pan as required.
3. Blend yoghurt with salt to taste and the crushed garlic.
4. Place a layer of cooled eggplant in serving dish, overlapping slices a little. Season with pepper and spread some yoghurt on top. Repeat, finishing with a layer of yoghurt. Cover and chill. Serve garnished with chopped walnuts if desired.

Note: Borani Bademjan may be layered in individual dishes for serving as a first course. If serving in place of a khoresh, dice the eggplant, fry until cooked through and fold into yoghurt with other ingredients.

BORANI ESFANAJ
SPINACH SALAD

Serves: 6
Cooking time: 20 minutes

750 g (1½ lb) spinach
1 medium-sized onion, finely chopped
1 tablespoon oil
2 cloves garlic, crushed
salt
freshly ground black pepper
2 cups drained yoghurt (page 21)
Nano Dok (page 297)

1. Trim off roots and coarse stalks from spinach. Wash leaves well, discarding any discoloured and damaged leaves. Drain and shred coarsely.
2. In a large frying pan gently fry onion in oil until transparent. Add spinach and toss over medium heat until wilted. Cook until moisture evaporates.
3. Add garlic, about 1 teaspoon salt and a good grind of pepper. Remove from heat and cool a little.
4. Pour yoghurt into a mixing bowl and add spinach mixture. Toss well and adjust seasoning. Make Nano Dok using small amount of ghee.
5. Turn borani into serving dish and pour on Nano Dok. Serve at room temperature.

SABZI KHORDAN (Mixed herb Platter) *recipe page 297*;
MAST VA KHIAR (Yoghurt with Cucumber and Sultanas) *recipe page 300.*

BORANI CHOGONDAR
BEETROOT SALAD

Serves: 6-8

3 medium-sized cooked or pickled beetroot
  (beets)
2 cups drained yoghurt (page 21)
salt
freshly ground black pepper
vinegar or lemon juice, optional
1 tablespoon chopped fresh or 1 teaspoon
  dried mint
fresh or dried mint to garnish

1. Peel and cool beetroot if freshly cooked. Cut fresh or pickled beetroot in 1 cm (½ inch) dice.
2. Reserve about a ¼ cup of diced beetroot and mix remainder into yoghurt with salt and pepper to taste. If using freshly cooked beetroot, it may be necessary to add a little vinegar or lemon juice to sharpen the flavour.
3. Blend in mint; rub dried mint to a coarse powder if this is used. Cover and chill.
4. Place in serving bowl and garnish with reserved beetroot and mint leaves or powdered dried mint.

MAST VA KHIAR
YOGHURT WITH CUCUMBER AND SULTANAS

Serves: 6-8

2 green cucumbers
2 cups drained yoghurt (page 21)
2 spring onions, finely chopped
½ cup sultanas, washed if necessary
¼ cup chopped walnuts, optional
salt
freshly ground white pepper
1 tablespoon chopped fresh mint or 1
  teaspoon dried mint

1. Choose slender, firm cucumbers and peel thinly. Halve lengthwise; if cucumber is very seedy, remove with the end of a teaspoon. Slice cucumber thinly into a colander and leave to drain.
2. Combine cucumber with yoghurt in a bowl. Stir in spring onions (including some of the green tops), sultanas, walnuts if used and salt and pepper to taste.
3. Add finely chopped fresh mint or dried mint rubbed to a coarse powder, stir well, cover and chill mixture for 1 hour at least.
4. Serve with flat bread cut in squares.

Note: This is classed as a borani. Another version of this recipe is served as a soup — see section on Soups.

TORSHI HOLU
PEACH PICKLES

500 g (1 lb) fresh peaches or 250 g (8 oz) dried
  peaches
1½ cups wine vinegar or cider vinegar
1 tablespoon grated fresh ginger
3 teaspoons ground coriander
3 cloves garlic, crushed
1½ teaspoons tamarind paste
½ cup granulated sugar
¼ teaspoon hot chilli powder
¼ teaspoon salt
¼ teaspoon freshly ground black pepper

1. Peel fresh peaches and slice. Place them in 1 cup vinegar in preserving pan as they are prepared. If using dried peaches, rinse well in cold water, drain, chop and soak overnight in 1 cup vinegar.
2. Add ginger to peaches with coriander and garlic. Dissolve tamarind paste in remaining vinegar and add with remaining ingredients.
3. Bring slowly to the boil, stirring gently until sugar is dissolved. Boil gently for 5 minutes.
4. Ladle into warm, sterilized jar and seal when cool with glass or plastic lid. Use after 1 week.

TORSHI BADEMJAN
EGGPLANT PICKLES

1 kg (2 lb) eggplants (aubergines)
   (3-4 medium-sized)
2 cups cider vinegar
piece of tamarind the size of an egg
½ cup hot water
1 tablespoon white mustard seeds
1 tablespoon coriander seeds, toasted
2 teaspoons fennel seeds
4-6 cloves garlic
1 teaspoon chopped ginger root
½ teaspoon hot chili powder
2 teaspoons freshly ground black pepper
2 teaspoons salt

1. Pierce eggplants with a fork and place on rungs of oven shelf. Bake at 200°C (400°F) for 20 minutes or until soft. Place a dish underneath to catch juices.
2. Hold onto the stem and peel skin from eggplants, then remove stems. Chop flesh into a bowl and immediately mix in ½ cup vinegar to prevent eggplant discolouring.
3. Soak tamarind in hot water for 10-15 minutes until softened. Rub with fingertips to separate pulp, then press through a sieve into the eggplant.
4. Put another ½ cup vinegar into blender jar and add mustard, toasted coriander and fennel seeds, peeled garlic cloves and ginger. Blend to a smooth paste.
5. Add this paste to eggplants with chili powder, pepper and salt. Add remaining vinegar and ladle into sterilized jars. Seal and store in a cool place.

TORSHI KHRAMLU
PERSIMMON PICKLES

1 kg (2 lb) ripe persimmons
2 limu omani (dried limes)
3 teaspoons white mustard seeds
2 teaspoons black peppercorns
1 teaspoon cardamom seeds
3 teaspoons toasted coriander seeds
1 teaspoon fennel seeds
4 whole cloves
2 small pieces cinnamon bark
10 cloves garlic, cracked
12 fresh or dried dates, pitted and halved
3 cups white vinegar
2 teaspoons salt
¼ cup sugar

1. Wash persimmons and dry well. Remove stems and core with a pointed knife. Halve persimmons, then slice into wedges.
2. Break dried limes into small pieces.
3. Mix spices except cinnamon, put in blender jar and grind to a coarse powder. Alternatively pound in a mortar with pestle.
4. In a large, sterilized jar, place some persimmon pieces in the base with 1 piece of cinnamon. Add a few pieces of lime and 2 cracked garlic cloves. Add a few halved dates and some of the ground spices. Repeat in layers until all ingredients are used, placing second piece of cinnamon towards top of jar.
5. Combine vinegar, sugar and salt in a pan and bring to the boil, stirring to dissolve the sugar.
6. Pour hot vinegar into jar. Remove air bubbles with a fine skewer inserted down sides of jar. Seal with glass or plastic lid and leave for 1 week before opening. Use within 3 months of making.

PERSIAN BREADS

With patience, a high powered mixer with dough hook attachment (or a strong arm) and a disregard for high fuel bills, it is possible to achieve acceptable results when making these delicious breads.

In bakers' language, Persian breads are classed as 'lean' — that is, not of definite flavour, as their role in the Persian meal is as an actual aid to eating other foods, rather than as a food to be enjoyed for its own sake. Personally I find the breads absolutely delicious on their own, but I like mine buttered — in Iran this is never done.

You will need a little extra equipment, such as a small cushion wrapped in a tea towel, with towel fastened on one side with a safety pin. Other side should be smooth as dough has to be placed on this. A cast iron or aluminium smooth-surfaced griddle is also necessary as bread has to cook as quickly as possible.

The bread freezes and reheats well, so once you have mastered the art, you can attempt larger quantities when you feel in the mood for bread making.

NANE LAVASH or TAFTOON
WHOLEMEAL FLAT BREAD

The only difference between these breads is the size. Nane Lavash is the better known of the Persian breads, but it is a very large bread and impossible to cook in the domestic oven because of its size. Taftoon is the same dough shaped in a smaller round, so you will be making Taftoon. Call it Nane Lavash if you like.

Makes 6 rounds
Oven temperature: 290°C (550°F)
Cooking time: 5 minutes each bread

1 cup plain white flour
3 cups wholemeal flour
1 sachet active dry yeast
2½ cups warm water
1½ teaspoons salt
oil for handling dough

1. Sift flours into a large mixing bowl, discarding any flakes left in sifter.
2. Dissolve yeast in ¼ cup warm water. Add 1½ cups of the remaining water and the salt.
3. Pour yeast mixture into the centre of the flour and gradually work in the flour.
4. Beat with the hand for 20-30 minutes, or use dough hook on electric mixer and beat for 20 minutes, gradually beating in as much of the remaining ¾ cup water as dough will take. As the dough is beaten, its ability to absorb water increases.
5. Preheat oven to very hot and place griddle on centre shelf for 10 minutes to heat. When hot, rub with wad of cloth dipped in oil.
6. As there is no need to prove this dough, turn it out of bowl onto an oiled board when oven is ready.
7. Oil hands and divide dough into 6 even-sized pieces, shaping each into a ball.
8. Roll out one ball of dough as thinly as possible with an oiled rolling pin. Prick well all over with a fork or run a pin wheel 3 or 4 times across surface.
9. Take round of dough and flip it across the backs of your hands to stretch it a little. Place dough on smooth side of cushion.
10. Pull out rack with heated griddle, quickly turn cushion over and press dough on to it. Close oven and cook 1 minute, then pat dough down again with cushion to prevent bread puffing up.
11. Bake until surface is bubbly — about 3 minutes — turn bread over and cook 2 minutes more. Remove and wrap in a cloth. Let oven temperature return to set heat before adding next lot. Rolled out dough should not rest before being baked, so prepare each round just before you are ready for baking.

SANGYAK (Pebble-baked Wholemeal Bread) and BARBARI (White Bread) *recipes page 304;*
NANE LAVASH or TAFTOON (Wholemeal Flat Bread) *recipe above*

SANGYAK
PEBBLE-BAKED WHOLEMEAL BREAD

The ingredients and method for making this fascinating bread are the same as for Nane Lavash. Instead of the griddle, you will require enough well-washed blue metal to cover the base of a large, shallow baking dish. Brush the blue metal with peanut oil when first making this bread. Once a few loaves have been cooked on it, the metal absorbs enough oil for further bakings.

Place blue metal in its dish on the lowest shelf in oven and turn oven on to heat to 290°C (550°F). If using a gas oven the centre shelf may be a better position as such ovens do not have the advantage of having a heating element directly under dish.

Divide dough into 6 pieces and roll out to an oval shape, or as near to oval as you can. Do not roll too thinly. Place on cushion and turn onto hot blue metal. Bake for 1 minute, then press dough with cushion, cook for further 3 minutes then turn over and cook for 2 minutes more or until bread is cooked. Remove from oven and pull off any pieces of blue metal, returning them to dish. After a few breads have been baked, metal is less likely to stick. Wrap bread as it comes out of the oven.

If bread has not browned sufficiently, place under a hot grill for a few seconds on each side.

BARBARI
WHITE BREAD

Makes 4 loaves
Oven temperature: 220°C (425°F)
Cooking time: 15 minutes

1 sachet active dry yeast
2 cups warm water
1½ teaspoons salt
5 cups plain flour
1 tablespoon oil
oil for shaping

1. Sprinkle yeast on ¼ cup of the warm water in a bowl. Leave to soak and stir to dissolve. Add remaining water and salt.
2. Sift flour into a mixing bowl, holding back 1 cup flour. Make a well in the centre and add yeast liquid. Stir in a little of the flour to slightly thicken liquid, cover bowl and leave in a warm place for 10 minutes or so until frothy.
3. Blend in remaining flour in bowl and beat by hand for 20 minutes, adding 1 tablespoon oil and reserved flour gradually. Knead in flour when dough becomes too stiff for beating, only adding enough to stop dough sticking. Alternatively beat on electric mixer using dough hook for 15 minutes, adding oil gradually, then reserved flour.
4. Cover bowl and leave in a warm place to rise until doubled in bulk — about 30 minutes to 1 hour.
5. Turn dough onto an oiled board and divide in four equal portions. Roll each into a ball. Oil hands and rolling pin. Shape each ball of dough into a rectangle and roll lightly into a long strip about 12 cm (5 inches) wide and 30 cm (12 inches) long. Loaf should be about 1 cm (½ inch) thick. Preheat oven.
6. Place loaves on lightly oiled trays, cover with cloths and leave in a warm place for 15-20 minutes.
7. Brush tops of loaves with oil and make four parallel grooves in each loaf running the length of the loaf, beginning and finishing 2 cm (¾ inch) in from ends. Make grooves with the side of your forefinger.
8. Bake loaves in hot oven, centre shelf, for 15 minutes or until cooked and golden brown.

CHELOU
STEAMED RICE

Serves: 6
Cooking time: 50 minutes

2 cups basmati rice or other good quality long
   grain rice
8 cups water
2 tablespoons salt
¼ cup butter or ghee
¼ cup water

1. Pick over rice and remove discoloured grains and stones. Place in a sieve and wash well under running water until water is clear. Drain.
2. Bring 8 cups water to the boil in a heavy based pan. Add salt and rice, and stir until water returns to the boil.
3. Boil rice for 5 minutes. Pour immediately into a large sieve or colander and drain.
4. In a small pan heat butter with ¼ cup water until bubbling. Pour half of this into pan in which rice was cooked and swirl to coat base and sides.
5. Spread half of partly cooked rice in base of pan, and even out with back of spoon.
6. Spoon remainder of rice on top in a mound. Make a hole in the centre with the end of a wooden spoon and pour remaining butter mixture on top.
7. Cover rim of pan with a doubled tea towel or 2 paper towels and place lid on firmly.
8. Cook rice over medium low heat for 10 minutes, reduce to low and cook for further 35 minutes. The cloth absorbs the steam and makes the rice fluffy and light.
9. Stir rice gently with a fork to distribute butter evenly and serve with kababs and khoreshes and use as a basis for polous.

CHELOU TA DIG
STEAMED CRUSTY RICE

This is the rice dish by which the expertise of a Persian cook is gauged. While plain chelou gives a rice so light and fragrant, each grain glistening separately, Chelou ta Dig is all this plus crusty crunchy golden brown rice for a completely new rice-eating experience — except to the Persians of course.

Follow the basic chelou method to Step 4. Blend about 1 cup of the partly cooked rice with a beaten egg yolk or ¼ cup yoghurt. Spread in base of prepared pan, mound remainder of rice on top and continue to Step 8. Cook on medium heat for 15 minutes, then reduce to medium low heat for further 30 minutes. By this time bottom of rice should be golden brown and crisp. Place pan on a cold surface for a few minutes to loosen rice from base. Spoon fluffy rice into a heated dish. Break up crusty layer into pieces and arrange around rice in dish, browned side up. Serve with khoreshes and kababs.

KATEH
RICE CAKE

This means of cooking rice is popular in the Caspian Sea region of northern Iran, an area where much of Iran's rice is grown. It is a simplified version of Chelou ta Dig, unmoulded like a cake and served cut in wedges. Basmati rice is best for Kateh.

Serves: 6
Cooking time: 1 hour

2 cups basmati rice
3½ cups water
2 teaspoons salt
¼ cup ghee or butter

1. Pick over rice, wash very well and drain. Place in a heavy pan, preferably one with a non-stick coating, and add water and salt.
2. Bring to the boil over medium heat, stirring occasionally. Cover, reduce heat a little and cook for 25 minutes until water is absorbed.
3. Add ghee or butter and stir through with a wooden spoon. Even out top of rice, pressing lightly.
4. Cover pan and return to medium low heat for 30 minutes. Move pan over hot plate or burner from time to time so that base becomes evenly browned.
5. Remove from heat and place pan in cold water for 10 minutes. Run a spatula or knife blade around sides to loosen and invert a plate on top. Holding plate and pot firmly, turn upside-down so that rice cake comes out cleanly. Serve cut in wedges with Khoresh. Kateh is often served cold in summer.

DAMI
BOILED RICE

Yet another method to cook rice. It is similar to Kateh except that heat is kept lower once rice begins to boil, and the rim of the pan is covered with a cloth or 2 paper towels before lid is placed in position. After 30 minutes pour melted ghee or butter over rice, replace lid without cloth and leave on low heat for further 30 minutes. Fluff up with fork and serve as an accompaniment to Khoresh, or mix with other ingredients before or halfway through cooking.

MIVEH DAMI
RICE WITH FRUIT

Serves: 6
Cooking time: 1 hour

2 cups basmati or other good quality long
    grain rice
¼ cup ghee or butter
1 small onion, finely chopped
250 g (1 lb) lean lamb or veal stew meat, diced
½ teaspoon ground cinnamon
1½ cups pitted sour cherries
½ cup chopped walnuts
¼ cup currants
½ cup chopped dried apricots
2 teaspoons salt
freshly ground black pepper
water

1. Wash rice well until water runs clear and drain in sieve.
2. In a heavy pan heat ghee and fry onion and meat until lightly browned. Stir in cinnamon, cherries, walnuts, currants and apricots and add salt and pepper to taste.
3. Add drained rice and stir to blend, then pour in enough cold water to come 2 cm (¾ inch) above level of rice. Cover rim of pan with a cloth or 2 paper towels, place lid on tightly and cook over very low heat for 50 minutes.

KHORESHE GORMEH SABZI (Green Vegetable and Meat Sauce) *recipe page 312.*

ESTANBOLI POLOU
LAMB, TOMATO AND RICE

For this recipe I have used a method which can be applied to other polous. Mrs Akhtar Ostowari, an Iranian residing in Sydney, Australia, makes many of her polous in this way. She has found that straight-sided utensils with a non-stick coating always ensure the perfect unmoulding of any crusted polou without the need to place the utensil on a cold surface to loosen the contents.

With the potato lining used in this recipe a straight-sided pan of heavy gauge aluminium works just as well. The potato-crusted rice section of the recipe has been placed separately so that you can use if for other polou recipes. For method follow from Step 4.

Serves: 6
Cooking time: 2¼ hours

750 g (1½ lb) lean boneless lamb or beef for
    braising
¼ cup ghee or butter
1 large onion, finely chopped
½ teaspoon ground cinnamon
1 teaspoon paprika
1 cup tomato purée
salt
freshly ground black pepper

Potato-crusted Rice:
2 cups basmati or other good quality long
    grain rice
water
salt
3-4 medium-sized potatoes
⅓ cup ghee

1. Trim meat and cut into 3 cm (1¼ inch) squares. Heat half the ghee or butter in a pan and brown meat on each side. Remove to a plate.
2. Add remaining ghee and onion to pan and fry onion gently until transparent. Sprinkle in spices and return meat to pan. Add tomato purée and salt and pepper to taste. Cover and simmer gently for 1 hour or until meat is just tender.
3. Meanwhile pick over rice if necessary and wash well. Bring 8 cups water to the boil, add 2 tablespoons salt and the rice and stir occasionally until boiling again. Boil uncovered for 8 minutes, then drain in a sieve.
4. Peel potatoes and cut in 5 mm (¼ inch) slices. Place in cold salted water and leave to soak until meat completes cooking.
5. Drain potatoes and dry well. Melt half the ghee in pan to be used for final cooking. Coat slices in ghee and arrange on base and sides.
6. Add half the rice, spreading it evenly, and top with meat mixture. Spread remaining rice on top and pour remaining ghee evenly over rice.
7. Cover rim of pan with 2 paper towels or a cloth and put lid on tightly. Cook on high heat for 3 minutes, then reduce to medium and cook for 30 minutes, then a little lower for further 30 minutes. Move pan on hot plate or burner from time to time so that potatoes brown evenly.
8. Run a knife blade around polou to loosen, then invert carefully onto serving platter. Cut in wedges to serve.

HAVIJ POLOU
CARROTS WITH RICE

Serves: 6
Cooking time: 1¼-1½ hours

1 kg (2 lb) chicken breasts or 1 whole chicken
500 g (1 lb) carrots
¼ cup ghee or butter
salt
freshly ground black pepper
1 large onion, finely chopped
1 teaspoon turmeric
¼ cup lemon juice
¼ cup brown sugar
½ cup water
1 quantity Chelou (page 305)

1. Cut chicken breasts into quarters; if using whole chicken, joint and halve larger pieces.
2. Scrape carrots and cut into sticks 5 mm (¼ inch) thick and 5 cm (2 inches) long.
3. In a frying pan heat half the ghee and brown chicken pieces on each side. Remove to a plate and season with salt and pepper.
4. Add remaining ghee to pan and gently fry onion until transparent. Sprinkle in turmeric, add carrots and cook, stirring often, for further 5 minutes.
5. Add lemon juice, brown sugar and water and stir to lift browned sediment. Return chicken to pan, cover and simmer gently for 10 minutes.
6. Prepare chelou up to Step 5. Place chicken pieces on top of rice and spread carrot mixture on top. Spread remaining rice over carrots and add the remaining ghee mixture from chelou recipe (Step 6).
7. Cover rim of pan with 2 paper towels. Put lid on and cook over medium low heat for 40 minutes. Alternatively polou may be layered in a casserole dish and cooked in a moderately slow oven 170°C (325°F) for 30 minutes.

KADO POLOU
RICE WITH PUMPKIN SQUASH

Serves: 4-5
Cooking time: 1½ hours

500 g (1 lb) finely ground lamb, beef or veal
1 small onion, grated
salt
freshly ground black pepper
½ teaspoon ground cinnamon
¼ teaspoon ground nutmeg
500 g (1 lb) butternut pumpkin squash
1 large onion
¼ cup butter or ghee
1 quantity Chelou (page 305)
3 teaspoons brown sugar

1. Combine ground meat with grated onion, 1 teaspoon salt, pepper and spices. Blend thoroughly and shape into balls the size of a large walnut, then flatten into thick patties.
2. Peel pumpkin squash and cut into slices 1 cm (½ inch) thick.
3. Halve onion lengthways and slice thinly. Heat half the butter or ghee in a frying pan and gently fry onion until transparent and lightly browned. Take care not to burn it. Remove and keep aside.
4. Add remaining butter to pan and brown meat patties on each side.
5. Prepare chelou up to Step 5, and place meat patties on top of rice. Cover meat with half the onion, then add prepared pumpkin squash. Sprinkle on the sugar and salt and pepper to taste. Top with remaining onion, then last of rice and butter mixture from chelou recipe (Step 6).
6. Cover top of pan with 2 paper towels, place lid on tightly and cook over medium heat for 10 minutes, reduce to low and cook for 45-50 minutes until pumpkin squash is tender. Alternatively polou may be cooked in a casserole dish in a moderate oven, 180°C (350°F).

MORGH POLOU
CHICKEN WITH RICE

Serves: 4-5
Cooking time: 1 ¼ hours

1 chicken, about 1.5 kg (3 lb)
salt
freshly ground black pepper
¼ cup butter or ghee
1 large onion, finely chopped
½ cup chopped dried apricots
½ cup sultanas
½ teaspoon cinnamon
water
½ teaspoon saffron threads
1 quantity Chelou (page 305)

1. Joint chicken and wipe dry with paper towels. Season pieces with salt and pepper.
2. Heat half the butter in a frying pan and brown chicken pieces on all sides. Remove and keep aside.
3. Add remaining butter to pan and fry onion gently until transparent. Add apricots and sultanas and cook for further 5 minutes. Stir in cinnamon and a little water to lift browned sediment.
4. Prepare chelou to Step 5 and place chicken pieces on top of rice. Spread apricot mixture over chicken and top with remaining rice and butter mixture from chelou recipe (Step 6).
5. Cover top of pan with 2 paper towels, place lid on tightly and cook over low heat for 50 minutes or until chicken is tender.
6. While polou is cooking, boil 2 tablespoons water and mix with saffron. Leave aside to steep.
7. Just before serving sprinkle saffron liquid over rice and stir in gently. Serve piled on a platter.

SHEVID BHAGALA POLOU
RICE WITH LAMB, BROAD BEANS AND DILL

Serves: 6
Cooking time: 2 hours

1.5 kg (3 lb) lamb shoulder chops
½ cup ghee or butter
1 large onion, finely chopped
½ teaspoon turmeric
water
salt
freshly ground black pepper
3 cups basmati or other good quality long
    grain rice
2 cups fresh shelled broad beans, skin
    removed (see page 12)
¾ cup chopped dill (fennel may be
    substituted)

1. Ask meat supplier to cut shoulder chops 4 cm (1½ inches) thick. In a heavy pan heat 1 tablespoon ghee and brown lamb on each side. Remove to a plate.
2. Add another tablespoon ghee to pan and gently fry onion until transparent. Add turmeric and cook 2 minutes longer. Stir in 1 cup water, return lamb to pan and add salt and pepper to taste. Cover and simmer gently for 1 hour until lamb is tender but not falling apart.
3. While lamb is cooking bring 8 cups water to the boil in a large pot. Add 2 tablespoons salt and well-washed rice. Stir until water returns to the boil and boil uncovered for 5 minutes. Drain immediately into a sieve.
4. Have broad beans and dill in a bowl and add half the hot rice. Toss to combine and add salt to taste.
5. Melt remaining ghee in a large casserole dish or Dutch oven and add 1 tablespoon water. Swirl to coat sides and pour most of ghee into a container.
6. Place the plain partly cooked rice in the base of the casserole. Top with lamb mixture including juices. Spread bean, dill and rice mixture on top. Pour half the reserved ghee evenly over the rice.
7. Cover casserole and cook in a moderate oven for 35-40 minutes until beans are tender.
8. Spoon rice from top and arrange around edge of serving platter. Remove lamb pieces to a plate. Put rice from bottom of dish in centre of platter and top with lamb pieces. Pour remaining ghee over lamb and rice and serve with yoghurt and pickles.

Note: Fresh shelled broad beans are skinned similarly to dried soaked broad beans.

KHORESHE FESENJAN
DUCK IN WALNUT AND POMEGRANATE SAUCE

Serves: 4
Cooking time: 2-2½ hours

1 duck, about 2 kg (4 lb)
salt
freshly ground black pepper
2 tablespoons ghee or butter
1 large onion, finely chopped
1 cup finely chopped or ground walnuts
½ cup coarsely ground walnuts
1½ cups pomegranate juice (see Glossary for substitutes)
3 tablespoons brown sugar
2 pieces cinnamon bark
1 tablespoon lime or lemon juice, optional

For serving:
¼ cup coarsely chopped walnuts
pomegranate seeds if available
Chelou or Chelou Ta Dig (page 305)

1. Remove pin feathers from cleaned duck and singe if necessary. Remove excess fat from cavity. Wipe dry with paper towels. Truss duck and season with salt and pepper.
2. Heat 1 tablespoon ghee in a large heavy pan and brown duck on all sides over medium heat. Remove when browned and keep aside. Drain off fat.
3. Add remaining ghee and gently fry onion until transparent. Add walnuts, pomegranate juice, sugar and cinnamon and bring to the boil. Reduce heat.
4. Return duck to pan and spoon sauce over it. Cover and simmer gently for 2-2½ hours until tender. Baste occasionally during cooking.
5. Adjust seasoning of sauce during cooking, adding lime or lemon juice if pomegranate juice lacks tartness.
6. Lift cooked duck onto platter and keep hot. Skim excess oil from sauce and return to the boil.
7. Spoon sauce over duck and garnish with walnuts. Add a dash of colour with pomegranate seeds when available.
8. To serve, joint duck into four portions and serve with chelou.

Note: Whole chicken or chicken pieces may be used instead of duck.

KHORESHE HOLU
PEACH SAUCE WITH CHICKEN

Serves: 5-6
Cooking time: 1½ hours

1.5 kg (3 lb) chicken pieces
salt
freshly ground black pepper
¼ cup ghee or butter
1 medium-sized onion, chopped
1 teaspoon turmeric
1 cup water
small piece cinnamon bark
3 firm peaches
¼ cup lemon or lime juice
2 tablespoons brown sugar
Chelou Ta Dig for serving (page 305)

1. Either joint a chicken of the weight given or use chicken pieces (breasts, legs and thighs or a mixture). Cut pieces if large and wipe dry with paper towels. Season with salt and pepper.
2. Heat half the ghee in a heavy pan and brown chicken pieces.
3. Add onion to fat in pan and fry gently until transparent. Sprinkle on turmeric and fry until onion begins to brown.
4. Add water to pan and stir to lift browned juices. Return chicken and add cinnamon stick. Cover and simmer gently for 45 minutes until almost tender.
5. Peel and stone peaches and slice in wedges. Heat remaining ghee and fry peaches until lightly coloured.
6. Arrange peaches on top of chicken. Sprinkle on lemon juice and brown sugar. Cover pan and simmer for further 20-25 minutes. Check flavour and adjust with seasoning, lemon juice and sugar if necessary. Serve hot with Chelou Ta Dig.

Note: When fresh peaches are out of season substitute frozen peach slices or drained canned peaches — about 1½-2 cups of slices are sufficient. Omit sugar if using canned peaches, then adjust flavour if necessary before serving.

KHORESHE GORMEH SABZI
GREEN VEGETABLE AND MEAT SAUCE

Serves: 6
Cooking time: 2-2¼ hours

750 g (1½ lb) boneless stewing lamb or beef
1 large onion, finely chopped
⅓ cup ghee or oil
1 teaspoon turmeric
1½ cups water
¼ cup lemon juice
salt
freshly ground black pepper
1½ cups diced potatoes
1 cup chopped spring onion tops
1½ cups chopped spinach
¼ cup chopped coriander, optional
½ cup chopped parsley
¼ cup tareh (garlic chives), optional

1. Trim meat and cut into 2 cm (¾ inch) cubes.
2. In a heavy pan gently fry onion in half of the ghee or oil until transparent. Add turmeric and fry for 2 minutes longer.
3. Increase heat, add meat cubes and stir over high heat until meat changes colour and begins to brown. Reduce heat.
4. Add water, lemon juice and salt and pepper to taste. Cover and simmer gently for 1-1½ hours until meat is just tender. Time depends on type of meat used.
5. Heat remaining ghee or oil in a large frying pan and add potatoes. Fry over high heat until lightly browned. Add to sauce, leaving fat in pan. Cover and simmer 10 minutes.
6. Add prepared greens to frying pan and fry over medium heat until wilted. Add to sauce, cover and simmer for further 15-20 minutes or until meat and potatoes are tender. Adjust seasoning and serve.

KHORESHE ALU
PRUNE AND MEAT SAUCE

Serves: 4-5
Cooking time: 2 hours

750 g (1½ lb) boneless stewing lamb or beef
1 large onion, chopped
1 tablespoon ghee or oil
½ teaspoon turmeric
pinch of ground cinnamon
1½ cups water
salt
freshly ground black pepper
1 cup prunes
2 teaspoons lemon juice
1 tablespoon brown sugar
Chelou for serving (page 305)

1. Trim meat and cut into 2 cm (¾ inch) cubes.
2. In a heavy pan gently fry onion in ghee until transparent, adding turmeric and cinnamon while onion cooks.
3. Increase heat and add meat. Stir frequently until meat begins to brown.
4. Add water, salt and pepper and bring to a slow simmer. Reduce heat, cover and simmer gently for 1 hour.
5. Rinse prunes if necessary and add to meat with lemon juice and sugar. Cover and simmer for further 45 minutes. Serve hot with chelou.

KHORESHE SIB
APPLE AND MEAT SAUCE

Follow directions for Khoreshe Alu, substituting 4 apples for prunes. Peel, core and slice apples and fry gently in 2 tablespoons ghee or butter for 5 minutes until lightly coloured. At Step 4 simmer sauce for 1½ hours, add apples and simmer for 10-15 minutes so that slices stay intact. Add lemon juice and sugar to achieve a pleasant sweet-sour flavour.

KOTAH DOLMEH
FRIED DOUGH WITH LENTILS

Makes 6 dozen
Cooking time: 1½ hours plus 3 minutes each lot for frying

Dough:
1 sachet active dry yeast
1 cup warm water
2 teaspoons rose water
3½ cups plain flour
1 teaspoon salt
½ teaspoon ground cardamom
¼ cup melted, cooled ghee or oil

Lentil Filling:
1 cup brown lentils
3 cups cold water
2 large onions, finely chopped
⅓ cup ghee
salt
2 tablespoons brown sugar

To finish:
oil for deep frying

1. Dissolve yeast in ¼ cup warm water, add remaining water and rose water.
2. Sift flour, salt and cardamom into a mixing bowl and remove ½ cup of the flour mixture.
3. Add yeast liquid to flour and mix to a soft dough. Work in ghee or oil with reserved flour, then knead until smooth and elastic — about 10 minutes. Cover and leave in a warm place for 45-60 minutes or until doubled in bulk.
4. Meanwhile wash lentils well, place in a pan and add cold water. Bring to the boil, cover and simmer over low heat for 1-1¼ hours or until water is absorbed and lentils are soft. Mash with a fork.
5. Gently fry onion in ghee or oil until transparent and lightly browned, add lentils and fry with onion for 5 minutes. Stir in salt to taste and brown sugar. Cool.
6. Punch down dough and divide into two portions. Roll out each portion thinly to a 45 cm (18 inch) circle as described on page 16.
7. Cut dough into 8 cm (3 inch) rounds with a biscuit cutter and place a generous teaspoon of lentil paste in centre of each round. Moisten edge of dough lightly with water, fold over and press firmly to seal. Press with tines of fork.
8. Beginning with kotah shaped first, deep fry 6-8 at a time for 3 minutes until golden brown and puffed, turning to brown evenly. Lift out with slotted spoon and drain on paper towels. Serve hot or warm as a snack or part of a meal, particularly a picnic meal.

AASHE JOE
BARLEY SOUP

Serves: 8-10
Cooking time: 3½ hours

½ cup chick peas
½ cup red beans
750 g (1½ lb) lamb neck or shoulder with bone
¾ cup pearl barley
¼ cup brown lentils
water
salt
freshly ground black pepper
½ cup chopped parsley
1-2 tablespoons chopped coriander
½ cup chopped tareh (garlic chives) or spring onion leaves
1 cup chopped shahat or watercress
1 tablespoon ghee
1 large onion, halved then sliced
1 teaspoon turmeric
1 teaspoon dried mint

1. Cover washed chick peas and red beans with 3 cups water and soak overnight.
2. Have lamb cut by meat retailer into chunky pieces. Rinse in cold water and place in large soup pot.
3. Add 8 cups water, chick peas and beans and their soaking water. Bring slowly to a simmer, skimming when necessary. Cover pot and simmer gently for 1 hour.
4. Rinse barley and lentils and add to soup with salt and pepper to taste. Cover and simmer for further 1½ hours or until meat is fork tender and beans, etc., are soft.
5. Remove meat and strip meat from bones. Cut meat into small pieces and return to pot with prepared herbs. Cover and leave on low heat for 15 minutes.
6. Meanwhile heat ghee in a frying pan and fry onion slices over medium heat until transparent and golden brown. Sprinkle on turmeric and continue to fry until onion becomes crisp — it may be necessary to lower heat so that onion does not burn. Rub mint to a powder and sprinkle into pan, stir and remove from heat.
7. Stir half the onion mixture into the soup. Ladle soup into tureen or bowls and garnish with remaining onion mixture. Serve with flat bread as a main meal.

ABGUSHTE MIVEH
DRIED FRUIT SOUP

Serves: 6
Cooking time: 2 hours

500 g (1 lb) lean lamb or beef stew meat
500 g (1 lb) lamb or beef soup bones
7 cups water
1 limu omani (dried lime), optional
salt
freshly ground black pepper
2 tablespoons ghee or butter
1 large onion, finely chopped
2 teaspoons turmeric
1 cup prunes, pitted
½ cup dried apricot halves
½ cup chopped dried peaches
⅓-½ cup brown sugar
1-2 tablespoons lemon or lime juice

1. Cut meat into small cubes and place in a soup pot with bones, water and dried lime if available. Bring slowly to the boil, skimming when necessary.
2. Add salt and pepper, cover and simmer gently for 1½ hours or until meat is almost tender. Remove bones and dried lime if used.
3. In a frying pan heat ghee or butter and fry onion until transparent, stir in turmeric and cook until lightly browned. Add to soup with dried fruits (these may be washed if necessary, but do not require soaking). Cover and simmer for 30 minutes.
4. Add sugar and lemon or lime juice to taste so that soup has a pleasant sweet-sour flavour. Serve hot.

ABGUSHTE BEH
QUINCE SOUP

Follow directions for Abgushte Miveh, replacing dried fruits with 3 cups chopped quince, previously peeled and cored. After browned onions and turmeric have been added to the soup, heat another 2 tablespoons ghee in pan and fry quince gently for 10 minutes, stirring often. Add to soup, cover and simmer for 30-45 minutes or until quince is tender. Adjust sweet-sour flavour at end of cooking.

MAST VA KHIAR
COLD YOGHURT SOUP

Serves: 6

2 green cucumbers
3 cups yoghurt
½ cup sultanas, washed if necessary
3 spring onions including green tops
1 tablespoon finely chopped parsley
1 tablespoon finely chopped dill
½ cup finely chopped walnuts, optional
2 hard-boiled eggs, finely chopped
salt
about 1 cup iced water
parsley and/or dill to garnish

1. Peel cucumber thinly and grate coarsely. Add flesh and juice to yoghurt.
2. Leave some of the green tops on the spring onions and slice finely. Add to yoghurt with chopped herbs, walnuts if used, and eggs. Season to taste with salt.
3. Blend in iced water to give a thick cream consistency, and adjust flavour with more salt if necessary. Cover and chill for 2 hours at least.
4. Serve in bowls garnished with chopped herbs or herb sprigs.

ABGUSHTE MIVEH (Dried Fruit Soup) *recipe above*

AASHE ANAR
POMEGRANATE SOUP

Serves: 6
Cooking time: 2-2½ hours

2 lamb or veal foreshanks, cracked
6 cups water
¼ cup yellow split peas
1 small beetroot (beet), peeled and diced
1 small onion, finely chopped
salt
freshly ground black pepper
1 cup finely chopped spinach
½ cup finely chopped parsley
2 tablespoons finely chopped coriander
    leaves, optional
2 tablespoons chopped tareh (garlic chives)
½ cup chopped spring onion tops
⅓ cup short grain rice, washed
1½ cups pomegranate juice (see Glossary)
1-2 tablespoons lemon or lime juice
sugar to taste
Nano Dok (page 297)

1. Rinse meat and place in soup pot with water. Add washed split peas and bring to a slow simmer, skimming when necessary.
2. When well skimmed and beginning to boil, add beetroot, onion and salt and pepper to taste. Cover and simmer on low heat for 1½-2 hours or until meat is very tender.
3. Remove shanks from pot and strip meat from bones. Chop meat in small pieces and return to soup with spinach, herbs, rice, pomegranate juice, lemon or lime juice and sugar to taste. Soup should have a tart but slightly sweet flavour. Cover and simmer for further 30 minutes.
4. Make Nano Dok, using larger amount of ghee. Pour half into soup. Serve soup in bowls, floating a little Nano Dok on top of each.

KUKU

These delicious egg dishes feature prominently in Persian menus because of their versatility. Cut into small squares they can be served with pre-dinner drinks; with yoghurt and bread they make an excellent luncheon or supper dish; for dinner in the Western tradition they make an excellent first course, and are almost always part of the menu for a Persian dinner; as they are just as delicious served cold, prepare one for the picnic hamper as they do in Iran.

The usual method of cooking is in the oven, a relatively recent adaptation since ovens were seldom part of the early Persian kitchen. The other and more authentic method is to cook the kuku in a frying pan on the range top. As the finished kuku should resemble a cake when served, lightly browned and crisp all over, the choice of utensil and cooking method can be determined by the equipment you have on hand.

Modern Persian cooks have been quick to see the advantage of non-stick cookware for many of their dishes — in particular for certain rice dishes and for kukus.

For oven cooking, choose a smooth-surfaced casserole dish, or a Dutch oven or cake pan with a non-stick coating. The straighter the sides the better.

For range top cooking a well-seasoned heavy frying pan, or one with a non-stick coating should be used. An omelet pan is far too small, unless you halve the recipe.

Where initial cooking of the vegetables is required use any pan for this, keeping your special pan for finishing the kuku.

To present the kuku for serving, it always looks better with the top uppermost. If unmoulding from an oven dish, invert onto plate then place serving plate on top and turn upright. Of course you can serve it straight from the dish it was cooked in if you find your kuku has stuck.

KUKUYE SIBZAMINI
POTATO OMELET

Serves: 4-6
Oven temperature: 180°C (350°F)
Cooking time: 50-60 minutes

500 g (1 lb) potatoes
2 medium-sized onions, grated
1 teaspoon turmeric
salt
freshly ground black pepper
6 eggs
¼ cup ghee

1. Boil potatoes, then drain well and mash to a purée. Blend in onion, turmeric and salt and pepper to taste. Leave until cold.
2. Beat eggs with a whisk and stir gradually into potato mixture. Blend thoroughly and adjust seasoning.
3. Heat ghee in a 20 cm (8 inch) casserole dish, non-stick Dutch oven or cake pan, swirling to coat sides.
4. Pour in egg mixture and bake in a moderate oven for 30 minutes until set and lightly browned on top. Brown top under a hot grill if necessary.
5. Turn out onto serving dish and serve cut in wedges.

Note: Alternatively kuku may be cooked in a frying pan on range top. Cook covered over medium heat until set, brown top under hot grill, loosen and slide onto serving dish.

KUKUYE KADOU HALVAII
PUMPKIN SQUASH OMELET

Follow Kukuye Sibzamini recipe, using 500 g (1 lb) butternut pumpkin squash or similar yellow firm pumpkin instead of the potatoes. Boil and drain, return to heat and let excess moisture evaporate. Mash to a purée, add a little sugar and continue as directed.

KUKUYE BADEMJAN
EGGPLANT OMELET

Serves: 4
Oven temperature: 180°C (350°F)
Cooking time: 1 hour

500 g (1 lb) eggplant
⅓ cup ghee or cooking oil
2 spring onions, chopped
6 eggs
1 teaspoon salt
freshly ground black pepper
1 tablespoon ghee
yoghurt for serving

1. Peel eggplant and cut into large cubes.
2. Heat ghee or cooking oil in a frying pan, add eggplant and fry over medium heat until lightly browned and tender.
3. Pour pan contents into a bowl, mash with a fork and add spring onions. Leave until cool.
4. Beat eggs well with a fork or whisk. Stir in salt and pepper and add to eggplant.
5. Melt ghee in a 23 cm (9 inch) round casserole dish or cake pan in oven. When melted swirl ghee to coat sides.
6. Pour in egg mixture and cook in a moderate oven for 40 minutes until firm and lightly browned on top. If insufficiently browned, place under a hot grill for a few seconds.
7. Serve hot, cut in wedges, with yoghurt and flat bread. Also good served cold.

KUKUYE SABZI
HERB OMELET

Serves: 4-6
Oven temperature: 180°C (350°F)
Cooking time: 45-50 minutes

2 cups finely chopped spinach
1½ cups finely chopped spring onions
   including green tops
½ cup finely chopped parsley
¼ cup finely chopped coriander
1 tablespoon chopped dill
1 tablespoon chopped tarragon, optional
2 tablespoons chopped garlic chives (tareh)
1 tablespoon flour
salt
freshly ground black pepper
8 eggs
¼ cup ghee or butter

1. Vegetables and herbs must be well washed and dried before chopping and measuring. Chopping can be done very speedily and efficiently in food processor. Accurate measuring of greens is not essential to success of dish.
2. Combine greens in a bowl. Mix flour with 1 teaspoon salt and pepper to taste and sprinkle over greens, then toss well.
3. Beat eggs until frothy and pour over greens. Stir well to combine and adjust seasoning.
4. Heat butter in a 23 cm (9 inch) round casserole dish or deep cake pan in a moderate oven. Swirl to coat sides and pour in egg mixture.
5. Bake in a moderate oven, one shelf above centre, for 45-50 minutes until set and top is lightly browned. If insufficiently browned when set, place briefly under a hot grill.
6. Serve hot, cut in wedges, with yoghurt and flat bread. Also good served cold.

KUKUYE KADOU
ZUCCHINI OMELET

Serves: 6
Oven temperature: 180°C (350°F)
Cooking time: 1 hour

1 large onion, grated or finely chopped
4-5 zucchini (courgettes), preferably the
   light-skinned variety
¼ cup ghee
1 teaspoon turmeric
salt
freshly ground black pepper
1 teaspoon sugar
6 eggs
1 tablespoon ghee or oil

1. In a frying pan gently fry onion in ghee until transparent.
2. Wash and trim zucchini and cut into 5 mm (¼ inch) slices (about 3 cups sliced zucchini).
3. Add zucchini to onion in pan, increase heat and fry over medium high heat for 15 minutes, stirring occasionally. Cook until vegetables are lightly coloured and any moisture has evaporated.
4. Remove from heat, stir in turmeric, about 1 teaspoon salt, a good grinding of pepper and the sugar. Leave until cooled.
5. Beat eggs with a whisk and season lightly. Stir in cooled zucchini mixture.
6. Heat 1 tablespoon ghee or oil in a 20 cm (8 inch) non-stick casserole dish, Dutch oven or cake pan in a moderate oven. Swirl ghee around dish to coat sides.
7. Pour in egg mixture and bake kuku in a moderate oven for 30 minutes until set, puffed and lightly browned on top. If insufficiently browned when set, place under a hot grill for a few seconds.
8. Unmould onto a plate and serve hot or cold cut in wedges. Serve with yoghurt and flat bread.

To cook in frying pan: Heat 1 tablespoon ghee in frying pan and swirl to coat sides. Pour in egg mixture, cover and cook over medium heat for 10-15 minutes until set and puffed in the centre. Place under a hot grill to brown top, loosen kuku, tilt and slide onto serving platter.

HAVIJ POLOU (Carrots with Rice) *recipe page 309.*

ESHKANEH
ONION SOUP

Many versions of this soup are prepared in Iran. Basically it is a meatless soup with onion and a sour juice as the principal ingredients. Walnuts, spinach or diced potatoes are added to give substance to the soup. The juice used can be lime, lemon, pomegranate or verjuice (the juice of unripened grapes), with the tartness counteracted by the addition of sugar. Sometimes apricots or sour cherries are used instead of fruit juice. In other words the soup is composed of ingredients the cook might have on hand; once you have tried this version, experiment with other combinations. The eggs, prepared in either of the two ways mentioned, are mandatory.

Serves: 5-6
Cooking time: 50-60 minutes

5 medium-sized onions
⅓ cup ghee
⅓ cup plain flour
½ cup finely chopped walnuts (or 2 cups finely chopped spinach or diced potatoes)
½ teaspoon turmeric
5 cups water
½ cup lime or lemon juice
about ½ cup brown sugar
salt
freshly ground black pepper
Nano Dok (page 297)
2-6 eggs

1. Halve onions lengthwise and slice thinly into semicircles.
2. Heat 1 tablespoon ghee in a pot, add about ½ cup of the onion slices and fry over medium high heat until brown and crisp. Remove and keep aside for garnishing.
3. Melt remaining ghee on medium heat and add remainder of onions. Fry gently until transparent. Stir in flour and cook until flour is golden.
4. Add walnuts, spinach or potatoes and turmeric and stir over heat for 2 minutes. Stir in water and cook until thickened and bubbling, stirring occasionally. Cover and simmer for 20 minutes.
5. Add lime or lemon juice, sugar, salt and pepper to taste. Cover and simmer for further 15 minutes.
6. Prepare Nano Dok as directed and add to soup.
7. Beat 2 eggs lightly and pour in slowly, stirring soup gently until eggs set in shreds. Alternatively break 5-6 eggs into simmering soup one at a time and simmer gently until eggs are set.
8. Serve in bowls; if using whole eggs add one to each bowl and fill with soup. Garnish with reserved browned onions and serve with bread, preferably flat bread.

MOHI SHEKUMPOUR
STUFFED BAKED FISH

Serves: 4-5
Cooking time: 40-50 minutes
Oven temperature: 190°C (375°F)

1 whole baking fish, about 1.5 kg (3 lb)
salt
freshly ground black pepper
½ cup finely chopped spring onion
2 cups chopped fresh herbs — parsley, coriander, dill, watercress, combined
juice of 1 lemon
¼ cup olive oil
herb sprigs and lemon wedges to garnish

1. Clean and scale fish if necessary. Rub inside and out with salt and pepper and leave aside.
2. Combine spring onions and herbs with 1 tablespoon each lemon juice and olive oil and season lightly. Fill cavity of fish with mixture and secure opening with cocktail picks or thread.
3. Cut 3 diagonal slashes on each side of fish. Place in a well-oiled baking dish and pour remaining lemon juice and oil over fish.
4. Bake in a moderately hot oven for 40-50 minutes until fish is tender. Test thickest part with a fork. Baste during cooking with juices in dish.
5. Lift carefully onto serving platter and garnish with fresh herb sprigs and lemon wedges. Serve with chelou and a borani (Persian salad).

MOHI POLOU
FISH WITH HERBED RICE

Serves: 6
Cooking time: 1 hour

750 g (1½ lb) fish steaks
salt
¼ cup ghee
1 teaspoon turmeric
1 cup chopped spring onion tops
1½ cups chopped spinach
¼ cup chopped coriander leaves
¼ cup chopped parsley
2 tablespoons chopped dill
freshly ground black pepper
1 quantity Chelou (page 305)

1. Dry fish with paper towels and sprinkle lightly with salt. Leave for 15 minutes.
2. Heat ghee in a frying pan and quickly brown fish steaks on each side — it is not necessary to cook them through. Remove to a plate.
3. Add turmeric to ghee in pan, fry for 2 minutes and remove from heat.
4. Prepare chelou as directed to the end of Step 3 and turn rice into a bowl after draining. Add prepared vegetables and herbs and salt and pepper to taste, and toss to combine thoroughly.
5. Follow Steps 4 and 5 of chelou recipe, using the rice and herb mixture. Arrange fish steaks on top of rice and pour turmeric flavoured ghee over fish. Top with remainder of rice and pour on remaining butter or ghee mixture from chelou recipe, Step 6.
6. Cover top of pan with 2 paper towels, fit lid on firmly and cook over low heat for 45 minutes.
7. Remove rice from top of polou and place in a ring on serving dish. Lift fish onto a plate. Spoon remaining rice into centre of platter and place fish steaks on top. Serve hot, garnished with fresh herb sprigs if desired.

KUKUYE MOHI
FISH OMELET

Serves: 4-6
Oven temperature: 180°C (350°F)
Cooking time: 50 minutes

500 g (1 lb) white fish fillets
salt
⅓ cup ghee
1 small onion, finely chopped
½ teaspoon turmeric
1 tablespoon finely chopped coriander leaves
1 tablespoon plain flour
6 eggs
freshly ground black pepper

1. Remove skin from fish fillets and dry fish with paper towels. Sprinkle lightly with salt and leave for 10 minutes.
2. Heat ¼ cup ghee in a frying pan and fry fish quickly on each side until cooked through — fish does not have to brown. Remove to a plate and flake with a fork, removing any bones. Turn into a bowl.
3. Fry onion gently in ghee left in pan. When transparent, stir in turmeric and cook 2 minutes. Mix into fish with coriander and flour.
4. Beat eggs well with a fork and add to fish mixture with salt and pepper to taste. Blend thoroughly.
5. Heat remaining ghee in a 20 cm (8 inch) non-stick cake pan, casserole dish or Dutch oven and swirl to coat base and sides. Pour in egg mixture and bake in a moderate oven for 30 minutes until set. Brown top lightly under grill if necessary.
6. Unmould onto serving platter and serve hot or cold, cut into wedges.

MORGH SHEKUMPOUR
STUFFED CHICKEN

Serves: 5-6
Oven temperature: 190°C (375°F)
Cooking time: 2 hours

1 medium-sized onion, finely chopped
⅓ cup ghee or butter
½ cup chopped pitted prunes
¼ cup sultanas (white raisins)
½ cup dried apricot halves
¼ cup water
1 apple, peeled, cored and diced
1 teaspoon ground cinnamon
salt
freshly ground black pepper
brown sugar to taste
1 chicken, about 1.5 kg (3 lb)
½ lemon
Chelou for serving (page 305)

1. In a frying pan gently fry onion in half the ghee or butter until transparent. Add prunes, sultanas and apricots and stir over heat for 2 minutes.
2. Add water, cover and simmer for 10 minutes until liquid is absorbed and fruit plump. Stir in apple and cinnamon and add salt, pepper and sugar to taste.
3. Check cavity of chicken and clean further if necessary. Wipe inside and out with paper towels. Washing chicken removes valuable juices and is not necessary.
4. Stuff chicken with fruit mixture, close cavity and truss. Rub skin with cut lemon and season with salt and pepper.
5. Place chicken in a greased roasting dish and spread top with remaining ghee or butter. Roast in a moderately hot oven for 2 hours or until cooked when tested. Turn during cooking to brown evenly, and baste often.
6. Before carving chicken, remove stuffing and place on top of chelou. Mix through just before serving. If desired ½ teaspoon saffron threads may be soaked in a little hot water for 10 minutes and liquid spooned over chelou.

JOOJEH KABAB
SKEWERED GRILLED CHICKEN

Serves: 6
Cooking time: 15 minutes

2 chickens, each about 1 kg (2 lb)
½ cup lemon juice
1 large onion, grated
2 teaspoons salt
freshly ground black pepper
¼ cup melted ghee or butter
1 teaspoon paprika
Chelou (page 305) for serving
cherry tomatoes for garnish

1. Halve chickens and remove backbone. Cut each half into 6 pieces of fairly even dimension — halve breast pieces and thighs, chop off bony end of leg, leave wing intact.
2. Combine lemon juice, grated onion, salt and pepper in a glass or ceramic dish and add chicken pieces, turning in marinade to coat. Leave to marinate for 3-4 hours in refrigerator, turning pieces occasionally.
3. Thread pieces onto 6 long flat skewers with thicker pieces in centre of skewers, and placing them close together.
4. Combine melted ghee or butter with paprika and brush over chicken. Cook over glowing charcoal or in grill unit under high heat reducing to medium. Baste frequently with ghee mixture during cooking and turn often.
5. Cook for 12-15 minutes, concentrating heat on centre pieces towards end of cooking.
6. When cooked, remove chicken from skewers if desired and serve with chelou. Garnish with blistered cherry tomatoes.

To blister cherry tomatoes: Cut a cross on the rounded end of each tomato, brush with butter and grill under high heat or over glowing coals until skin blisters and browns lightly.

DOLMEH SIB (Stuffed Apples) *recipe page 324.*

DOLMEH BEH
STUFFED QUINCES

Serves: 6
Cooking time: 2 hours

1 medium-sized onion, finely chopped
¼ cup ghee or butter
500 g (1 lb) lean ground beef or veal
¼ cup water
2 tablespoons rice
½ teaspoon ground cinnamon
salt
freshly ground black pepper
6 medium-sized quinces
2 teaspoons sugar
1 cup water
¼ cup cider vinegar or lemon juice
¼ cup brown sugar

1. In a frying pan gently fry onion in half of the ghee or butter until transparent, add meat and stir over high heat until juices evaporate and meat begins to brown. Stir in water, rice and cinnamon. Add salt and pepper to taste and remove from heat.
2. Wash quinces well, rubbing off fuzz. Dry and cut off tops (stem end), reserving tops. Scoop out core and most of quince flesh with a melon baller, leaving a cavity of reasonable size in each. Sprinkle cavities with sugar and fill with meat mixture. Replace tops.
3. Place water in a deep pan large enough to take quinces side by side, and arrange quinces upright in pan. Top each quince with a knob of the remaining ghee. Place about a cup of the quince flesh around quinces.
4. Place 2 paper towels on rim of pan and cover tightly with lid. Set on medium heat, bring to a simmer, then lower heat and cook gently for 1 hour.
5. Add vinegar or lemon juice and brown sugar to liquid, tilt pan to combine, then baste quinces with sauce. Cook for further 45 minutes or until quinces are tender, basting occasionally during cooking.
6. Remove quinces carefully to a serving dish and keep hot. Pass liquid and quince pulp through a sieve and return to pan. Reduce by half and adjust sweet-sour flavour with sugar and vinegar or lemon juice. Pour sauce over quinces and serve with flat bread as a first course.

DOLMEH SIB
STUFFED APPLES

Follow directions for Dolmeh Beh, using 12 apples in place of the quinces. Arrange stuffed apples in a baking dish, adding half the apple pulp to the water. Dot apples with butter, cover dish with foil and bake in a moderate oven, 180°C (350°F) for 30 minutes. Remove foil and continue from Step 5, cooking apples uncovered for 15-20 minutes until tender.

Note: Eating apples are less likely to disintegrate during cooking — choose a variety with a tart flavour.

KHORESHE ALBALOO
SOUR CHERRY AND MEAT SAUCE

Sour black cherries are not readily available in many areas. As I found the table cherry can give almost the same flavour with the addition of more lime or lemon juice, the making of this khoresh is possible. Perhaps the flavour will not be quite the same, but it will be just as enjoyable. Morello cherries, though not the same as the sour black cherries of Persia, may be used with less adjustment to the tartness of the dish — the Morello is thought to be a descendant of the Albaloo, the Persian sour cherry.

If one wishs to be pedantic, when using the sweet table cherry, the name of the dish should be Khoreshe Guillass. However a Persian would not have heard of such a dish.

Serves: 6
Cooking time: 1½ hours

500 g (1 lb) lean lamb or veal stew meat
¼ cup ghee or oil
1 large onion, finely chopped
½ teaspoon turmeric
½ teaspoon ground cinnamon
½ cup water
salt
freshly ground black pepper
250 g (8 oz) pitted black cherries, sour for
    preference
1-3 tablespoons lime or lemon juice
brown sugar to taste

1. Trim meat and cut into 2 cm (¾ inch) cubes.
2. Heat half the ghee or oil in a heavy pan and brown meat cubes on each side. Remove meat to a plate. Reduce heat.
3. Add onion to pan with remaining ghee or oil and fry gently until transparent. Stir in turmeric and cook 2 minutes longer.
4. Return meat to pan and add cinnamon, water, and salt and pepper to taste. Cover and simmer gently for 40 minutes.
5. Add pitted cherries, simmer for 10 minutes so that their flavour may be released, then taste sauce. If cherries are sufficiently sour add 1 tablespoon lime or lemon juice and enough brown sugar to give a pleasant sweet-sour flavour; if sweet cherries are used, then add more lime or lemon juice and sugar if necessary to balance the flavour.
6. Cover and simmer for further 20 minutes or until meat is tender. Serve with chelou, polou or kateh (see Rice section of this chapter).

DOLMEH KALAM
STUFFED CABBAGE LEAVES WITH SWEET-SOUR SAUCE

Serves: 6
Cooking time: 1½ hours

18 cabbage leaves
water
750 g (1½ lb) finely ground beef or lamb
1 large onion, finely chopped
¼ cup short grain rice
¼ cup finely chopped parsley
2 tablespoons finely chopped coriander
1 teaspoon turmeric
salt
freshly ground black pepper
½ cup brown sugar
½ cup cider vinegar

1. Separate leaves carefully from head of cabbage. Larger leaves may be halved and counted as 2. Blanch in a large pot of boiling water for 5 minutes until limp — do not overcook. Drain in a colander. Cut out thick section (ribs), only removing lower portion.
2. Combine ground meat with onion, rice, herbs and turmeric. Add 1½ teaspoons salt and pepper to taste. Divide mixture into 18 portions.
3. Spread a cabbage leaf flat on work surface and place one portion of filling on base of leaf. Roll once, fold in sides and roll up into a firm package. Repeat with remaining ingredients.
4. Line a heavy pan with cabbage trimmings or a well-washed outer leaf. Pack rolls in close together in layers. Add 1 cup cold water and invert a heavy plate over rolls.
5. Cover, bring to simmering point and simmer gently for 45 minutes.
6. Blend sugar and vinegar and add to pan. Tilt pan to blend liquids. Cover and cook for further 30 minutes. Serve with chelou or flat bread.

325

CHELOU KABAB
GRILLED LAMB WITH RICE

Serves: 6
Cooking time: 5 minutes

3 loins of lamb
1 cup grated or minced onion
¾ cup lemon juice
freshly ground black pepper
melted ghee
salt
6-8 small tomatoes

For serving:
Chelou (page 305), using 2 or 3 cups rice
   according to number of serves required
6-8 egg yolks in half shells
butter pats
sumak (see Glossary)
yoghurt

1. Have meat retailer remove backbones from loins, or do this yourself with a boning knife. Each loin should be about 20 cm (8 inches) long (6 ribs).
2. Remove fillets from loins. Trim all fat and gristle from main (eye) muscles. Slice each piece lengthwise, with the grain, into three, giving strips of lamb about 8 cm (3 inches) wide, 20 cm (8 inches) long and 8 mm (⅜ inch) thick. Split each fillet without cutting right through, and open out.
3. Lightly hammer meat with a heavy-bladed knife to make fine, shallow incisions along the length of the meat.
4. Place onion in a sieve over a bowl and press to extract as much juice as possible. Discard pulp. Add lemon juice and a good grinding of black pepper.
5. Place lamb in this marinade, stir to coat, cover and leave to marinate in refrigerator for 12 hours or longer. Turn meat occasionally.
6. Pass a flat, sword-like skewer through the length of each strip of lamb.
7. Brush meat lightly with melted ghee and cook over a glowing charcoal fire for about 5 minutes, turning frequently, until meat is lightly browned and just cooked through. Meat will flop somewhat at beginning of cooking. As it cooks it flattens out — a good indication that it is ready.
8. Cut a cross on rounded end of each tomato, place tomatoes on a skewer and brush with ghee. Cook on fire till skin blisters — about 4 minutes.
9. Slide lamb off skewers and serve on hot chelou on individual plates, with a tomato as garnish for each serve.
10. Each diner places an egg yolk in centre of hot chelou and stirs it into the rice. Butter, sumak, salt and pepper are then stirred into the rice. Yoghurt is added if desired. Speed is the essence of a good Chelou Kabab meal, as it is more enjoyable when very hot.

Note: Chelou Kabab may be prepared more economically with lamb leg, although the dish will be slightly less authentic. Bone leg and trim off all fat and fine sinew and cut into 8 cm (3 inch) squares instead of long strips. Hammer as in Step 3. Place 4 pieces on each skewer. Serves 8.

KHORESHE ALBALOO (Sour Cherry and Meat Sauce) *recipe page 325.*

LULEH KABAB
GROUND LAMB ON SKEWERS

Serves: 4-6
Cooking time: 5-7 minutes

500 g (1 lb) lean boneless lamb
1 large onion
1 teaspoon salt
freshly ground black pepper to taste
½ teaspoon ground cinnamon, optional
melted ghee or butter
4-6 small tomatoes
1 quantity Chelou (page 305)
4-6 egg yolks in shells
sumak
butter for serving

1. Pass lamb through meat grinder twice, then grind onion.
2. Blend in salt, pepper and cinnamon if used, then beat well with a wooden spoon until paste-like.
3. Divide mixture into 12 equal portions and shape portions around moistened, long sword-like skewers, making thin sausage shapes about 12 cm (5 inches) long. Moisten hands frequently to mould mixture more easily.
4. Cook over glowing charcoal, placing skewers across supports so that meat does not touch grid. Remove grid if possible. Turn skewers frequently to brown meat evenly. Cook for about 5-7 minutes, brushing occasionally with ghee.
5. Cross-cut rounded end of tomatoes, brush with ghee, place on a skewer and grill quickly next to kababs.
6. Slide kababs off skewers and serve immediately with hot chelou, garnished with a tomato. An egg yolk, a teaspoon or two of sumak and a piece of butter are stirred into the hot rice before eating.

TAH CHIN
YOGHURT, LAMB AND RICE

Serves: 6
Oven temperature: 160°C (325°F)
Cooking time: 1¾ hours

1 kg (2 lb) lean lamb from leg
2½ cups yoghurt
salt
freshly ground black pepper
1 teaspoon turmeric or ½ teaspoon saffron
   threads
3 cups basmati or other good quality long
   grain rice
8 cups water
2 egg yolks
¼ cup melted ghee or butter
1 tablespoon hot water

1. Cut lamb into 3 cm (1¼ inch) cubes. Combine in a bowl with 2 cups yoghurt, 2 teaspoons salt, a good grinding of black pepper and the turmeric or pounded saffron threads. Cover and marinate in refrigerator for 6 hours or overnight.
2. Pick over rice and wash well until water runs clear. Boil water, add 2 tablespoons salt and the rice, stir and return to the boil. Leave uncovered and boil for 5 minutes. Drain in colander or large sieve.
3. Beat egg yolks in a bowl, stir in ½ cup yoghurt and 1½ cups of the rice.
4. Place melted ghee and hot water in a 10-cup casserole or Dutch oven. Swirl to coat sides. Spread egg, yoghurt and rice mixture evenly over base.
5. Arrange half the lamb cubes over this with some of the yoghurt marinade. Add a layer of rice, remaining lamb mixture and all but ½ cup of marinade. Top with remaining rice and spread reserved yoghurt marinade on top.
6. Cover casserole or Dutch oven with lid and cook tah chin in a moderate oven for 1½ hours.
7. Spoon rice and lamb mixture into centre of serving dish. Lift off crusty layer from bottom of dish and break into large pieces. Arrange around edge of dish. Alternatively if Dutch oven has been used, place on cold surface or in cold water for 5-10 minutes, run a knife blade round edge of contents and invert serving dish on top. Tip upside down so that contents can come out like a cake. Cut in wedges to serve.

ABGUSHT

The literal translation of abgusht is 'the water of the meat'. Translated into Persian cookery language, it can be a substantial soup or a stew. In fact, what might begin to be a stew, could end up as a soup if unexpected guests arrive at meal time. Then again it may serve as two courses from the one pot, with the flavoursome liquid ladled into bowls and served as soup, leaving enough liquid in the pot for the remainder to be served as a moist stew.

Though I have placed abgusht recipes in both the Soups section and the section dealing with more substantial meat dishes, you may add more or less water according to your particular situation at the time of cooking.

Whichever abgusht is being made, the essence of a good one lies in the long, slow cooking. Though my cooking times are considerably shorter than those used in Iran, I have taken into account the nature of ingredients available to the Western cook. Our lamb and beef is considerably more tender, dried beans and fruit take less time to cook than was the case in the past — and we usually tend to hurry things up considerably.

However as I have already said in the introduction, we have come full circle, and the era of slow cooking is upon us once more. Though I have not specified its use in all recipes, abgusht cooked in a slow cooker takes on excitingly different dimensions. For a guide to using such an appliance, see end of Abgushte Lubia Ghermez recipe, below.

ABGUSHTE LUBIA GHERMEZ
LAMB AND BEAN STEW

Serves: 6
Cooking time: 2½ hours

1 cup red kidney beans (lubia ghermez)
water
1.5 kg (3 lb) lamb shoulder on the bone or 6
    lamb foreshanks
1 large onion, finely chopped
¼ cup ghee or butter
1 teaspoon turmeric
½ cup tomato purée
1 limu omani (dried lime) or 1 tablespoon
    lemon juice
salt
freshly ground black pepper

1. Wash kidney beans well and place in a pan with 3 cups water. Bring to the boil, boil 2 minutes. Cover and leave off the heat for 30 minutes until plump.
2. Have meat retailer cut shoulder into 6 pieces. Trim off excess fat. If lamb shanks are used, have these cracked. Heat half the ghee in a deep heavy pan and brown meat on all sides. Remove to a plate.
3. Add remaining ghee to pan and gently fry onion until transparent. Stir in turmeric and cook 2 minutes.
4. Return lamb to pan with plumped beans and their soaking liquid, tomato purée and dried lime (pierced twice with a skewer) or the lemon juice. Add another 2 cups water and bring to the boil.
5. Cover pan and simmer over low heat for 1 hour. Season with salt and pepper to taste and cook a further hour or until meat and beans are tender. Remove dried lime if used.
6. Serve in deep plates with a piece of lamb in each. Pickles, fresh herbs, chopped onion, radishes and flat bread should be served as accompaniments.

Using a slow cooker: At Step 4 place all ingredients in a slow cooker and cook on low setting for 9-10 hours, or high setting for 5-6 hours. Use a little less water and add more only if necessary as evaporation is less when using this appliance.

ABGUSHTE BADEMJAN
LAMB AND EGGPLANT STEW

Follow Abgushte Lubia Ghermez recipe, omitting red beans and the 3 cups soaking water. Cut 2 medium-sized eggplants into chunky pieces with skin on. Sprinkle liberally with salt and leave for 30 minutes. Pat dry with paper towels and fry until lightly coloured in additional ghee. At Step 4 return lamb to pan with all ingredients except beans and their liquid and add salt and pepper as well. Cook for 1½ hours, add prepared eggplant and cook for further 30 minutes or until meat and eggplant are tender. Add more water only if necessary. If using a slow cooker, add eggplant after 8 hours on low setting, or after 4 hours on high setting.

BAQLAWA
ALMOND AND CARDAMOM PASTRY

Though baklava is regarded as a Greek pastry, its popularity extends throughout the Middle East. The Persian version differs considerably in that it uses a greater proportion of nuts to pastry, is perfumed with rose water and flavoured with cardamom.

To the Persian, Baqlawa and the celebration of Now Rooz (their New Year) go hand in hand. It is one of the special foods prepared in abundance for this joyful celebration.

Makes about 40 pieces
Oven temperature: 180°C (350°F)
Cooking time: 35-40 minutes

3 cups ground almonds
1 cup finely chopped almonds
1 cup caster sugar
1 teaspoon ground cardamom
10 sheets fillo pastry
¾ cup melted clarified butter or ghee

Syrup:
2 cups sugar
1½ cups water
1 teaspoon lemon juice
½ teaspoon ground cardamom
1 tablespoon rose water

1. Combine ground and chopped almonds with sugar and cardamom. For best flavour use freshly ground or pounded cardamom unless the quality of the ready-ground product is good.
2. Brush a 25 x 33 cm (10 x 13 inch) baking dish with clarified butter or ghee. Place 3 sheets of fillo pastry in dish, brushing each with butter.
3. Brush top sheet with butter and sprinkle in one-third of nut mixture. Top with 2 more buttered sheets, buttering top of second sheet. Repeat with another two layers of nuts, with 2 sheets of buttered fillo in between.
4. Top last layer of nuts with 3 sheets fillo, buttering each as before, including top.
5. Trim edges with a sharp knife and cut carefully through pastry and nut layers in diamond shapes. Pour remaining butter over top, letting it run into cuts and around sides of baqlawa.
6. Bake on centre shelf in a moderate oven for 35-40 minutes, raising it one shelf above centre after 30 minutes.
7. Meanwhile prepare syrup. In a heavy pan dissolve sugar in water over medium heat, stirring occasionally. Bring to the boil, add lemon juice and cardamom and boil rapidly for 15-18 minutes or until thick when a little is tested on a cold saucer. Add rose water and remove from heat. Leave aside until pastry is cooked.
8. When baqlawa is a pale golden brown, remove from oven and pour warm syrup evenly over hot pastry. Leave for at least 2 hours before cutting again and removing from dish. Pastry may be left in dish, covered lightly with a fine cloth to protect it from dust, etc., and will remain crisp for 3-4 days. Any left after serving may be stored in a sealed container for several days, though crispness will decrease. Do not refrigerate.

BAQLAWA (Almond and Cardamom Pastry) *recipe above*

KHARBOOZEH VA HOLOO MAKHLOOT
MELON AND PEACH DESSERT

Serves: 8

1 Persian or honey-dew melon
1 rock melon (cantaloupe)
½ cup caster sugar
½ teaspoon salt
4 firm, ripe peaches
¼ cup lemon juice
2-3 tablespoons rose water
shaved or crushed ice for serving

1. Halve melons and scoop seeds into a sieve set over a bowl. Let juice drip into bowl, then discard seeds.
2. Working over the bowl, scoop the melon into neat balls with a melon ball scoop, letting juices fall into bowl with the melon balls.
3. Add sugar and salt and stir gently to combine.
4. Peel peaches, halve and slice into a bowl containing the lemon juice. As each peach is added to bowl, stir gently to coat it with lemon juice to prevent discoloration.
5. When all are prepared, add peach slices and lemon juice to bowl of melon balls. Stir gently, add rose water to taste, amount depending on strength of rose water used. Cover bowl and chill for several hours.
6. To serve, pile into individual dessert glasses, top with a little shaved or crushed ice and serve immediately.

HALVAYE SHIR
MILK PUDDING

Serves: 5-6
Cooking time: 15 minutes

¼ cup ghee or unsalted butter
½ cup ground rice
1½ cups milk
¼ cup granulated sugar
3 teaspoons rose water
¼-½ teaspoon ground cardamom
¼ cup chopped blanched almonds or
    pistachio nuts

1. Heat ghee or butter in a heavy pan, preferably one with a non-stick coating. Stir in rice flour and cook, stirring often, for 3 minutes without allowing flour to colour. Keep heat at medium.
2. Add milk, stirring constantly, and keep stirring until thickened and bubbling. Blend in sugar, rose water and cardamom to taste. Stir over heat for further 5 minutes.
3. Pour into small bowls, sprinkle with nuts and serve warm or at room temperature. Alternatively pour into a lightly buttered 20 cm (8 inch) square cake pan and sprinkle with nuts. Leave until cold and cut into squares to serve.

SHIR BERENJ
RICE PUDDING

Serves: 6
Cooking time: 1-1¼ hours

½ cup short grain rice
1½ cups cold water
4 cups milk
pinch of salt
¼ cup granulated sugar
2-3 teaspoons rose water
½ teaspoon ground cardamom
honey for serving, optional

1. Rinse rice only if it is necessary. Place in a heavy pan with water and bring to the boil, stirring occasionally. Boil gently, uncovered, for 15 minutes until water is absorbed.
2. Stir in milk, add salt and bring to a slow simmer. Simmer gently, uncovered, for 40 minutes until pudding is thick. Take care that pudding does not scorch. Stir occasionally with a wooden spoon.
3. Add sugar, rose water to taste and cardamom. Stir to blend and turn into small bowls. Serve warm or chilled with a little honey drizzled on top if desired.

LAUZE BADAM
ALMOND SWEETMEAT

Sweetmeats are much appreciated in Iran, and their making is a long and ancient art. In order to assure the Western cook has success, I have followed basic candy making principles without sacrificing the Persian flavour of the sweetmeat. The following recipes use a base so similar to a cooked fondant that I have given basic fondant as the basis from which to work.

Makes about 45 pieces
Cooking time: 40-45 minutes

Fondant:
½ cup water
2 cups granulated sugar
¼ teaspoon cream of tartar

To finish:
2 cups finely ground almonds
½ teaspoon vanilla essence

1. Put water in a heavy pan, add sugar and leave on very low heat so that sugar may dissolve slowly — do not stir.
2. When sugar is completely dissolved bring to the boil, add cream of tartar and boil for 20-25 minutes to 115°C (240°F) on a candy thermometer — soft ball stage.
3. Put 1¾ cups of the ground almonds into a heatproof bowl and sprinkle half of the remaining almonds in the base of an 18 cm (7 inch) square cake pan.
4. Pour syrup onto almonds in bowl and leave until a skin begins to form around the edge, about 15 minutes.
5. Take a spatula and work it into the fondant in a figure-8 movement, continuing to work fondant until it begins to grain. Add vanilla essence during this process.
6. When mixture is cool enough to handle, knead into a ball.
7. Press fondant out flat on work surface and put onto almonds in prepared pan. Press into shape of pan. Sprinkle remaining almonds on top and press into fondant.
8. Leave until firm, about 3 hours, then cut into small diamonds (lozenges) with an oiled knife.

LAUZE NARJEEL
COCONUT SWEETMEAT

Follow Lauze Badam recipe, replacing ground almonds with 2 cups desiccated coconut.

LAUZE TOOT
MULBERRY SWEETMEAT

The shape, rather than the ingredients, gives this confection its name. Follow Lauze Badam recipe, using all the almonds in the fondant mixture. When cool enough to handle, shape into small pieces the size and shape of a mulberry and roll in granulated sugar. Insert a sliver of blanched pistachio nut in the top of each one to resemble the stem.

KALUCHEH BERENJ
RICE COOKIES

Makes 5 dozen
Oven temperature: 180°C (350°F)
Cooking time: 15 minutes

1 cup butter
1 cup icing (confectioner's) sugar, sifted
2 egg yolks
2½ cups ground rice
½-1 teaspoon ground cardamom
1 egg white, lightly beaten
½ cup finely chopped pistachio nuts or
   almonds

1. Cream butter and sugar until light and fluffy. Gradually add egg yolks, beating well.
2. Sift ground rice with cardamom and fold into butter mixture to form a soft dough. Knead for 2 minutes, cover bowl and let dough rest for 1 hour.
3. Take generous teaspoonfuls of dough and shape into balls. Place on ungreased baking sheets. Using a thimble, make 3 crescent shapes on each cookie.
4. Brush cookies very lightly with egg white and sprinkle lightly with chopped nuts. Bake in a moderate oven for 15 minutes. Do not let tops colour; base should be golden brown.
5. Leave on baking sheets for 5 minutes, then lift off onto wire racks to cool completely. Store in a sealed container.

MORABAYE HENDEVANEH
WATERMELON RIND PRESERVE

Cooking time: 1¾ hours

750 g (1½ lb) watermelon rind
water
3 cups sugar
1 tablespoon lemon juice
1 teaspoon cardamom seeds

1. Peel green skin from rind and remove any pink flesh. Weigh after peeling or cut into 2 cm (¾ inch) cubes and measure. You will require 4 cups cubed rind.
2. Put rind in a preserving pan and cover with cold water. Bring to the boil and simmer gently for 1 hour or until rind is tender and translucent. Drain in colander.
3. Dissolve sugar in 2 cups water in same pan placed over medium heat. Add lemon juice and bring to the boil.
4. Add drained rind and return to the boil. Boil for 15 minutes, skimming when necessary.
5. Crush cardamom seeds in a mortar and stir into preserve, boil 1 minute and remove from heat. Cover and leave for 12 hours or overnight.
6. Remove cover and place pan on medium heat. Bring to the boil and boil gently for 15-20 minutes until syrup is thick. Test a little on a cold saucer.
7. Ladle into warm, sterilized jars and seal when cooled.

SHARBAT ALBALOO
CHERRY SHERBET

The black sour cherries of Iran are used for this sherbet. If sour cherries such as Morello are unavailable, use the table varieties and increase the lemon juice to give the characteristic sharp tang.

500 g (1 lb) sour or other cherries
1½ cups water
granulated sugar
strained lemon juice

1. Wash cherries, remove stems and seeds. Place in a pan with the water and bring to the boil. Cover and simmer on low heat for 15 minutes or until cherries are soft.
2. Strain cherries through a sieve set over a bowl. Leave for 30 minutes to drain thoroughly.
3. Measure juice back into pan and add an equal volume of sugar, that is 1 cup sugar to each cup juice. Add lemon juice and bring to the boil over medium heat, stirring occasionally to dissolve sugar. Boil uncovered for 8-10 minutes without stirring. Skim when required. Cool and bottle. Store at room temperature.
4. To serve, place 2 to 3 tablespoons syrup in a glass, add ice cubes and cold water to taste. Stir gently.

KHARBOOZEH VA HOLOO MAKHLOOT (Melon and Peach Dessert) *recipe page 332;*
SEKANJABIN (Sweet-Sour Mint Syrup) *recipe page 336.*

SHARBAT BEH
QUINCE SHERBET

Traditionally this is made by grating the fruit into water. Care must be taken not to allow fruit to discolour so lemon juice is rubbed on the fruit and added to the water. It seems like such a lot of trouble when the resultant juice is cooked anyway. The method given works just as well, and gives a better colour to the syrup.

2 large quinces
2 cups water
granulated sugar
juice of ½ lemon

1. Peel quince and core. Chop into small pieces. Place in a stainless steel or enamelled pan and add water.
2. Bring slowly to the boil and simmer gently for 40 minutes or until fruit is very soft and quinces have coloured to a pinky orange.
3. Place a doubled piece of butter muslin in a bowl, draping ends over side. Pour fruit and juice into centre of muslin, gather ends and tie with string. Lift up and suspend over bowl. Leave to drip for several hours, as you would for jelly making.
4. Measure juice back into pan and add sugar in the proportion of 1 cup to each cup of juice. Add lemon juice and bring to the boil, stirring occasionally to dissolve sugar. Boil for 10 minutes, skimming when necessary. Cool and bottle.
5. To serve, place 2 to 3 tablespoons syrup in a glass, add ice cubes and cold water to taste. Stir gently.

Note: Quince pulp may be used for making Quince Paste (page 76).

SEKANJABIN
SWEET-SOUR MINT SYRUP

The Persian penchant for sweet-sour flavours extends to desserts and beverages. Sekanjabin, a sweet-sour syrup with a flavour reminiscent of mint sauce, plays more than one role in the Persian household: it may be served as a dip for crisp cos (romaine) lettuce leaves for an unusual dessert; with bread as an accompaniment to the lettuce and syrup it becomes a light meal; with water or soda water and ice it makes a refreshing drink; and with grated cucumber, soda water and ice, a very pleasant punch can be made, though this last innovation bears Western influence.

Medicinally, Persians in the past treated jaundice attacks with a diet of Sekanjabin and lettuce – no bread – until the patient recovered.

Makes about 1½ cups

2 cups granulated sugar
1 cup water
½ cup white vinegar
juice of ½ lemon
6 large sprigs fresh mint

1. In a pan stir sugar and water over medium heat until sugar dissolves. Bring to the boil.
2. Add vinegar and lemon juice and return to a steady boil. Boil over medium heat for 15-18 minutes until thick, skimming as required. Test a little on a cold saucer — when cool syrup should have a thin honey consistency.
3. Have mint sprigs well washed and drained and add to boiling syrup. Boil for 1 minute, then remove pan from heat and leave until cool.
4. Strain syrup, pour into a bottle, seal and store.

To serve as a dessert: Pour some syrup into a shallow bowl and float mint sprigs on top if desired. In a separate dish have cos (romaine) lettuce leaves, washed and crisped. Lettuce is folded, dipped into syrup and eaten.

As a beverage: One-third fill a glass with syrup, add ice cubes and top with water or soda water. Stir gently and float a mint sprig on top.

As a punch: Coarsely grate a young, peeled cucumber into punch bowl. Add 1 quantity Sekanjabin syrup, plenty of ice cubes and soda water to taste. Garnish with mint sprigs and thin slices of cucumber.

AFGHANISTAN

In early history Alexander the Great conquered Afghanistan on his way to India; the country was plundered by Genghis Khan and his Mongol hordes in their surge to the Middle and Near East; and it served as a route to Marco Polo on his journey to China. It is the land of the Khyber Pass which features in the annals of military history in Britain's attempts to maintain her colonies in India. Babur, founder of the Moghul Empire in India and a direct descendant of Genghis Khan, began his rise to power in Kabul and returned there to die.

It was not until the eighteenth century that Afghanistan was proclaimed an independent kingdom. With the advent of steamships and aeroplanes, however, Afghanistan was passed around and over by modern trade caravans, and consequently it remained backward, traditional, fiercely tribal and under-developed. In 1973 General Mohammad Daoud formed the Republic of Afghanistan and became the country's President. It is a Moslem country, but though clinging to tradition, many modern Afghan women would be considered as liberated.

Being a land-locked country it is to be expected that the foods of Afghanistan would reflect those of her neighbours, Pakistan, India and Iran. Though she shares a border with Russia, there is little evidence that Russia has influenced her cuisine.

THE FLAVOUR OF AFGHAN FOOD

The Pakistan-Indian influence is prevalent in Afghan spices and palaus. Garam masala is a popular spicing, with saffron, cinnamon, cloves, peppers and hot chilis echoing the same influence; cardamom, dill, mint, cumin and coriander reflect the Persian and Arabic influence. Gashneez, fresh coriander, is referred to as Afghan parsley and is used extensively. Though history shows that Persia influenced India in her cooking in early times, Afghanistan seems to have taken the best of both worlds. The Mongol influence can be seen in noodle-type dishes such as Aushak and Aush, though it is possible that any grain-producing area could have conceived the noodle without outside influence.

Maust (yoghurt) is a necessary part of Afghan cooking and is frequently drained to make a thick, cream-cheese-like substance called chakah. Yoghurt or sour milk is drained and dried for a cheese called Quroot which is then painstakingly dissolved in water to reconstitute it; instructions for making a similar-tasting cheese condiment are given among the recipes.

The breads of Afghanistan are similar to those of Pakistan, India and Iran though they are prepared a little differently. Naun and Lawash are two different breads, Naun being similar to the Punjabi (North Indian) Naan, and Lawash similar to the Nane Lavash of Iran. This perhaps shows clearly the influences of each of the countries on the other's cooking.

The Chalau and Palau of Afghanistan are again similar to the rice dishes of both Iran and Pakistan-India. Basmati rice is used in Afghanistan, though another good quality long grain rice may be substituted.

The Korma (meat sauce) of Afghanistan has a parallel in the Korma of India, though it's not as spicy, and Khoreshe Gormeh Sabzi is a related dish from Persia. Here again another similarity is apparent. The sabzee and sabzi of Afghanistan and Persia are also to be found in Pakistan-Indian cooking. Persian sabzi refers to green herbs, Afghan sabzee to spinach, and Pakistan-Indian sabzi to a variety of vegetables. The point is, of course, that the Indo-Iranian sub-family of languages is the basis of the languages spoken in these four countries. Language aside, their foods are closely linked in many areas.

The kabaub is a convenient way to cook cubes of meat and Afghans like to serve them between pieces of Lawash. Favoured meats are beef and lamb, though occasionally goat or camel meat is used. As much of the meat is rather tough, ground meat is used extensively either in sauces or made into Kofta Kabaub.

The fat from the tail of the Awassi sheep is highly favoured and added to ground meat, or cubed and placed between meat cubes when preparing kabaubs. For a somewhat similar flavour use lamb with a proportion of fat — lamb shoulder is a good choice. The Afghans like their foods to be oily, either from the lamb fat or from the use of rather large amounts of vegetable oil or ghee.

The latter is the preferred fat, but in short supply in Afghanistan. The amounts of these fats have been reduced in recipes to cater for Western tastes, and may be reduced even further if necessary.

A wide variety of vegetables is used in cooking, with leeks being particularly popular, fired with chili and used as a filling for boiled and fried doughs for Aushak and Boolawnee. Vegetables are frequently combined with meats for Korma, with spinach, turnip, potato and carrot being the most popular. Though I have called such recipes Korma Sabzee, Korma Zardak and so on, when the korma is served with chalau the correct titles become Sabzee Chalau or Zardak Chalau — rather confusing, but this is how the Afghans refer to them.

Yellow split peas are frequently used to thicken sauces and soups, just as they are in Iran. The use of mung beans in Maushawa interested me as this is the only recipe I have ever encountered using the whole mung bean. Usually these beans are used for the Chinese bean sprouts, or ground into a flour for Asian sweet making.

Choi, the tea of Afghanistan, is ever present. It is usually served black, very strong, sometimes flavoured with cardamom, and can be taken with or without sugar. Afghans are renowned for their hospitality and when serving a guest with tea they are likely to add copious quantities of sugar. If your tea is served very, very, sweet, you can count yourself as a very honoured guest indeed. Generally tea is served at the end of a meal with each person being provided with their own teapot, cup, and a bowl for the tea dregs. Tea with milk, sheer choi, is usually served on more formal occasions, green tea being used for this brew.

EATING AFGHAN STYLE

The food is served in large platters or pots and placed on a cloth spread over a mat or carpet. Sometimes individual plates or bowls are provided though this varies according to location, whether in a house or a tent. Cushions are provided for seating and the food is generally eaten with the fingers of the right hand, after the traditional hand washing. A chalau or palau is always served, usually with Korma. Kabaub, chicken or Aushak plus a thick soup could also be served, particularly if the occasion is festive. The Afghans are noted for serving foods in large quantities. Vegetables, salad, pickles, yoghurt and bread are always served. The bread is used to scoop up soft foods. Dug (yoghurt drink) or murgh (buttermilk) is often served as the beverage during the meal. Fresh fruit is plentiful and very good and is always part of the meal. Puddings or sweet pastries frequently follow the meal, with teas being served quite some time later.

COOKING METHODS

Rice is cooked in a traditional pot called a *degh* and stirred and served with a *gafgeer*. These are pictured at the beginning of this chapter. Cooking over the embers of a wood fire is a popular method for kabaubs, the same fire also being used to cook the other components of the meal. The oven for bread making is the *tandour*, the beehive oven of Iran, Iraq and Asia, and as this is not suitable for baking pastries, the sweet tooth of the Afghan is satisfied with copious amounts of fried pastries, though Baqlawa and Kalucheh Berenj, the rice cookies of Iran, are available at pastry shops. One fried pastry which intrigued

me considerably was the Abraysham Kabaub, actually a kind of sweet omelet. You might enjoy tackling the recipe I have given.

INGREDIENTS FOR AFGHAN COOKING

There are few ingredients which you might not already have on your pantry shelf or in your vegetable bin. Fresh coriander is a must and can be grown from seed. Pick it before flowering. Coriander is a delicate herb and if it is washed, allowed to dry well, then packed loosely into a plastic bag, it should keep in the refrigerator for four days or so.

You will require lots of garlic, onions and dried mint, and a few hot chilis for flavouring; leeks for special recipes; plenty of yoghurt — try making your own, instructions on page 20. Spices required are cinnamon, cloves, nutmeg, cardamom, cumin, black cumin, or the ready-prepared garam masala if you would rather not make your own. For sweet pastries, saffron threads, rose water, unsalted pistachio nuts, almonds and walnuts. Use ghee or vegetable oil for cooking. Fresh limes and lemons are also necessary.

QUROOT
YOGHURT CHEESE

Quroot is a ball of very dry Afghan cheese made from drained, salted and dried yoghurt. To prepare quroot for serving with particular dishes, the ball is soaked in hot water in a special bowl containing a stone. The quroot is then rubbed against the stone and the sides of the bowl, and gradually worked into the water to form a thick sauce.

Afghans living abroad have found a substitute in combining chakah (drained yoghurt) and mature cheddar cheese. The cheese provides the tang associated with ripened cheese. Another substitute is a combination of undrained yoghurt, mature cheddar and sour cream.

2 cups Chakah (drained yoghurt, see page 21)
½ cup finely grated mature cheddar cheese
salt to taste

Mix a little of the chakah into the grated cheese, working mixture with back of a wooden spoon to blend ingredients. Gradually stir in remaining chakah and add salt to taste. Pile into a small bowl or serve as directed in recipes.

Alternative mixture:
1 cup undrained yoghurt
½ cup grated mature cheddar cheese
1 cup sour cream
salt to taste

Mix as above, blending yoghurt into cheese, then adding sour cream and salt to taste.

KORMA
MEAT SAUCE

Serves: 6
Cooking time: 1½-2 hours

750 g (1½ lb) lean stewing beef or lamb
½ cup oil
1 large onion, finely chopped
2 cloves garlic, crushed
1½ cups water
salt
freshly ground black pepper
¼-½ teaspoon hot chili pepper
¼ cup daul nakhud (yellow split peas)
1 teaspoon cumin
2-3 tablespoons chopped coriander leaves
Chalau (page 346) for serving

1. Cut meat into 2 cm (¾ inch) cubes.
2. Heat oil in a heavy pan, add onion and fry gently until transparent. Increase heat, add garlic and meat cubes and fry, stirring often, until juices evaporate and meat begins to brown.
3. Add water, salt and pepper to taste, chili pepper, washed split peas and cumin. Bring to a slow simmer and reduce heat. Cover pan and simmer gently for 1-1½ hours until meat is tender. Time depends on cut of meat used.
4. Add coriander and cook for further 10 minutes.
5. Mound chalau on a platter and spoon some of the sauce on top. Serve remainder in a separate bowl.

KORMA SABZEE
MEAT AND SPINACH SAUCE

Prepare basic Korma as above, omitting split peas. At Step 4 add 3 cups chopped fresh spinach with the coriander. Cook for further 10-15 minutes.

KORMA SHULGUN or KORMA KACHALO
MEAT AND TURNIP SAUCE or MEAT AND POTATO SAUCE

Prepare basic Korma, omitting split peas. About 20 minutes before meat is cooked add 3 white turnips or 3 medium-sized potatoes, peeled and cut into 2 cm (¾ inch) cubes. Continue on from Step 4.

KORMA ZARDAK
MEAT AND CARROT SAUCE

Prepare basic Korma with Korma Shulgun variation. Add 2 cups diced carrots instead of turnips.

BOURANEE BAUNJAUN
EGGPLANT WITH YOGHURT SAUCE

Serves: 6
Cooking time: 30-40 minutes

4 medium-sized eggplants, about 1 kg (2 lb)
   in all
salt
oil for frying
2 medium-sized onions, sliced
1 sweet green pepper, seeded and sliced in
   rings
2 large, ripe tomatoes, peeled
salt
¼ teaspoon hot chili pepper
¼ cup water

Chakah (Yoghurt Sauce):
2 cups Chakah (drained yoghurt, see page 21)
2-3 cloves garlic, crushed
salt to taste

1. Cut stems from eggplants and leave peel on. Cut into slices 1 cm (½ inch) thick. Spread on a tray and sprinkle slices liberally with salt. Leave for 30 minutes, then dry well with paper towels.
2. Pour enough oil into a deep frying pan (with lid to fit) to cover base well. Fry eggplant until lightly browned on each side. Do not cook completely. Lift onto a plate when browned. Add more oil to pan as required for remaining slices.
3. As oil drains out of eggplant on standing, return this to the pan and add onion. Fry gently until transparent. Remove to another plate.
4. Place a layer of eggplant back into the pan. Top with some sliced onion, green pepper rings and tomato slices. Repeat using remaining ingredients and adding a little salt and the chili pepper between layers. Pour in any remaining oil from eggplant and onion and add the water. Cover and simmer gently for 10-15 minutes until eggplant is tender.
5. Combine chakah ingredients and spread half of the sauce into base of serving dish. Top with vegetables, lifting eggplant carefully to keep slices intact. Leave some of the juices in the pan.
6. Top vegetables with remainder of chakah and drizzle vegetable juices over it. Serve with Kabaub and Lawash (flat bread).

GARAM MASALA
FRAGRANT SPICE MIX

5 cardamom pods
2 pieces cinnamon bark, each about 8 cm
   (3 inches) long
½ teaspoon whole cloves
2 tablespoons cumin seeds
1 teaspoon black cumin seeds
½ nutmeg, grated

1. Combine all spices except nutmeg in a small pan and roast over medium heat, stirring occasionally, until spices smell fragrant. Remove to a plate and cool.
2. Remove pods from cardamoms and discard. Place roasted spices with cardamom seeds in jar of blender and blend to a fine powder.
3. Grate nutmeg and add to ground spices. Store in a sealed jar.

BOOLAWNEE
FRIED LEEK PASTRIES

Makes about 32

Pastry:
2 cups plain flour
½ teaspoon salt
⅔ cup cold water

Leek Filling:
2 leeks (3 cups chopped)
2 teaspoons salt
¼ teaspoon hot chili pepper
3 teaspoons oil

To finish:
oil for deep frying

1. Sift flour and salt into a bowl, make a well in the centre and add water. Mix to a firm dough and knead for 5 minutes until elastic, dusting with more flour if necessary. Wrap in plastic film and leave to rest for 30 minutes.
2. Cut most of green tops from leeks, halve lengthwise and rinse well to remove all traces of soil between leaves. Remove roots and dry leeks with paper towels. Place flat on board, cut along length at 5 mm (¼ inch) intervals then across to dice. Measure in cup measure and place in bowl.
3. Add salt and chili pepper and knead with hand to soften leeks. Stir in oil.
4. Roll pieces of dough into balls the size of a large hazelnut and roll thinly into a 10 cm (4 inch) circle. Alternatively roll out dough and cut into 10 cm (4 inch) rounds.
5. Place about 2 teaspoons leek filling in centre of circle, moisten pastry half way round edge of circle and fold pastry over filling. Press edge to seal well, and using the edge of a thimble, (the traditional method) or a coffee spoon make little crescent-shaped marks around the edge, or press with fork.
6. Fry 3 or 4 at a time in hot oil until golden brown, turning to brown evenly. Drain on paper towels and serve hot or warm.

CHATNI GASHNEEZ
CORIANDER CHUTNEY

1 cup roughly chopped coriander leaves
2 cloves garlic
1 green chili
½ cup coarsely chopped walnuts
¼ cup lemon juice or vinegar
salt

1. Pack chopped coriander firmly into cup to measure. Peel garlic and chop roughly; slit chili, remove seeds and chop roughly.
2. Place prepared ingredients and walnuts in blender or food processor container and process until a textured paste is achieved, adding lemon juice or vinegar gradually while processing.
3. Add salt to taste, place in a bowl and chill until required. Serve with kabaubs.

Note: If you have no processor or blender, pass ingredients through food grinder with fine screen, or chop ingredients finely, then pound with a pestle in a mortar. Gradually stir in lemon juice or vinegar and add salt to taste.

AFGHAN BREADS
AFGHANISTAN

The breads of Afghanistan are rather similar to those of neighbouring Iran on one side, and India on the other. Basically there are two breads widely used: one is the large, flat lawash or parakee baked on the wall of a beehive oven called the tandoor; the other is naun, similar to the Punjabi naan in shape.

Wholemeal flour is generally used, and the bread is leavened with a fermented starter. As you really have to know how to handle such a starter, it is better to use conventional yeast, though the flavour is not quite the same.

BOOLAWNEE (Fried Leek Pastries) *recipe above*

LAWASH
WHOLEMEAL FLAT BREAD

Follow recipe for Nane Lavash in chapter on Iran, page 302.

Use as directed in recipes or as an accompaniment to foods. The readily available Lebanese flat bread may be used instead. When lawash is required in the serving of food, split a Lebanese bread and use the two rounds separately instead of the lawash. Though the flavour is not the same, the basic effect is there.

To warm lawash, wrap in foil and heat in a moderate oven for 5 minutes.

NAUN
WHOLEMEAL BREAD

Makes 8 loaves
Oven temperature: 220°C (425°F)
Cooking time: 15 minutes

1 sachet active dry yeast
2 cups warm water
3 cups wholemeal flour
2 cups plain white flour
1½ teaspoons salt
oil for shaping

1. Dissolve yeast in ¼ cup warm water.
2. Combine flours and salt and sift into mixing bowl, discarding any flakes left in sifter. Remove about 1 cup flour and keep aside.
3. Add remaining warm water to yeast mixture and pour into centre of flour. Stir a little flour into liquid to thicken it slightly, cover bowl and leave in a warm place for 10 minutes or until frothy.
4. Blend in remaining flour in bowl and beat by hand for 20 minutes, adding reserved flour gradually. Knead in flour towards end of time. Alternatively beat in electric mixer using dough hook for 15 minutes, gradually adding as much of the reserved flour as mixture will take.
5. Cover bowl and leave in a warm place to rise until doubled in bulk — 30 minutes to 1 hour.
6. With oiled hands divide dough into 8 equal portions, rolling each into a ball. Preheat oven.
7. Take a ball of dough and press into a tear shape about 1 cm (½ inch) thick. Work on an oiled board and oil hands lightly. Place shaped loaves on baking sheets, cover with cloth and leave for 15 minutes.
8. Dip forefinger in oil and make 3 parallel grooves in each loaf by pressing side of finger along length of bread. Begin and finish grooves about 2 cm (¾ inch) in from edge. You will end up with ridged, tear-shaped loaves each with 3 grooves, the centre one longer than the other two.
9. Bake loaves on centre shelf of hot oven for 15 minutes or until lightly browned and cooked. Wrap in a cloth as they are removed from oven.

ZARDA PALAU
SWEET RICE WITH ORANGE AND CHICKEN

Serves: 5-6
Oven temperature: 150°C (300°F)
Cooking time: 1¾ hours

thinly peeled rind of 2 oranges
water
1 cup granulated sugar
¼ cup ghee or oil
½ cup blanched slivered almonds
1 kg (2 lb) chicken breasts, quartered
salt
freshly ground black pepper
1 medium-sized onion, sliced
2 cups basmati or other good quality long
    grain rice
½ teaspoon saffron threads
2 tablespoons hot water
¼ cup blanched pistachio nuts, optional

1. Cut orange peel into fine shreds about 3 cm (1¼ inches) long. Boil in 2 cups water for 5 minutes, drain and rinse.
2. Dissolve sugar in 1 cup water, add orange peel and boil gently for 5 minutes or until syrup is thick. Remove from heat and keep aside.
3. In a frying pan heat 1 tablespoon ghee, add almonds and fry gently until golden. Remove and keep aside.
4. Heat remaining ghee in pan and brown chicken pieces on all sides. Remove, leaving fat in pan. Season chicken with salt and pepper.
5. Add onion to pan and fry gently until soft and slightly browned. Add 1 cup water and stir to lift browned juices. Return chicken, cover and simmer gently for 20 minutes.
6. Bring 8 cups water to the boil in a large pot, add washed rice and 1 tablespoon salt. Return to the boil and boil for 8 minutes. Drain in a colander or sieve.
7. Turn rice into a bowl and strain syrup from orange peel over rice, reserving peel. Toss rice and spread half into a greased casserole dish.
8. Arrange chicken pieces on top with the onion and half the cooking liquid. Sprinkle with half the shredded peel and browned almonds.
9. Spread remaining rice on top, pour on chicken liquid evenly, cover casserole and cook in a slow oven for 40 minutes.
10. Meanwhile steep pounded saffron threads in hot water.
11. When palau is cooked remove top layer of rice and arrange around edge of warm serving platter. Put chicken pieces aside and place bottom layer of rice in centre of platter. Top with chicken pieces and garnish with reserved orange shreds and almonds. Sprinkle on pistachio nuts if used. Pour saffron liquid over the rice border and serve immediately.

CHALAU
STEAMED RICE

Serves: 6-8
Cooking time: 40 minutes

3 cups basmati or other good quality long
    grain rice
¼ cup oil
water
2 teaspoons salt

1. Pick over rice if necessary and place in a sieve. Wash under cold running water until water runs clear. Drain in sieve for 30 minutes.
2. Heat oil in a heavy pan and add rice. Stir over medium heat for 5 minutes.
3. Add cold water to a level 2 cm (¾ inch) above surface of rice (reaching up to first joint of forefinger is a reliable indication of level required). Stir in salt.
4. Bring to the boil, stirring occasionally until boiling, reduce heat to low. Cover rim of pan with a cloth or 2 paper towels and fit lid on tightly.
5. Cook gently for 30 minutes over low heat. Fluff up with fork and mound on platter to serve.

Alternative method:
1. Wash rice only if necessary. Bring 8 cups water to the boil in a heavy pot and add rice and 1 tablespoon salt. Stir until water re-boils and boil, uncovered, for 8 minutes.
2. Drain into a large sieve or colander.
3. Place rice in a casserole dish, add oil and toss to coat grains with oil. Add 1 teaspoon salt and ½ cup cold water.
4. Cover rim of casserole with a cloth or 2 paper towels and fit lid on tightly.
5. Cook in a slow oven, 150°C (300°F) for 30 minutes.

MAUSHAWA
BEAN AND MEAT BALL SOUP

Serves: 6
Cooking time: 2½ hours

½ cup lubia (dried red beans), washed and
    soaked overnight
water
½ cup daul nakhud (yellow split peas)
½ cup maush (mung beans)
½ cup short grain rice
salt

Meat Balls:
250 g (8 oz) finely ground beef or lamb
½ teaspoon salt
½ teaspoon freshly ground black pepper
¼ teaspoon hot chili pepper
¼ teaspoon ground cinnamon

To finish:
½ cup oil
1 large onion, finely chopped
water
½ cup chopped peeled tomatoes
1 teaspoon shabit (dill weed) or 1 tablespoon
    chopped fresh dill
1 cup yoghurt

1. Place red beans in a large pot with their soaking water. Bring to the boil, cover and simmer gently for 1 hour.
2. Wash split peas and mung beans and add to beans with 2 cups water. Return to the boil and simmer for 30 minutes.
3. Wash rice and add to pot with 2 teaspoons salt. Simmer for further 30 minutes until ingredients are soft.
4. Combine ground meat with seasonings and shape into balls the size of a hazelnut.
5. Heat oil in a large heavy pot and fry onion until transparent and lightly browned. Add meat balls and fry, stirring often, until browned. Stir in water and tomatoes, cover and simmer for 30 minutes.
6. Add cooked bean mixture, another 2 cups water and shabit or fresh dill. Bring to the boil, then add yoghurt, stirring over low heat until almost boiling. Adjust seasoning with salt and more chili pepper if desired. Serve hot in deep plates with Lawash or Naun.

ZARDA PALAU (Sweet Rice with Orange and Chicken) *recipe page 345*

KABAB-E-MURGH
ROAST CHICKEN

Serves: 5-6
Oven temperature: 190°C (375°F)
Cooking time: 2-2½ hours

1 chicken, about 1.5 kg (3 lb)
1-2 cloves garlic, crushed
salt
freshly ground black pepper
½ cup melted ghee or oil
1 onion, finely chopped
1 cup chopped, peeled tomatoes

For serving:
2 Lawash (page 344)
3 hard-boiled eggs, sliced
fresh coriander

1. Check cavity of bird and clean further if necessary. Wipe inside and out with paper towels.
2. Season cavity with salt and pepper and rub seasoning and crushed garlic over skin of bird. Truss if desired.
3. Brush chicken all over with ghee or oil and place in roasting dish. Roast in a moderately hot oven for 1½ hours, basting occasionally with ghee. Turn to brown evenly.
4. Meanwhile gently fry onion in 1 tablespoon of the ghee until soft, add tomatoes and season to taste. Simmer uncovered for 15 minutes, then pass through a sieve or food mill.
5. Combine thick sauce with last of ghee and brush frequently over chicken during last 30-45 minutes of cooking.
6. To serve put 1 lawash on platter and place chicken in centre. Garnish with egg slices and coriander leaves and top with second lawash. Carve or joint chicken at the table. Cut each lawash into quarters and serve with the chicken.

Note: If you have a rotisserie, place chicken on spit and cook, basting with ghee, then later with tomato sauce.

KOFTA KABAUB SURKH SHUDA
FRIED GROUND LAMB KEBAB

Serves: 6
Cooking time: 1½ hours

1 kg (2 lb) boneless stewing lamb
2 cups water
2 medium-sized onions, chopped
½ cup daul nakhud (yellow split peas)
salt
¼ cup chopped coriander leaves
1 clove garlic, optional
½ teaspoon Garam Masala (page 341)
1 egg, beaten
½ teaspoon freshly ground black pepper
about ¼ cup wholemeal flour
oil for frying
4 medium-sized potatoes, peeled and each cut into 8 wedges

For serving:
2 Lawash (page 344), optional
lemon or lime wedges
coriander leaves

1. Cut lamb into cubes and place in pan with water. Add 1 chopped onion and bring slowly to the boil, skimming when necessary. Cover and simmer for 30 minutes.
2. Rinse split peas and add to pan with 2 teaspoons salt, cover and cook for further 30 minutes until lamb and split peas are tender and water is absorbed. Leave lid off pan and cook over medium heat for a few minutes to evaporate some of the moisture.
3. Cool a little, then mix with remaining chopped onion, coriander and chopped garlic if used. Pass through meat grinder using fine screen, or process in food processor using steel blade.
4. Turn into a bowl and leave until cold. Blend in garam masala, egg, salt to taste and pepper. Add enough flour to make a manageable paste.
5. With moistened hands shape about 2 tablespoons of the paste into sausage shapes 10 cm (4 inches) long.
6. Heat enough oil to cover base of frying pan to depth of 5 mm (¼ inch) and fry kabaubs until golden brown on all sides. Drain and keep hot.
7. While kabaubs are cooking, deep-fry potatoes in another pan until golden brown and cooked through. Drain.
8. Arrange kabaubs on one lawash placed on a platter, garnish with lemon or lime wedges and coriander. Top with second lawash and arrange potatoes on platter. If lawash is not used, arrange kabaubs, potatoes and garnish on platter and serve with other flat bread.

AUSHAK
BOILED LEEK PASTRIES WITH YOGHURT AND MEAT SAUCE

It is popularly believed Marco Polo introduced noodles to Italy from China. Some fifty years before his travels Arabs and Indians were eating noodles, called rishta *in Arabic (a name still used today and derived from the Persian word for 'thread'), and* sevika *by the Indians. It may be assumed that the same dough was used when freshly made in other ways. As Afghanistan was the natural land route from one area to the other, it is anybody's guess where rishta, sevika or aush (page 350) originated.*

All this preamble because the usual English description of Aushak is Leek Ravioli with Yoghurt and Meat Sauce! With all due respect to the Italians, I have refrained from using Italian words to prevent confusion. The recipe is of ancient origin, and without doubt Afghan. Only the tomato is a recent introduction and probably replaced tamarind or some such acid ingredient.

Serves: 6
Cooking time: 1¼ hours

1 quantity Aush Dough (page 350)
2 leeks (about 3 cups chopped)
1 teaspoon salt
¼ teaspoon hot chili pepper
1 tablespoon oil

Keema (Meat Sauce):
½ cup oil
1 large onion, finely chopped
500 g (1 lb) lean ground lamb or beef
½ cup tomato purée
1 cup water
salt
freshly ground black pepper

Chakah (Yoghurt Sauce):
2 cups drained yoghurt (page 21)
3-4 cloves garlic, crushed
1 teaspoon salt

To finish:
8 cups water
1 teaspoon salt
1 tablespoon oil
2-3 teaspoons dried mint

1. Make dough as directed, wrap in plastic and rest for 30 minutes.
2. Cut most of green top and roots from leeks, halve lengthwise and wash well. Dry with paper towels, chop finely and measure, preparing more if necessary.
3. Combine leeks in a bowl with salt, chili pepper and oil. If desired, leeks may be fried gently in oil until soft.
4. Divide dough in two and roll out very thinly on a lightly floured board. Cut into 5 cm (2 inch) rounds or squares. Stack and cover as shapes are made; roll out trimmings and cut to shape.
5. Place a teaspoon of leek filling in centre of dough, moisten edge with water and fold over to make semicircles; fold squares into triangles. Seal edges by pressing with edge of thimble or tines of fork. Put prepared aushaks on a cloth-lined tray and keep covered with another cloth.
6. Heat oil in a pan and gently fry onion until transparent. Increase heat, add meat and stir until crumbly. Cook until juices evaporate and meat browns. Reduce heat and add remaining keema ingredients. Cover and simmer gently for 20 minutes, remove lid and cook until moisture evaporates and mixture is oily. Keep hot.
7. To make chakah combine ingredients in a bowl and keep aside.
8. Bring 8 cups water to the boil in a large pot and add salt and oil. Drop in about 20 aushaks and boil for 10 minutes. Remove with slotted spoon to a colander set over simmering water. Cover and keep warm while cooking remaining aushaks.
9. Spread half the chakah on an oval platter. Top with hot aushaks and cover with remaining chakah. Rub dried mint to a powder and sprinkle over chakah. Top with hot keema and serve immediately.

AUSH
NOODLES WITH PULSES, MEAT AND YOGHURT

Serves: 6
Cooking time: 1-1¼ hours

Aush Dough:
2 cups plain flour
1 teaspoon salt
⅔ cup cold water
additional flour

Pulse and Noodle Mixture:
½ cup daul nakhud (yellow split peas)
cold water
1 cup canned red kidney beans with liquid
salt
1 tablespoon oil
2 cups finely chopped spinach

Keema (Meat Sauce):
½ cup oil
1 medium-sized onion, finely chopped
750 g (1½ lb) ground lamb or beef
salt
freshly ground black pepper
½ cup tomato purée
½ cup water

Chakah (Yoghurt Sauce):
1½ cups drained yoghurt (see page 21)
3 teaspoons dried mint, rubbed
¼-½ teaspoon hot chili pepper
¼ cup finely chopped coriander leaves
salt to taste

1. Sift flour and salt into a bowl, add water and mix to a firm dough, adding more flour if necessary. Divide into 2 balls and wrap in plastic. Rest for 30 minutes.
2. On a floured board roll out each ball of dough very thinly. Cut into 5 mm (¼ inch) strips either while it is flat or by rolling up each sheet of dough and slicing with a sharp knife.
3. Place noodles on a floured cloth, dust with flour and leave to dry for about 30 minutes.
4. Wash split peas well and place in a pan with 1½ cups cold water. Bring to the boil and boil gently for 30 minutes or until tender. Add red beans and liquid and keep warm.
5. In a large pot bring 8 cups water to the boil, add 2 teaspoons salt, oil and noodles. Put noodles in gradually, stirring after each addition. Return to the boil and cook uncovered for 5 minutes. Add spinach and cook for further 5 minutes. Drain in a colander and return to the pot.
6. Add split peas and bean mixture with its liquid, toss ingredients lightly and keep hot over low heat.
7. In a frying pan heat the ½ cup oil, fry onion until soft and add ground meat. Stir over high heat until juices evaporate and meat browns lightly. Add salt and pepper to taste, tomato purée and water, cover and simmer 10 minutes, then remove cover and let moisture evaporate. Sauce should be oily.
8. Combine chakah ingredients, add to noodles and toss well. Mixture should be moist.
9. Place noodle mixture in a deep dish and top with keema. Stir at the table and serve in deep plates.

FIRNEE (Almond and Cardamom Cream Pudding) *recipe page 357.*

KABAUB
LAMB KEBABS WITH YOGHURT MARINADE

Traditionally this kebab uses pieces of lean lamb alternated on skewers with similar sized pieces of lamb tail fat. As this kind of lamb, the Awassi or fat-tailed sheep, is not available outside the Middle East, I have used lamb shoulder. The cubes will contain fat either running through the meat or on one side to give the desired effect. The fat flavours and moistens the meat.

Serves: 5-6
Cooking time: about 15 minutes

750 g (1½ lb) boneless lamb shoulder
1 cup yoghurt
2 cloves garlic, crushed
1 teaspoon salt
freshly ground black pepper

For serving:
5-6 Lawash (page 344) or other flat bread
sliced tomatoes
sliced onions
lemon wedges and coriander sprigs

1. Cut lamb into 3 cm (1¼ inch) cubes.
2. Combine yoghurt, garlic, salt and a generous grind of pepper in a glass or ceramic bowl. Add meat, stir to coat, cover and refrigerate for 4-5 hours or overnight.
3. When ready to cook kebabs, thread 5-6 pieces of lamb on to each of 5 or 6 skewers, leaving a little space between cubes. Brush off excess marinade, though meat should be coated with a thin film.
4. Cook over glowing charcoal. If possible rest across sides of barbecue so that meat is not directly on grid. Grid should be removed if possible. Turn kebabs frequently during cooking.
5. Push meat off skewer onto one half of flat bread. Add tomato and onion slices. Fold bread over top to keep meat warm and serve immediately, garnished with lemon wedges and coriander.

KHABLI PALAU
SPICED LAMB PILAF

Serves: 4-5
Cooking time: 2 hours

¼ cup ghee or oil
2 medium-sized onions, chopped
500 g (1 lb) boneless lamb
½ teaspoon Garam Masala (page 341)
¼ teaspoon ground cardamom
¼ teaspoon ground cinnamon
¼ teaspoon ground black pepper
1 teaspoon salt
1½ cups water
¼ cup butter or ghee
¼ cup blanched, slivered almonds
2 medium-sized carrots cut in
    matchstick lengths
1 cup seedless raisins
2 teaspoons sugar
2 cups long grain rice
6 cups water
salt

1. Heat half the ghee or oil in a deep heavy pan. Add onion and fry over medium heat for 15 minutes until transparent and golden brown. Remove and keep aside.
2. Trim lamb and cut into 2 cm (¾ inch) cubes. Add to pan with remaining ghee and fry over high heat until brown, stirring often. Sprinkle on spices and salt, stir over heat 1 minute, add 1½ cups water and return onion to pan. Cover and simmer for 1 hour.
3. While meat is cooking lightly brown the almonds in butter or ghee in a separate pan. Remove and set aside, leaving fat in pan. Add carrots and fry over medium heat until lightly coloured, stirring often. Add raisins and continue to fry and stir until raisins become plump. Sprinkle with sugar and set aside.
4. Wash rice well and strain. Bring 6 cups water to the boil with 1 tablespoon salt, add rice, return to the boil and boil for 6 minutes. Strain.
5. Remove cooked meat and about ½ cup liquid from pan. Stir partly cooked rice and 1 teaspoon salt into juices in pan. Make 3 or 4 holes in the rice with end of a wooden spoon. Place cooked meat on one side on top of rice, and place carrot and raisin mixture over rest of rice. Spoon reserved meat juices over meat and carrot mixture.
6. Cover rim of pan with two paper towels and cover tightly with lid. Cook over medium heat for 5 minutes, reduce heat to low and cook for further 25 minutes. Leave off the heat, covered, for 5 minutes.
7. Pile meat pieces in centre of platter, and top with carrot-raisin mixture. Fluff up rice with fork and mound around edge of dish. Sprinkle top with reserved browned almonds and serve.

KECHEREE QUROOT-E-KOFTA
RICE AND MUNG BEANS WITH MEAT BALL AND YOGHURT SAUCE

Serves: 6
Cooking time: 1 hour

Kofta (Meat Ball Sauce):
750 g (1½ lb) finely ground lamb
1 medium-sized onion, grated
1 teaspoon ground coriander
1 teaspoon ground cumin
½ teaspoon hot chili pepper
salt
1 large onion, finely chopped
½ cup oil or ghee
1½ cups chopped, peeled tomatoes
1 cup water

Kecheree (Rice and Mung Beans):
1 cup maush (mung beans)
1½ cups short grain rice
½ cup oil or ghee
2 medium-sized onions, chopped
4 cups water
2 teaspoons salt
freshly ground black pepper
½ teaspoon Garam Masala (page 341)
1 teaspoon dried mint, rubbed

For serving:
¼ cup ghee or butter
3 cloves garlic, finely chopped
Quroot (Yoghurt Cheese Sauce, page 340)

1. Combine lamb with grated onion, coriander, cumin, chili pepper and 1½ teaspoons salt. Shape into balls the size of a walnut.
2. Fry chopped onion in oil or ghee until lightly browned, add tomatoes, water and salt to taste. Bring to the boil and add kofta balls. Cover and simmer for 30 minutes, remove lid and cook until most of liquid has evaporated. Stir occasionally at this stage.
3. Meanwhile wash mung beans and rice separately and drain.
4. Heat oil or ghee in a heavy pan, add onion and fry gently until lightly browned.
5. Add 4 cups water and bring to the boil, stir in mung beans, return to the boil and simmer, covered, for 10 minutes.
6. Add rice, salt, pepper, garam masala and mint, return to the boil and lower heat. Cover pan with cloth and lid and simmer gently over low heat for 30 minutes.
7. Mound kecheree onto platter, hollowing centre. Fill hollow with some of the kofta and sauce. Place remaining kofta in a bowl alongside platter.
8. In a small pan heat ghee or butter and fry garlic gently until lightly coloured. Have quroot in a bowl and pour hot garlic mixture over quroot. Serve immediately with other dishes so that it may be added to individual taste.

HALWAU-E AURD-E SUJEE
SEMOLINA SWEETMEAT

This halwau is very similar in preparation to a Greek halva I have been making for years. The ghee, cardamom and rose water give it a typically Oriental flavour.

Cooking time: 30-35 minutes

1 cup sugar
2 cups water
¾ cup ghee
1 cup coarse semolina
¼ cup blanched pistachio nuts
¼ cup blanched, slivered almonds
½-1 teaspoon ground cardamom
1-2 teaspoons rose water
additional pistachio nuts or almonds to
   decorate

1. Combine sugar and water in a pan and stir occasionally until dissolved over medium heat. Bring to the boil, and boil briskly for 5 minutes without stirring. Remove from heat and leave aside in pan.
2. In a heavy deep pan heat ghee and add semolina. Stir over medium heat for 5 minutes. Semolina should not colour.
3. Pour hot syrup into semolina, stirring constantly. When smoothly blended, reduce heat a little and leave to cook, uncovered, until liquid is absorbed. Mixture should be thick, but still moist at this stage. Stir in nuts, and cardamom and rose water to taste.
4. Cover rim of pan with a cloth or 2 paper towels, put lid on tightly and leave on low heat for 5 minutes. Turn off heat and leave pan undisturbed for 10 minutes.
5. Spread halwau on a flat, lightly oiled platter and decorate with nuts. Serve warm or cold, cutting pieces into diamond shapes or squares.

SAMBOSAY GOSHTI
FRIED MEAT TRIANGLES

Makes 40
Cooking time: about 1 minute each lot

Filling:
500 g (1 lb) lean beef or lamb
salt
1 cup water
¼ cup oil
1 small onion, finely chopped
freshly ground black pepper
½ teaspoon Garam Masala (page 341)

Pastry:
2 cups plain flour
1 teaspoon salt
¼ cup butter or ghee
1 egg
cold water
oil for deep frying

1. Cube meat and place in a pan with about 1 teaspoon salt and the water. Bring slowly to the boil and simmer for 1-1½ hours until tender.
2. Lift meat from liquid and chop finely or grind using coarse screen.
3. Heat oil in pan and gently fry onion until transparent. Add meat, increase heat and fry until lightly browned. Add a little of the cooking liquid to moisten and add pepper, garam masala and salt if necessary. Remove from heat and cool.
4. Sift flour and salt into a bowl. Add butter or ghee and rub into flour lightly with fingertips until well distributed. Beat egg lightly in cup measure and make up to ½ cup liquid with cold water.
5. Pour liquid into flour mixture and mix to a soft dough. Cover with plastic wrap and leave to rest for 15 minutes.
6. Roll out half the pastry thinly using method described on page 16. Circle should be about 50 cm (20 inches) in diameter.
7. Fold pastry back on itself in 8 cm (3 inch) pleats, so that you finish with a strip of that width and the length of the circle's diameter. Press lightly with rolling pin and cut strip in half for easier handling.
8. Roll each strip lengthwise to a strip about 75 cm (30 inches) long and about 9 cm (3½ inches) wide. Cut into squares and stack. Repeat with other strip, then with remaining pastry.
9. Place a generous teaspoon of filling in centre of square of pastry, moisten two adjacent edges with water and fold over to form a triangle. Press edges to seal, then press with edge of thimble in crescents, or with fork. Place finished pastries on a tray.
10. Deep fry 3 or 4 at a time in hot oil, turning to cook evenly. Fry until golden brown, then lift out and drain on paper towels. Serve hot.

SAMBOSAY SHEEREEN
FRIED SWEET PASTRIES

Makes 40
Cooking time: about 1 minute each lot

1 quantity pastry (see Sambosay Goshti, above)
½ cup icing (confectioner's) sugar
½ cup ground blanched pistachio nuts, optional
oil for deep frying

Filling:
1 cup ground walnuts
1 cup ground seedless raisins

1. Make pastry as directed (Steps 4 and 5). Roll out and cut into squares as directed (Steps 6, 7 and 8). Combine icing sugar and nuts and keep aside.
2. Combine walnuts and raisins to form a coarse paste.
3. Place a generous teaspoon of filling in centre of square, moisten two adjacent edges of pastry and fold pastry diagonally to form a triangle. Press edges to seal, then press with thimble in crescents, or with a fork. Place finished pastries on a tray.
4. Deep fry 3 or 4 at a time in hot oil, turning to brown evenly. Cook until golden brown, lift out and drain on paper towels.
5. Sprinkle warm pastries with sugar-nut mixture and serve warm or cold. Store remaining pastries in a sealed container.

GOSH FEEL (Elephant Ear Pastries), *recipe page 357;*
SAMBOOSAY SHEEREEN (Fried Sweet Pastries) *recipe above;*
ABRAYSHAM KABAUB (Silk Kebab) *recipe page 356*

ABRAYSHAM KABAUB
SILK KEBAB

This fascinating sweet is actually a sweet omelet cooked in a most unusual way. Afghan cooks differ on how the silken thread omelet should be prepared. I have given the method which works best for me — once you have the idea you might devise a simpler method.

This is regarded as one of the great delicacies of Afghan cooking, but the 'kebab' part of the name is rather confusing. Perhaps it is because the final pieces resemble kebab meats; personally I cannot see it.

Makes about 30 pieces
Cooking time: 20-30 minutes

Syrup:
1½ cups granulated sugar
1 cup water
1 teaspoon lemon juice
¼ teaspoon saffron threads, optional

Omelet:
8 eggs
pinch of salt

To finish:
2 cups oil
¾ cup finely chopped pistachio nuts or walnuts
½ teaspoon ground cardamom

1. Dissolve sugar in water in a heavy pan over medium heat. Bring to the boil, add lemon juice and saffron and boil for 10 minutes. Cool and strain into a 25 cm (10 inch) pie plate. Keep aside.
2. Break eggs into a casserole dish about 20 cm (8 inches) in diameter. The size and the flat base are important. Add salt and mix eggs with a fork until yolks and whites are thoroughly combined — do not beat as eggs must not be foamy.
3. Heat oil in an electric frypan to 190°C (375°F) or in a 25 cm (10 inch) frypan placed on a thermostatically controlled hot plate or burner.
4. Have ready nearby a long skewer, the plate of syrup, a baking sheet and the nuts mixed with the cardamom. A bowl of water and a cloth for drying hands are also necessary.
5. Hold dish with eggs in one hand next to the pan of oil and slightly above it. Put hand into egg, palm down, so that egg covers back of hand. Lift out hand, curling fingers slightly inwards, then open out over hot oil, fingers pointing down. Move hand across surface of oil so that egg falls in streams from fingertips. Dip hand in egg again and make more strands across those already in pan. Repeat 3 or 4 times until about an eighth of the egg is used. There should be a closely meshed layer of egg strands about 20 cm (8 inches) across. Work quickly so that the last lot of egg is added not long after the first lot.
6. Rinse hand quickly and dry. Take skewer and slide under bubbling omelet, lift up and turn over to lightly brown other side. The first side will be bubbly, the underside somewhat smoother. When golden brown lift out with skewer and drain over pan.
7. Place omelet flat in the syrup, spoon syrup over the top and lift out with skewer onto baking sheet. Roll up with bubbly side inwards. Finished roll should be about 3 cm (1¼ inches) in diameter. Put to one side and sprinkle with nuts.
8. Repeat with remaining egg, making 7 or 8 rolls in all. Though depth of egg diminishes, you will become so adept that somehow you will get it into the pan in fine strands.
9. When cool, cut kabaubs into 4-5 cm (1½-2 inch) pieces and serve. These keep well in a sealed container in a cool place.

GOSH FEEL
ELEPHANT EAR PASTRIES

Makes about 40
Cooking time: about 45 seconds each

2 eggs
2 teaspoons caster sugar
¼ teaspoon salt
½ cup milk
4 teaspoons oil
2½ cups plain flour plus ¼ cup for kneading
½ teaspoon ground cardamom
oil for deep frying

To finish:
1 cup icing (confectioner's) sugar
½ teaspoon ground cardamom, optional
½ cup finely chopped blanched pistachio nuts
OR ½ cup finely chopped walnuts

1. Beat eggs until frothy, beat in sugar and salt. Stir in milk and oil. Sift flour, add half to egg mixture and blend in with wooden spoon. Gradually stir in remainder of flour, holding back about ½ cup.
2. Turn onto floured board and dust with some of reserved flour. Knead for 10 minutes until smooth and glossy, using more flour as required. Dough will still be slightly sticky. Cover with plastic wrap and rest for 2 hours.
3. Take a piece of dough about the size of a large hazelnut and roll out on floured board to a circle about 8-10 cm (3-4 inches) in diameter. Gather up dough on one side and pinch, forming a shape resembling an elephant ear. Place on a cloth and cover. Repeat with remaining dough.
4. Deep fry one at a time in oil heated to 190°C (375°F), turning to cook evenly. Fry until golden, do not over-brown. As dough is rather elastic, the pastry tends to contract with handling, so just before dropping pastry into hot oil, pull out lightly with fingers to enlarge.
5. Drain pastries on paper towels.
6. Sift icing sugar with cardamom if used and dust pastries with mixture. Sprinkle with nuts and serve warm or cold. Store in a sealed container.

Alternative topping: Make a syrup with 1 cup sugar and ½ cup water. Bring to the boil when sugar is dissolved and boil for 5 minutes. Dribble syrup onto warm pastries and sprinkle with cardamom and nuts.

FIRNEE
ALMOND AND CARDAMOM CREAM PUDDING

Serves: 6-8
Cooking time: 15 minutes

3 cups milk
pinch salt
⅓ cup granulated sugar
½ cup cornflour (cornstarch)
¼ cup cold water
½ cup slivered or chopped blanched almonds
¼-½ teaspoon ground cardamom
¼ teaspoon saffron threads, pounded
¼ cup finely chopped blanched pistachio nuts

1. Put all but ½ cup milk into a heavy pan and add salt and sugar. Put on to heat gently, stirring to dissolve sugar.
2. Blend cornflour into reserved milk with the ¼ cup water and pour into warm milk, stirring constantly. Add almonds and keep stirring until mixture thickens and bubbles. Use a whisk if mixture becomes lumpy.
3. Add cardamom to taste and the pounded saffron. Cook on low heat for 5 minutes, letting pudding simmer very gently. Stir occasionally.
4. Pour into 6 or 8 individual sweet dishes, spreading evenly. Sprinkle pistachio nuts around edge of each dish. To serve firnee in the traditional manner, the pudding should be poured into two plates, decorated with pistachio nuts and cut into quarters to serve in wedges.

USING THE WEIGHTS AND MEASURES IN THIS BOOK

Cooking is not an exact science: one does not require finely calibrated scales, pipettes and scientific equipment to cook, yet the conversion to metric measures in some countries and its interpretations must have intimidated many a good cook. I am a cup and spoon cook myself, long having been a fan of this U.S. method of measures; metrication has given me the opportunity to put this into practice.

Weights are given in the recipes only for ingredients such as meats, fish, poultry and some vegetables, necessary for marketing anyway, though a few grams or ounces one way or another will not affect the success of your dish.

Though recipes have been tested using the Australian Standard 250 ml cup, 20 ml tablespoon and 5 ml teaspoon, they will work just as well with the U.S. and Canadian 8 fluid ounce cup, or the U.K. 300 ml cup, as I have used graduated cup measures in preference to tablespoon measures so that proportions are always the same. Where tablespoon measures have been given, these are not crucial measures, so using the smaller tablespoon of the U.S. or U.K. will not affect the recipe's success. At least we all agree on the teaspoon size.

For breads, cakes, pastries, etc., the only area which might cause concern is where eggs are used, as proportions will then vary. If working with a 250 ml or 300 ml cup, use large eggs (60 g or 2 oz), adding a little more liquid to the recipe for 300 ml cup measures if it seems necessary. Use medium-sized eggs (55 g or 1¾ oz) with 8 fl oz cup measure. A graduated set of measuring cups and spoons is recommended, the cups in particular for measuring dry ingredients. Remember to level such ingredients.

Butter has been given in cups and fractions of cups. So that you can relate these measures to the block or stick as purchased, follow this guide:

> 250 g butter = 1 x 250 ml cup
> 8 oz butter (2 sticks) = 1 x 8 fl oz cup
> 300 g butter = 1 x 300 ml cup

The metric measures given are not equivalent to the Imperial measures — figures have been rounded off and the metric measures are slightly higher than the Imperial. If following a recipe using metric measures, your yield will be 10 per cent greater.

RELATING SPOON MEASURES TO CUPS

While working on the recipes I devised a method whereby I could convert weights and measures to cup and fractional cup measures. Knowing the tablespoon and teaspoon capacities of the various cup measures could be of some assistance to you, as it was to me.

12½ x 20 ml tablespoons or 50 teaspoons
    to 1 x 250 ml cup
15 x 20 ml tablespoons or 60 teaspoons
    to 1 x 300 ml cup
20 x 15 ml tablespoons or 60 teaspoons
    to 1 x 300 ml cup
16 x ½ fl oz tablespoon or 48 teaspoons
    to 1 x 8 fl oz cup

Standard teaspoon measures in Australia, U.S. and U.K. are 5 ml in capacity (one-sixth of a fluid ounce)

OVEN TEMPERATURES

Though recipes give temperatures in degrees Celsius and Fahrenheit (°C and °F), a scale including Regulo numbers for gas cookers might be an advantage. This is meant as a guide only since stoves vary — follow the manufacturer's temperature guide, relating it to oven description given in recipe.

	°C	°F	Regulo
very slow	120	250	1
slow	150	300	2
moderately slow	160-170	325	3
moderate	180-190	350-375	4-5
moderately hot	190-200	375-400	6
hot	220	425	7
very hot	230-290	450-550	8-10

FALAFEL (Dried Bean Croquettes) *recipe page 192.*

GLOSSARY

ALLSPICE
Bot: *Pimenta officinalis*
Fam: *Myrtaceae*
Arabic: *bhar hub wa na'im, bahar*
Turkish: *yeni bahar*
Though it is a spice from the new world, allspice has been adopted in Middle East cooking for its similarity to the combined flavours of clove, cinnamon and nutmeg. Commonly referred to as bahar.

BAHAR
See Allspice.

BAHARAT
A mixture of spices used in Gulf Arabic and Iraqi cooking, it is a combination of cinnamon, cloves, nutmeg, cumin, coriander and pepper with paprika added for colour.

BAKALIAROS
Dried salt cod. A favourite in Greece and Cyprus. Requires soaking for several hours, changing water often. Usually par-boiled, coated with batter and fried, with garlic sauce an essential accompaniment. Also used in stews or rissoles.

BAY LEAF
Bot: *Laurus nobilis*
Fam: *Lauraceae*
Arabic: *warak al gar*
Greek: *thaphne*
Turkish: *dafne yapregi*
Used in Greek, Turkish and Cypriot cooking as a flavouring herb in meat stews and in marinades for lamb and fish. Pieces of bay leaves are frequently placed on skewers between food pieces. Occasionally used in Arabic cooking.

BEANS, DRIED
See individual entries under Broad beans, Black-eyed beans and Mung beans. Only the lesser known dried beans are detailed.

BLACK-EYED BEANS
Bot: *Vigna unguiculata*
Fam: *Leguminosae*
Arabic: *lubyi msallat*
Greek: *fassoulia mavromatica*
Greek Cypriot: *louvi mavromati*
The black-eyed bean is a variety of the cowpea, and native to Central Africa. It should not be confused with the dried bean of *Vigna sesquipendalis*, which,
when-immature, is the yard-long asparagus or snake bean so popular in Mediterranean countries. Black-eyed beans have a pleasant, slightly sweet flavour and cook more quickly than other dried beans. Though they discolour the liquid in which they are cooked, I prefer these beans to any other for making Fassoulatha (Bean Soup).

BROAD BEANS (FAVA BEANS)
Bot: *Vicia faba*
Fam: *Leguminosae*
Arabic: *ful nabed*
Iranian: *bhagala*
Greek: *koukia*
Turkish: *fava*
Used fresh in Greek, Cypriot, Turkish and Arabic cooking. When very young, the whole bean is used, topped, tailed and strings removed. Mature beans are shelled and used in most countries of the region. Very good when cooked with globe artichoke hearts. In Iranian cooking the skin is removed from the fresh, shelled beans. Frozen broad beans are a good year-round standby and are easily skinned.

Dried broad beans vary in colour from olive green to a purplish hue. The green beans are usually new season's beans and take less soaking and cooking than the darker coloured beans. Used in Egyptian and Arabic cooking for Ful Nabed, Tameya and Falafel. See page 12 for instructions on soaking and skinning. Sometimes available ready skinned — when skinned the beans are white.

BROAD BEANS, SMALL
Bot: *Vicia faba* var. *minor*
Fam: *Leguminosae*
Arabic: *ful*
Greek: *fava*
Turkish: *bakla*
Also called Egyptian brown beans, tick, horse, fava and ful beans, these are only used when dried. Essential for the Egyptian Ful Medamis, a dish popular throughout most of the region, though the name varies occasionally. They range in colour from beige to purple and require soaking and long, slow cooking. Native to the Mediterranean region, their use as a food goes back to pre-history.

BURGHUL
Arabic: *burghul, bulkar*
Greek: *pourgouri*
Turkish: *bulgar*
Hulled wheat, steamed until partly cooked, dried then ground. Available in fine and coarse grades.

Recipes specify which grade to use. It has a nut-like flavour making it a popular food for those following natural food diets. It is widely used in Lebanon, Syria and neighbouring countries. Available at Middle East, Greek and Armenian food stores and specialty food stores.

CAPSICUM
See Peppers, sweet.

CARDAMOM
Bot: *Elettaria cardamomum*
Fam: *Zingiberceae*
Afghan: *hale*
Arabic: *hell, hail*
Iranian: *hell*

An expensive spice but necessary to Gulf Arabic, Iranian and Afghan cooking. Available in pods, as seeds or ground. Where ground cardamom is required, better flavour is obtained with freshly ground seeds particularly for sweet recipes. A necessary spice for Arabic coffee.

CAROB
Bot: *Ceratonia siliqua*
Fam: *Leguminosae*
Arabic: *kharrub*

An evergreen tree native to the Mediterranean region yielding long fleshy pods. The dried pods are sold in the Middle East as a snack food — the slightly sweet, chocolate flavour appeals particularly to children. In the carob, the Western natural food advocate has found a substitute for chocolate, a substitute with far less fat. See Dibs.

CASSIA
Bot: *Cinnamomum cassia*
Fam: *Lauraceae*
Arabic: *darseen, kerfee*
Greek: *kanella*

Also known as Chinese cassia, it is considered an inferior form of cinnamon. The thick pieces of bark are widely used in Arabic and Greek cooking in savoury dishes and sweet syrups, and though cinnamon is specified in recipes, either cassia or cinnamon may be used.

CHESTNUTS
Bot: *Castanea sativa*
Fam: *Fagaceae*
Arabic: *kestani, abu farwe*
Greek: *kastana*
Turkish: *kestane*

Native to Mediterranean regions, chestnuts have been used from ancient times. The chestnut sellers with their charcoal braziers ply their trade in cities around the Mediterranean, but are a less frequent sight today for crops are dwindling as fungus diseases affect the trees. Chestnuts are used in stuffings for poultry; in Greece chestnut purée is a favourite dessert, and the Zaharoplasti (sweetmaker) excels in preparing glace chestnuts. To prepare for cooking, cut through shell at each end, cover with water and boil for 10 minutes. Remove a few at a time and peel off shell and inner covering on nut. To roast, cut a cross on one side of shell, place in a moderate oven and cook for 10-15 minutes. Peel while hot.

CHICK PEAS, GARBANZO BEANS
Bot: *Cicer arietinium*
Fam: *Leguminosae*
Arabic: *hummus*
Armenian: *siser-noghud*
Greek: *revithia*
Iranian: *nakhod*
Turkish: *nohut*

Used as a food from ancient times in Egypt and Greece, they are popular throughout the region. They must be soaked before cooking and some recipes require the removal of the skins — see page 12. Armenian food stores sometimes stock ready-skinned chick peas. Also sold roasted as a snack food.

CHILI
Bot: *Capsicum frutescens*
Fam: *Solanaceae*
Arabic: *felfel, bishas*
Afghan: *murgh*

The long, slender green or red hot chili is favoured in Gulf and Yemeni cooking. Frequently the whole pod is used, including seeds, but as the seeds are very hot indeed it is better to remove them. Take care when handling chilis, keeping fingers away from mouth and eyes. Dried chilis or hot ground chili pepper may be substituted. Seed dried chili and soak in hot water for 5 minutes. Use hot chili pepper cautiously, adding a small amount at a time and tasting until the desired heat is obtained.

CINNAMON
Bot: *Cinnamomum zeylanicum*
Fam: *Lauraceae*
Afghan: *dolchini*
Arabic: *darseen, kerfee*
Armenian: *dartchin*
Greek: *kanella*
Iranian: *derchin*
Turkish: *tarcin*

A popular spice for both savoury and sweet dishes; either ground cinnamon or pieces of bark are used. It is an essential ingredient in the baharat of the Gulf States and Iraq, and the garam masala of Afghanistan and India. Sticks are comprised of fine sheets of the inner layer of the cinnamon bark, dried and inter-leaved to form sticks or quills. Though in recipes a small piece of bark refers to a stick about 4 cm (1½ inches) long, and a large piece one twice as long, there is no need to be very accurate in measuring.

CLOVES

Bot: *Syzygium aromaticum*
Syn: *Eugenia aromatica*
Fam: *Myrtaceae*
Afghan: *kala*
Arabic: *habahan, gharanful-mesmar*
Greek: *garifala*
Iranian: *nebos*
Turkish: *karinfil*

The dried flower bud of an evergreen tree native to tropical Asia. Used in both savoury and sweet dishes. A clove is sometimes added to simmering chicken to remove unwanted flavours, perhaps necessary for range-fed chickens or boiling fowls, but not for specially raised birds. It is claimed to sweeten the breath after eating garlic. In the Gulf States it is infused for a spicy tea.

CORIANDER (CILANTRO)

Bot: *Coriandrum sativum*
Fam: *Umbelliferae*
Afghan: *gashneez*
Arabic: *kazbarah*
Greek Cypriot: *koliandros*
Iranian: *geshniez*
Turkish: *kişniş*

A member of the parsley family. Both the green leaves and seeds are widely used in the Middle East. The flavour of the leaves is an acquired taste—the name of this pungent herb comes from the Greek koris, meaning bug, indicative of its aroma. However it is also similar to the aroma of dried orange peel, a more acceptable comparison. Used in the cooking of Afghanistan, Iran, the Gulf States, Yemen and Cyprus. Known as cilantro in the USA.

Ground coriander seeds are also widely used and feature in the baharat of the Gulf States and Iraq. The crushed seeds are an essential ingredient in the Afelias of Cyprus.

CORNFLOUR

Cornstarch — a white starch used for thickening milk puddings and essential for making Turkish Delight. Not to be confused with yellow cornflour.

CRESS

Bot: *Arabis caucasica*
Fam: *Cruciferae*
Arabic: *barbeen*
Iranian: *shahat*

A green herb much used in Iran, Iraq and the Gulf States as a salad herb. In Iran it is also used for the pot. Very similar to watercress in appearance and flavour, though the leaves are larger and more closely bunched on the stems.

CUMIN

Bot: *Cuminum cyminum*
Fam: *Umbelliferae*
Afghan: *zeera*
Arabic: *kamoon*
Armenian: *kimion*
Greek: *kimino*
Iranian: *zire*
Turkish: *cemen*

Native to Egypt, the seeds have been widely used as a spice from ancient times in Egyptian and Eastern Mediterranean cooking. In Cyprus a seed called artisha is used in Tavas, and though similar in appearance and flavour to cumin, it is claimed to be different by the Cypriots and is rarely available outside Cyprus. Some herbs and spices do vary in flavour when grown in differing climates and soils; perhaps this can explain the difference.

CUMIN, BLACK

Bot: *Nigella sativa*
Fam: *Ranunculaceae*
Afghan: *kala zeera*
Arabic: *habet el sauda*
Armenian: *shoushma*
Greek: *mavrokoko*

This small black aromatic seed bears no relationship to cumin. It is used on sweet yeast breads and cakes in Cyprus, Lebanon, Syria and Armenia; for flavouring haloumy cheese in Lebanon; and is one of the spices in the garam masala of Afghanistan.

DIBS

A syrup made from the carob pod which has a chocolate flavour. Popular in Lebanon and Syria where it is mixed with tahini as a spread for bread.

DIBS ROMAN

Pomegranate molasses or syrup used in Lebanese and Syrian cooking. See Pomegranate.

DILL

Bot: *Anethum graveolens*
Fam: *Umbelliferae*
Afghan: *shabit*
Armenian: *samit*
Greek: *anitho*
Turkish: *dereotu*

Native to the Mediterranean region, dill was much favoured as a medicinal herb in ancient times. The feathery leaves are blue-green in colour and give a distinctive, slightly aniseed flavour to meat, vegetable and rice dishes and pickles. An excellent herb for globe artichokes. Fennel may be substituted.

DRIED LIMES
Arabic: *loomi, noomi, noomi besra*
Iranian: *limu omani*
Also called black limes, these are available in the Gulf States either light grey-brown in colour or almost black. In Iran and Iraq the lighter limes are used. They come from Oman and also from Thailand and are dried on the trees. As they are not readily available to the Westerner, directions are given to make your own, page 245.

FENUGREEK
Bot: *Trigonella foenum-graecum*
Fam: *Leguminosae*
Arabic: *hulba, hilbeh*
Armenian: *chaiman*
Iranian: *shambalileh*
Though indigenous to the Eastern Mediterranean countries, the fawn, three-sided seed is used in Yemeni cooking for a potent paste called hulba or hilbeh, according to the dialect of the region; it is also a principal ingredient for pastourma (dried, spiced beef). The seeds have a slightly bitter flavour and are an essential ingredient in Indian curry blends.

The small, oval leaves are used in Iran in dishes such as Sabzi Khordan, Kukuye Sabzi and Khoreshe Gormeh Sabzi. Though some recipes do not include the herb because it is not readily available, add a small quantity if you have it on hand.

FETA
Greek in origin, feta is a soft, crumbly, white cheese made from goat's or ewe's milk. Turkey's beyaz peynir and Iran's panir are both feta-style cheeses, and as these are not exported, feta is the only substitute. Feta is made in many other countries and quality varies according to the milk used. Greek, Bulgarian and Romanian fetas are the best for serving as appetizers or in salads. Firmer fetas are made from cow's milk; usually less expensive, these are suitable for cooking purposes. To keep feta for a considerable time, take a wide-necked jar with you when purchasing so that the cheese may be covered with the whey in which it is packed. Alternatively reserve whey when making Mizithra (page 27), boil, cool and pour over feta. Seal container and store in refrigerator.

FLOUR
The plain flour used in these recipes is known in North America as all-purpose flour; wholemeal flour is known as whole-wheat flour. Unbleached plain (all-purpose) flour can be used in recipes if preferred, especially for bread. See also All About Bread, page 13.

FUL, FUL MEDAMIS
See Broad Beans, Small.

GARBANZO BEANS
See Chick Peas, garbanzo beans.

GARLIC
Bot: *Allium sativum*
Fam: *Liliaceae*
Afghan: *seer*
Arabic: *tum*
Armenian: *sekhdor*
Greek: *skortho*
Iranian: *sir*
Turkish: *sarmısak*
Known and used from ancient times for the medicinal properties attributed to it, garlic is essential to Middle East foods and should not be omitted from recipes using it. Remember that the flavour of garlic becomes more pronounced if browned, so avoid browning if a strong flavour is not desired. Raw garlic, finely chopped, is often mixed through boiled greens. Any recipe using raw garlic will leave you with an unpleasant breath. Chewing on a clove or drinking milk are favourite antidotes.

GARLIC CHIVES
Bot: *Allium tuberosum*
Fam: *Liliaceae*
Iranian: *tareh*
This flat-bladed green herb is used extensively in Iranian cooking and has a garlic-like flavour. If unavailable it may be omitted from the ingredients, or add onion flavoured chives and half a crushed clove of garlic.

GHEE
Afghan: *roghan*
Arabic: *samneh*
Iranian: *roghani kare*
Pure butter fat. Because of the absence of milk solids, ghee can be heated to high temperatures without burning and imparts a special fragrance to foods. When ghee is heated a degree of oxidation occurs, evident in the white colour of the ghee when it solidifies. Food laws in some countries are not as stringent as in others, and ghee often includes other fats or vegetable oils; for this reason clarified butter is given as the alternative in recipes where the flavour of ghee is necessary.

HALOUMY
A salty, sheep's milk cheese made in Cyprus and

Lebanon, and matured in whey. It is string-like in texture as it is kneaded after the drained curd is boiled in the whey. Cyprus haloumy is flavoured with dried mint; the Lebanese haloumy uses black cumin. The cheese can be made in the home using cow's milk; recipe gives details.

HALVA

Halva, with its many variations in spelling, generally means sweet, and is frequently a thickened pudding or sweetmeat. The confection called halva is made from ground raw sesame seeds; as its preparation requires cooking under pressure and the skill of a professional confectioner, it is not possible to duplicate the process in the home. Halva often contains almonds or pistachio nuts. It is a delicious confection, and though high in calories, it has good nutritive value and is highly recommended if you wish to gain weight.

HILOPITES

Small, square noodles used in Greek and Cypriot cooking in dishes such as Yiouvetsi, or simply boiled and served with a tomato or meat sauce and grated cheese.

KASSERI

A Greek sheep or goat's milk cheese, creamy white, firm textured with a few very small holes. It is a good table cheese, is excellent fried in butter or olive oil and served with a squeeze of lemon juice, and is frequently used diced on top of lamb stews. Kaşer, a Turkish cheese, and kashkaval, a Romanian cheese, may be used in place of kasseri.

KATAIFI

Greek: *kataifi*
Turkish: *kadaif*
Arabic: *konafa, k'nafi*
A shredded pastry which looks rather like slightly soft vermicelli noodles. A dough, somewhat similar to fillo dough, is forced through a finely perforated metal plate. The fine pastry strands drop onto a solid, heated metal plate, cooked briefly then scooped off while still pliable. Kataifi is usually packaged in plastic and keeps well in the refrigerator or freezer, providing package is sealed and overwrapped if stored in freezer. It has a longer storage life than fillo pastry. Bring to room temperature, in its package, before attempting to loosen strands. Available at Greek and Middle Eastern food stores and pastry shops.

KEFALOTIRI

Literally means 'head cheese'. A popular Greek grating cheese. The Italian parmesan cheese may be substituted.

KISHK

Burghul fermented with milk and yoghurt in a lengthy process. After fermentation it is salted, spread on a cloth to dry, then ground to a fine powder and stored for winter use. Cooked with water, kishk becomes a nourishing breakfast; it is also added to soups for extra nourishment. Used in Lebanon and Syria, and to a lesser extent in Iran where it is called kashk. Available from Middle East food stores.

LIMU OMANI

See Dried limes.

LOOMI

See Dried limes.

MAHLAB

Greek: *mahlepi*
A Syrian spice from the kernel of the black cherry stone, with a sweet spicy fragrance. The spice is always sold whole and is a small husked seed, pale brown in colour and a little smaller than a coriander seed. Pound in a mortar before using to flavour sweet yeast breads.

MASTICHA

Bot: *Pistacia lentiscus*
Fam: *Anacardiaceae*
Arabic: *mistki*
Greek: *masticha*
Mastic is a resin from a small evergreen tree, with most of the world's supply coming from the Greek island of Chios. From ancient times it has been used as a chewing gum. The powdered resin is used to flavour sweet yeast breads and a Greek liqueur of the same name. In Egypt a small piece of masticha is often added to boiling chicken to remove unwanted flavours.

MELOKHIA

Bot: *Corchorus olitorius*
Fam: *Tiliaceae*
A secondary source of jute grown in Egypt and India. In Egypt the younger shoots are harvested and the oval leaves, 4-8 cm (1½-3 inches) long, are stripped from the long stalks and used as a pot herb for a soup of the same name. The herb has the viscous properties of okra and it is favoured more for this than for its flavour. Melokhia sometimes makes its appearance in Western city markets during late spring and summer. Strip leaves from stalks, wash well, drain and shred very finely, using about 500g (1 lb) leaves in place of the 1½ cups dried leaves given in the recipe, page 287. Dried melokhia is available at Greek and Middle East food stores.

MINT
Bot: *Mentha spicata* or *M. viridis*
Fam: *Labiatae*
Afghan: *nauna*
Arabic: *na'na*
Armenian: *ananoukh*
Greek: *thiosmos*
Iranian: *nano*
Turkish: *nane*

The mint most favoured throughout the region is spearmint, and it is used in fresh or dried form. Used in meat and vegetable dishes, fragrant when fried in butter or ghee for a final touch to yoghurt soups and salads, mint gives Middle East cooking a distinct and appealing flavour. Dried mint is readily available at any store carrying a wide range of dried herbs.

MUNG BEANS
Bot: *Vigna radiata*
Fam: *Leguminosae*
Afghan: *maush*

Also known as green beans, golden gram or green gram, mung beans have been cultivated in Asia for centuries. While mainly used for bean sprouts or ground to a flour for Asian sweets, they are used whole in Afghan cooking. Mung beans do not require pre-soaking as they cook quickly.

NOOMI
See Dried limes.

NUTMEG
Bot: *Myristica fragrans*
Fam: *Myristicaceae*
Arabic: *josat al teeb*
Greek: *mostokaritho*
Turkish: *küçük hindistancevizi*

The hard inner kernel of the fruit of a tropical tree grown in the West Indies, Sri Lanka and South East Asian countries. An essential ingredient in the baharat of the Gulf States. In Greek cooking a small quantity of ground nutmeg is added to cream and meat sauces and spinach pie fillings.

OKRA
Bot: *Abelmoschus esculentus* or *Hibiscus esculentus*
Fam: *Malvaceae*
Arabic: *bamia*
Greek: *bamye*
Turkish: *bamya*

Also called ladies' fingers and gumbo. Native to Africa, it is an angular pod tapering to a point. Young okra are preferred. The vegetable has viscous properties, and while it is used for these properties in Western cooking, the preparation of the vegetable in the Middle East, particularly in Greece, is so devised that these properties are lessened. See page 9 for prepara-

tion. If you like the glutinous texture, then do not use the vinegar treatment given, though a brief blanching will firm the vegetable. Okra is also available dried, canned and frozen.

OLIVES
Bot: *Olea europaea*
Fam: *Oleaceae*
Arabic: *zaytun*
Greek: *elies*
Turkish: *zeytin*

Native to Eastern Mediterranean regions, the olive has been enjoyed as a fruit and for its oil from ancient times. The fresh fruit is bitter and must be treated to make it edible. Though recommended methods use a lye solution initially, home-cured olives are prepared in other ways. Ripe olives are dry-salted in wicker baskets and left for several days until the bitter juices have run out, then placed in wooden casks to mature, giving olives a wrinkled appearance. Another method for both ripe and green olives requires water soaking for 3-7 days (the longer period for green olives) with water changed daily; they are then left in brine to mature. Slitting or cracking the fruit hastens curing.

Oil is extracted by pressing, the first pressing yielding the finest oil which is greenish in colour. The pulp is treated and subsequent pressings give oil of gradually lessening quality. Better quality oils keep longest. If you find high quality oil strong in flavour, blend a small amount at a time with a bland salad oil.

ORANGE FLOWER WATER
Arabic: *ma'ez zahr*
Greek: *neroli*
Turkish: *portakal çiçeği suyu*

A fragrant liquid distilled from orange blossoms and used to flavour syrups and pastries. Available at Middle East and Greek food stores. Chemists (druggists) sell a concentrated essence; if this is all you can obtain, use in drops rather than the teaspoon or tablespoon measures given.

ORZO
Flat, oval noodles with a shape similar to rice grains. Used in soups or for Yiouvetsi.

PARSLEY
Bot: *Petroselinum crispum neapolitanum*
Fam: *Umbelliferae*
Arabic: *bakdounis*
Armenian: *azadkegh*
Greek: *maidano*
Iranian: *jafari*
Turkish: *maydanoz*

Only the flat leaf parsley is used in the region, being regarded as more flavoursome than its curly leafed cousin. Where small quantities are used in recipes, use the curly leaf variety if that is all you have on hand, adding some of the finely chopped stalks for more flavour. For dishes such as Tabouleh, and Iranian recipes using large quantities of herbs, the flat leaf variety is essential. It is now more widely available at greengrocers, and is easily grown from seed.

PASTOURMA
Armenian: *basderma, arboukht*
Greek: *pastourma*
Turkish: *pastirma*
Dried, highly spiced beef popular in Turkey, Greece and Armenia. Pastourma is the most widely used term as it is generally available at Greek food stores. Fenugreek, garlic, paprika, black and chili pepper are the main ingredients used in the thick, spicy coating. Slice very thinly and eat with bread, or fry in butter and serve with fried eggs.

PEPPERS, SWEET
Bot: *Capsicum* spp.
Fam: *Solanaceae*
Arabic: *felfel, felfel bard*
Armenian: *ganantch biber*
Greek: *piperies*
Iranian: *felfel sabz*
Also known as bell peppers, capsicum and pimento, they are green, ripening to a deep red with a change in flavour when ripe. The spice paprika is made from the ripe pepper. Though native to tropical America, peppers are very popular throughout the Middle East.

PINE NUTS
Bot: *Pinus pinea*
Fam: *Pinaceae*
Arabic: *snoober*
Greek: *koukounaria*
Turkish: *cam sistigi*
Also called pignolia nuts, they are the kernels from the cones of the stone or umbrella pine native to the Mediterranean region. Pine nuts are evenly oval and slender; there is another nut sold as pine nuts — it is tear shaped and is actually the pinon (pronounced pi'nyon) nut from pines native to north-west America. Pinon nuts are less expensive.

POMEGRANATE
Bot: *Punica granatum*
Fam: *Punicaceae*
Arabic: *roman*
Iranian: *anar*
A fruit known from ancient times and native to south-western Asia. The fruit well keep for months in a cool, dry place if picked before full maturity. Much used in the cooking of Iran where its sour juice is highly favoured. As some varieties are not very sour,

the addition of lime or lemon juice may be necessary. In Lebanon and Syria the juice is used in cooking, and the colourful seeds are a popular garnish. To juice the fruit, place a handful of seeds at a time in muslin and squeeze juice into a bowl. Freeze in ice-cube trays, then pack cubes in plastic bags and store in freezer. The seeds also freeze well if required for garnish. If fresh pomegranate juice is not available, use pomegranate molasses or syrup, dibs roman, available at Middle East food stores. Use 3-4 teaspoons dibs roman in 1 cup water for 1 cup pomegranate juice. The syrup grenadine is made from pomegranates, but cannot be used in savoury dishes.

POURGOURI
See Burghul.

PURSLANE, PURSLEY
Bot: *Portulaca oleracea*
Fam: *Portulacaceae*
Arabic: *ba'le, bakli, farfhin*
Armenian: *perper*
Greek: *glystiritha*
A wild green with fleshy leaves, popular as a salad ingredient for the Fattoush of Syria and Lebanon. In Armenian cookery it is added to yoghurt with cucumber for a refreshing salad; in Greece and Cyprus it is used in raw vegetable salads. Pick the young leaves and tender leafy tips from the reddish-coloured stalks.

RIGANI
Bot: *Origanum vulgare*
Fam: *Labiatae*
A pungent Greek herb and an essential flavouring for many Greek lamb dishes. It is wild marjoram, made that little more pungent because of the hot, dry climate. Picked when the flowers are in bud, the herb is dried before use. Though oregano grown elsewhere, picked at the bud stage and dried, is a reasonable substitute, it lacks the special, pleasantly pungent flavour of that grown in Greece. Available at Greek food stores either in dried bunches or stripped from the stalks.

ROSEMARY
Bot: *Rosmarinus officinalis*
Fam: *Libiatae*
Greek: *thendrolivano*
Turkish: *biberiye*
Widely used in ancient times, being regarded as beneficial to the head in ways ranging from curing headaches to aiding the memory. Occasionally used in Greek, Turkish and Cypriot cooking in lamb or fish dishes.

ROSE WATER

Arabic: *ma'el ward*
Iranian: *golab*
Turkish: *gül suyu*

Distilled from fragrant rose petals, rose water is used for both savoury and sweet dishes. As the strength varies according to the quality, when using a new brand add cautiously and taste to judge how much is required. Price is usually indicative of quality, with the more expensive brands being stronger. Rose water essence is a concentrate available from chemists (druggists); it should be used in drops rather than spoon measures. Rose water is available at Middle East and Greek food stores.

SAFFRON

Bot: *Crocus sativus*
Fam:*Iridaceae*
Afghan: *zaffaron*
Arabic: *zaffaran*
Iranian: *zaffaron*

When it takes the stamens of almost a quarter million blooms to produce 500 grams of saffron, is it any wonder that saffron is the world's most expensive spice? The use of saffron originated in Asia Minor in ancient times. Buy a reliable brand as there are cheaper versions sold which are not true saffron. Pound threads in a mortar and soak in liquid specified to bring out the fragrance and colour.

SALEP

Arabic: *sahlab*
Greek: *salepi*
Iranian: *neshasteh*
Turkish: *salep*

A fawn-coloured powder from the dried tubers of various species of *Orchis*. It has a gelatinous quality similar to cornflour (cornstarch) or arrowroot. In Greece and Turkey it is made into a hot beverage with milk and sugar (1 teaspoon salep to 1 cup cold milk, stir and heat till boiling), served with a dusting of cinnamon. In Lebanon and Syria it is the thickener for the custard base for buza (ice cream). The falooda of Iran is a cream pudding thickened with salep, chilled and served with fruit syrup and crushed ice.

SESAME SEEDS

Bot: *Sesamum indicum* or *S. orientale*
Fam: *Pedaliaceae*
Arabic: *simsum*
Armenian: *sousma*
Greek: *sousame*
Turkish: *susam*

Pale cream seeds of a plant widely grown in tropical regions. Sesame seeds are oily and highly nutritious and used since ancient times in the Middle East. The seeds are used on breads and cookies, for pastelli, a confection made with honey, for another confection called halva, and for tahini (see Glossary entries for last two).

SPRING ONIONS

Bot: *Allium Cepa*

Also known as scallions and green onions, these are the long green shoots of an immature onion. Unless otherwise specified in recipe, use some of the tender green tops as well as the white section.

SUMAK

The dried, crushed red berries of a species of sumach tree. It has a pleasant sour taste, rather lemony in flavour. As many trees of related species are poisonous, I have deliberately omitted the botanical name — it is advisable that sumak be purchased at Middle East and Armenian food stores.

TAHINI

Also called tahina in some countries, it is an oily paste made from toasted sesame seeds. The flavour of different brands varies, so it might be necessary to try various tahinis to find one to your liking. Smooth peanut butter is frequently given as a substitute; though it is a good substitute in cakes and cookies, only tahini should be used for any other recipes. Tahini separates on standing for a considerable time and requires blending before use. Storing unopened cans upside-down for some days makes blending easier.

TAMARIND

Bot: *Tamarindus indica*
Fam: *Leguminosae*
Arabic: *shar, tamar hindi*

The word tamarind comes from the Arabic, and literally means 'date of India'. The large bean pod of this tropical tree is strongly acid and favoured for this quality. Dried pods, compressed and packaged, are available at Asian food stores and require soaking and straining to separate the pulp from the seeds and fibres. Tamarind is used in the Gulf States and Iraq for dishes which include okra, as well as in other Gulf dishes. Tamarind pulp is also combined with a syrup for a cooling beverage popular in Egypt.

TARO

Bot: *Colocasia esculenta*
Fam: *Araceae*
Arabic: *kolkas*
Greek Cypriot: *kolokassi*

Though there are species of *Colocasia* native to tropical Asia and Africa, the kolokassi used in Cyprus is the same species as that of the Pacific Islands. It is a large, starchy tuber with side tubers or corms. The taro is toxic if eaten raw; heating destroys the toxicity.

TOMATO PASTE

A thick concentrated paste made from tomatoes, it is also known as tomato purée in the U.K. The tomato purée used in recipes, however, refers to a thick, pourable tomato concentrate, which is thicker than canned tomato juice but thinner than tomato paste; it is available in cans. See also recipe for Tomato Paste, page 26.

TROUMIS

Bot: *Lupinus luteus*
Fam: *Leguminosae*
Certain lupins have been used as a food in the Mediterranean region from 2000 B.C. With the wide variety of pulses now available, lupins are now used only as a snack food. Troumis is the Arabic for dried white lupins, and as these look rather like dried lima beans (though close inspection reveals differences) an explanation is necessary. As they are bitter, troumis should not be prepared similarly to other pulses. Soak for 4 days in cold water, changing water twice each day. Boil until tender, adding salt after 1½ hours. Drain and serve cold with olive oil and lemon juice as an appetizer.

TURMERIC

Bot: *Curcuma domestica*
Fam: *Zingiberaceae*
Afghan: *zarchoba*
Arabic: *kurkum*
Iranian: *zarchubeh*
Though often regarded as a spice for colouring food rather than flavouring it, turmeric does impart a pleasant, mildly pungent aroma to foods. It is used only in small quantities in Gulf Arabic and Iranian cooking for both colour and flavour, and is an essential ingredient in Indian curry blends.

WALNUT OIL

To extract oil from walnuts, chop shelled walnuts roughly and press a few pieces at a time in a garlic press. For 1 tablespoon oil, you will require 6-7 walnuts. In Turkey the chopped nuts are enclosed in butter muslin and squeezed — but the garlic press is much easier. Used as a garnish combined with paprika for Çerkes Tavüğü. Walnut oil is available commercially, but it is very expensive. A bland salad oil may be substituted for this particular garnish.

YOGHURT DRINK

Afghanistan: *dugh*
Arabic: *aryaan, laban bi sikkar*
Armenia: *tan*
Iranian: *abdug*
Turkish: *ayran*
Yoghurt blended with cold water, usually 2 parts yoghurt to 1 part water, though this varies according to the thickness of the yoghurt. Salt is usually added, though in Lebanon, Syria and Jordan, sugar is sometimes used (laban bi sikkar). In Iran, abdug is prepared commercially, carbonated and bottled.

ZA'TAR

A blend of powdered herbs, including thyme, marjoram and sumak, with salt added. Sprinkle an oiled khoubiz before baking for a flavourful flat bread; occasionally used as a flavouring spice mix in cooked meat dishes. Za'tar also refers to the herb thyme.

INDEX